Politics and Dependency in the Third World

Ronaldo Munck

'The Philosophers have only *interpreted* the world, in various ways; the point is to *change* it.'

Karl Marx

Politics and Dependency in the Third World

The Case of Latin America

Ronaldo Munck

University of Ulster at Jordanstown, Newtonabbey, Co. Antrim

Zed Books Ltd, 57 Caledonian Road, London N1 9BU.

Politics and Dependency in the Third World was first
published by Zed Books Ltd., 57 Caledonian Road, London
N1 9BU and University of Ulster at Jordanstown, Newtonabbey,
Co. Antrim, in 1985

First Reprint, 1985

Copyright © Ronaldo Munck, 1984

Typeset by Jo Marsh
Proofread by Tony Berrett
Cover design by Jacque Solomons
Printed by The Bath Press, Avon

British Library Cataloguing in Publication Data

Munck, Ronaldo
Politics and dependency in the Third World:
the case of Latin America
1. Dependency
I. Title
330'.9172'4   HB199

ISBN 0-86232-165-4
ISBN 0-86232-166-2 Pbk

U.S. Distributor
Biblio Distribution Center, 81 Adams Drive, Totowa,
New Jersey 07512

Contents

Tables

Figures

Acknowledgements

This book was generated by an ongoing political concern with the fate of the struggle for liberation in Latin America. At another level it began to materialise to answer my needs as a teacher of courses on the sociology of development. Some of the chapters spring from articles I have written for various journals over the past few years, and I am grateful to them for allowing me to air my views. For my formative intellectual experience I owe a great deal to Ernesto Laclau, Fernando Henrique Cardoso and the late Nicos Poulantzas. For extremely helpful comments on an earlier draft of this book I must thank Ronald Chilcote, Aidan Foster-Carter and Robert Molteno of Zed Press.

I also wish to formally acknowledge the indispensable support of the University Publications Committee, in particular Professors Ellis and Saunders. Finally, my thanks to Lesley for typing an illegible script and much else besides, to Felisa for not complaining (too much), *y para los viejos un gracias tambien.*

Ronaldo Munck
University of Ulster
at Jordanstown
Northern Ireland

Preface

There have been many books written about the economics and the sociology of development, showing how hunger and poverty prevail throughout the Third World. In practice, however, neither sympathetic reports to international agencies nor 'policy recommendations' to governments have changed conditions fundamentally. The reason is that only the people of the Third World themselves can overcome oppression, through radical social and economic transformations. And it is not Third World nations or societies but *particular* social classes within the Third World which might carry out these changes. So this book is less about 'social problems' in the Third World and more about the political struggles to overcome them. Class and politics in Third World development are the main themes. Development however is not seen as a one way path to social and economic progress but a *relation* in which there is a dominant and a dominated or dependent element. In the Third World, we are thus dealing with a particular form of 'dependent development'. In this sense, development refers to the historical process of capital accumulation and its extension to the far reaches of the globe.

It was with some hesitation that I retained the term 'Third World' in this book. One derivation of the term springs from a policy of the Soviet Union in the 1950s which described the regimes of Nehru, Nasser, and Nkrumah as a 'third way' between socialism and capitalism. These countries were given dispensation to embark on a 'non-capitalist' path to development without recourse to a proletarian revolution. In this sense, the term 'Third World' is just as ambiguous as the terms 'underdeveloped', 'less developed' or 'developing' countries advanced by Western economists. There is a vast economic and political diversity amongst the countries embraced by the 'Third World' label. Furthermore, the domination of the world economy by advanced capitalism (primarily the USA) makes it more appropriate to speak of *one* world rather than three, or four or five, as some people do. But on the other hand, the term is instantly recognised as a shorthand for the dependent or peripheral capitalist countries of Africa, Asia and Latin America and so can be retained with mental quotation marks around it. There is of course another derivation of the term from the '*tiers état*' of the French Revolution — the diverse social sectors oppressed by the clergy and the nobility. In this usage one is making no judgement about two other

1

'worlds' or some alternative to revolution. In this sense it can be retained without reservations.

Chapter 1 (Dependent Development), examines the main critical alternatives to the now widely discredited 'sociology of modernisation' which assumed that the Third World would follow the same path to development as the at present advanced societies did. The theory of dependency shows how the Third World has always been dominated by these 'central' countries and its development prospects, therefore, thwarted. Dependency analysis sometimes operated within a more global Marxist theory of imperialism, which we must examine critically. Dissatisfaction with what was considered the vagueness of dependency theories, has also prompted a return to the more explicitly Marxist 'modes of production' analysis. This has remained at a rather abstract theoretical level and I believe we should now move beyond this counterposition of rival theories. The concept of 'reproduction' seems to provide the key to a more dynamic yet concrete approach. Finally, a thumbnail statistical sketch and a broad classification of the Latin American countries helps to keep our real 'object of analysis' in mind.

Chapter 2 (Capitalism and Imperialism) appears at first glance 'an unfinished history of the world' (title of a recent book by Hugh Thomas). Its aims are more limited and are, in fact, to provide a summary historical illustration of the previous chapter's theoretical analysis. It is also the framework in which our subsequent analysis of particular countries for limited periods must be set. Capitalism is the mainspring, and imperialism its manifestation on the world scene. We trace this development from the 'primitive accumulation' phase through to the current period of late capitalism and the development of a so-called 'new international economic order'. The 'centre' and 'periphery' of the world system are considered together, just as economic and political analysis is integrated. This closes Part I on 'Dependent Development'.

Chapter 3 (Class and Politics) takes up the internal social structure of the Third World which is often absent in 'Third Worldist' analysis that sees nations exploiting whole nations. We see how classes are generated by the process of economic development but also how they react on this process. The question of class, in fact, runs right through the two themes of this book — politics and development — and informs all our case studies. We examine first the general theory of class, and then move through the major social classes and their sub-groupings. Particular attention is paid to questions such as the 'national bourgeoisie' and 'marginality', which can supposedly distinguish the social structure of the Third World from that of the industrialised nations. It is also necessary, however, to consider those non-class cleavages such as nation, race, or sex, which are of such vital importance in the Third World. Chapter 4 (Beyond Class) attempts to remedy the lack of attention to these divisions on the part of traditional economistic Marxism. Our case study for this chapter is the economic and political role of women in Latin America.

In Chapter 5 (Urban Social Movements) we move on to consider the comparative role of the labour movements in Argentina and Brazil. Reversing a classical Marxist dictum I try to show how men and women 'make their own history' even though we act 'in conditions not of our own choosing'. As the vast majority of the working population in the Third World are still peasants it is necessary in Chapter 6 (Rural Social Movements) to examine the question of agrarian reform and peasant movements, using Chile as our case study. A key element in the study of development and politics in the Third World must be the reproduction of social classes through the class struggle of dependent capitalism. This means, above all, a study of the formation and reproduction of the working class which is the essence of the capital relation and the basis of its undoing. This closes Part II on 'Class'.

Chapter 7 (State and Development) brings the vital concept of 'dependent capitalist state' into our analysis, through a detailed study of the role of the state in Brazil from 1930 to 1980. We examine the process of capital accumulation and the distinctive 'state forms' which emerge: oligarchic, bonapartist and military states. We also assess the question of the relative weight which must be given to external constraints and internal developments in shaping a Third World country's destiny. In the process of late or dependent development, the state plays a particularly important economic role, so we turn finally to a consideration of 'state capitalism'. Though this analysis focuses on Brazil, it has wider relevance to the issue of state and development in the Third World generally. Chapter 8 (Comprador Regimes) is the first in our study of specific state forms in the Third World. It examines the simplest and most brutal form of dependency — where the local ruling class becomes a simple agent for imperialism opening up the country to unbridled exploitation. We use various examples from Central America to illustrate the concept of 'comprador regimes'.

Chapter 9 (Nationalism) turns to the study of the Peronist movement in Argentina, which is taken as an archetypal example of Third World nationalism. Chapter 10 (Militarism), examines in turn the various theories put forward to account for the rise of the 'new' military dictatorships in Latin America. Again, Argentina provides the source material to illustrate the theoretical debates.

Chapter 11 (Socialism) shows that there is an alternative to dependent capitalist development in the Third World. Of course, many will argue that Cuba (our case study) has merely exchanged one form of dependency (on the USA) for another (on the Soviet Union). We confront that argument squarely, but first we assess the achievements of the Cuban Revolution and carry out a broad critical survey of developments since 1959. This is posed in the context of the major issues considered relevant to the 'transition to socialism' in the Third World. Cuba is for many the 'showcase' for socialism in the Western world, but we should not allow this uniqueness to cloud our critical judgement. Cuba has, of course, had an immense political impact on the rest of Latin America over the last 20 years, and for that reason alone this study is necessary here. This closes Part III on 'Politics'.

The conclusion (Chapter 12) aims to provide 'elements towards a theory' of Third World politics. Though our case studies were all drawn from Latin America I believe the concepts developed are of wider relevance.

In Part I we examined the theory of dependent development and its concrete unfolding since the formation of the world economy. In Part II various aspects of class were examined, and in Part III the main forms of political regime were sketched in. It is necessary to *relate* dependent reproduction and the different state forms, class conflict and its internal/external determination. On that basis we are able to pull together the various theoretical threads running through the book and develop an understanding of political power and social class in the Third World. The aim, however, is not a global theory, but rather theoretical elements which might provide a fruitful research agenda. That didactic element of the text is pursued in the Bibliography, which provides a guide to further reading on the topics developed in each part of the book. It is broader in scope than the particular case studies examined in the hope that it will encourage comparative research. A comparative focus (developed in Chapter 5) is seen as essential to a critical awareness of national reality. In this sense our discussions on Latin America could be broadened to encompass trends and perspectives in the rest of the Third World.

PART I
Dependent
Development

1. Dependency and Modes of Production

> Development is the 'struggle' of opposites. The two basic
> ... conceptions of development (evolution) are: develop-
> ment as decrease and increase, as repetition *and* develop-
> ment as a unity of opposites ... The first conception is
> lifeless, pale and dry. The second is living. The second
> *alone* furnishes the key to the 'self-movement' of everything
> existing; it alone furnishes the key to the 'leaps', to the
> 'break in continuity' to the 'transformation into the
> opposite', to the destruction of the old and the emergence
> of the new.   V.I. Lenin[1]

During the 1950s there was a certain naive optimism in the mainstream of
development studies that the Third World would move towards modernisation
if a magical 'take-off' point was reached. Development was a one-way process,
a continuum along which all countries passed — some were just further ahead
than others. The theory of dependency put forward the simple and now so
obvious point, that development and underdevelopment were but different
sides of the same coin — the advance of one took place at the cost of the
other. Dependency writings helped to reawaken interest in the classical
Marxist theories of imperialism which earlier had sought to explain the
differentiation between nations. It was the perceived weakness of dependency
theory in specifying the exact nature of underdevelopment which led in part
to work on the 'modes of production' in the Third World. We examine each
of these theoretical perspectives — dependency, imperialism and modes of
production — highlighting their strengths and weaknesses. A final section
attempts to move beyond the apparent impasse between the various radical
theories of development and underdevelopment.

Dependency Theories

The genesis of dependency theory is inseparable from the crisis of modernisation theory in the mid 1960s. The theoretical credibility of this approach had
been in question for some time, and there was a considerable output of

historical analysis in Latin America which implicitly questioned modernisation theory postulates. The determinant factor, however, was the crisis of modernisation in the real world, or more specifically the failure to achieve its stated aims and objectives. In this context a number of Latin American writers began a systematic critique of modernisation theory assumptions and misconceptions. It was no coincidence that Brazilian writers figured prominently in this enterprise because, we shall see in Chapter 7, the whole model of national autonomous development collapsed with the 1964 military coup in that country. The Cuban Revolution had become rapidly radicalised around this period, and was also a powerful catalyst. The Cuban experience led to a radical questioning of the very possibility of sustained national development in a capitalist context. Brazil showed that the 'national bourgeoisie' could easily give up the objective of *national* development and political participation. Cuba showed that another non-capitalist road to social and economic development was possible in Latin America. Orthodox modernisation and development theories gave way to a new paradigm, known as 'dependency', which gained the upper hand in Latin America and later spread to Europe and North America. The main differences between the two theories are summarised in Figure 1.1. Clearly, each step of modernisation theory discourse is challenged by the new approach. The assumptions of the first centred around a diffusion model whereby technology, capital and 'progress' will trickle down from the advanced to the Third World countries and from the cities to the countryside. Foreign investment is obviously a key factor in this, and foreign aid a benevolent contribution from the advanced to the backward areas. Dependency theory disputes the underlying conception of dualism (feudalism/capitalism) and shows how the historical *relation* with the metropolis is the key to underdevelopment. It rejects an assumption that Latin America is simply at an *un*developed stage heading towards progress, in favour of a conception of *under*development caused by the very process of development in the central industrialised countries. Any analogy with the original transition to capitalism in Western Europe must be rejected from this perspective, because it ignores that *those* countries at *that* period of history became dominant precisely through the building up of their overseas empires. Quite clearly the political conclusions of both theories are diametrically opposed – for one, *more* capital is required, whereas for the other a *break* with capitalism is a prerequisite for development.

Through the critique of modernisation theory and the influence of the United Nations' Economic Commission for Latin America (ECLA) a new paradigm in the study of underdevelopment emerged. Its basic concept was quite simple. Dos Santos wrote that 'dependence is a *conditioning situation* in which the economies of one group of countries are conditioned by the development and expansion of others. . . . [They] can only expand as a reflection of the expansion of the dominant countries. . . .'[2] A theory of imperialism obviously underlies this definition of 'dependence' but the influence of ECLA's work was probably just as important. Since 1950, this influential body had been producing reports on Latin America's economic

Figure 1.1
Modernization and Dependency Theories

Issue	*Modernization theory*	*Dependency theory*
Nature of society	A feudal aristocracy evolved in Latin America and was to predominate to the present day. This aristocracy was to impede the development of capitalism and the rise of a progressive national bourgeoisie. In the cities of Latin America, capitalism was introduced through commercial contact with more modern nations.	The Iberian countries conquered America in order to incorporate it within a new system of capitalist production, not to reproduce the European feudal cycle. A bourgeoisie evolved which had no interest in developing the domestic market and national industry because its main source of income lay in the export trade.
Nature of progress	Through capital and technology the development of the metropolitan nations was diffused to the urban centres of Latin America. As this process accelerates there should be a breakdown of the two societies (feudal/capitalist) through a diffusion from city to countryside.	The market system imposed in Latin America creates underdevelopment rather than development. The poverty of the countryside is reinforced by its relationship to the city and the outside world. There is no dualism between city and countryside.
Nature of ruling class	The national bourgeoisie will promote development through the diffusion of innovations and enterprising spirit to the backward areas. They will lead in the drive for social reforms and political democracy.	The diffusion of capital results in stagnation and decapitalization of the rural areas. The industrial bourgeoisie is dominated by imperialism and subordinated to agrarian interests. They have no particular democratic urge and will support stable authoritarian government.
Development	The diffusion of capital and modern values into the backward areas is the key to development.	Development can only be brought about with the overthrow of capitalism and imperialism.

Source: adapted from Chilcote, R. and Edelstein, J. (eds)(1974) *Latin America: The Struggle with Dependency and Beyond*. New York, Schenkman Publishing Co, pp.49 and 53.

development problems within a model of the world economy which set an industrial 'centre' against a primary-goods producing 'periphery', in the international division of labour. Analysing a long term trend for the terms of trade to move against the periphery they advocated a policy of 'import-substitution' industrialisation. Development was to move from an export orientation towards inward-directed growth. In practice, however, this process only increased 'dependence' on the advanced industrial societies for the machinery and technology necessary for industrialisation. The sharp increase of foreign investment in the Latin American economies from the mid 1950s onwards — 'external co-operation' in ECLA's vocabulary — led to growing dissatisfaction with dominant economic theories from a wide sector of nationalist opinion. Nevertheless, in relation to some of the basic assumptions of 'dependency theory' which began to take shape in the early 1960s, the work of ECLA was supportive. The failure of the Christian Democratic government's bid at conservative modernisation in Chile in the mid 1960s gave these theories their decisive boost. Under the Allende regime in Chile (1970–73) a Latin American intellectual community flourished, producing much of the essential dependency work.

Outside Latin America, it was the work of Gunder Frank which symbolised this new radical perspective, but this oversimplifies the origins of dependency theory and its diversity. The first main approach we must distinguish is that of economists such as Celso Furtado and Osvaldo Sunkel, which aimed at reformulating the original ECLA analysis. The stagnation of capitalist development in the 1960s made it necessary to rethink ECLA's positive attitude towards foreign investment. Early hopes of the local industrial bourgeoisie vanquishing the traditional agrarian oligarchy were replaced by the reality of the multinational corporations. There was growing foreign control of industry, and a massive increase in unemployment, because of its 'capital-intensive' nature. Sunkel presented an analysis of how this process of 'international integration' led to an increase of 'national disintegration' in the Third World.[3] Furtado, for his part, advanced a wide-ranging structural and historical interpretation of economic development in Latin America.[4] These authors distinguished between economic growth and economic development, which entailed a redistribution of income, and national control over the economic and political spheres. They concentrated on the obstacles to *national* development caused by the *distortions* in the process of economic growth. In other words, they did not move beyond ECLA to analyse the class structure of underdevelopment and they did not question the essence of capitalism, only its perverse pattern of growth in the periphery. Simplifying slightly this could be considered the conservative wing of the dependency school.

Another, more radical wing, centred around the work of a number of economists and sociologists based in Chile: Theotonio Dos Santos, Ruy Mauro Marini, Vania Bambirra and many others. Their objective was nothing less than the construction of a systematic theory of Latin American underdevelopment. Dos Santos provided the well-known definition of dependency quoted above, which is rather formal and static. Nevertheless, this author went on to produce a remarkable empirical analysis of the 'new dependency' — based on the investment carried out by the multinational corporations since the Second World War.[5] This technological dependence is distinguished from earlier financial dependence which predominated when Britain was the dominant power.

Vania Bambirra provided a systematic typology of different forms of dependency according to the particular social and economic structure of the country concerned, and the contradictions of 'dependent capitalism'. The most sophisticated *theory* of dependency is that of Marini, whose book on the 'dialectics of dependency' attempted to uncover the 'laws' of dependent capitalism, based on the super-exploitation of labour, and limited by the restricted nature of the internal market.[7] Taking these writers as a group we can note the much greater influence of the Cuban revolution on their position compared to the 'structuralist' group analysed above. In fact, in their bid to show that 'socialism or fascism' were the only historical alternatives open in Latin America, they often tried to show that dependent capitalist development was simply impossible. Thus, Caputo and Pizarro could state that 'it is impossible to develop our countries within the capitalist system'.[8]

It was André Gunder Frank who eclectically absorbed all these theories and, strongly influenced by the work of the Monthly Review school, began to popularise the notion of 'development of underdevelopment'.[9] The main thrust of his early writing was to undermine the theory of dualism which posited a 'traditional' sector holding back a 'modern' sector from development. He showed conclusively how there was an integral relation between the two, with capitalism moulding the whole economy, including 'backward' sectors of agriculture, to its needs. The key tenet of modernisation theory — that the 'diffusion' of Western technology and values would lead to development in the Third World — was also soundly rebutted with ample historical evidence. More questionably, Gunder Frank advanced a notion of a chain-type metropolis/satellite relation — an exploitative link stretching from the central powers through to the landowners, the peasants and the landless labourers, each extracting an economic surplus from the one below. Changes in this chain, from the 16th Century until today, represent only 'continuity in change' for Frank. From Paul Baran (part of the Monthly Review school) he borrowed the concept of 'potential' economic surplus which would be available if dependency could be overcome, as against the 'actual' surplus which at present is expropriated by external and internal monopolies.[10] Under conditions of dependent capitalism the most that can happen is the 'development of underdevelopment' — the deepening of the structure of dependence. Given the capitalist nature of the Latin American economies (from the Spanish Conquest in fact) a socialist revolution is the only way of breaking the metropolis/satellite network and achieving sustained development.

The third variant of dependency studies is best represented by the work of Fernando Henrique Cardoso, which aims at establishing a *methodology* for

11

the analysis of concrete situations of dependency. Against a general emphasis on the 'external' factors causing underdevelopment, this current stresses the 'internal' factors and in particular the relationships and struggles between social classes. Cardoso rejects the attempts to elaborate a 'theory of dependent capitalism', seeking rather to elaborate the historical process involved. Against the stagnationist perspective of both previous currents mentioned Cardoso recognises the possibility of dependent development – the fact that it brings poverty and unemployment in its wake does not alter this fact. Instead of simply labelling the national bourgeoisie in Latin America as a 'lumpen' bourgeoisie, as Frank did, Cardoso examined the *particular* structure and attitudes of the industrial bourgeoisie in Argentina and Brazil.[11] In the classical study of dependent development in Latin America, written with Enzo Faletto, Cardoso examines the different phases and forms of dependency, and the specific class alliances which corresponded to them. They examine 'diversity within unity' rather than 'unity within diversity' as does Frank. To sum up this approach – 'the relationship between external and internal forces [in] a complex whole rooted in coincidences of interests between local dominant classes and international ones, and, on the other side, are challenged by local dominated groups and classes.'[12] Against the rather economistic tendencies of some of the other writers, Cardoso affirms that the history of capital accumulation is the history of class struggles.

The critics of 'dependency theory' soon began pointing out the weaknesses and inconsistencies in its main postulates.[13] We shall try to examine these systematically. It could be said firstly, that dependency operates with a simple tautology: the Third World countries are poor because they are dependent and all the characteristics they display are signs of dependency. This type of circularity, however, is only apparent in the crudest simplifications. Another of these 'terminological' objections would be that dependence is a redundant concept, in so far as all countries are *inter*dependent. More pertinent, is the point that it is not really an operational concept. To remedy this a number of writers, particularly in the USA, have devised various means to 'test' dependency theory.[14] Various criteria of dependency are isolated and measured against a cross cultural matrix through a full panoply of quantitative methods. The results supposedly measure different 'degrees' of dependency conceived as a simple continuum (dependency/independence) quite similar to that used in the modernisation theories. Cardoso has rightly accused this type of analysis of a formal and ahistorical approach that distorts the original intentions of its proponents.[15] In a sense dependency was never a 'theory' but a number of divergent approaches to the question of underdevelopment in Latin America. The attempt at 'model building' and 'theory testing' results from the same type of empiricism which produced modernisation theory, and is just as sterile.

To my mind, the most far reaching critique of dependency is that it oscillates theoretically between a national and a class approach.[16] When taking the Third World nation as the appropriate unit of analysis there is an inevitable tendency to reduce the importance of the class struggle. Even

Cardoso, who stresses the role of classes, tends to mention only the 'incorporation' of the middle class and, in passing, the 'exclusion' of the working class. Other writers go further and explicitly aim for national independence without a revolution. That is why the 'progressive' Peruvian generals who came to power in 1968 were able to speak in terms of their country's 'dependency'. It would, though, be reducing all the dependency theorists to this level to say, as have some critics recently, that they simply 'express' the interests of national competitive capital against the multi-nationals.[17] Dependency is not a simple 'apology' for nationalism, although there is clearly a nationalist element in most of its versions. Perhaps more telling is the criticism that dependency is inherently teleological – the assumption that there is an ideal, unrealised but potentially achievable state of autonomous 'non-dependent' development.[18] It is very easy to slip into the idea that, breaking the links with the world market will automatically allow for development, if these are seen as the basic 'cause' of backwardness. In this sense, the 'tradition/modernity' schema is only replaced by an equally distorting 'dependent/autonomous' dichotomy.

The general neglect of class analysis is now seen as the major failure of dependency writers. Though many writers paid ritual homage to the need for a class analysis, social classes very rarely appeared as prime movers of history in their accounts. As Petras has recently pointed out, the emphasis on a metropolis/satellite relation rides roughshod over the specific processes that shaped historical development – the different configurations of capital and the particular class relationships and conflict between capital and labour.[19] In Gunder Frank's chain of exploitation between the centre and the periphery, we have a strange reduction of class relations to spatial relations, as though geography determined relations of exploitation. In general, we see an almost totally 'external' determination of history in the Third World and a neglect of the internal social relations of production. This general tendency towards economism in the dependency theorists is matched by the attempt to prove that socialism is necessary because dependent capitalist development is somehow not possible. This stagnationist perspective (clearly rejected by Cardoso) is based on a theory of under-consumption that is simply not valid. Basically, it was thought that dependent capitalism could not expand because it would not find a market for its products. The internal consumption market of a country like Brazil is certainly not that narrow, and anyway, the export market is obviously another outlet. On both counts – neglect of class analysis and a misconception of capital's ability to expand in the Third World – the dependency theories showed an impoverished linear conception of history based on simplified models of exploitation.

To summarise, Gunder Frank 'constructs a mechanico-formal model which is no more than a set of equations of general equilibrium (static and unhistorical), in which the extraction of the surplus takes place through a series of satellite-metropolis relationships. . . .'[20] This emphasis, by Gabriel Palma, on the economism of Frank's analysis is, I think, correct. This is precisely the reason why classes are displaced from his analysis, except in a very formal sense. In a way Frank has constructed a model which is the mirror opposite of the modernisation theories: the dichotomies of rich/poor, traditional/modern are replaced by those of dominant/dependent, and centre/periphery. The latter are equally static, and totally impoverish the real process of history. Even imperialism is reduced to a simple causal force, without due attention to its internal contradictions. The multinational corporations act as one conscious agent instead of as quite specific and competing entities. It is here that the inherent nationalism of much dependency writings emerges most starkly — the multinationals are condemned for their extraction of surplus from the economic system but basically because they are *foreign*. We must seriously question whether the class relation and the system of exploitation changes radically because a capital unit is not in national hands. It is at this point that dependency theory parts company with Marxism and becomes a sophisticated variant of nationalist ideology.

The systematic critique of dependency theory over the last 10 to 15 years has, of course, affected its early protagonists. Cardoso has ceased to situate his work within the dependency 'paradigm' and has turned his attention more to the concrete questions of the state and authoritarianism in Brazil.[21] Bambirra, on the other hand, has written a vigorous 'anti-critique' directed at all the detractors of the approach.[22] Marini has also continued working on a general theory of underdevelopment and has strongly attacked what he sees as Cardoso's adaptation to ECLAs 'developmentalism'.[23] Dos Santos has continued his general investigations into the nature of capitalism in Latin America today, but much more within an explicitly Marxist theory of imperialism.[24] Sunkel has developed his notion of a 'transnational system', moving beyond the old distinction of centre and periphery. This has proved to be a fruitful research programme, which has already produced a useful volume on different aspects of dependence.[25] What, perhaps is most interesting is that the dependence approach has been extended to the study of African situations. In particular, there has been a vigorous debate on the nature of the bourgeoisie in Kenya and this has moved the terms of the debate beyond the cruder 'dependency' formulations.[26] The preoccupation of early writers with international relations of 'dependence' has been replaced by more detailed studies of the concrete structures of dependent capitalism. In particular, there has been a growing focus on the realm of production (not just circulation) and on class relations, including the growing role of the labour movement.

For his part, Gunder Frank has explicitly moved out of the dependency tradition to work on the broad historical process which gave rise to the formation of the world economy. In this, he is following the path of Immanuel Wallerstein who pioneered the 'world-systems' analysis, centred around the belief that the world has experienced a single all-embracing process of capital accumulation centred on Western Europe.[27] As the back cover of one of Frank's latest books says, he 'transcends neo-Marxist theory and his own previous contributions to the theory of "dependence" and "development of underdevelopment" in his treatment of modern history as a single world-wide process driven by the motor force of . . . capital accumulation.'[28] In shifting his analysis to the level of capital accumulation on a world scale he has joined forces with the earlier work of Samir Amin, although Frank is more concerned with the early genesis of the world system.[29] The same criticism that is levelled at dependency theories can be directed at the newer world-systems analysis — by focusing on the relations between systems or nations they neglect the internal process of class formation. The class conflict, as Petras notes correctly, 'shapes relations between countries as much as it is shaped by intersystem relations.'[30] Much of this new work is at a very high level of generalisation based on empirical observations without a sound theoretical framework — the very notion of 'world system' is taken as given rather than theoretically constructed. On the broad canvas painted by these writers, differences between countries (and regions, and classes) tend to disappear. Above all, they have continued the dependency theory emphasis on circulation (trade) rather than production relations within the Third World countries. Politically, they retreat from the interventionist stance of the dependency theorists and offer no guidelines to politics at the national level, which is still the site of the class struggle.

Theories of Imperialism

Dependency theory emerged out of the failure of modernisation theories, but also due to the weakness of the Marxist theory of imperialism, which was seen to neglect the effects it had on the underdeveloped countries themselves. In other words, its concern with the motive forces of imperialist expansion and its general mechanisms was not followed up by any detailed investigation of the Third World. This is probably true for all the early Marxist theorists of imperialism, except Rosa Luxembourg. Her work on imperialism, published in 1913, begins with a criticism of Marx's analysis of expanded reproduction in Volume II of *Capital*. She maintained that it was impossible for a closed capitalist system to realise (exchange for money) the goods produced in each period of production without an 'outside' non-capitalist outlet. At this level she can be criticised, as Lenin did the Russian Populists, for holding an under-consumptionist view of capitalism.[31] Popular consumption is of far less importance to capitalism than the productive consumption of means of production (machinery etc). The strength of Luxembourg's contribution lies in her concrete analysis of how capitalism emerged historically and was maintained in a non-capitalist environment:

> Capitalism arises and develops historically amidst a non-capitalist society . . . after having swallowed up the feudal system, it exists mainly in an environment of peasants and artisans . . . European capitalism is further surrounded by vast territories of non-European civilisation ranging over all levels of development. . . . This is the setting for the accumulation of capital.[32]

Imperialism, in Britain, in an analogy with Marx's analysis of 'primitive accumulation', is directed at bringing the 'national economy' under the subjection of capital, coercing labour power into its service and gaining possession of land, minerals, precious stones; in short, introducing a commodity economy. To do this, 'Force is the only solution open to capital: the accumulation of capital, seen as an historical process, employs force as a permanent weapon, not only at its genesis, but further on down to the present day.'[33]

Though Marx himself did not dedicate sustained attention to the world economy he does mention how a,

> new and international division of labour springs up, one suited to the requirements of the main industrial countries, and it converts one part of the globe into a chiefly agricultural field of production, for supplying the other part which remains a pre-eminently industrial field.[34]

The main drift of his analysis looks towards capitalism as a dynamic, expanding force which will bring the whole globe under its power, creating new societies in its own image. In his journalistic articles on India he shows how this 'progressive' side of capital operates:

> England has to fulfill a double mission in India: one destructive, the other regenerating — the annihilation of old Asiatic society, and the laying of the material foundations of Western society in Asia.[35]

Destruction of the pre-existing communities and the uprooting of native industry was carried out by British colonialism but 'the work of regeneration hardly transpires through a heap of ruins'.[36] His stress is still on the modernising and integrating role of capital:

> [The political unity of India] imposed by the British sword, will now be strengthened and perpetuated by the electric telegraph. . . . The free press . . . is a new and powerful agent of reconstruction. . . . Steam has brought India into regular and rapid communication with Europe . . . has revindicated it from its isolated position which was the prime law of its stagnation.[37]

There is a similarity here with modernisation theory, both seeing capitalism pulling the Third World out of its state of stagnation, but not quite, because Marx also made clear that:

> the Indians themselves will not reap the fruits of the new elements of society scattered among them by the British bourgeoisie, till in Great Britain itself the now ruling classes shall have been supplanted by the industrial proletariat, or till the Hindoos themselves shall have grown

strong enough to throw off the English yoke altogether.[38]

Marx's view of 1853, that British rule in India would lead to the development of industrial capitalism, was proved wrong. Capitalism as colonialism did not lead to capitalist development but rather to underdevelopment. Marx's belief that 'the country that is more developed industrially only shows the less developed the image of its own future'[39] was proved to be hopelessly optimistic. Marx's position, however, changed considerably through involvement with the Irish question during the 1860s and after. In a passage close to the conception of 'development of underdevelopment' Engels says that 'Ireland has been stunted in her development by the English invasion and thrown centuries back'.[40] Ireland was, according to Marx, compelled to contribute cheap labour power and capital for Britain's industrial development, and 'every time Ireland was about to develop industrially, she was crushed and reconverted into a purely agricultural land'.[41] Whereas Marx thought the destruction of native industry in India was progressive, he was now saying the Irish needed: 1) self-government and independence from England, 2) an agrarian revolution and 3) protective tariffs against England.[42] Though he had once thought the separation of Ireland from England 'impossible', by 1867 he was writing to Engels that he thought it 'inevitable'. It was in relation to the Irish struggle for self-determination that Marxism developed its first progressive policy on the national question, through the unstinting support Marx and Engels gave the radical Fenian movement. This is summed up in Marx's prediction in 1870 that 'any nation that oppresses another forges its own chains'.

It was, of course, Lenin, in the period of the First World War, who developed what has become known as the 'classical' theory of imperialism. His own famous work was preceded by that of two other Marxists — Rudolf Hilferding and Nicolai Bukharin — on whom he relied heavily. Hilferding's book *Finance Capital* develops Marx's theory of capitalism into the era of monopoly (as against competitive) capitalism.[43] In particular, he shows how there is an accelerated centralisation of capital with the emergence of joint stock companies. A central element in this growth of monopoly were the banks which, together with industrial capital, fuse into 'finance capital' — separation of financial and industrial capital having become an anachronism. The unification of the magnates of industry and banks under the control of high finance is a key element in the subsequent evolution of monopoly capitalism. Finance capital was to support the expansionist policies of the European countries in a bid to extend their markets. Bukharin's book *Imperialism and World Economy* was to have an even more direct influence on Lenin.[44] In it, he pursued the theme of growing international interdependence as the world market expanded, and its simultaneous division into national blocks. The conflict between these two tendencies lies at the heart of imperialism's propensity to wars. Bukharin traces how the expansion of international trade has led to a social division of labour on a world scale. In his own words:

world capitalism, the world system of production, assumes in our times the following aspect: a few consolidated, organised economic bodies ('the great civilised powers') on the one hand, and a periphery of underdeveloped countries with a semi agrarian or agrarian system on the other.[45]

The formation of 'state capitalist trusts' at the centre leads inevitably to imperialist annexations.

Lenin's work on imperialism was tied closely to the political struggles of the time and displays his constant linking of theory with practice. He took up the contributions of Hilferding and Bukharin, together with that of the liberal writer Hobson, to produce his famous 'popular outline' of imperialism.[46] From Hobson he derived the key argument that the economic driving force of colonial expansionism was the need for investment outlets at the centre. The export of capital to the Third World thus occurs because of the 'over-ripeness' of capitalism, as well as the fact that 'in these backward countries profits are usually high, for capital is scarce, the price of land is relatively low, wages are low, raw materials are cheap.'[47] The tendencies of capitalism which lead to imperialism are, for Lenin, the following:

1) the concentration of production and capital has developed to such a high stage that it has created monopolies which play a decisive role in economic life;
2) the merging of bank capital with industrial capital, and the creation, on the basis of this 'finance capital' of a financial oligarchy;.
3) the export of capital as distinguished from the export of commodities acquires exceptional importance;
4) the formation of international monopolist capitalist combines which share the world amongst themselves; and
5) the territorial division of the world amongst the biggest capitalist powers is completed.[48]

Lenin summed up his definition of imperialism as 'the highest stage of capitalism' and in this way he was distancing himself from Karl Kautsky's understanding of imperialism as the 'policy' preferred by finance capitalism (which implied that industrial capital might not find imperialism necessary). Above all, Lenin opposed Kautsky's theory of 'ultra-imperialism' – which saw the major powers agreeing peacefully to exploit the world together.[49] In his view, militarism was an intrinsic part of imperialism, and World War I simply the inevitable expression of inter-imperialist rivalry.

Lenin's theory of imperialism was 'frozen' by Stalinist orthodoxy from 1930 onwards, and the changes which followed the Second World War were met by improvised 'updatings' of his work. So, as Arrighi writes,

by the end of the sixties, what had once been 'the pride' of Marxism – the theory of imperialism – has become a 'Tower of Babel', in which not even Marxists know any longer how to find their way.[50]

The ritual tributes to Lenin began to give way to systematic criticism in later years, and great stress was laid by some on the 'lack of scientific pretensions' of his short booklet on imperialism. Many of these criticisms centred around the relationship among Lenin's five tendencies outlined above. It is, for example, unclear why or how monopoly, capital export and the division of the world are linked together causally. Decolonisation has shown that the territorial division of the world amongst the powers is not essential to maintain the domination of capitalist combines (today the multinationals). A weaker line of criticism is put forward by several liberal writers, to the effect that the driving force behind Britain's colonisation of Africa was political and strategic, and did not have a clearly defined economic basis.[51] This simply confuses colonialism and imperialism, which Lenin maintains quite separate — one can exist without the other. More substantial is the point that Britain engaged in capital exports from the inception of industrial capitalism (the 1820s onwards) and there was no noticeable increment of this at the various phases Lenin mentioned as the commencement of a 'new' imperialist stage (1880s or 1890s). The monopolies generally developed after the 'partition of the world' and only in Germany can we detect any connection between monopolisation and imperialism. Above all, imperialism was to prove to be not the sign of a 'decaying' or 'over-ripe' capitalism as Lenin wrote, but rather a sign of its vigorous expansion.

It seems clear that Lenin's work on imperialism suffers from grave internal contradictions, mistaken timing of trends and lack of clear integration between them. Ironically, it became far more of a model of real processes in the 1920s and 1930s, but it then underwent a subtle transformation. In his original work, Lenin had maintained Marx's own views of capital's 'progressive' role in the Third World:

> the export of capital influences and greatly accelerates the development of capitalism in those countries to which it is exported, [and referred to it] expanding and deepening the further development of capitalism throughout the world.[52]

The victorious Russian Revolution (1917) had led to the formation of the Third (Communist) International in opposition to the social democratic Second International. The Comintern, unlike its predecessor, was a fervent supporter of the struggle for liberation in the colonial and semi-colonial countries, and the Leninist theory of imperialism was its cornerstone. In one fundamental sense it was altered — imperialism was gradually seen as an impediment to the capitalist development of the Third World. At its Sixth Congress (1928) a Comintern resolution on the colonial and semi-colonial countries declared that:

> Imperialism is related to the colonial country primarily as a parasite, sucking the blood from its economic organisms. . . . The specific colonial forms of capitalist exploitation . . . hinder the development of

the productive forces . . . Real industrialisation of the colonial country . . . is hindered by the metropolis. This is the essence of its function. . . .[53]

According to Bill Warren, 'the resolutions of this congress formalised the surrender of the Marxist analysis of imperialism to the requirements of bourgeois anti-imperialist propaganda.'[54] We shall return to this criticism shortly, but we must now see how the post-Second World War theories of imperialism developed along this new line of interpretation.

Paul Baran's *Political Economy of Growth*, published in 1957, represents an important shift in the Marxist theory of imperialism.[55] Monopoly capitalism is seen as the cause of stagnation at the centre and underdevelopment at the periphery. Unlike the classics (including Luxembourg) Baran saw the development of capitalism in the Third World following an intrinsically different path to that of the original industrialisers. His study of the 'morphology of backwardness' marks a systematic turn towards analysis of the Third World countries themselves (not just their role in a global imperialist system). Capitalist development of one area is shown to lead to the underdevelopment of another area, as the 'economic surplus' is drained from it. This concept of surplus is, of course, different from Marx's theory of surplus-value and directs attention away from the particular relations of production. His concept of development is thus quantitative (the size of the surplus) and teleological, in that he constantly refers to the 'potential surplus' a growth-oriented rationally ordered society could achieve. Whatever its shortcomings, this book was something of a breakthrough and generated a whole series of studies of imperialism and the Third World. The work by Harry Magdoff on US imperialism showed how it differed from the European imperialism analysed by Lenin.[56] A series of books by Pierre Jalée broadened the picture to analyse the role of the Third World in the world economy, and the nature of imperialism in the 1970s.[57] The emphasis was now on the 'pillage' of the Third World — how imperialism drained off basic raw materials and oil, and exploited cheap labour in the peripheral countries.

The new Marxist emphasis on the problems of *under*development and the reorientation of the theory of imperialism has recently been challenged by a number of writers. Against the turn of the 'Leninist' theory of imperialism towards growing concentration on the distortion or 'blocking' of Third World development, they called for a 'return to Marx'. Geoffrey Kay, standing on Marx's words, put it bluntly that 'capital created underdevelopment not because it exploited the underdeveloped world, but because it did not exploit it enough'.[58] Marx had, in fact, said that the more backward country will 'suffer not only from the development of capitalist production, but *also* from the incompleteness of that development'.[59] Nevertheless, the point is clear — all the symptoms of 'underdevelopment' are due to the lack of thoroughness in capital's transformation of the Third World in its own image. That capital's growth is endogenous or exogenous (introduced from outside) can make no difference to its laws of motion and general tendency towards accelerated accumulation and reproduction. Bill Warren goes even further, arguing that Lenin's theory of imperialism had begun a process 'through which the view that capitalism could be an instrument of social advance in pre-capitalist societies was erased from Marxism'.[60] In Warren's view, this is incorrect, because in fact:

> imperialism was the means through which the techniques, culture and institutions that had evolved in Western Europe over several centuries ... sowed their revolutionary seeds in the rest of the world.[61]

That this is not merely the generally 'progressive' nature of capitalism that Marx referred to (i.e., development of the forces of production) is clear from Warren's conclusion that 'capitalism and democracy are, I would argue, linked virtually as Siamese twins'.[62] We are certainly a long way from Lenin, but also a long way from what Marx would say today.

A response to this onslaught must be at several levels, because although it is polemical it raises fundamental problems that must be confronted. Warren has shown conclusively that the spread of capitalism into the Third World has often been underestimated by writers in the 'sociology of underdevelopment' tradition. But Brazil, Taiwan and South Korea are not the Third World — capitalist penetration has advanced in an uneven and partial manner.[63] Some of the purely consumption-oriented emphasis on income redistribution by development economists is surely naive, but Warren maybe goes too far when he says that 'the pursuit of income equality for its own sake is both unjust and undemocratic'.[64] The rational kernel of Warren's polemic is that the development of capitalism in the Third World is leading to the formation of an industrial proletariat which could act as the 'gravedigger' of capitalism as Marx foresaw. It is for that reason that he is so keen to draw the lines between nationalism and socialism. Dependency writers tended to reduce one to the other, but on the other hand, it is hard to conceive of a transition to socialism in the Third World which does not 'pass through' the resolution of the national question. Warren has denied *any* ethical element in socialism.[65] This renews Marx's cool-headed analysis of India but ignores his unconditional support of the rights of self-determination in Ireland. Marx never sat back to await the logical unfolding of capital's contradiction, as Warren seems to suggest doing in the Third World. Above all Warren ignores Marx's *dialectical* analysis, even in the case of India, where he pointed to the simultaneously destructive/progressive nature of capitalism. It still remains a fact that the second element is not in much evidence in Africa, Asia or Latin America.

In the belief that the Marxist theory of imperialism cannot remain at the level of fitting the facts to Lenin's work of 1916, we turn now to two of the main current debates.[66]

One of the most original contributions in the last decades is Arghiri Emmanuel's theory of 'unequal exchange', which he identifies as the mainspring of modern imperialism.[67] This 'imperialism of free trade' is based on the different level of wages and of exploitation which obtain between the advanced and the Third World countries. Capital is assumed to move freely round the world and hence the rate of profit is evened out, but wages, determined by social and historical elements, are maintained at subsistence level in the dependent countries. Then, when exchange of commodities occurs, those of the dependent country (low value of labour power) are exchanged below their value, but those of the imperialist country above it. The deterioration of the terms of exchange noted by the Economic Commission for Latin America is thus explained at a theoretical level. The criticisms of the 'unequal exchange' theory are many.[68] It is probably wrong to consider wages as an 'independent variable' as Emmanuel does, and the fact that they are low in the Third World is more a *result* of imperialism than a cause of it. By presenting the relation between 'rich' and 'poor' nations in terms of 'exploitation' Emmanuel is simplifying the complexity of the economic relations between countries and especially the international social relations of production. As with Lenin's original theory of imperialism, Emmanuel tends to see the proletariat of the industrial countries as co-beneficiaries of this exploitation of the Third World. In this sense he plays down the class struggle at the centre and accords an uncritical support to the nationalist movements — the dangerous logic is that if 'unequal exchange' is ended, imperialism and class domination will fade away.

From the underlying process of unequal exchange we pass to the very visible exploitation by the multinational or transnational corporations. These firms are today the 'bearers' of the international relations of production, and their mode of operation has understandably received a great deal of attention.[69] As the concrete institutional form of modern imperialism they can be studied only at the level of internationalisation of production and of capital, and not merely at the level of the firm. They are the result of a process of concentration and centralisation of capital on a world scale as analysed by Bukharin and Lenin, and amenable to explanation in these 'classical' terms. They have not led to the irrelevance of the nation-state, as some theorists believe, nor do they seem to be leading to the 'world trust' envisaged by Kautsky. In short, the multinationals have still not been adequately integrated into a Marxist theory of imperialism. Related to the conception of these international firms as somehow above the national boundaries of the 20th Century is the question of inter-imperialist rivalry. In spite of their name, the multinationals do have a national base, and rivalries between nations have not disappeared. Broadly, there are two positions competing today — one holds that the United States has achieved undisputed hegemony in the inter-imperialist system, whereas others argue that Western Europe and Japan pose a serious threat to US dominance.[70] If the latter trend is proved correct, Lenin's analysis of the inherent instability and trend towards militarism in imperialism may yet become political reality again.

Modes of Production Theory

Interest in 'modes of production', at least in Latin America, arose out of a directly political debate. As with 'modernisation theory' we cannot divorce this analytical category from the particular political context within which it arose. During the 1960s, a major area of debate in the political analysis of the Latin American social formations was the question of whether the relations of production in the countryside were 'feudal' or 'capitalist'. The traditional view of the Communist Parties, since around 1930, was that the agrarian tasks of the proletariat were 'anti-feudal'. Other writers argued that the cattle ranchers, mine owners and the big landholders were essentially new capitalist classes. Spain, itself, had been in transition to capitalism when the conquest of America took place, so feudalism could hardly have been transplanted there. Politically, this meant that a struggle against capitalism, and not just against feudalism, was necessary, even for a bourgeois-democratic revolution.[71] Gunder Frank was to codify this type of analysis and popularise it abroad. This advance on Marxist 'orthodoxy' led to a serious error however — the idea that the relations of production in Latin America were capitalist from the days of the Conquest. Clearly, insertion in the world capitalist economic system did not determine a capitalist mode of production throughout the continent. There was a distinct tendency to ignore the real persistence of non-capitalist relations of production in many agrarian areas of Latin America.

The critique of Gunder Frank is probably best exemplified by the article 'Feudalism and Capitalism in Latin America' by Ernesto Laclau.[72] Frank's 'circulationist' perspective (i.e., deriving the capitalist nature of these societies from insertion in the world market) is criticised on the basis of the orthodox Marxist prioritisation of the realm of production. Laclau points correctly to Frank's simplistic concept of 'exploitation' which stretches from the days of Pizarro (the Conquistador) to General Motors. He shows how the relations of production in the plantations, for example, are clearly non-capitalist in character. Laclau, however, takes a step backwards when he argues, as do the Communist Parties, that 'socialists should therefore seek an alliance with the national bourgeoisie, and form a united front with it against the oligarchy and imperialism'.[73] In fact, Laclau's critique of Frank for ignoring Marx's definition of capitalism as a mode of *production* is sound as far as it goes, but it could have situated the debate better in terms of the classical conception of 'combined and uneven development'.[74] I think it is important to note in this context that Marx is not unambiguously a 'productionist' as the following passage makes clear:

> Whether the commodities are the product of production based on slavery, the product of peasants (Chinese, Indian ryots), of a community (Dutch East Indies), of state production (such as existed in earlier epochs of Russian history, based on serfdom) or of half-savage hunting people, etc — as commodities and money they confront the money and

commodities in which industrial capital presents itself. . . . The character of the production process from which they derive is immaterial . . . the circulation process of industrial capital is characterized by the many-sided character of its origins, and the existence of the market as a world market.[75]

In conclusion, Marx was also a 'circulationist', or rather he did not separate the realm of production and circulation, counterposing one to the other.

The debate in Latin America was a continuation of an earlier polemic over the transition from feudalism to capitalism in Western Europe. One school, typified by Maurice Dobb, concentrated on the internal transformations of the feudal mode of production and the elements within it which brought it to a crisis — in Marxist terms, how the relations of production became a barrier to the further expansion of the forces of production. The other 'circulationist' perspective advanced by Paul Sweezy in a polemic with Dobb, concentrated on how the growth of international commerce had a dissolving effect on feudalism.[76] The stress is on how exchange brought a percolation of money into the largely self-sufficient manorial economy and broke up the links of personal bondage. The property relations perspective of Dobb, and in Latin America Laclau, is clearly closer to Marx's own conception, though Wallerstein argues that Sweezy and Frank are closer to the 'spirit' of his writings. However that may be, Perry Anderson's recent broad survey of the debate has helped us break out of this sterile counterposition.[77] He shows how, only under capitalism will the mode of surplus extraction take a purely 'economic' form, with pre-capitalist modes of production there is need for 'extra economic' coercion. Serfdom is, in fact, legally enforced labour services performed for the feudal lord in exchange for his 'protection'. The crisis of feudalism can, therefore, not be explained by purely economic factors. He refers to the 'parcellisation of sovereignty' (fragmentation of feudal authority) as a key factor in the transition. This occurs alongside the 'spontaneous combustion' of the forces of production through technological advance and the voyages of discovery. In Figure 1.2 we can see the main positions of the classical debate on the transition, and their respective Latin American supporters.

The position of Marx himself was that 'what new mode of production arises in place of the old, does not depend on trade, but rather on the character of the old mode of production itself'.[78] Having said that, though production is *determinant*, circulation may be a *dominant* factor in certain historical conjunctures.

The real point is that, as Brenner says:

the mere rise of trade cannot, in itself, determine the processes of dissolution. They are understandable only in terms of the conflictual processes, processes of class transformation and class struggle. . . .[79]

The development of capitalism in Western Europe was not simply owing to the 'profit motive' of overseas traders, but rather to the emergence of a new

Figure 1.2
The Transition from Feudalism to Capitalism

Author	Characterisation of feudalism	Characterisation of capitalism	Dynamic of feudal decline and capitalist rise
SWEEZY FRANK	Near-subsistence system with low division of labour. Only limited development of trade.	Production for profit through market exchange. Trade-based division of labour.	International trade and forms 'external' to feudalism. Mercantile development.
DOBB LACLAU	Agrarian society based on coerced serf labour, consistent with trade and some urbanisation.	Expansive capital accumulation. "Free" wage-labour (peasant land appropriation) acts as a commodity.	Endogenous class struggle between lords and serfs over control of the surplus. Priority of agrarian transformations.
ANDER-SON	Land-based economy with neither land nor labour as commodities. Extra-economic coercion through politico-legal sovereignty of feudal lord.	Economic surplus extraction through commodified wage-labour.	Combination of urbanisation and feudal parcellised sovereignty with "spontaneous combustion of the forces of production".

Source: adapted from Holton, R. (1981) Marxist theories of social change and the transition from feudalism to capitalism. *Theory and Society*, No.10, p.839.

system of class relations and surplus extraction (separation of artisans from the means of production and development of 'free' labour). Likewise, the 'underdevelopment' of the Third World cannot be reduced to the effects of Europe's predatory needs — it is the social and historically determined class structures that determined what type of relations imperialism would establish. It is not an abstract process of capitalist expansion which determines development/underdevelopment — this is mediated by particular class structures.

It was the work of the French Marxist school of Louis Althusser, and particularly his collaborator Etienne Balibar, which systematically elaborated a conception of modes of production.[80] In this analysis, work is the basic and fundamental condition of all human life and this labour process is always carried out under a specific social form. The instruments of this work process, and the correlated forms of co-operation between workers, constitute the *forces of production*; these develop within specific *relations of production* between the direct producers, the non-producers, and the material means of production. All class societies are composed of productive workers and a class of non-producers who appropriate the means of production, giving rise to a form of exploitation of social labour. A *mode of production* then consists of the specific historical combination of the forces of production and the relations of production. Each mode of production determines a particular mode of appropriation of surplus labour, i.e., a surplus of the product of labour over and above the costs of maintenance of the labour. Actual societies are composed of more than one mode of production which together make up a socio-economic formation or, more simply, a *social formation*. The major modes of production analysed by Marx were: the classless primitive community, the slave-based society of classical times, the feudal society based on serfdom, the modern bourgeois society based on the capitalist mode of production and the classless communist society of the future.[81] He also referred to an Asiatic mode of production in which primitive communities were combined with a state power which controlled essential economic resources.

Balibar, who had developed a 'systematic' analysis of modes of production, later launched the sharpest attack on the *formalism* of his original analysis based on a series of invariant elements (forces of production and relations of production, etc) which 'combined' to form a mode of production. This formalistic and static conception was not improved by a general 'theory of transition' which ignored history and simply rearranged the constituent elements.

Balibar now maintains correctly that:

> there is not, and cannot be, a *general theory of modes of production* in the strong sense of the word theory: it would become inevitably a theory of universal history. By definition, each mode of production implies a specific theory, at once with regards to its form of social process, its tendential laws, and as regards the historical conditions in which it is constituted, it is reproduced and it is transformed.[82]

In this way, we can break away from the futile model-building characteristic of most modernisation theories. We are seeking explanations for real history and not just an abstract typology of 'modes of production'. It should be clear now that the modes listed above are neither historically complete, nor can they be seen as a neat historical sequence. History is simply not a struggle between structures — the modes of production — its 'motor' is always the class struggle.

It is the recent work by John Taylor, *From Modernisation to Modes of Production*, which most clearly sets the Althusserian concepts to work analysing Third World social formations. He begins with a systematic criticism of the sociologies of development *and* underdevelopment as equally economistic and teleological. They are both seen to work within a framework where 'the present is defined in terms of the potentiality of a future state, and the extent to which elements of the present could function to bring this about.'[83] Taylor, on the other hand, examines how a capitalist mode of production comes to exist in the Third World through the subordination of previously dominant non-capitalist modes. He rejects the notions of 'underdevelopment' and 'modernising society', in favour of a Marxist concept of 'transitional social formations'. What is specific about this transition is that it is brought about by imperialist penetration which works to separate direct producers from the means of production. As he says, 'the Third World formation can, therefore, be analysed as being structured (or determined in the last instance) by an articulation which is produced largely as an effect of imperialist penetration.'[84] This is seen to provide a rigorous basis from which to analyse the historical development of the different levels of the social formation: economic, political and ideological in the Althusserian system.[85] Finally, he refers to a whole series of 'dislocations' characteristic of Third World social formations owing to the coexistence of political and ideological forms required for different modes of production in contradiction. An example would be the patrimonial ideology of the 'semi-feudal' mode that supports the landowning class, which may be in contradiction with an agrarian reform suited to the general requirements of a capitalist reproduction.

Taylor's book has systematically drawn together the criticisms of the conventional theory of modernisation and the theory of underdevelopment associated with Frank which never quite established itself as a viable theoretical alternative. By situating his project within the Althusserian theoretical universe he is led into a structural determinism where real history takes second place. So, for example, he sees the uneven and restricted development of capitalism as owing to imperialist restrictions (marketing requirements) and what he calls 'the resistance put up against imperialist penetration by the non-capitalist mode. . . .'[86] It is not, however, modes of production which 'resist' anything but concrete social classes. In Taylor's scheme, it is the articulation of modes of production that explains the particular class structures of the Third World, not the other way round. All social phenomena are reduced to mere effects of structural determinations.[87] The 'requirements' of modes of production (defined by whom?) dictate the course of history, and the class struggle appears only at the level of 'conjunctural analysis'. Taylor spends some pages discussing Chile in the decades preceding the Popular Unity government (1970–73) and he concludes that 'the holding of state power by an alliance between fractions of the capitalist class, in opposition to a non-capitalist class . . . is extremely precarious. . . .'[88] In short, Allende came to power with a socialist programme because a 'non-capitalist' landowning class had blocked attempts at agrarian reform by the Christian Democrats. Thus, politics and conscious intervention by various social forces is left out of the account and we really have no explanation at all. This type of project may seem rigorous, but it ultimately detracts from (theoretically guided) empirical research because it can only study the 'phenomenal forms' of articulations and dislocations of modes of production.

In the Third World there has also been considerable interest in the 'articulation' of modes of production for the analysis of the colonial period and the agrarian question. The concept of 'articulation' seeks to provide a more sophisticated analysis than the mere 'combination' or 'coexistence' of modes of production. According to Wolpe, articulation:

> refers to the relationship between the reproduction of the capitalist economy on the one hand and the reproduction of productive units organised according to pre-capitalist relations and forces of production on the other.[89]

This definition leaves it open for us to conceive of a capitalist mode of production which subsumes other, non-capitalist relations of exploitation – whether slave, feudal or subsistence – under its laws of motion. When, however, it comes to *specifying* what the modes of production in the Third World actually are, more problems arise.

The first area which presents a difficulty lies in the attempts to specify a particular 'colonial' mode of production. Hamza Alavi has attempted to do this in relation to colonial India, which he sees as neither feudal (there was widespread commodity production) nor capitalist (there was little accumulation).[90] He goes on to refer to a 'colonial mode of production' characterised by subordination to the needs of imperialism, and with internally disarticulated economies (i.e., articulated only via their links with the metropolis). There is then, logically, a 'post-colonial mode of production' when colonial state power is overthrown but many of the old features continue. It is doubtful whether Alavi's model of colonialism differs substantially from that Paul Baran paints of a typical underdeveloped country, or what Samir Amin calls 'peripheral capitalism'. The truth of the matter is, as Brewer points out, that:

> Alavi is entitled to call this a mode of production if he wishes, but it is not remotely like any other Marxist concept of a mode of production. It is not an abstract conceptual construction, it has no defining relation of production, it does not define any specific class opposition.[91]

Much the same could be said of the attempts to construct a theory of an African mode of production.[92] This is not to say that the concept is useless – there has been interesting work done on the Incas in terms of the Asiatic mode of production[93] – but that one cannot apply a linear model of modes of production to the dependent countries.

There was an attempt to construct a 'colonial slavery mode of production' in relation to Latin America, but this encountered severe criticism.[94] During the 19th Century, mining based on slavery was a predominant economic sector in some areas. Some writers concluded that the social formation was dominated by the slavery mode of production. Now, for one there were hardly any *national* social formations during this period but rather, distinct regional economies. At most, slavery would be dominant in a given region and the slave owners' political representation in the power bloc would hardly be predominant. Slavery, as an institution, was furthermore in decline throughout the century being finally dissolved between 1850–80. One must seriously question how a declining mode of production can be dominant. Taking the Brazilian case, that slavery existed in the sugar plantations of the north-east did not, for one moment, make Brazil a slave society comparable to Ancient Greece. At most we can speak of slave *forms* of production being employed in a mercantile setting (i.e., commercial exchanges with the metropolis) determined by the logic of a developing capitalism.

A more fruitful area for modes of production analysis has been the question of subsistence production within a capitalist economy. Wolpe has shown conclusively how the overall rate of surplus value in South Africa's apartheid capitalism depends above all on the maintenance of non-capitalist relations of production in the (Black) Reserves.[95] These furnish part of the means of reproduction of the migrant labour force which turns the wheels of South Africa's industry. In Nigeria, the colonial government once turned down a proposal by Unilever to establish a plantation there because it would create a large rural proletariat. Instead, they strove to reinforce the 'tribal community' to provide a permanent reserve of cheap labour-power without the attendant political risks of permanent proletarianisation. Of more general application is the concept of 'petty-commodity production', based on ownership of the means of production and very little division of labour. This is a relation from capitalism's 'pre-history', which survives and prospers in the dependent capitalist development of the Third World. One variant arises from wage rates that are insufficient to maintain and reproduce a family. Widespread female production in the Third World has led some authors to distinguish a 'domestic mode of production'. Meillasoux shows how it has been crushed and divided as a mode of production so it cannot reproduce itself in a coherent fashion, but:

> *domestic relations of production* have not disappeared completely. They still support millions of productive units integrated to a greater or lesser extent in the capitalist economy, disgorging goods and energy under the crushing weight of imperialism.[96]

Initial reaction to the modes of production analysis on the part of some dependency writers was that it represented an intellectual fashion and, even worse, an attempt to resurrect a discredited, dogmatic Marxism. Our quick survey has indicated that it can, however, be a fruitful guide to analysis in certain areas, though there are still serious problems to overcome. There has been a tendency to extend the term 'mode of production' to just about any distinctive productive system: colonial, African, subsistence, etc. We must question whether we are really dealing with a distinct mode of production in the Marxist sense, or simply a combination of non-capitalist labour processes under the overall domination of the capitalist world economy.[97] Certainly, there was slavery in the Southern states of North America but is that equivalent to the slavery of Antiquity? Gunder Frank was quite correct to show that, in the first case it was developed as part of *capitalist* expansion overseas. If peasants in the north-east of Brazil still pay rent-in-kind to the landlord, does this mean there is a coexistence of capitalist and feudal modes of production there? These non-capitalist labour relations constitute distinct *forms* of production, but they hardly operate as distinct modes of production with a dynamic of their own. They are rather moulded, destroyed and re-created by capitalism, they are not competitors on equal terms as implied in the term 'articulation'. Capitalism subordinates these non-capitalist forms of production to *its* logic, even though it has not overcome all pre-capitalist relations, as Marx, writing on India, tended to believe.

The most serious criticism of the modes of production approach is that it tends to displace systematic concern with the historical class struggle. This reaches its peak in the work of Hindness and Hirst for whom 'the study of history is not only scientifically, but also politically valueless'.[98] These authors, after their earlier formalist typology of pre-capitalist modes,[99] went on in a subsequent work to reject even the conception of modes of production. Their direction was away from Marxism towards a form of empiricism. Pierre-Philipe Rey, on the other hand, went on from his seminal study of the articulation of modes of production to a very different type of 'autocritique'.[100] In it, he soundly criticised intellectualising for its own sake, and turned the study of modes of production towards an understanding of the basis and operation of *class alliances*. This is in contrast to most work in this area, which Foster-Carter rightly criticises for raising modes of production to 'entities occupying the totality of explanatory space' and, when not omitting the political level, relegating it to 'a minor and preordained place'.[101] Many who criticised making classes the 'subjects of history' now place modes of production in that role. If we must reject a conception of modes of production as a structural grid along which history moves in a logical progression, it must be recognised that its general impact has been to raise the theoretical level of 'dependency' analysis. Above all, it has directed our attention to Marx's concept of the *social relations of production*:

> The specific economic form in which unpaid surplus labour is pumped out of the direct producers determines the relationship of domination and servitude. . . . It is in each case the direct relationship of the owners of the conditions of production to the immediate producers in which we find the innermost secret, the hidden basis of the entire social edifice and, hence also the political form of the relationship of sovereignty and dependence, in short, the specific form of state in each case.[102]

Dependent Reproduction

There has been a realisation in recent years that we must move beyond the sterile counterposition between the broad (but vague) dependency analysis on the one hand and the more precise (yet abstract) modes of production approach.[103] The theory of imperialism – yet to be fully developed – can serve as the general context in which we study the Third World social formations, but it does not itself provide a guide to the internal development process. Bearing that in mind we now move to elaborate a conception of 'dependent reproduction' which accepts the basic premise of dependency theory (domination by imperialism) but seeks in the modes of production approach the adequate theoretical tools (principally relations of production) to conceptualise the precise mechanisms of dependency.

As Marx notes in *Capital*:

> whatever the social form of the production process, it has to be continuous, it must periodically repeat the same phases. A society can no more cease to produce than it can cease to consume. When viewed, therefore, as a connected whole, and in the constant flux of its incessant renewal, every social process of production is at the same time a process of reproduction. The conditions of production are at the same time the conditions of reproduction.[104]

Viewed as a process of reproduction, capitalism produces not only commodities but must constantly recreate the capital-relation itself: the capitalist and the wage-labourer. As Marx says, 'this incessant reproduction, this perpetuation of the worker, is the absolutely necessary condition for capitalist production.'[105] This reproduction by the relations of production has obviously an international dimension, and at this general level we should move towards a conception of imperialism as a mode of reproduction of cheap labour power.[106] Unless we move to the level of reproduction we are bound to have a flat, static and distorted view of society. Again quoting Marx:

> capital, as self-valorising value, does not just comprise class relations, a definite social character that depends on the existence of labour as wage-labour. It is a movement, a circulatory process through different stages. . . . Hence it can only be grasped as a movement, and not as a static thing.[107]

We must distinguish firstly between 'simple' reproduction (all surplus value produced in the course of the year is consumed by the capitalist) and reproduction 'on an extended scale' (accumulation assumes that part of surplus value and becomes extra capital). The second distinction is between the two major 'departments' into which the total production of society can be divided: Department I, production of the means of production or, in

31

economic parlance, 'capital goods', and Department II, production of the means of consumption, or 'consumer goods'. The second can further be broken down into: (a) the necessary means of consumption, or those which enter the consumption of the working class, and (b) luxury means of consumption which enter the consumption only of the capitalist class. In the reproduction schemas of Volume II of *Capital* Marx shows the conditions of proportionality that must obtain between the departments for reproduction to prosper. The concept of expanded reproduction points to the tremendous self-expansion drive of capital, which constantly moves on to a greater and higher level of accumulation. Finally, the movement of capital must be seen as a combination of three different 'functional forms' or circuits: capital in the form of money that buys the elements of production ('money capital'); capital in the form of the industrial labour process that combines productively the elements of production ('productive capital') and finally, capital in the form of industrial products, which are sold as commodities containing surplus-value ('commodity capital').

There are several fundamental differences between Marx's reproduction schemas and the nature of dependent reproduction.[108] The 'laws of motion' of capital may be the same everywhere, but their concrete working out will be subject to great variations. In the first place, it is unrealistic to operate on the assumption of a closed economy, and the element of foreign trade must be an integral element of a dependent reproduction schema. Owing to the lack of a substantial internal market and the moulding of the dependent economy by imperialism, most of the realisation (sale) of commodity takes place on the foreign market. Next, the division of labour between the departments of social capital are complicated by the presence of non-capitalist relations of production. Finally, apart from the most industrialised countries of the Third World, there is no internal capital-goods sector; although, arguably, the export sector fulfils this role (by earning the currency which buys machinery). This means that increases in productive capacity may lead to further exports, but not to an internal expansion of Department I which is the main dynamic element in the capitalist mode of production. That is why there is not an integrated expansion of the means of subsistence and the means of production in the process of expanded reproduction. It is the exchange relations established with international capital which determine (to a greater or lesser extent) the conditions of capital accumulation in the Third World. The consumption of the working class is not an important dynamic element in this form of capitalism: Department II(a) is often 'stagnant' and traditional, whereas Department II(b) (luxury goods) is, with Department I, the dynamic sector. Foreign capitalists also 'consume' (through profit repatriations) a large part of surplus value rather than reinvest, making for a very uneven and partial extended reproduction of capital in the Third World.

In the graphic representation of dependent reproduction in Figure 1.3 we can see some of the complex interrelationships involved. The subsistence sector is essential to the cheap reproduction of labour-power by, for example, providing cheap housing and food and thus keeping wages low. The vast

Figure 1.3
Dependent Reproduction: Inter-sectoral Flows

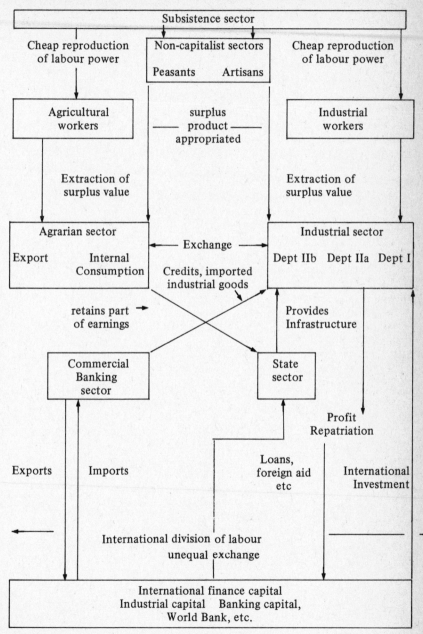

range of non-capitalist relations of production — from peasants to urban artisans — are indirectly exploited by the capitalist sector, which appropriates surplus labour through them. Industrial and agricultural workers are directly exploited by capital, which extracts surplus value from them. The industrial sector is usually dominated by international investment through the transnational corporations which repatriate most of their profits abroad. A few Third World countries have a Department I producing means of production, but even then, the high technology sector is situated abroad ('technological dependence'). Department II(a) producing wage goods, has a limited market in the Third World (owing to low wages) and must engage in exports to survive. Department II(b) produces the luxury and durable consumer goods for the bourgeoisie and, in some cases, the middle class. The state sector may retain some of the foreign exchange earnings of the agrarian export sector to promote industrialisation, and in all cases, provide the necessary infra-structure (e.g. transport network) and cheap inputs (e.g. power). The agrarian sector is divided primarily between the export-oriented enterprises and those directed towards internal consumption. The commercial sector usually intermediates with the international market through the import-export houses (often dominated by foreign capital), and the banking sector (also with heavy foreign participation) maintains the circuit of monetary capital which is the necessary complement of productive capital. The dependent economy is finally integrated into the world economy through the international division of labour in which a process of unequal exchange operates to its disadvantage.

It would be wrong to think that dependent reproduction was a purely economic process. Certainly the mode of extraction of surplus value provides a key to the 'innermost secret' of the social structure, but these political, legal, ideological and social elements have their own 'relative autonomy'. If the social system must be reproduced so must its political structures. The intellectual élite is educated in the universities of Europe and the USA, so that in Chile we have the 'Chicago boys' running the economy. The military élite must receive its counter-insurgency training and this is provided in various US schools. Trade union bureaucrats must have a sound 'business unionism' attitude so they often have their courses in the USA. As against the diffusion theories, magazines such as *Life* and *Reader's Digest* do not 'modernise' Latin America, but rather promote ideological dependency. Even children are integrated into the process of dependent reproduction: it has been shown how, for example, the Donald Duck comics read in Latin America are a powerful element in ideological subordination.[109] There is a broad range of 'extra-economic coercion' in the process of dependent reproduction, as under feudalism. The machinations of the CIA in Latin America, so well documented by ex-agent Philip Agee, and the role of ITT against the Allende government in Chile, are merely the tip of the iceberg.[110] If I do not spend more time detailing this process it is because it has been dealt with at length elsewhere, and not because I consider it unimportant. In fact, the social contradictions engendered by dependent reproduction would probably burst out into the open without this 'foreign aid' to the local ruling class.

We can now briefly summarize the conclusions of this chapter. Dependency writers carried out a trenchant critique of hitherto prevalent modernisation and development theories. However, whereas the evolutionism of the first saw advanced capitalism as a general paradigm of development, devoid of all contradictions, dependency theory tended towards an abstract conception of the world economy, imposing primary goods production on certain areas and blocking development. At its best, this school points towards historical analysis focused particularity on social classes. This we can retain, also bearing in mind that the Marxist critics of dependency *theory* do not deny the existence of dependency as the basic trait of Third World countries. A simple return to the orthodox Marxist/Leninist theories of imperialism and modes of production is no panacea for the admitted weaknesses of dependency theory.[111] In both areas there is little agreement as to what actually constitutes the 'correct' version, but we should retain the focus on underlying economic processes which are essential to a rigorous understanding of social class. Any static or formalistic theory of development will fail to uncover the essential relations involved. To remedy this, we advanced a concept of dependent reproduction which could account for the dynamics of under-development. This is, of course, only a framework and the historical element — only formally present in most dependency works and largely absent from the modes of production debates — must now be introduced. As Lenin was fond of saying, theory is grey but the tree of life grows green.

The Statistics of Dependent Development

As we noted in the preface, the Third World label covers a multitude of political and economic situations. Statistical analysis is also notoriously unreliable, because if we take Libya's Gross National Product 'per capita' of $8,640 in 1980 it compares favourably with Britain's $7,920, and even the USA's $9,363 but this cannot suffice to take Libya out of the Third World. But whatever the problems, it is necessary to provide a statistical breakdown of the Latin American countries if we are not to remain at an abstract theoretical level.

We have used the 1982 World Development Report to elaborate a chart of the Latin American republics in Table 1:1 even though the categories employed are far from satisfactory. Gross National Product (GNP) measures a country's total annual income including net earnings from abroad. The first column shows the absolute amount of GNP, or national income, theoretically available per head of population measured in US dollars. The second column indicates the average annual growth rate between 1960 and 1980 in percentage form. These are the conventional 'indicators' of economic development, to which we must add just two 'social indicators', namely, infant mortality rates and number of population served by each doctor. Other so called 'indices of modernisation' would be the proportion of inhabitants living in cities, life

Table 1.1
Latin America: Social and Economic Indicators

COUNTRY	GROSS NATIONAL PRODUCT PER CAPITA (1960-1980)		SOCIAL INDICATORS		DISTRIBUTION OF GROSS DOMESTIC PRODUCT (%) (1960-1980)							
	Dollars 1980	Average annual growth rate (percentage) 1960-1980	Infant mortality rate (aged 0-1) 1980	Population per doctor 1977	Agriculture 1960-1980		Industry 1960-1980		Manufacturing* 1960-1980		Services 1960-1980	
Argentina	2,390	2.2	45	530	16	13	38	46	32	37	46	41
Bolivia	570	2.1	131	1,850	26	18	25	29	15	14	49	53
Brazil	2,050	5.1	77	1,700	16	10	35	37	26	28	49	53
Chile	2,150	1.6	43	1,620	10	7	51	37	29	21	39	56
Colombia	1,180	3.0	56	1,970	34	28	26	30	17	22	40	42
Costa Rica	1,730	2.2	24	1,390	26	17	20	29	14	20	54	54
Cuba	1,410	4.4	21	626	25	16	65	68			(+ construction: 15%)	
										1974**		
Dominican Rep.	1,160	3.4	68	–	27	18	23	27	17	15	50	55
Ecudor	1,270	4.5	82	1,620	29	13	19	38	13	8	48	49
El Salvador	660	1.6	78	3,600	32	27	19	21	15	15	49	52
Guatemala	1,080	2.8	70	2,490	31	26	13	19	10	13	56	55
Haiti	270	0.5	115	5,940	47	40	14	22	10	13	39	38
Honduras	560	1.1	88	3,290	37	31	19	25	13	17	44	44
Mexico	2,090	2.6	56	1,820	16	10	29	38	19	24	55	52
Nicaragua	740	0.9	91	1,670	24	23	21	31	16	25	55	46
Panama	1,730	3.3	22	1,220	23	14	21	24	13	14	56	62
Paraguay	1,300	3.2	47	2,160	36	30	20	25	17	17	44	45
Peru	930	1.1	88	1,560	18	8	33	45	24	27	49	47
Uruguay	2,810	1.4	40	540	19	10	28	33	21	25	53	57
Venezuela	3,630	2.6	42	930	6	6	22	47	–	16	72	47

*Manufacturing is part of the industrial sector, but its share of GDP is shown separately because it typically is the most dynamic part of the industrial sector.

**The data on Cuba is not comparable as it refers to material production in agriculture and industry alone.

Source: The World Bank (1982) *World Development Report 1982*. New York; Oxford University Press. Data for Panama, Guatemala and Haiti were elaborated from tables in Inter-American Bank (1982). *Economic and Social Progress in Latin America*. Washington. Date for Cuba

expectancy and literacy rates. The two indicators we use are sufficient to indicate the value placed on human life in the different countries. Development in GNP terms does not always lead to socio-economic growth defined in more global social terms.

The following set of figures are for the distribution of Gross Domestic Product (GDP) which simply measures the total wealth generated within a country each year, i.e., excludes income from abroad or payable abroad. The figures indicate the percentage of goods and services generated respectively by the agricultural sector (agriculture, forestry, hunting and fishing), the industrial sector (mining, manufacturing, construction, electricity, water and gas), the manufacturing sector taken separately on its own – and the services sector (all other branches of the economy). In the colonial and semi-colonial mode of accumulation, the bulk of production consisted of agrarian or mining products destined almost exclusively for the external market. The post-war expansion of international capitalism has led to a partial and uneven industrialisation in most of Latin America, which is reflected in the general rise of industry between 1960 and 1980. The services sector is a 'catch-all which covers economic activities as diverse as the big banks and the car washer in the streets below. A relatively large services sector can go along with a dynamic expanding capitalism (Brazil) or a more stagnant 'traditional' society (Bolivia).

In interpreting the data we must bear in mind some further reservations about the categories used. National income statistics are ill-equipped to deal with non-monetary sources of value, such as subsistence production or domestic labour. Not only does this write out the bulk of the population from the statistics, but a rise in GNP could simply refer to the expansion of the monetary economy and not a genuine development of the forces of production. Furthermore, the use of a particular national currency (the US dollar) as an international standard causes problems. As the authors of the very useful *State of the World Atlas* point out:

> even under conditions of monetary stability, a national currency is significantly affected by both the performance of the related national economy and by shifts in the international investment. In a period of floating exchange rates, when the value of the dollar standard in other currencies moves constantly and often sharply, the distortions are enormous.[112]

Most important of all, GNP per capita tells us nothing about the *internal* distribution of wealth in each country, which classes profit from the expansion of the economy and which provide the surplus value which makes it possible. Additionally, the figures for 'agriculture' do not tell us which modes or forms of production prevail, nor does 'industry' distinguish between the multinational corporation and the artisanal workshop. In Part II we shall examine all these questions in a qualitative analysis of the class structure of the Third World, but the quantitative breakdown provided here can serve as a starting point. We require, however, the elaboration of more concepts before we can make full sense of the social reality lying behind this statistical 'raw material'.

As a guide to the broad categories of capitalist development in Latin America we can elaborate a typology based on the shifting patterns of capital accumulation. These provide a very rough classification of the countries listed in Table 1.1:[113]

1) in a few countries a fairly high degree of previous industrialisation resulted in the incorporation of certain sectors of the economy into the international circuit of expanded reproduction. As industrial activity expands it begins to act as the axis for an internal circuit of capital accumulation and realisation of surplus value. These economies take on functions of *intermediation* within the international economic system (what Wallerstein calls the 'semi-periphery'). Brazil is, without doubt, the most advanced example, but Mexico, and to a lesser extent Argentina, can be added.

2) another larger group of countries has a relatively significant industrial sector but this is much more recent and hardly incorporated into capital's international circuit of reproduction. It has resulted, however, in the expansion of the internal circuit of capital accumulation and there is local realisation of an important part of the surplus value generated. Non-capitalist relations of production persist, but are becoming rapidly subordinated to the dictates of capitalism. We can include Colombia, Chile, Venezuela, Peru, Uruguay, and possibly Ecuador, in this category in spite of their specific differences.

3) a final group of countries is only beginning to take the path of the countries listed above, and they are still tied fundamentally to a pattern of semi-colonial accumulation. The internal circuit of capital accumulation is still very weak, and agriculture or mining, based on non-capitalist forms of production, dominate the economy. This is the case for Paraguay, Bolivia and most of the countries of Central America.

References

1. Lenin, V.I. (1972) *Collected Works*, Volume 38. Moscow, Progress Publishers, p.360.
2. Dos Santos, T. (1976) The crisis of development theory and the problem of dependence in Latin America. *Underdevelopment and Development*, (ed) H. Bernstein. London, Penguin Books, p.76.
3. Sunkel, O. and Paz, P. (1970) *El Subdesarollo Latino-americano y la Teoría del Desarollo*. Mexico Siglo XXI.
4. Furtado, C. (1970) *Economic Development in Latin America. A Survey from Colonial Times to the Cuban Revolution*. Cambridge, Cambridge

University Press.

5. Dos Santos, T. (1972) *Socialismo o Fascismo. El Nuevo caracter de la dependencia y el dilemma latinoamericano*. Buenos Aires, Ediciones Periferia.
6. Bambirra, V. (1973) *Capitalismo Dependiente Latinoamericano*. Santiago, Prensa Latinoamericana.
7. Marini, R.M. (1973) *Dialéctica de la Dependencia*. Mexico/Ediciones Era.
8. Caputo, O. and Pizarro, R. (1974) *Dependencia y Relaciones Internacionales*. Costa Rica: Ediciones Educa. p.51.
9. Frank, A.G. (1967) *Capitalism and Underdevelopment in Latin America*. New York, Monthly Review Press, and (1969) *Latin America: Underdevelopment or Revolution.* New York, Monthly Review Press. For an assessment of this work see Booth, D. (1975) André Gunder Frank: an introduction and appreciation. *Beyond the Sociology of Development*, (eds) I. Oxaal, T. Barnett and D. Booth. London, Routledge and Kegan Paul, pp.50–8.
10. For a critique of this school see Cypher, J. (1979) Internationalization of Capital and the Transformation of Social Formations. A Critique of the Monthly Review School. *Review of Radical Political Economy*, Vol.II No.4, 33–49.
11. Cardoso, F.H. (1971) *Ideologías de la burguesía industrial en sociedades dependientes (Argentina y Brasil)*. Mexico, Siglo XXI.
12. Cardoso, F.H. and Faletto, E. (1979) *Dependency and Development in Latin America*. California, University of California Press, p.xvi. For a review of Cardoso's work see Kahl, J. (1976) *Modernization, Exploitation and Dependency in Latin America – Germani, González Casanova and Cardoso*. New Jersey, Transaction Books.
13. For a general survey of the dependency literature see O'Brien, P. (1975) A critique of Latin American theories of dependency. *Beyond the Sociology of Development*, op. cit. pp.7–27; Palma, G. (1978) Dependency: A formal theory of underdevelopment or a methodology for the analysis of concrete situations. *World Development*, Vol.6: 881–924, and Chilcote, R. (ed)(1982) *Dependency and Marxism. Towards a Resolution of the Debate*. Boulder, Colorado. West View Press.
14. See for example Chase-Dunn, C. (1975) The Effect of international economic dependence on development and inequality: a cross-national study. *American Sociological Review*, Vol.40 No.12: 720–30, and Kaufman, R., Chernotsky, H. and Geller, D. (1975) A Preliminary Test of the Theory of Dependency. *Comparative Politics*, Vol.7 No.3: 303–30.
15. Cardoso, F.H. (1977) The consumption of dependency theory in the US. *Latin American Research Review*, Vol.XII No.3: 7–24.
16. See Weffort F. (1971) Nota sôbre a 'Teoria da dependência': teoria de classe ou ideologia nacional. *Estudos CEBRAP* No.1: 3–45. (São Paulo, Brazil).

17. See for example Johnson, C. (1981) Dependency Theory and the Processes of Capitalism and Socialism. *Dependency and Marxism*, op. cit. pp.55–81.

18. For a development of this critique see Bernstein, H. (1979) Sociology of underdevelopment as sociology of development? *Development Theory: Four Critical Studies*, (ed) D. Lehman. London, Frank Cass, pp.77–106.

19. Petras, J. (1981) Dependency and World System Theory: A critique and new directions. *Dependency and Marxism*, op. cit. p.150.

20. Palma, G. (1978) *Dependency*, op. cit. p.900.

21. Cardoso, F.H. (1975) *Autoritarismo e Democratizacão*. Rio de Janeiro, Paz e Terra.

22. Bambirra, V. (1978) *Teoría de la dependencia: una anticritica*. Mexico, Siglo XXI.

23. See Cardoso, F.H. and Serra, J. (1978) Las desventuras de la dialéctica de la dependencia, and Marini, R.M. (1978) Las razones del neodesarollismo (respuesta a F.M. Cardoso y J. Serra) *Revista Mexicana de Sociología*, Vol XL, E, 9–55, pp.57–106.

24. Dos Santos, T. (1978) *Imperialismo y Dependencia*. Mexico, Ediciones Era.

25. See Villamil, J. (ed)(1978) *Transnational Capitalism and National Development – New Perspectives on Dependence*. Brighton, Harvester Press.

26. Kaplinsky, R., Henley, J.S. and Leys, C. (1980) *Review of African Political Economy*, No 17, pp.83–113; for a pioneering analysis of the African continent from a dependency perspective see Rodney, W. (1972) *How Europe Underdeveloped Africa*. London, Bogle – L'Ouverture Publications.

27. See Wallerstein, I. (1979) *The Capitalist World Economy*. Cambridge, Cambridge University Press; and Hopkins, T. and Wallerstein, I. (eds) (1982) *World-System Analysis – Theory and Methodology*. London, Sage Publications. For a critique of this perspective see Skopcol, T. (1977) Wallerstein's World Capitalist System: A Theoretical and Historical Critique. *American Journal of Sociology*, Vol.82 No.5: 1075–90; and also Navarro, V. (1982) The Limits of the World Systems Theory in Defining Capitalist and Socialist Formations. *Science and Society*, Vol.XLVI No.1: 77–90.

28. Frank, A.G. (1978) *Dependent Accumulation and Underdevelopment*. London, Macmillan.

29. See Amin, S. (1974) *Accumulation on a World Scale*. New York, Monthly Review Press.

30. Petras, J. (1981) *State and Power in the Third World*. London, Zed Press, p.68.

31. See Lenin, V.I. (1974) *The Development of Capitalism in Russia*. Moscow, Progress Publishers. For a contemporary critique see Bleaney, M. (1976) *Under-Consumption Theories – A History and Critical*

Analysis. London, Lawrence and Wishart.
32. Luxemburg, R. (1971) *The Accumulation of Capital.* London, Routledge and Kegan Paul, p.368.
33. Ibid., p.371.
34. Marx, K. (1976) *Capital* Vol 1. Harmondsworth, Penguin, pp.579–80.
35. Avineri, S. (ed)(1969) *Karl Marx on Colonialism and Modernization.* New York, Anchor Books, pp.132–3. For an analysis of Marx's writings on India see Chandra, B. (1981) Karl Marx, His Theories of Asian societies and colonial rule. *Review,* Vol.V 1: 13–91.
36. Ibid., p.133.
37. Ibid.
38. Ibid., p.137.
39. Marx, K. (1976) *Capital* Vol 1, op. cit. p.91.
40. Marx, K. and Engels, F. (1971) *Ireland and the Irish Question,* Moscow, Progress Publishers, p.286. For a discussion of how this work represents a break with his position on India see Mohri, K. (1979) Marx and 'Underdevelopment'. *Monthly Review,* Vol.30 No.11; 32–43; and, more generally, Cummings, M. (1980) *Marx, Engels and National Movements.* London, Croom Helm. On Marx's singular lack of understanding with regard to Latin America, see Aricó, J. (1982) *Marx y América Latina.* Mexico, Alianza Editorial Mexicana.
41. Ibid., p.132.
42. Ibid., p.148.
43. Hilferding, R. (1981) *Finance Capital: A Study of the Latest Phase of Capitalist Development.* London, Routledge and Kegan Paul.
44. Bukharin, N. (1972) *Imperialism and World Economy.* London. Merlin Press. See also his polemic with Luxemburg in Luxemburg, R. and Bukharin, N. (1972) *Imperialism and the Accumulation of Capital.* London, Allen Lane.
45. Bukharin, op. cit., p.74.
46. See Hobson, J.A. (1938) *Imperialism – A Study.* London, Allen and Unwin.
47. Lenin, V.I. (1970) Imperialism, The Highest Stage of Capitalism. *Selected Works,* Vol 1. Moscow, Progress Publishers, p.716.
48. Ibid., p.732.
49. See Kautsky, K. (1970) Ultra-Imperialism. *New Left Review,* No.59.
50. Arrighi, G. (1978) *The Geometry of Imperialism – The Limits of Hobson's Paradigm.* London, New Left Books, p.17. For a useful guide through this 'tower of Babel' see Brewer, A. (1980) *Marxist Theories of Imperialism.* London, Routledge and Kegan Paul.
51. See, for example, Fieldhouse, D.K. (1969) *The Theory of Capitalist Imperialism.* London, Longmans. For further consideration of these issues from a Marxist perspective see Barratt Brown, M. (1974) *The Economics of Imperialism.* London, Penguin.
52. Lenin, V.I. (1970) *Imperialism,* op. cit. p.718.
53. Degras, J. (ed)(1970) *The Communist International 1919–1943 –*

Documents, Vol 2. London, Oxford University Press, p.534.

54.   Warren, B. (1980) *Imperialism: Pioneer of Capitalism*. London, New Left Books, p.107.

55.   Baran, P. (1957) *The Political Economy of Growth*. New York, Monthly Review Press.

56.   Magdoff, H. (1969) *The Age of Imperialism*. New York, Monthly Review Press. See also Magdoff, H. (1978) *Imperialism: From the Colonial Age to the Present*. New York, Monthly Review Press.

57.   Jalée, P. (1969) *The Pillage of the Third World*. New York, Monthly Review Press; and Jalée, P. (1972) *Imperialism in the Seventies*. New York, The Third World Press.

58.   Kay, G. (1975) *Development and Underdevelopment – A Marxist Analysis*. London, Macmillan. For the traditional Marxist view of imperialism as an impediment to industrialisation see Sutcliffe, B. (1972) Imperialism and Industrialization in the Third World. *Studies in the Theory of Imperialism*, (eds) R. Owen and B. Sutcliffe. London, Longmans; 171-92.

59.   Marx, K. (1976) *Capital*, Vol I, op. cit. p.91. (emphasis added)

60.   Warren, B. (1980) *Imperialism*, op. cit. p.138.

61.   Ibid., p.136.

62.   Ibid., p.28.

63.   For a general critique of Warren see McMichael, P., Petras, J. and Rhodes, R. (1974) Imperialism and the Contradictions of Imperialism. *New Left Review*, No.85: 83-104; and Lipietz, A. (1982) Marx or Rostow? *New Left Review*, No.132: 48-58.

64.   Warren, B. (1980) *Imperialism*, op. cit. p.210.

65.   For an alternative critique of populism in development studies see Kitching, G. (1982) *Development and Underdevelopment in Historical Perspective – Populism, Nationalism and Industrialization*. London, Methuen & Co.

66.   On recent debates see; Facing the 1980s: New Directions in the Theory of Imperialism. *The Review of Radical Political Economics*, Vol.II No.4 (1979).

67.   Emmanuel, A. (1972) *Unequal Exchange – A Study of the Imperialism of Trade*. London, New Left Books.

68.   For a guide to the controversy see Mandel, E. (1975) *Late Capitalism*, Ch.11. London, New Left Books. See also the rather premature closure of the debate in Amin, S. (1977) *Imperialism and Unequal Exchange*; Part IV. New York, Monthly Review Press.

69.   See for example Radice, H. (ed)(1975) *International Firms and Modern Imperialism*. London, Penguin Books; Barnet, R. and Muller, R. (1974) *Global Reach: The power of the Multinational Corporations*. London, Cape; and Hymer, S. (1979) *The Multinational Corporation – A radical approach*. Cambridge, Cambridge University Press.

70.   For a survey of this debate see Poulantzas, N. (1975) *Classes in Contemporary Capitalism*. London, New Left Books, pp.38-88.

71. See for example Vitale, L. (1968) Latin America: Feudal or Capitalist? *Latin America: Reform or Revolution?* (eds) J. Petras and M. Zeitlin. New York, Fawcett Publications.
72. Laclau, E. (1971) Feudalism and Capitalism in Latin America. *New Left Review*, No.67; reproduced in Laclau, E. (1977) *Politics and Ideology in Marxist Theory*. London, New Left Books.
73. Ibid., p.19.
74. This was a concept used by Lenin and developed by Trotsky. For an attempt to apply it at a global level see Löwy, M. (1981) *The Politics of Combined and Uneven Development*. London, New Left Books.
75. Marx, K. (1978) *Capital* Vol 2. London, Penguin Books. pp.189-90.
76. The whole debate is reproduced in Hilton, R. (ed)(1976) *The Transition from Feudalism to Capitalism*. London, New Left Books.
77. See Anderson, P. (1974) *Lineages of the Absolutist State*. London, New Left Books, and Anderson, P. (1974) *Passages from Antiquity to Feudalism*. London, New Left Books.
78. Marx, K. (1981) *Capital*, Vol 3 London, Lawrence & Wishart, p.390.
79. Brenner, R. (1977) The Origins of Capitalist Development: A Critique of Neo-Smithian Marxism. *New Left Review*, No 104: 53.
80. See Balibar, E. (1970) The basic concepts of historical materialism. *Reading Capital*, L. Althusser and E. Balibar. London, New Left Books.
81. For a broad historical sweep which breaks with this unilinear conception see Melotti, U. (1977) *Marx and the Third World*. London, Macmillan, and Dhoquois, G. (1971) *Pour l'histoire*. Paris, Anthropos.
82. Balibar, E. (1975) *Cinco Estudos do Materialismo Histórico* Vol II. Lisbon, Editorial Presença, p.29. (Emphasis in original.)
83. Taylor, J. (1979) *From Modernization to Modes of Production. A critique of the sociologies of development and underdevelopment.* London, Macmillan, p.93.
84. Ibid., p.103.
85. There are many critiques of Althusser, but see particularly Clarke, S. (1980) Althusserian Marxism. *One-Dimensional Marxism*, S. Clarke, et al. London, Alison and Busby.
86. Taylor, J. (1979) *From Modernization to Modes of Production*. op. cit. p.221.
87. See the critical review of Taylor in Mouzelis, N. (1980) Modernization, Underdevelopment, Uneven Development: Prospects for a Theory of Third World Formations. *The Journal of Peasant Studies*, Vol.7 No.3: 352-74.
88. Taylor, J. (1979) *From Modernization to Modes of Production*, op. cit. p.264.
89. Wolpe, P. (1980) Introduction. *The Articulation of Modes of Production*, (ed) H. Wolpe. London, Routledge & Kegan Paul, p.41.
90. Alavi, H. (1975) India and the colonial mode of production. *Socialist Register 1975*. 160-97.
91. Brewer, A. (1980) *Marxist Theories of Imperialism*, op. cit. p.271.

92. See Coquery-Vidrovitch, C. (1978) Research on an African mode of production. *Relations of Production*, (ed) D. Seddon. London, Cass.

93. See Godelier, M. (1977) The concept of 'social and economic formation' the Inca example. *Perspectives in Marxist Anthropology*, M. Godelier. Cambridge, Cambridge University Press; and Golte, J. (1981) The economy of the Inca state and the notion of the AMP. *The Asiatic Mode of Production*, (eds) A. Bailey and J.R. Llobera. London, Macmil

94. See Cardoso, C.F.S. (1973) El modo de producción esclavista colonial e América. C.S. Assadourian et al *Modos de Producción en América Latin* Buenos Aires, Pasado y Presente. 135–59 (this article is available in English in *Critique of Anthropology* No 4/5, 1975, 1–36); and Cardoso C.F.S. (1975) Los modes de producción coloniales. *Historia Sociedad*, No.5: 90–106. Taken together these two volumes are a representative sample of the debate on modes of production in Latin America.

95. See Wolpe, H. (1980) Capitalism and cheap labour-power in South Africa: from segregation to apartheid. *The Articulation of Modes of Production*, (ed) H. Wolpe, op.cit.

96. Meillasoux, C. (1981) *Maidens, Meal and Money – Capitalism and the Domestic Community*. Cambridge, Cambridge University Press, p.87.

97. See the discussion in Banaji, J. (1977) Modes of Production in a materialist conception of history. *Capital and Class*, No.3: 1–44.

98. Hindness, B. and Hirst, P. (1975) *Pre-Capitalist Modes of Production*. London, Routledge & Kegan Paul.

99. Hindness, B. and Hirst, P. (1977) *Modes of Production and Social Formation – An Auto-Critique of Pre-Capitalist Modes of Production*. London, Macmillan.

100. Rey, P.P. (1973) Matérialisme Historique et Luttes de Classes. *Les Alliances de Classes*, P.P. Rey. Paris, Maspero.

101. Foster-Carter, A. (1978) The Modes of Production Controversy. *New Left Review*, No.107: 55. This is a very useful introduction to the modes of production debate.

102. Marx, K. (1981) *Capital* Vol 3, op. cit. p.927.

103. See for example Henfrey, C. (1981) Dependency, Modes of Production and the Class Analysis of Latin America. *Dependency and Marxism*, op. cit., pp.17–54. Also the various contributions in Chilcote, R. and Johnson, D. (eds)(1983) *Theories of Development – Mode of Producti or Dependency?* London, Sage.

104. Marx, K. (1976) *Capital* Vol I, op. cit. p.711. For a discussion of Marx' reproduction schemes see Rosdolsky, R. (1977) *The Making of Marx's Capital*. London, Pluto Press.

105. Ibid., p.716.

106. See Meillassoux, M. (1981) The exploitation of the domestic communi imperialism as a mode of reproduction of cheap labour power. *Maidens Meal and Money*, M. Meillasoux, op. cit.

107. Marx, K. (1978) *Capital* Vol 2, op. cit. p.185.

108. For further discussion see Kalmanovitz, S. (1980) Teoría de la

reproducción dependiente. *Criticas de la Economía Política*, No 11, pp.1–45; and Sorj, B. and Zamosc, L. (1977) La reproducción del capitalismo periférico: estructura y contradicciones. *Caderno do Departmento de Ciencia Política* (Federal University of Minas Gerais, Brazil), No 4: 1–80.

109. See Dorfman, A. and Matellart, A. (1976) *How to Read Donald Duck, Imperialist Ideology in the Disney Comic*. New York, International General Publishers; and more generally, Mattellart, A. (1979) *Multinational Corporations and the Control of Culture: The Ideological Apparatures of Imperialism*. Brighton, Harvester Press.

110. See Agee, P. (1975) *Inside the Company – CIA Diary*. Harmondsworth, Penguin; and Bertrand Russell Peace Foundation (1972) *Subversion in Chile: A Case Study of US Corporate Intrigue in the Third World*. Nottingham, Spokesman Books.

111. An example of this problem is Castañeda, J. and Hett, E. (1981) *El economismo dependentista*. Mexico, Siglo XXI, which criticises the economism of the dependency approach and advocates an uncritical 'return to Lenin' as an alternative.

112. Kidron, M. and Segal, R. (1981) *The State of the World Atlas*. London, Pan, p.2.

113. This typology is developed in Quijano, A. (1974) *Crisis Imperialista y Clase Obrera en América Latina*. Lima, no publisher.

2. Capitalism and Imperialism

In the previous chapter we put forward the concept of 'dependent reproduction' as a framework for the process of development in the Third World. Dependent development is conditioned by the insertion of these countries in the international capitalist economy. Our earlier discussion of imperialism pointed to the dynamics of this system, but it is now necessary to add a historical dimension. We begin with a succinct outline of the formation of the world economy from 'primitive accumulation' to the 'industrial revolution', and then turn to the classical 'age of imperialism' and the prolonged period of inter-imperialist crises and revolutions which followed the First World War. An examination of the basis of the 'post-war boom' of the 1950s and 1960s and the nature of the present system of 'late capitalism' follows. Finally, the significance of recent discussions on the emergence or desirability of a 'new international economic order' is assessed. At each step of our analysis we examine capitalism in the central economies and its impact through imperialism on the Third World (more specifically Latin America). Development and underdevelopment ('the unity of opposites' as Lenin has said) can be understood *only* in this integrated fashion. It is hoped that some of the rather abstract discussions in the previous chapter, are now clarified by our historical sketch. A chart at the end provides a summary of this chapter, bearing in mind that the periodisation is only approximate and that there is always an overlap of different phases and forms of imperialism.

Primitive Accumulation

> The discovery of gold and silver in America, the extirpation, enslavement and entombment in mines of the indigenous population of that continent, the beginnings of the conquest and plunder of India, and the conversion of Africa into a preserve for the commercial hunting of blackskins, are all things which characterize the dawn of the era of capitalist production. These idyllic proceedings are the chief moments of primitive accumulation.
>
> Karl Marx[1]

The basic condition for the development of capitalism is the separation of direct producers from the means of production and the emergence of 'free' labourers who must sell their labour-power in order to survive. In Tudor Britain this process took the form of expropriation of land from the peasants through the enclosure movement by which common lands were transformed into consolidated farms. This process, whereby 'sheep devoured men', accelerated in the mid-18th Century with dispossession mounting and, consequently, the concentration of land holdings. As the first proletariat was being born so a parallel history was giving rise to its historical counterpart: capital. As Marx put it, capital came into the world 'dripping from head to foot, from every pore, with blood and dirt'. In short, it was based on its pillage of the Third World. The gallant Drake set out on an expedition costing £5,000 and returned with a booty of £5,000,000. During the 17th Century the East India Company averaged a rate of profit of around 100% but Sir Walter Raleigh considered this 'a small return'. The African slave trade was even more lucrative, bringing in up to 300% in profits. From the pillage of Mexico and Peru by the Spaniards, the sacking of Indonesia by the Portuguese and the Dutch, to the exploitation of India by the British, we see a relentless concentration of capital in Western Europe. As Ernest Mandel sums up,

> the contribution made by this stolen capital was decisive for the accumulation of the commercial capital and money capital which, between 1500 and 1750, created the conditions which proved propitious for the industrial revolution.[2]

Capitalism as a mode of production did not of course emerge overnight. Capital had existed 'in the pores' of earlier societies right back to antiquity, but the mode of production remained clearly pre-capitalist.

Merchant capital arises before capital has brought production itself under its control, and this phase of the world economy is best characterised as mercantilism. In his polemic with Dobb over the origins of capitalism, Paul Sweezy was heavily influenced by the historian Henri Pirenne who spoke of capitalism in 12th Century Netherlands. For a modes of production approach, however, as Dobb notes, the opening phases of capitalism cannot be located:

> even in the fourteenth century with its urban trade and guild handicrafts, as others have done, but in the latter half of the sixteenth and early seventeenth century when capital began to penetrate production on a considerable scale, either in the form of a fairly matured relationship between capitalist and hired wage-earners or in the less developed form of the subordination of domestic handicraftsmen working in their own homes to a capitalist on the so-called 'putting out system'.[3]

Feudalism had, in fact, entered a period of crisis in the 14th Century but what emerged was the petty-commodity mode of production — characterised by the worker-owner, the artisan and the peasant — not capitalism. Merchant capital, as it expanded between the 14th and 16th Centuries did, however, have a profound dissolving influence on the old order, as did the towns where the petty-commodity production flourished.

The emerging capitalism moved inevitably to secure its control over the old mode of production in order to extract a greater surplus labour and to expand it in the interests of profit and the foreign market. According to Marx, this process of transformation follows two historical paths: in one, 'the really revolutionary way', a section of the producers themselves (from amongst the artisans and the yeomanry) began to organise production for the foreign market on a capitalist basis free from the restrictions of the medieval guilds. The second path saw part of the existing merchant class move into production, thus serving historically as a mode of transition, but 'this method always stands in the way of the genuine capitalist mode of production and disappears with its development'.[4] Thus was born that historical figure – the half-manufacturer half-merchant – who helped achieve Britain's preeminence over the old mercantilist powers of the Mediterranean and the Low Countries. Mercantilism was based on the exploitation of a dependent colonial system,[5] the merchants-manufacturers taking their manufactured products to trade for the raw materials in the colonies. Before Britain could extend its preeminent position to Latin America, however, Spanish and Portuguese colonialism had to run its course.

The discovery of America by Christopher Columbus in 1492 opened up a period of destruction of the preexisting civilisations and naked pillage which lasted until 1550.[6] The whole fabric of the Inca and Maya societies was subverted by the Spanish 'Conquistadores' who came seeking gold and silver. The most common relation of exploitation established was known as the *encomienda*, by which a colonizer was granted a certain number of Indians from whom he extracted a tribute in kind or a labour-rent. The surplus extracted by the *encomienda* relations of production – either mineral or agrarian – was destined primarily for transfer to Europe. Though extra-economic coercion was present in this relation, making it clearly non-capitalist in nature, it did not represent a 'transfer' of the old European feudal cycle as though the Conquistadores had brought their 'mode of production' along in their luggage. Rather the *encomienda* was a stage in the development of a mercantile economy in America, inextricably bound up with the circulation of money-capital on the growing world market. This is the process which links up the nascent capitalist mode of production with the pre-capitalist modes in the rest of the world. The 'thirst for gold' was rationalised half way through the 16th Century, and for the next 100 years it was based on more systematic exploitation. With the collapse of the mining industry, the *encomienda* began to lose its preeminence. Exploitation of the land came to be based on the huge *haciendas* which tied down the Indian and growing *mestizo* population through various mechanisms of bondage, such as debt-peonage or the *obligación* (rent in services). The other dominant form of land-holding, the plantation, was based on black slaves and was oriented mainly towards tropical products (coffee, sugar, tobacco, etc). Far more than the *hacienda*, this economic unit was developed as a function of the requirements of the European market.[7] They were not, however, linked to the internal economy and the creation of an internal market since they operated as virtual enclaves. By the end of the 18th Century, capitalist penetration gained ground, threatening the already precarious stability of the non-capitalist relations of production. This will be taken up in the next section dealing with the independence phase.

The other two areas mentioned by Marx in the quotation at the beginning of this section are India and Africa. The British East India Company began operations in 1612, but it was 1708 before it obtained a monopoly position and total subordination of the Indian sub-continent. It not only made a profit for trade, but gathered a great deal of political power in its hands, financing wars and annexations out of its revenues. After displacing a section of the indigenous ruling class and disarticulating the previous mode of production, the Company became engaged in the direct exploitation of the peasantry. It is estimated that the drain of surplus from Bengal over the period of 1757 and 1780 was around £38 millions, which was a considerable boost to capital formation in Britain.[8] The period from Clive's victory over the Bengalis in 1757 to 1793, when the operation of the Company came under tighter control because it jeopardised overall British policy, is known with very little exaggeration as 'the rape of Bengal'. Africa's exploitation in this phase is symbolised by the trade in human beings. After the initial voyages of discovery, in 1444, for the first time, a Portuguese ship transported 235 slaves 'acquired' on the African coast. During the 16th Century, nearly one million African slaves were shipped to the Americas, the figure jumped to 2.75 million in the 17th Century, and seven million in the 18th Century. Overall, it is calculated that up to 100 million Africans were directly affected by the slave trade. As an Angolan author writes:

> the exploitation and internal trade of slaves represented a deep blow against the Angolan economy, whose negative effects persist to this day. Loss of most valuable productive force . . . disequilibrium of agriculture . . . iron ring of inhumanity . . . breakup of traditional mode of production.[9]

According to Gunder Frank

> the three decades from 1762 to 1789 decidedly were marked by recurrent and predominant economic depression — and they in turn mark what is probably the decisive turning point in the modern history of humanity.[10]

Spain and Portugal in particular were to experience grave economic and political contradictions, which paved the way for the loss of their colonies in America from 1810 onwards. It was a period of growing unrest in the colonies, marked by the Communero revolt of 1780 in New Granada, and the great rising of the descendants of the Incas under Tupac Amaru which collapsed only with his death in 1783. Better known, because it was successful, is the American War of Independence, which culminated in the formation of the United States of America. In global historical terms, the French Revolution of 1789 marks a key transition — to the age of bourgeois revolutions.

If one were to characterise the period from the Conquest until the French Revolution as a whole, it would have to be by the formation of the world economy.[11] The growing integration of the world market during the 18th Century is perhaps best epitomized by the so called 'triangular trade'.[12] Ships left England with manufactured goods, and sailed to Africa where they were sold in exchange for slaves. The slaves were taken to the plantations in America, sold for further profit, and colonial produce was taken on board for sale back in England. The North American colonies played an intermediary role in this rational trading arrangement, which set them on a course towards becoming an imperialist power in their own right. It is quite true as Banaji notes, that:

> the idea of world economy as already dominated from its inception by the requirements of capital-reproduction is a false abstraction [because] the initial impulse which sustained the vast network of world commodity exchanges before the eighteenth century derived from the expanding consumption requirements of the lords. Moreover, at its inception the colonization of Latin America was a *feudal* colonization, a response to the crisis of feudal profitability which all the landowning classes of Europe were facing down to the latter part of the sixteenth century.[13]

By the close of the 18th Century, however, the bourgeois mode of production had become firmly implanted in England and elsewhere, and henceforth, Latin America was to be dominated by the worldwide requirements of capital reproduction.

Industrial Revolution

> As soon as manufacture becomes somewhat stronger, still more so large-scale industry, it creates a market for itself and uses its commodities to conquer it. Trade now becomes the servant of industrial production. . . .   Karl Marx[14]

If the French Revolution of 1789 symbolised the political bourgeois revolution the Industrial Revolution in Britain launched the real 'Age of Capital'.[15] Towards the end of the last period, domestic industry was beginning to give way to the manufacturing workshops where the labour process was still based on handicraft instruments and not power-driven machinery, but where a more complex stage of co-operation was involved.

The Industrial Revolution, based fundamentally on the textile mill and the steam-engine, was, however, well established by 1815. This launched the first expansive phase of capitalism which was to last until 1840. Based mainly on England, Belgium and the north-east of France, this phase marked the consolidation of competitive capitalism. Once production was subordinated to capital it would take only the great technical innovations of the Industrial Revolution to complete the transition to capitalism. At the same time, cottage industry had to be totally destroyed to complete the separation of the rural semi-proletarian from the land. Only then, could the twins of capital and 'free' labour meet directly in the market place. Factory production *per se*, however, did not impose itself in a short time. This is sometimes forgotten by those who compare the distorted industrialisation process in the Third World with a somewhat mythical original Industrial Revolution. In fact, well into the second half of the 19th Century domestic industry, and particularly manufactory — atomised work process, low division of labour — survived and even prospered.[16]

The democratic revolutions across Europe in 1848 close this phase of early capitalist development. At once an economic and political crisis, the defeat of the working class in 1848, allowed capital to establish the conditions for another long, expansive phase, from 1849 to 1873. But the 1840s had seen the growth of Chartism in the English working class and 1848 was a real watershed, with the appearance of Marxism in the form of the Communist Manifesto. Here, as later, we see how closely the economic and political histories of capitalism are intertwined, the distinction being more of an analytical convenience than anything else. Our focus is also integrated in dealing with the central and peripheral development of capitalism. The key concept is the internationalisation of the various cycles of capital. The period we are dealing with (1790–1848) sees the internationalisation of the commodity-capital cycle. Direct pillage of the Third World receded in importance during this phase, giving way to the commercial exchange of commodities.

If violence was the midwife of capitalism through the process of primitive accumulation, the 'imperialism of free trade' now began to take over. More concretely, unequal trade relations were imposed by political and military force and then free trade was declared. This had the effect of destroying the artisan industries of the Third World when confronted with competition by the highly productive new industries. One clear example is India which, by the 18th Century, had achieved a high level of pre-industrial development: artisans produced advanced manufactured goods for the home market and foreign trade, and iron and coal were readily available. Development did not advance, quite simply because of the colonial domination by Britain. At the beginning of the 19th Century, India was still one of the world's largest suppliers of textile products. The expanding textile mills of Lancashire led to Britain imposing protectionist measures against Indian textiles, whereas the East India Company for its part, imposed a policy of free-exchange in India. By mid 19th Century the superiority of British manufacture was ensured;

in 1815 Britain had imported £1.3 million worth of Indian textiles, by 1850 India was taking 50% of Lancashire's exports. The artisans returned to agriculture, often working for British owned cotton plantations.[17]

In Latin America, meanwhile, the end of the 18th Century saw the emergence of an anti-colonial class alliance in the context of a weakening of Spain and Portugal during the Napoleonic Wars. As the commercial monopoly imposed by the colonial powers was relaxed, a new power stepped into the breach — Britain. Trade relations with the latter greatly strengthened a *criollo* bourgeoisie dedicated to the production of raw materials. As Vitale notes in his history of Chile, it —

> controlled the principal sources of wealth, but the government remained in the hands of the representatives of the Spanish monarchy. This contradiction between economic power monopolised by the Spaniards is the motivating force which set the revolutionary process of 1810 in motion.[18]

The move to seize political power was determined by the need for a new economic policy — increased trade with Britain, the new world power — and not by any desire to transform the colonial social structure with all its inequalities. Between 1810 and 1826, political independence had been achieved in most of the countries of Latin America, but the reality was to be a reinforcement of economic dependency. In 1824, the British Foreign Secretary Lord Canning, is reputed to have said that 'Spanish America is free, and if we do not mismanage our affairs, she is English'.[19]

Before this ambition could be realised fully, however, a civil war had to be settled in Latin America. This pitted a 'European' agro-exporting bourgeoisie, based on the most fertile regions and standing on the platform of free-trade, against a provincial 'American' or nationalist force, who wanted protectionist measures to defend their regional industries against the fate of India's artisans. The most remarkable experience of the latter current was the Francia presidency in Paraguay (1814–40) based on isolation from the web of international economic dependency. The subsequent Paraguay War (1864–70) declared by Argentina, Brazil and Uruguay, wiped out six-seventh's of the country's male population and imposed 'civilization' in the form of the Europeanist policy.[20]

The great boom of external trade after the settling of the civil wars sharpened the drive of the landowners for profit. In countries such as Argentina and Uruguay and the south of Brazil, the capital-wage labour relation was consolidated. In other countries, the tenant-labourers moved to gain their personal freedom against the bondage mechanisms. The landowner's aims, especially in the context of a growing European labour migration, could be achieved only by relaxing the chains of bondage. In Eastern Europe after the Thirty Years War, the so-called 'second servitude' was reimposed precisely as links with the world economy intensified, but the resistance of labour in many parts of Latin America prevented, for a time at least, this reversal of history. During this phase of the world economy, the forms of labour control changed considerably. The slave trade was abolished in 1807 but it continued in British colonies until 1833 and in Brazil up to 1888. In slave-based society, as Aristotle noted, 'the slave is an animated instrument and the instrument is an inanimate slave'. In Ancient Rome, slaves were literally classified as 'human cattle'. In was this sharp antagonism between classes which led to the downfall of slave society. With the development of commercial capital in the pores of the slave society the need for an increased social division of labour arose. The productivity of the slave, however, could not be increased beyond a certain point, because 'human cattle' could have no interest in raising their technical proficiency or intensifying their labour. In general, slavery declined in importance during this period but gave way to 'free' wage labour only partially in most parts of the Third World. Forced and indentured labour often took its place, and in the rural areas diverse forms of extra-economic coercion evolved to maintain the subordination of the working population.

Looking at this period as a whole, we can see how it is a transition from mercantilism to classical imperialism. Marx notes how:

> the colonies provided a market for the budding manufactures, and a vast increase in accumulation which was guaranteed by the mother country's monopoly of the market. . . . Today, industrial supremacy brings with it commercial supremacy. In the period of manufacture it is the reverse: commercial supremacy produces industrial predominance.[21]

Marx, in fact, refers to the preponderant role played by the colonial system during the first phase. As manufacture gave way to the factory system *laissez faire* became the main element in Britain's domination. Though British industry had been consolidated behind a barrier of protective tariffs, the virtues of free trade were now proclaimed to the world. The repeal of the Corn Laws, in 1846, marked the end of the protection of British landlords at the expense of the rising industrial bourgeoisie. In 1849, the repeal of the Navigation Acts saw the opening up of colonial trade and the end of imperial preferences. As Barratt Brown concludes:

> by the middle of the nineteenth century, free trade had made Britain the workshop of the world. The fact was that British naval and military victories of the early nineteenth century, consolidated by Britain's industrial advance far ahead of any other nation, made the whole world, in a sense, Britain's colony.[22]

The old colonial Empires of the 16th and 17th Centuries had served their purpose, but now British industrialists had won the battle for tree trade, which was elevated to the status of a scientific law. In 1848, Marx discussed the free traders ideology as follows:

> We are told that free trade would create an international division of labour, and thereby give to each country the production which is most in harmony with its natural advantages. . . . If the free-traders cannot understand how one nation can grow rich at the expense of another, we need not wonder, since these same gentlemen also refuse to understand how within one country one class can enrich itself at the expense of another.[23]

Age of Imperialism

> Imperialism is a policy of conquest. But not every policy of conquest is imperialism. Finance capital cannot pursue any other policy. This is why, when we speak of imperialism as the policy of finance capital, its conquest character is self understood; at the same time, however, we . . . imply highly developed economic organisms and, consequently, a certain scope and intensity of world relations; in a word we imply the existence of a developed world economy . . . a certain interrelation of classes and also a certain *future* of economic relations.
> Nikolai Bukharin[24]

Competitive capitalism was a spur to capital accumulation on an extended scale, but it also led inevitably to the concentration and centralisation of capitalism. Monopolies thus appeared sporadically during the 1860s, which was the heyday of competitive capitalism. A major element in this expansive phase was the consolidation of industrial capitalism in the USA after the Civil War (1861–65) along the first steps to advanced capitalism.[25] Imperialism, in a nutshell, was to be the age of monopoly capitalism. The early phase of this new model of accumulation was based on the steel industry and the development of the railways. An intensification of the class struggle, culminating in the great Paris Commune of 1871 (which prefigured the dictatorship of the proletariat) however, seriously weakened this model. The economic crisis of 1873 led to a new expansive phase, lasting until the eve of the First World War and interrupted only by the Great Depression of 1893–95. It was in this period that capitalist accumulation took the form of monopoly capitalism. This 'second' industrial revolution was marked, fundamentally, by the development of the internal-combustion engine and the electric motor, but also by an underlying change in the labour process itself towards mass production and the assembly line (Fordism).

As we mentioned above, the internationalisation of capital is a key concept to an understanding of dependent development. We can see in Figure 2.1 each of the circuits of social capital which are successively internationalised. Under free-trade imperialism, and even earlier, the circuit of commodity capital (trade) has become internationalised. Now, under classical imperialism as defined by Lenin, money-capital was becoming internationalised. Finally, after

Figure 2.1
Circuits of Social Capital

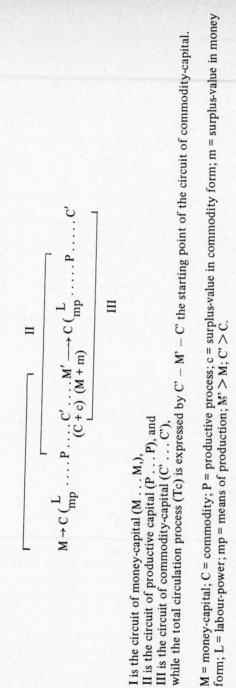

$$M \rightarrow C \left({}_{mp}^{L} \right. \ldots \ldots P \ldots C' \ldots \ldots M' \longrightarrow C \left({}_{mp}^{L} \ldots \ldots P \ldots \ldots C' \right.$$
$$(C+c) \quad (M+m)$$

I is the circuit of money-capital $(M \ldots M_{,})$,
II is the circuit of productive capital $(P \ldots P)$, and
III is the circuit of commodity-capital $(C' \ldots C')$,
while the total circulation process (Tc) is expressed by $C' - M' - C'$ the starting point of the circuit of commodity-capital.

M = money-capital; C = commodity; P = productive process; c = surplus-value in commodity form; m = surplus-value in money form; L = labour-power; mp = means of production; $M' > M$; $C' > C$.

Source: adapted from Palloix, C. (1975) The Internationalization of Capital and the Circuit of Social Capital. *International Firms and Modern Imperialism*, (ed) H. Radice. Harmondsworth, Penguin Books, P.65.

55

the Second World War, productive capital was to become internationalised as direct foreign investment in the productive sphere increased.

The export of capital by the central nations was the means whereby the process of internationalisation of the cycle of money-capital was accomplished. The export of surplus capital which could not find a profitable outlet at home was a key factor in the post-Depression boom. This was caused by the increase in the organic composition of capital (ratio between capital investment and wages-bill) and the consequent falling rate of profit. Investment was directed towards the non-industrialised areas of the British Empire (Canada, South Africa, Australia), the colonial countries of Africa and Asia, and finally, the dependent economies of Latin America. According to Dobb, 'railways, docks, public utilities, telegraphs and tramways, mining, plantations, land mortgage companies, banks, insurance and trading companies were the favourite objects of this investment boom.'[26] By the end of this period (1913) British capital investment abroad made up nearly a third of total capital holdings. Of this, around half was directed to the British colonies and most of the rest to North and South America. An extraordinary extension of communications, especially shipping, went alongside this process of capital export. It constituted in its totality an unprecedented expansion of capitalist relations of production into non-capitalist spheres, as Rosa Luxemburg stresses in her variant of the theory of imperialism.

The spread of capitalist relations of production across the globe led to the consolidation of an international division of labour — a hierarchy of national units in the reproduction of capital — that Lenin called the imperialist chain. The destruction of the old modes of production in the Third World did not lead to the organic growth of capitalism in their place, but rather saw a moulding of the economies according to the international needs of capital. For example, during the 'age of railroads' these were built purely to service the export sector and quite often were ill-suited in their planning to the needs of *internal* development. Likewise, the development of ports took place at the expense of the development of internal communications. The needs of the central countries were primarily agrarian and mineral raw materials, and this is what the Third World had to produce. Thus, in the north-east of Brazil for example, because conditions were ripe for sugar that is what was produced, to the exclusion of fruits or vegetables. The consequence is still felt today in regular famines. What could make a few rich — Brazilian sugar or Bolivian tin — could make a region and its people poor. This international division of labour also gives rise to a particular unequal exchange between the industrialised countries and the producers of foodstuffs and raw materials, although during this stage 'super profits' are the main source of surplus.

Colonial domination had led to a certain structure of dependency based on the drive for precious metals, and resulting in a commercial monopoly of the dominant powers. The relations of production and the class structure of this period were directly determined by the requirements of the colonial economy. A movement for independence emerged, however, based partly on international conditions (defeat of the previously dominant colonial powers) and partly on internal developments – the need for the local bourgeoisie to seek new markets. This power bloc which emerged was able to adapt itself with considerable ease to the requirements of the new dominant power in the region – British industrial capitalism. There followed a long period, lasting effectively to the world crisis of 1929, in which the Latin American economies rested almost exclusively on the export of the primary commodities needed for European industrialisation. The heyday of imperialism (1880–1914) led to the consolidation of a British 'informal empire' in Latin America. During the previous period (1840–60 approximately) some of the countries of Latin America, and particularly Argentina, had begun a serious process of development.[27] It was on this basis that British financial imperialism operated, greatly accelerating the process of 'outward-oriented' growth. It did not lead to a bourgeois revolution, however, because this period was precisely the high-point of the agrarian oligarchy's rule in Latin America. What this period did promote – at least outside of the 'company-nations' in Central America – was a process of national integration, intensive urbanisation and a limited industrialisation, mainly processing of agrarian produce. The point to make is that the subsequent process of industrialisation did not take place simply because of external influence. It was based rather on an internal process of social differentiation and an increased division of labour, in fact, the internal Third World equivalent of 'primitive accumulation', however distorted or limited in its consequences.

The super-exploitation of labour in the dependent countries allowed for the increased productivity of labour at the centre through the provision of cheaper means of subsistence. In particular, the export of foodstuffs from Latin America during this period led to a cheapening of the costs involved in the reproduction of European labour – necessary labour was less and, therefore, surplus value greater. On the other hand, the export of cheap raw materials to the centre lessened the amount of fixed capital expended and therefore counteracted the tendency of the rate of profit to fall. Both processes (cheap foodstuffs and raw materials) depend on the over (or super) exploitation of labour in the Third World. This is possible without seriously affecting accumulation (usually workers are buyers too) because circulation is separated from production, with the product being realised (i.e. sold) on the foreign market. In conclusion, the low individual consumption of the Third World worker is irrelevant to the process of accumulation during this phase, except in so far as it allows for the increased extraction of super profits.[28]

Crisis, War and Revolution

Capitalism has grown into a world system of colonial oppression and the financial strangulation of the over-whelming majority of the population of the world by a handful of 'advanced' countries. And this 'booty' is shared

> between two or three powerful world plunderers armed to
> the teeth (America, Great Britain, Japan), who are drawing
> the whole world into *their* war over the division of *their*
> booty.   V.I. Lenin[29]

The age of imperialism gave way to the age of inter-imperialist rivalries. A
number of powers occupied the centre of the world stage — Britain, France,
Germany and the USA, with Russia, Austria-Hungary, Japan and Italy occupying a second-rank position. With the world already divided into colonies and
'zones of influence', inter-imperialist conflicts were bound to emerge. Mandel
mentions, amongst others, the following flash points: the Anglo-French
conflict over equatorial Africa and Morocco, Anglo-Russian conflict in Persia
and Afghanistan, Russo-Japanese conflict over the partition of Manchuria
(leading to the 1904–5 war), Anglo-German conflict over the partition of
Turkey and the Middle East, and the conflict between Russia and the Austro-
Hungarian Empire over the partition of the Balkans.[30] These last two conflicts
set alight the powder-barrel of the First World War in 1914. Europe as a whole
emerged weakened out of the conflict, and a new power, the USA, began
rising as the process of international concentration and centralisation of
capital was accelerated.

Ten years after the war when everything seemed 'back to normal' the Great
Slump of 1929 came like a thunderbolt out of a clear sky. The economic
crisis of 1929 and the depression of the 1930s led to a profound transformation
of capitalism, in particular an increased economic role of the state —
Keynesianism. Unemployment, the real social consequence of the slump,
as against the Wall Street bankers and investors who jumped out of their
windows on Black Thursday, was also here to stay. As Michael Kalecki says
'under a regime of permanent full employment, "the sack" would cease to
play its role as a disciplinary measure. The social position of the boss would
be undermined and the self-assurance and class consciousness of the working
class would grow. . . .'[31]

Class consciousness *had* in fact been growing in Russia, and the 1905
Revolution was succeeded by the October Revolution of 1917. A new social
system was born and a large part of the world threatened to withdraw from
the world capitalist economy. Barely ten years later the Civil War began in
China and by the end of the Second World War socialism was victorious there
too. This last war (1939–45) which was also the result of inter-imperialist
rivalries, led to a rearticulation of the capitalist world — Germany was out,
Britain had lost the Empire, and the USA at last emerged as the uncontested
leader of the 'West'. The war, however, also led to the emergence of the
People's Democracies in Eastern Europe which went to swell the non-capitalist,
if not socialist world system.[32] From now on there are two competing world
systems, and reference to a 'world economy' as such is not strictly correct.
One has only to recall that while the USA and the whole capitalist world was
in the throes of the Depression the Soviet Union was going through a process
of intensive industrialisation quite unaffected by this. It is true, however,

that the Soviet bloc later became more integrated through trade with the Western 'market economies', in countries such as Yugoslavia to a marked degree. Commodities still exchange on the world market according to the law of value. Nor must we neglect the fact that Soviet stress on the competition between the two 'world blocs' was the main arena of the struggle for socialism, as against the Third World or the internal struggle of the advanced countries themselves. Basically, we can say that the cycle of revolutions after 1917 opened up a political, rather than an economic alternative, one that remained attractive to millions across the world, at least until after the Second World War. Today, of course, the reality of bureaucratic state socialism is not the clear-cut alternative it once was.

If the First World War was fought over the repartitioning of the colonial world it led precisely to the emergence of nationalism is these countries. The period from 1917 to 1945 is the beginning of the crisis of imperialism's colonial system. The upsurge of national liberation movements led to the conquest of independence, or its defence, in Turkey, Iran, Afghanistan, Egypt, and Ethiopia amongst other countries. It was, however, in the aftermath of the Second World War that the anti-colonial movement began to reap the fruits of its efforts.[33] In 1946, the Philippines became independent, in 1947 India, in 1950 Indonesia, and in 1960 fully 17 countries of Africa gained their independence. The consequences of nationalism in the Third World would be felt in the subsequent period, but its roots lie in what is now increasingly becoming seen as an integrated crisis period – 1914–45.

In Latin America this period is one of transition between the agro-export model we discussed earlier, and a new industrial-associated model which was consolidated after the First World War. It was also a period of revolutionary upsurge – the communist insurrections in El Salvador (1932) and Brazil (1935), the war in Nicaragua against US troops (1927–34), Cuba's aborted revolution (1933–34) as well as a whole series of more confused episodes.[34] As to the economy from 1914, and more particularly after 1929, the basic pattern of Latin American dependence began to change. The collapse of the international capitalist market caused by the First World War, which produced a crisis within the Latin American primary goods/exporting sectors, coinciding with war-time limits on imports, spurred several countries into a process of import-substitution industrialisation. This process was extended and accelerated under similar conditions following the crisis of 1929. The success of this industrialisation was, however, largely dependent on the nature of the internal market and the degree of development previously achieved, so that only countries such as Brazil, Mexico and Argentina were able at this stage to create a light industry capable of satisfying the internal demand for non-durable consumption goods.

In those countries where the local dominant class did not have control over the forces of production, foreign domination led to the 'enclave' economies (see Chapter 8).[35] This involves a foreign company, producing for the foreign market, established in a country with a largely pre-capitalist mode of production. These companies usually have little contact with the 'host' country and are solely capitalist 'enclaves' within it. Their administrative autonomy can lead to their virtual control over large parts of the national territory. One of the most glaring examples of this type of operation was the United Fruit Co. (today United Brands) in Central America. In 1955 it owned 680,000 hectares of land in the area, and it is estimated that it controlled up to 85% of the land favourable to the production of bananas, its main crop. It controlled the railway lines in these countries and owned a large shipping company, so that even distribution remained in company hands. Its political weight was such, that in 1954, when the Guatemalan government moved to nationalise the company, it was able to call on the US government to organise an armed invasion of the country. Its economic impact could be equally devastating. If the land in one area became fallow the company would move out, even taking with it the railway lines, and from one day to another whole areas would become economic deserts. Tin in Bolivia, oil in Venezuela and copper in Chile, all represented similarly an 'enclave' economy.

Where import-substituting industrialisation was able to take place on a significant scale, the old agrarian-mercantile bourgeoisie and the ascendant industrial bourgeoisie established a compromise state which reflected their complementary interests. The precise expression of this compromise at the level of the state varies a good deal from case to case, reflecting notably the degree to which the urban petty bourgeoisie was admitted to the ruling bloc. There were, likewise, wide variations in the behaviour of these economies where foreign capital directly controlled the export sector. But in general, these experienced little industrialisation, and the crisis of the 1930s saw the maintenance of the hegemony of the 'oligarchy' and the often brutal repression of popular movements. The reason these latter did not achieve the transition from 'outward-oriented' to 'inward-oriented' development, is fundamentally because the class structure had not developed sufficiently in the previous period to allow for the emergence of industrial capitalism and its expanded reproduction. That is to say, the external impact of the world capitalist crisis, which encouraged the local substitution of previously imported products, acted upon deep-seated, preexisting internal transformations of the social structure. In short, capital accumulation is a social and not simply a technical process.

The acceleration of industrialisation during the Second World War led to a sharper difference of interests between the two fractions of the bourgeoisie in the most industrialised countries, the industrial bourgeoisie attempting to channel the pressure of the popular masses in its favour through 'populist' regimes, of which Perón's in Argentina (see Chapter 9) was perhaps the clearest example. This situation corresponded to the end of the first phase of industrialisation, which had substituted local production for imported non-durable consumption goods, and to the need to launch a new phase based on heavy industry producing durable consumption and 'capital' goods. The new phase of industrialisation coincided with the reorganisation of the world market under the hegemony of United States capital, and the associated tendency of imperialism to integrate systems of production on a world scale.

This tendency led to the export of capital from the imperialist centres (mainly the USA) in the form of direct investments which, to a great extent, were now directed towards the industrial sectors.

Post-War Boom

> The bourgeoisie, historically, has played a most revolutionary role. . . . The bourgeoisie cannot exist without constantly revolutionising the instruments of production, and thereby the relations of production, and with them the whole relations of society.
>
> The development of modern industry, cuts from under its feet the very foundation on which the bourgeoisie produces and appropriates products. What the bourgeoisie therefore produces, above all, are its own grave-diggers.[36]

The first quote from the Communist Manifesto seemed amply confirmed in the period after the Second World War, and in particular after the Korean War. The second warning was virtually forgotten. What then was the basis of this great expansive phase? It was in many ways a Third Industrial Revolution based, this time, on the exploitation of nuclear energy and the great leap forward in electronics. In the labour process itself, Fordism began to give way to a neo-Fordism as automation and a policy of 'responsible autonomy' (as against direct control) was imposed on labour.[37] With the great expansion of durable goods production the car becomes the symbol of this age. The changes in production were accompanied by expansion of circulation (unity of production/circulation); a strong growth of the world economy during 1948-68 contrasted with the stagnation of 1914-48 and even surpassed the exceptional rhythm of expansion during the 1890-1914 period. As a whole, these phenomena led to an immense increase in productivity in the Western capitalist nations. This was the period when 'we never had it so good' according to bourgeois politicians.

A major element in this new phase of capitalist development was the growing intervention of the state. In the realm of production this began after the slump of the 1930s in a bid to cushion the cyclical pattern of capitalist growth. The nationalisation of coal and steel in Britain after the war was a sign that, from now on, the state would assume a direct role in the process of capitalist production. The other major area of expansion of the state was in the realm of reproduction – the continuous renewal of the social relations of production. This meant, fundamentally, the 'welfare state', which began to take over some of the costs of reproduction of labour-power. Several authors have characterised this overall process as one of 'state monopoly capitalism'. Thus, the Soviet author Kirsanov, refers to:

the combining of the strength of the monopolies with the strength of the state in a simple mechanism [which] was the qualitatively new element in the development of monopoly capitalism, in its growth into state-monopoly-capitalism.[38]

The Communist parties tend to draw from this analysis that state monopoly capitalism is the most complete material preparation for socialism, and from that derive a type of 'state socialism' which uncritically supports nationalisations and state run firms. Though one cannot neglect the theoretical weaknesses of 'state monopoly capitalism' as a full economic and political theory, it seems clearly an apt *description* of this new period of monopoly capitalism in which the state acquired a preeminent role.[39]

Above all else, this phase is characterised by the internationalisation of the cycle of productive-capital. First it was commodities, then money-capital, and now production itself which becomes an international process. The multinational (or transnational) corporations become the 'bearers' (agents) of these new international relations of production. These are the successors of the 19th Century trusts and cartels. This process involves a shift in the composition of the investment abroad carried out by the central economies. Prior to 1914 three-quarters of foreign investment was in portfolio terms (i.e. through financial investment) and only one quarter was direct investment in production. On the other hand, after 1945 these ratios were reversed, with three-quarters going into direct investment and only one quarter into portfolio investment. This, in short, was the difference between British and US imperialism.[40] A clearer idea of these transformations can be gained from an examination of US foreign investment in Latin America as shown in Table 2.1. Since 1929 there has been a clear shift in the pattern of US investment away from agro-mineral and public utilities towards petroleum, finance, trade and, above all, manufacturing. Thus, imperialism is not restricted to its grip over a few strategic 'enclaves' but spreads its web throughout the productive structure of the dependent society. It is worth noting, furthermore, that in 1976, Latin America accounted for 81% of US investment in the Third World. Within Latin America, Brazil accounted for 40% of US manufacturing investment, and together with Mexico and Argentina, fully three-quarters of that total. In this way the North American corporations had gained privileged access to the internal markets of the major Latin American economies.[41]

The neo-imperialism of the USA led to a phase of neo-dependency in Latin America. Fundamentally, this involves an 'internationalisation of the internal market', to use Cardoso's term, with internal consumption assuming an important role. This is all part and parcel of the new international division of labour, which began to take shape in the 1960s. Certain basic lines of industrial production (for example, cars) were shifted to the Third World, with the advanced countries retaining those branches involving sophisticated technology — although now, for example, several countries in Latin America have nuclear power. In this 'new' dependency it is technological dependence which assumes a major role, with control exercised through

Table 2.1
US Investment in Latin America (in $ millions)

	1929		1950		1957		1966		1976	
Agriculture	817	23.3%	523	11.4%	571	7.0%	232	2.4%	–	
Mining	732	21%	666	15%	1,232	15%	1,340	14%	1,600	7%
Public Utilities	887	25%	942	21%	1,049	13%	542	6%	285	1%
Petroleum	617	18%	1,303	28%	2,998	37%	2,454	25%	1,653	7%
Manufacturing	231	6%	781	17%	1,280	16%	2,973	30%	9,242	39%
Finance	–		–		–		957	10%	5,478	23%
Trade	–		–		–		1,135	12%	2,402	10%
Total	*3,519*		*4,576*		*8,053*		*9,752*		*23,536*	

Source: Petras, J. (1981) *Class, State and Power in the Third World*.
London, Zed Press, p.74.

patents, payment of royalties etc. which arise from the advanced countries'
monopoly over technological advance.[42] This, in turn, leads to renewed
financial dependency — these countries borrow in order to pay for this
technology. The American dollar is, in fact, the world currency that acts as a
determining power in this process of international economic integration,
either directly or through organs such as the World Bank and the International
Monetary Fund.[43]

The new dependency in Latin America led to a renegotiation of the internal
conditions of dependency — a compromise between the landed oligarchy,
the industrialists, the state and, of course, foreign capital. In some cases,
populist regimes even attempted to incorporate sections of the urban masses
into the new 'development pact'. The state began to play a growing role in
this process in 'regulating' the capital/wage-labour relation and through
'joint ventures' with foreign capital (see Chapter 7). This period (1946-68)
began with a number of nationalist-statist regimes promoting a form of
autonomous development. By the mid 1950s, the inflow of foreign capital
had begun to alter the whole pattern of capital accumulation, giving rise to the
phase of 'dependent development'. By the mid 1960s this model of
dependent accumulation had become incompatible with the 'populist' or
nationalist political regimes. A new era of military regimes on the one hand
excluded the masses from political life and on the other hand, opened up the
country's economy more fully towards the world capitalist system (see
Chapter 10). The multinational corporations, using mainly local financial
resources, operated very successfully in this schema, remitting huge sums back
to their home country. According to the US Department of Commerce, the
total US private capital investment between 1960 and 1965 amounted to
US$3,800 million, whereas over the same period US$11,300 million
were repatriated by these companies. The pillage of the continent's resources
during the period of the Conquistadores was being repeated now in a more
'civilised' fashion by the giant international firms.[44] So, when Gunder Frank

traces a direct line from Pizarro to General Motors he is, in essence, correct, so long as one distinguishes the different *form* of exploitation.

The post-war new dependency in Latin America had its counterpart in the phase of neo-colonialism which opened up on the African continent. Faced by the upsurge of the colonial revolution in this period, imperialism reverted to a more subtle form of domination than colonialism. We cannot examine African neo-colonialism here, but we should mention that it was the old colonial powers, such as Britain and France, but most particularly the now dominant USA, which benefited from this.[45] In the 1960s, the African countries began the process of import-substitution industrialisation which had started in Latin America during the 1940s, but this time under the direct economic aegis of imperialism from the start. In this case, in bowing to the inevitable (decolonisation), imperialism managed to impose a profitable new relationship (neo-colonialism) which actually corresponded better to its current needs (export of light-machinery, durable consumer goods, etc).

Not all, however, went the way of imperialism during this phase. The nationalisation of the Suez Canal by Egypt in 1956, and the subsequent fiasco of the Anglo-French intervention, marked the real end of Britain's days of owning an empire 'where the sun never set'.[46] The final victory of the Algerian war for independence in 1962 represented a similar blow for France. Perhaps, most significant in retrospect, was the Cuban Revolution's victory in 1959 (see Chapter 11) which represented a serious blow to the prestige, if not the material might, of the United States of America.

Late Capitalism

> The capitalist mode of production . . . is a mode of
> production of a particular kind and a specific historical
> determinacy . . . it assumes a given level of social productive
> forces and of their forms of development as its historical
> precondition, a condition that is itself the historical result
> and product of a previous process . . . [The] relations of
> production corresponding to the specific and historically
> determined mode of production — relations into which
> men enter in their social life — have a specific historical
> and transitory character . . .   Karl Marx[47]

If May 1968 was a warning sign and dark clouds were to roll over the horizon with the 'oil crisis' of 1973, by 1979, when the 50th anniversary of the Great Crash was commemorated, even 'crisis' seemed a mild term. In May 1968 the French student revolt and workers' general strike, showed that the social relations of neo-capitalism were, after all, neither secure nor immutable. This was followed in 1969 by the international monetary crisis (leading to the 1971 declaration that the dollar was no longer convertible

against gold) and the beginning of a series of extremely militant actions by
the Italian working class.[48] The following years were punctuated by the
brief Portuguese 'revolution' of 1974–75 — a remarkable interaction of the
colonial revolution and the crisis of advanced capitalism. Without doubt,
this period of imperialist crisis is symbolised by the final defeat of the most
powerful military machine in history by the people of Vietnam in 1975.
This was followed by anti-imperialist victories in Southern Africa, and later,
the revolutions in Iran and Nicaragua which severely shook the self-confidence
of imperialism. What justifies calling this period a crisis of imperialism as such
is the combination of the anti-imperialist revolution and the continuous
obstacles to the valorisation of capital precipitated by the working-class
resistance practices in the core nations.

The phase which opens up in 1969 can rightly be characterised as 'late
capitalism', not in the sense of a final great collapse, but in the sense Marx
refers to in the quotation at the beginning of this section. Capitalism is a
historically determined mode of production which is limited (not timeless)
and specific to a particular phase of human development. There is no
possible class society which can replace capitalism, and in that sense we
live in the age of 'late capitalism'.[49] Take nuclear power, for example. This
tremendously powerful *productive* force is now in flagrant contradiction
with the prevailing relations of production which are leading inevitably to
its (ultimate) *destructive* application. More concretely, we can turn to the
economic crises of the 1970s which brought back memories of 1929 to capital
and labour alike.

The long, post-war boom had never really altered the cyclical fluctuations
of capital accumulation, it could only cushion them. Nor did the hegemony
of the USA, established after the war, alter the basic tendency of monopoly
capitalism towards inter-imperialist rivalry. In economic terms this is reflected
in the *relative* decline in the share of American exports in the total world
trade (from 20% in 1950 to 12% in 1978), compared to the rise of West
Germany (from 4% in 1950 to 12% in 1978) and Japan (from 1% in 1950
to 8% in 1978). The European Economic Community has, from the early
1970s, begun to rival the USA, and Japan's spectacular growth of
productivity is leading it towards an even more threatening position. Though
a static comparison of this nature is of limited value, Table 2.2 shows quite
clearly the growing power of non-US capital units in recent decades. On the
basis of this, and further data on average growth rates and relative size ratios
of these firms, one recent article points to 'the serious erosion of the position
of American enterprises and the gradually developing challenge of European
and Japanese firms during the last two decades'.[50] The position is not of
course static and the positions of US 'ultra-imperialism' and of the 'European
(or Japanese) challenge' tend to simplify what is in fact a constantly shifting
pattern of rivalry and relative advantages.

In this context of renewed inter-imperialist rivalry the economic crisis
hit the advanced capitalist world. There are many open questions about the
series of economic crises since 1969 which we cannot really discuss here.

Table 2.2
Largest 100 Industrial Companies (in terms of sales)

Country(ies)	1957	1967	1977
U.S.	74	69	48
Japan	–	9	10
EEC	24	21	34
Others	2	1	8
Total	*100*	*100*	*100*

Source: Adapted from Droucopoulos, V. (1981) The Non-American
Challenge: A Report on the size of the World's Largest Firms.
Capital and Class, No 14, p.38.

It is, however, worth pointing out that the raising of the oil price by the
OPEC countries in 1973 was in no real way the 'cause' of the 1974–75
recession. Its roots lie deep in the contradictory expansion of the capitalist
mode of production itself.[51] Be that as it may, this recession, as Gunder
Frank says, was:

> by far the deepest, longest and most universal of the post-war period so
> far . . . the three most important features of this recession — low
> investment and high unemployment as well as inflation — have, however,
> persisted until the present [1980] and are destined to continue doing
> so into the foreseeable future. This scenario is all the more likely as
> another recession has begun.[52]

Effectively, the 1976–79 'recovery' was sporadic, uneven and superficial,
doing little to overcome the real causes of 'stagflation'. In 1981 the 24
industrialised capitalist countries of the OECD had 25 million officially
registered unemployed workers which, with their families, meant that some
90 million people were affected. The forecast for 1985 is 35 million unemployed,
which is, of course, still low compared to 300–500 million unemployed in
the rest of the world. The crisis of the automobile industry, with all its
economic ramifications and social impact was, in particular, a sign that the
Big American Dream was over. Capitalism had gone through crises before,
recovered, and advanced at a higher level, but under late capitalism this is
simply not occurring. A sustained upturn of the world capitalist economy
depends essentially on a severe defeat of the working class in advanced
industrialised countries and of the Third World. As Mandel notes

> The international working class enjoys much more favourable
> conditions today than in the past to emerge from their battles victorious.
> But the stakes are enormous. Because of the gravity of the crisis of the
> system [and] the accumulation of weapons of massive destruction
> . . . the present crisis confronts humanity with an apocalyptic version

of the alternative 'socialism or barbarism' . . .[53]

The synchronised recession of the capitalist system could not but have its effects on the dependent economies of the Third World. Being more closely enmeshed in the web of international capitalist relations than in the previous period of imperialist crisis (1914–45) these countries were not able to launch independent industrialising initiatives; the effects of the 1980–82 recession were even worse in this respect than those of 1974–75. The economic redeployment of the Western economies after the crisis, however, helped consolidate the new international division of labour that began taking shape in the previous phase. By the late 1970s, a particular form of industrial development in certain Third World countries (the NICs-newly industrialising countries) had led to a growth of Third World *industrial* exports to the advanced capitalist countries. As one economist notes, however,

> in these countries, industrialisation through exportation cannot, in the present conditions, be considered capable of making a major contribution to their development, nor as a solution to the problem of their international indebtedness, *except in a small number of these countries.*[54]

Still, limited as it is to certain nations and certain sectors, this process does mean that the 'old' dependency model cannot be applied unthinkingly. We see, in fact, the real limitations of the 'centre-periphery' analogy, which can no longer account for the reproduction of the industrial labour process in today's world. Many labour-intensive labour processes are being delocalised towards the Third World (electronics in Taiwan or the 'runaway industries' in Mexico), even though the advanced countries retain control over the means of reproduction (essentially technology). These countries play an important role of *intermediation* in the international division of labour.

Taken to its limits, the thesis of a 'new international division of labour' operates with a concept of a world market for labour, a worldwide industrial reserve army and a world market for production sites.[55] Production is split into sub-processes and is then simply carried out wherever capital and labour can be put together most cheaply. Certainly, fragmentation of the production process, with some sections relocated in cheap labour areas, has deepened the internationalisation of production. The 'free trade zones', however, which the proponents of this thesis put so much stress upon, employ only 7.25 million people – a mere fraction of the labouring poor in the Third World. In other words, the new division of labour does not completely displace the old based on raw materials production. In 1980, 80% of the total exports of the 'low income countries' were still primary commodities and raw materials. Perhaps the most important element to emerge from the new international division of labour is that we are moving towards a global extension of Fordism, as exploitation of absolute surplus value gives way to one based on relative surplus value.[56] As this process advances, so we can expect an explosive combination of anti-imperialist revolts in the classical mould combined with proletarian resistance against the tyranny of the assembly line.

The huge rise in the foreign debt of a group of Third World countries was a major new feature of the late 1970s. Whereas, in 1970, the public debt of the 'developing countries' was 'only' $67.7 billion, by 1980 it had reached $438.7 billion, a sixfold rise. Of this, the Latin American countries accounted for around one-third. Certainly, the temporary improvement of the terms of trade for primary products against manufactures around 1972-73 provided a boost for the financing of imports in some Third World countries,[57] but the major source of finance was international credit operations with a noticeably greater proportion coming from private (12% in 1970; 43% in 1980) as against multilateral (e.g. IMF) and bilateral (i.e. 'foreign aid') sources. In fact, it is estimated that nearly half of all credits for the Third World are held in the portfolios of just 30 major banks. As Parboni writes:

> through their control of the flow of finance, the great imperialist powers are seeking to control the economic development of the debtor countries, forcing them to open their markets and to abandon control of multi-national investment within their border; they are also seeking to influence the foreign policy of the debtor countries.[58]

The main reason for this unprecedented level of international credit expansion has been to open up a market for capital goods in the Third World — a sort of pump-priming exercise, as it were. Of course, the danger of this situation — in some countries the total accumulated debt is nearly as large as their Gross National Product — is that the next international capitalist recession will see a wave of bankruptcies and massive defaulting on the foreign debt in the Third World.[59] The financial collapse in Mexico towards the end of 1982 brought all these contradictions into the open, and showed how easily the recession could turn into a major depression. In the meantime, a new form of international 'debt peonage' is imposed on the Third World as countries fall deeper and deeper into debt.[60]

The 1982 war in the South Atlantic was a dramatic confirmation that the imperialist system was inherently unstable and prone to wars, as Lenin had predicted. It pitted one declining imperialist power (Britain) against an important intermediary state (Argentina) thus affecting the vital interests of the hegemonic imperialist state (USA). Argentina was already involved in the Central American conflict and was about to embark on an extended anti-communist crusade in El Salvador as a US proxy force. The whole basis of US foreign policy in the Southern Cone was thrown into disarray as the forces of nationalism were rekindled. Colonial adventures were revived in the late 20th Century, and the speed at which inter-imperialist conflict could develop was fully revealed. Above all, the Malvinas represented no fundamental economic or strategic interest for Britain, yet the biggest naval task force since the Second World War was mobilised to recover them. War fever and patriotic fervour gripped British labourism and showed that Lenin's polemic against the social-chauvinists on the eve of the First World War had lost none of its relevance. In Argentina, the overwhelming degree of popular support for what could be objectively called a military adventure showed that nationalism and self-determination were not simply ideologies of the past. The Malvinas war showed, not the strength of imperialism (because the defeat of Argentina by a technologically superior armed force was inevitable) but the weakness of a system which allowed a major crisis to emerge from a rather minor issue.

A New International Economic Order?

The current debates on the need for a 'new international economic order' have their roots in the formation of a movement of non-aligned countries in the mid 1950s. United by their anti-colonialism, these countries were pledged to neutrality between the political/military power blocs, and to an independent economic policy. After the 1973 summit in Algeria, the campaign for a new international economic order (NIEO) became the main axis of the movement's activity.[61] Concrete actions that year, such as the raising of oil prices by the OPEC countries, stimulated a campaign to bring the natural resources of the Third World under national control. One slogan put forward was to call for 'Two, three, many OPECs' in a pale, economistic reflection of Ché Guevara's calls for 'Two, three, many Vietnams'. The aims of the NIEO were set out as a thorough rearticulation of 'North-South' relations through a policy of 'collective self-reliance' in the Third World. Its main demands were: for an increase in the price of raw materials, access to the market by the industrialised countries for their manufactured exports, and an accelerated transfer of technology to the Third World. The aim was to build up an autonomous self-centred development dynamic. These hopes were fundamentally shattered by the Cancún summit in 1981 between Western heads of state. The underlying logic of the NIEO was rejected out of hand by the USA and its allies such as Britain, and not a single specific agreement to do anything concrete emerged. Austerity and monetarism — or survival of the fittest — were to be the order of the day for the 1980s.

The Cancún summit had been called as a response to the Brandt Report issued by a Commission promoted by Robert McNamara, until recently President of the World Bank. Prominent politicians, bankers and diplomats were set the task of charting 'a programme for survival' in the 1980s, tackling problems of pollution, food and energy.[62] Their recommendations echoed many of the demands contained in the NIEO proposals put forward by some Third World governments. They recommended 'a new system of economic relationships that acknowledges . . . mutual needs and human interests.'[63] Countries would be taxed on a sliding scale, related to national income, to provide resources for a World Development Fund. The Report contains many rational suggestions on development of the sea bed, alternative energy sources and so on, but it is essentially ambiguous. That is because it is never clear whether it is putting forward a strategy to meet 'human needs and interests' or those of capitalist reproduction. It shares in the rather vague and utopian nature of the whole NIEO debate and it is, in fact, surprising that so many socialists in the advanced industrialised countries actually support it as a progressive step in the right direction. It never asks what type of social system will emerge from the new 'auto-dynamic' model of development, nor what type of government will or can promote it. It slips over the heterogeneous economic and political objectives of the various social classes in the 'South' and overestimates the rationality of the 'North' as displayed in their negative attitude at the Cancún summit. Protectionism made more sense in the short term than the massive recycling of financial resources suggested by the Brandt Report.

Our critique must go deeper than this questioning of the internal consistency of the NIEO. Basically, I think we are dealing with a common strategy of sections of the Third World bourgeoisie and an enlightened fraction of international capital. In fact, the multinational corporations operating in the Third World would be the first to benefit from access to the metropolitan markets for their industrial exports, and likewise from an increase in aid through loans and grants for industrialisation of the Third World. In this case, we are dealing with a scheme to 'modernise' dependency – not to 'liberate' the Third World. Professor Angelopoulos (Honorary Governor of the National Bank of Greece) seems to admit as much in his plea for a NIEO:

> To maintain the present situation is to risk in a short time a financial crash deeper than that of 1929, with repercussions which could result in ruin for the foundations of the international economic and monetary system. What can be done to avoid such a crisis? ... The great problem for the industrialised countries today is to produce 'creative demand' with maximum effectiveness ... there is, thus, a need for new consumers capable of absorbing the goods produced. If consumers cannot be found inside a country [because of massive unemployment? (Author)] they must be sought elsewhere. Where can they be found? Only in the developing countries which have such a great need to accelerate their economic and social progress. These countries have vast requirements for capital equipment and services, but they lack the means of acquiring them. This is the key to the problem.[64]

Whose problem . . . ?

In one sense only is the Brandt Report positive, because it shows beyond doubt the integrated international networks of the world economy. This may lead us to conclude that any autarkic strategy for Third World socialist development – as proposed by the dependency writers and taken to its limits in Kampuchea – is bound to fail. The main impact is, however, of an abstractly rational programme which is utopian in present circumstances.

The essential flaw is captured by Diane Elson:

> Rather than a strategy, the Brandt Report offers an illusion. It is an illusion that has been common enough in the North: the illusion that the undesirable effects of capitalism can be reformed away through negotiation, without the necessity of grass-roots struggle against their basic causes.[65]

At another level, the 'South' is hardly united in its demands for a NIEO. It is, in fact, the whole dynamic of 'non-alignment' which is being called into question today, as was made evident in the serious arguments at the 1979 Havana World Conference of the Non-Aligned Movement.[66] An essential component of the movement since the 1950s was a model of independent economic development as exemplified by that of India. Given a fairly self-sufficient internal market and effective protective measures, an industrial base could be built. This strategy was reflected in Latin America during the 1960s with the formation of regional markets such as the Central American Common Market, the Andean Pact and the Latin American Free Trade Association. Regional association was seen as a measure to enlarge internal consumption markets and provide the muscle to regulate the multinational corporations. Essentially, this economic strategy aimed to minimise subordination to the emerging international division of labour. Other countries, such as Taiwan, Singapore and the Philippines, and later Brazil, began opening their doors to foreign capital, accepting fully a subordinated yet dynamic role in the imperialist productive chain. As Parboni concludes:

> There was a profound divergence between the dependent and independent countries in the seventies. The former were rewarded for their subordination to the international division of labour imposed by the metropolitan countries and received considerable foreign investment and credit financing.[67]

It is more questionable that 'in the space of a decade, these countries were able to cross the threshold of development', but the basic point is sound. The material economic base of 'non-alignment' was disappearing — Egypt after Nasser, Argentina after Perón, Chile after Allende were just the frontrunners. The Group of 77, which is the economic counterpart of the Non-Aligned Movement and mainstay of the NIEO, will be swimming against the current in the 1980s although it will clearly serve as a self-defence organ for the more prosperous Third World ruling classes. As the model of dependent capitalist development spreads, so the very notion of a Third World will lose any value it may still have. Parboni is absolutely right when he says that:

> It is the end of an era: the development exigencies of world capital are destroying the dream of neutrality, peace and independent

71

Figure 2.2
World Economy and Dependent Development

Phase	*Central Economies*	*Dependent Economies*	*Form of Exploitation*
Formation of the World Economy 1492–1789	Development of capitalism. Expansion of mercantilism. British hegemony achieved. French Revolution – 1789.	The age of discoveries and primitive accumulation. Destruction of pre-existing modes of production. Colonialism in Latin America.	Direct plunder of captive markets. Force as the midwife of international capitalist economy.
Free-Trade Imperialism 1790–1848	Consolidation of competitive capitalism. Internationalisation of commodity-capital. Industrial Revolution (steam engine, textiles). 1848 Revolutions.	Artisan and handicraft industries destroyed by political measures and economic competition. The replacement of slavery by other non-capitalist relations of production. Neo-colonialism begins in Latin America.	Under 'laisser-faire' system, Third World provides cheap raw materials and buys manufactured goods of Industrial Revolution.
Classical Imperialism 1849–1913	Rise of monopoly capitalism. Internationalisation of money-capital. Second Industrial Revolution (internal-combustion engine, electric motors). Paris Commune – 1871.	The age of imperialism consolidates neo-colonial relation in Latin America. The scramble for Africa and the repartitioning of the world. British 'informal empire' in Latin America.	Colonial super-profits are the chief form of exploitation. Unequal exchange is a secondary form.

Inter-Imperialist Crisis 1914-1945	First World War – 1914-1918 Russian Revolution – 1917 The Great Slump – 1929-1932 Second World War – 1938-1945	Economic expansion during inter-imperialist crisis. Rise of the nationalist/socialist movements. Transition from agro-export to industrial/associated model in Latin America.	As above. This phase marks the transition from exploitation based on extraction of absolute surplus value to relative surplus value.
Neo-Imperialism 1946-1968	'State-monopoly capitalism'. Internationalisation of productive capital. Third Industrial Revolution (nuclear energy, electronics) US hegemony consolidated, May 1968.	The colonial revolution. Foreign investment shifts to industry. Neo-colonialism in Africa. The 'new' dependency in Latin America.	Unequal exchange becomes the main form of exploitation. Technological dependence increases.
Crisis of Imperialism 1969-1982	Late capitalism. Renewed inter-imperialist rivalry (US, EEC, Japan). Economic crisis – 1974-75; 1980-82 Austerity and unemployment.	Effects of imperialist crisis. A new international division of labour is consolidated. Debate on 'new international economic order'. Third World impact on Centre – Vietnam, Southern Africa, Iran, Nicaragua, Malvinas.	As above. Growing role of banks and so-called debt peonage.

development of the Third World. War is again becoming a permanent feature of capitalism.[68]

To summarise this chapter, I have elaborated a chart (Figure 2.2) tracing the main phases of the world economy and its impact on dependent development. Several warnings are called for in reading it. The chronological phases are only approximate and other transition points could have been suggested — 1770 instead of 1790, 1870 instead of 1850 and so on. Under the heading of 'central economies' are listed some of the major transformation within the capitalist system, with some significant political dates added to set the context. Clearly we are barely scratching the surface of history — the aim is the more modest one of pointing to the major 'determinant' transformations. The 'dependent economies' column takes us through the major phases of Third World development, stressing the global effects of multinational capitalist domination. Finally, we list the dominant form of exploitation which characterises each phase, emphasising that, in reality, there is always a combination of different forms operating together. In conclusion, this chapter has provided a skeletal analysis of capitalist accumulation on a world scale from a historical perspective. We have seen how we cannot separate the dominant from the dominated pole of international capitalist development, nor the economic and political moments of this process. From the laws of motion of capitalism as a whole we can now pass to the more concrete investigation of class struggle and state forms in the dependent countries of Latin America. Constantly, one must bear in mind the international setting or context of that development which is only apparently 'abstract'.

References

1. Marx, K. (1976) *Capital*, Vol.1. Harmondsworth, Penguin, p.915.
2. Mandel, E. (1971) *Marxist Economic Theory*. London, Merlin Press, p.
3. Dobb, M. (1972) *Studies in the Development of Capitalism*. London, Routledge & Kegan Paul, p.18. On this proto-industrialisation of the 16th and 17th Centuries, see Kriedte, P., Medick, H. and Schlumbohm, J. (1981) *Industrialization Before Industrialization*. Cambridge, Cambri University Press.
4. Marx, K. (1981) *Capital*, Vol.3. Harmondsworth, Penguin, pp.452-3.
5. The importance of merchant capital is stressed in Kay, G. (1975) *Development and Underdevelopment — A Marxist Analysis*. London, Macmillan.
6. The best general treatment of the colonial period is probably Stein, S. and Stein B. (1980) *The Colonial Heritage of Latin America*. Cambridge Cambridge University Press.
8. Davey, B. (1975) *The Economic Development of India*. Nottingham,

Spokesman Books, p.43.

9. Ferreira, E. (1979) *Feiras e Presidios*. Luanda, União dos Escritores Angolanos, p.55.

10. Frank, A.G. (1978) *World Accumulation 1492-1789*. London, Macmillan, p.167.

11. See a full historical account in Wallerstein, I. (1980) *The Modern World System II – Mercantilism and the Consolidation of the European World Economy, 1600-1750*. New York, Academic Press.

12. Williams, E. (1967) *Capitalism and Slavery*. London, Andre Deutsch, pp.51-2

13. Banaji, J. (1977) Modes of production in a materialist conception of history. *Capital and Class*, No.3:31. For a historical analysis of Latin America following this interpretation see Carmagnani, M. (1978) *Formación y crisis de un sistema feudal: América Latina del Siglo XVI a nuestros dias*. Mexico, Siglo XXI.

14. Marx, K. (1981) *Capital*, Vol.3, op.cit. p.454.

15. Title of a remarkable book by Hobsbawm, E. (1977) *The Age of Capital: 1848-1875*. London, Abacus; which, together with its predecessor, Hobsbawm E. (1977) *The Age of Revolution: Europe 1789-1848*. London, Abacus, is an excellent historical guide to the periods referred to.

16. See the challenge of orthodox versions in Samuel, R. (1977) The Workshop of the World: Steam Power and Hand Technology in mid-Victorian Britain. *History Workshop*:6-72.

17. See Mandel, E. (1971) *Marxist Economic Theory*. op.cit. p.447.

18. Quoted by Frank, A.G. (1972) *Lumpen-Bourgeoisie Lumpen-Development*. New York, Monthly Review Press, p.47.

19. Ibid., p.51. For a discussion of Britain's 'informal empire' in Latin America see Platt, D.C.M. (ed.) (1977) *Business Imperialism 1840-1930 An Enquiry Based on British Experience in Latin America*. Oxford, Oxford University Press.

20. For a full discussion see White, R.A. (1979) The Denied Revolution: Paraguay's Economics of Independence. *Latin American Perspectives*, Vol.VI No.2:4-24.

21. Marx, K. (1976) *Capital*, Vol.1, op.cit., p.918.

22. Barratt Brown, M. (1970) *After Imperialism*. London, Merlin Press, p.53.

23. Marx, K. (1971) On the question of free trade. *The Poverty of Philosophy*, K. Marx. New York, International Publishers, pp.222-3.

24. Bukharin, N. (1972) *Imperialism and World Economy*. London, Merlin Press, p.114.

25. See Aglietta, M. (1976) *A Theory of Capitalist Regulation – the US Experience*. London, New Left Books, for a remarkable analysis of capitalist development in the USA.

26. Dobb, M. (1972) *Studies in the Development of Capitalism*, op.cit., p.315.

27. On the process of industrialisation as a whole see Weaver, F.S. (1981) *Class, State and Industrial Structure – The Historical Process of South American Industrial Growth*. Connecticut, Greenwood Press, and also Cueva, A. (1979) *El desarollo del capitalismo en América Latina*. Mexico, Siglo XXI.

28. See Marini, R.M. (1973) *La dialéctica de la dependencia*. Mexico, Ediciones Era.

29. Lenin, V.I. (1970) Imperialism: The Highest Stage of Capitalism. *Selected Works*, Vol.1. Moscow, Progress Publishers, p.674.

30. See Mandel, E. (1970) *Marxist Economic Theory*, op.cit., p.453.

31. Kalecki, M. (1972) *The Last Phase of the Transformation of Capitalism* New York, Monthly Review Press, p.78.

32. I say this, because many argue that the Soviet Union exploits the Third World in the same way as the West – see Clawson, P. (1979) The Character of Soviet Economic Relations with Third World Countries. *Review of Radical Political Economics* Vol.13 No.1:76–84. On the 'nature of the USSR' debate generally see Szymanski, A. (1978) *Is the Red Flag Flying?* London, Zed Press, and the journal *Critique*.

33. On the process of decolonisation see Fieldhouse, D.K. (1979) Decolonisation. *Imperialism, Intervention and Development*, (ed) A. Mack, D. Plant, and U. Doyle. London, Croom Helm. This is a good general reader.

34. On these early revolts and the subsequent development of the communist movement see Aguilar, A. (ed) (1968) *Marxism in Latin America*. New York, Borzoi Books; and the far superior Lowy, M. (ed) (1980) *Le Marxisme en Amérique Latine*. Paris, Maspero.

35. The distinction between 'enclave' economies and those under national control is stressed by Cardoso, F.H. and Faletto, E. (1979) *Dependency and Development in Latin America*. California, The University of California Press.

36. Marx, K. (1973) *The Revolutions of 1848*. Harmondsworth, Penguin Books, p.70 and p.79.

37. This theme is elaborated in Friedman, A. (1977) *Industry and Labour*. London, Macmillan.

38. Kirsanov, A. (1975) *USA and Western Europe*. Moscow, Progress Publishers, p.181.

39. See, for example, Wirth, M. (1977) Towards a Critique of State Monopoly Capitalism. *Economy and Society*, Vol.6 No.3:284–313. Also Dupuy, A. and Truchill, B. (1979) Problems in the Theory of Sta Capitalism. *Theory and Society*, Vol.8 No.1:1–38.

40. For a general discussion see Alavi, H. (1964) Imperialism old and new. *Socialist Register 1964*, pp.104–26.

41. The literature on the changing pattern of US investment is vast but see amongst others: Cardoso, F.H. (1972) Dependent Capitalist Development in Latin America, *New Left Review*, No.74, pp.83–95; Dos Santos, T. (1968) The changing structure of foreign investment in

Latin America, (eds) J. Petras and M. Zeitlin *Latin America: Reform or Revolution?* New York, Fawcett Publications; and North American Congress on Latin America (1978). *Yankee Dollar: The Contribution of US Private Investment to Underdevelopment in Latin America.* (Berkeley, 1972).

42. On 'technological dependence' see, apart from the dependency literature generally, Merhav, M. (1969) *Technological Dependence, Monopoly and Growth.* Oxford, Pergamon Press; and Stewart, F. (1977) *Technology and Underdevelopment.* London, Macmillan.

43. On the World Bank and the IMF see respectively Hayter, T. (1971) *Aid as Imperialism.* London, Penguin Books; and Payer, C. (1974) *The IMF and the Third World.* London, Penguin Books.

44. An interpretation developed eloquently in Galeano, E. (1973) *Open Veins of Latin America – Five Centuries of the Pillage of a Continent.* New York, Monthly Review Press.

45. For an analysis of the aftermath of decolonisation, see Morris-Jones, W.H. and Fischer, G. (eds) (1980) *Decolonization and After – The British and French Experience.* London, Frank Cass. For a brilliant study of the development of neo-colonialism in Algeria since independence see Dersa (1981) *L'Algérie en débat – Luttes et développement.* Paris, Maspero.

46. The decline of Britain is examined thoroughly in Gamble, A. (1981) *Britain in Decline.* London, Macmillan.

47. Marx, K. (1981) *Capital*, Vol.3, op.cit., p.1018.

48. On the dollar crisis, see Morrell, J. (1981) *The Future of the Dollar and the World Reserve System.* London, Butterworths.

49. The term was developed by Mandel, E. (1975) *Late Capitalism.* London, New Left Books.

50. Droucopoulos, V. (1981) The Non-American Challenge: A Report on the size and growth of the world's largest firms. *Capital and Class*, No.14:43.

51. For a full analysis of the crisis see Mandel, E. (1979) *The Second Slump.* London, New Left Books. Also Amin, A., Arrighi, G., Gunder Frank, A. and Wallerstein, I. (1982) *Dynamics of Global Crisis.* New York, Monthly Review Press.

52. Frank, A.G. (1980) *Crisis: In the World Economy.* London, Heineman, p.68. The companion volume, Frank A.G. (1981) *Crisis: In the Third World.* London, Heineman, is particularly useful on the impact of the recession on the Third World countries.

53. Mandel, E. (1979) *The Second Slump.* op.cit., p.192.

54. Faire, A. (1981) The strategies of economic redeployment in the West. *Review*, Vol.V No.2:199.

55. I am referring to the remarkable study by Frobel, F., Heinrichs, J., and Kreye, O. (1981) *The New International Division of Labour.* Cambridge, Cambridge University Press.

56. For a useful current discussion of this process see Lipietz, A. (1982)

Towards a Global Fordism? *New Left Review*, No.132:33-47. Also Trajtenberg, R. (1978) *Transnacionales y fuerza de trabajo en la periferia.* Mexico, Instituto Latinoamericano de Estudios Transnacionales.

57. See Hone, A. (1973) The Primary Commodities Boom. *New Left Review*, No.81:82-92.

58. Parboni, R. (1980) *The Dollar and Its Rivals – Recession, Inflation and International Finance.* London, New Left Books, p.182.

59. See Wachtel, H. (1977) *The New Gnomes: Multinational Banks in the Third World.* Washington, Transnational Institute; and, The Brandt Commission (1983) *Common Crisis North South.* London, Pan.

60. See the discussion in Franklin, B. (1981) Debt Peonage: the Highest Form of Imperialism? *Monthly Review*, Vol.33 No.10:15-31.

61. For a general study of the NIEO see Anell, L. and Nygren, B. (1980) *The Developing Countries and the World Economic Order.* London, Methuen. For the debate as applied to Latin America see Lozoya, J. and Estevez, J. (eds) (1981) *Latin America and the New International Economic Order.* New York, Pergamon Press; and, Muñoz, H. (ed) (1981) *From Dependency to Development:Strategies to Overcome Underdevelopment and Inequality.* Boulder, Colorado, Westview Press; also Jacobsen, H. and Sidjanski, D. (1982) *The Emerging International Economic Order.* London, Sage Publications.

62. See Report of the Independent Commission on International Development Issues (1981) *North-South: A Programme for Survival.* London, Pan Books. For a point by point critique see Hayter, D. (1981) *The Creation of World Poverty – An alternative to the Brandt Report.* London, Pluto Press.

63. Ibid., p.270.

64. Angelopulos, A. (1980) The urgent need for adoption of an effective new international economic order. *UNITAR Conference*, New Delhi, pp.5-6.

65. Elson, D. (1982) The Brandt Report: A Programme for Survival? *Capital and Class*, No.16:119.

66. On the non-aligned movement, see Willetts, P. (1978) *The Non-Aligned Movement – The Origin of a Third World Alliance.* London, Frances Pinter and Singham, A.W. (ed) (1980) *The Nonaligned Movement in World Politics.* Connecticut, Lawrence Hill. For a recent reassessment see Verlet, M. (1980) Le mouvement des non-alignés après La Havane: Contradictions et dynamique. *Revue Tiers Monde*, Vol.XXI No.81: 185-95.

67. Parboni, R. (1980) *The Dollar and its Rivals*, op. cit. p.192.

68. Ibid., p.195.

PART II
Class

3. Class and Politics

> Classes are large groups of people differing from each
> other by the place they occupy in a historically determined
> system of social production, by their relation . . . to the
> means of production, by their role in the social organisation
> of labour, and, consequently, by the dimensions of the
> share of social wealth of which they dispose and the mode
> of acquiring it. Classes are groups of people one of which
> can appropriate the labour of another owing to the different
> places they occupy in a definite system of social economy.
> V.I. Lenin[1]

The Marxist theory of social class has advanced considerably since Lenin
offered his summary definition in 1919, but it can serve as a useful starting
point. Development studies have generally neglected the role of social classes
operating at the level of 'society' or, at best, with a simple 'mass/élite'
distinction. In an attempt to remedy this gap we will go through the major
social groupings present in a 'typical' Third World country which is
summarised in the graphic representation of social structure at the end of
this chapter. This is not, however, a simple exercise in the stratification studies
mould and we shall constantly refer to the political dimension of class and, of
course, class conflict. Before going on to examine classes and politics in the
Third World, however, we must cast a brief look over theories of class as
developed in recent Marxist debates. Class is probably *the* key concept for
understanding the dynamic of dependent development, its origins and its
inherent contradictions.

Class Theories

As is well known, the third volume of *Capital* breaks off precisely when Marx
was beginning to discuss social class. He referred to:

> The owners of mere labour-power, the owners of capital and the
> landowners, whose respective sources of income are wages, profit and

ground-rent – in other words wage-labourers, capitalists and landowners – form the three great classes of modern society based on the capitalist mode of production.[2]

Marx saw that even in England, where the development of capitalism had proceeded furthest, this articulation of classes did not emerge in its pure form and referred to 'middle and transitional levels [which] always conceal the boundaries'.[3] In fact, Marx did not develop a sustained theoretical discussion of class, pointing simply to the major social groupings who live off the valorisation of their labour-power, capital and landed property respectively. As to the politics of class, Marx established the fundamental distinction between 'class in itself' i.e., objectively determined by its position in the social relations of production – and 'class for itself' – i.e., conscious of its own interests and acting accordingly. At certain points, Marx seems to be saying in fact that classes are *only* constituted when they acquire a political consciousness. Thus, a resolution of the First International of 1871 drafted by Marx stated that against the 'collective power of the propertied classes the working class cannot act, as a class; except by constituting itself into a political party'.[4] This objective/subjective element in the definition of class was to frame much of the subsequent Marxist discussion of social classes.

In *History and Class Consciousness*, Lukács emphasised the role of consciousness in historical development, culminating with the self-consciousness of the proletariat and the abolition of classes. For Lukács,

> the self-understanding of the proletariat is . . . simultaneously the objective understanding of the nature of society. When the proletariat furthers its own class aims it simultaneously achieves the conscious realisation of the – objective – aims of society. . . .[5]

In this conception of the proletariat as 'subject of history' there is a clear unity between class as economic category and political agency. Lukács distinguishes between objective class interests and 'imputed class consciousness' on the one hand, and the empirically given 'psychological consciousness' of a class on the other. In the latter case, if a class cannot perceive its own 'true' class interests it simply suffers from 'false consciousness'. There are several problems in this construction. Althusser has shown that one cannot reduce history to the actions of class subjects, nor is class simply an inter-subjective unity. As Cutler and his co-authors note:

> Lukács reproduces at the level of the class subject all the problems of the subjectivist conception of history as a function of the will and consciousness of actors.[6]

It is also sheer idealism to see the proletariat as the class/subject of history moving inexorably to a predetermined end. Furthermore, the distinction between an 'actual' consciousness (what workers think) and a 'possible' consciousness (what Marxists think they should think) ignores the real complexity and contradictory nature of class consciousness. Ideology is not simply 'false', rather it reflects, in a distorted fashion, real relations — labour-power *is* a commodity under capitalism, workers *are* alienated and so on.[7]

The critique of Lukács has led, amongst other things, to a conception of class as the effect of structures — men and women become simply the 'bearers' of the relations of production and 'agents' occupying their alloted place in the class structure. Poulantzas has tried to break out of the Hegelian schema of class in itself (economic class situation) and class for itself (endowed with class consciousness). This reduces class definition to the economic level, leaving the class struggle to the political and ideological level. According to Poulantzas, rather, 'from the start structural class determination involves economic, political and ideological class struggle'.[8] Classes thus result from a process of 'structural causality' and the unity of class simply reflects the unity of the structure of which it is an effect.[9] This structure that Althusser resorts to for an explanation is rather mystically conceived of

> as a cause immanent in its effects in the Spinozist sense of the term, that *the whole existence of the structure consists in its effects*, in short that the structure, which is merely a specific combination of its peculiar elements, is nothing outside its effects.[10]

The class struggle, as much as the classes themselves, is seen as an 'effect' of this immanent structure, which hardly squares with the Althusserian support of the Marxist conception of the 'class struggle as the motor of history'. In rejecting the teleology of Lukács — the proletariat advancing inexorably to its goal as the forces of production develop — Althusser has ended up with a form of functionalism where the mode of production is eternal and classes are simply reproduced to serve its functional requirements.

The work of Poulantzas cannot be reduced simply to a mechanical application of Althusser to the political domain. Certainly, it shares many of its shortcomings, but also it has developed a conceptual armoury (drawing largely on Gramsci's work) which has passed into widespread use and guided a number of sound, concrete studies.[11] He starts from the fundamental premiss that:

> for Marxism, social classes involve in one and the same process both class contradictions and class struggle; social classes do not firstly exist as such, and only then enter into a class struggle'.[12]

In other words, classes are not 'things' but a relation, just as Marx saw capital not as money but a relation. Classes, or class fractions, take up positions which do not correspond with their objective structural determination, such as the 'labour aristocracy' which adopts bourgeois positions, or technicians who take up proletarian positions. In analysing class boundaries Poulantzas centres on the economic *and* political-ideological criteria which determine class positions within the social division of labour, refusing to relegate the latter to the process of transformation of 'class in itself' into a 'class for itself'. In this, he rejects the economism which reduces social relations to economic structures, and he also distances himself from Althusser's structural causality, which, for Poulantzas, sets 'limits of variation of class struggle' but does not determine class practices. In fact, in his distinction between 'class interests' determined by the structure of society and the 'class positions' adopted in practice, which do not necessarily correspond, Poulantzas has returned to the same problematic as Lukács recasting the terms but hardly resolving the problem.

Perhaps the most radical resolution of the objective-subjective aspect of class is provided by the historian E.P. Thompson for whom,

> classes arise because men and women, in determinative productive relations, identify their antagonistic interests, and come to struggle, to think and to value in class ways: thus the process of class formation is a process of self-making . . .[13]

Whereas, for Althusser, history is 'a process without a subject', for Thompson it is 'unmastered human practice', and Althusser's 'conjuncture' is seen 'as a moment of *becoming*, of alternative possibilities, of ascendant and descendant forces, of opposing (class) definitions. . . .'[14] The key element in this construction is that of human agency, and the criterion of consciousness becomes the cornerstone of class. At one point in *The Making of the English Working Class*, Thompson says bluntly that 'class is defined by men as they live their own history, and, in the end, this is the only definition'.[15] This book is a landmark in labour history but, as Anderson points out, there is

> a disconcerting lack of objective coordinates as the narrative of class formation unfolds. It comes as something of a shock to realise, at the end of 900 pages, that one has never learnt such an elementary fact as the approximate size of the English working class, or its proportion within the population as a whole . . .[16]

What is called for is a simultaneous analysis of how classes are objectively assembled and transformed by the capital accumulation process, and how class consciousness arises from this. Certainly this is a *social* process determined by the overall reproduction cycle of social capital, but one cannot reject objective class determination as a futile structural/functionalist exercise.

The American writer, Erik Wright, has criticised the theory of class advancement by Poulantzas from another angle, its inability to deal with ambiguous positions within the class structure.[17] In Poulantzas's analysis of the working class, any deviation from the various political and ideological criteria is sufficient for exclusion from the proletariat. As Wright points out, this type of analysis does not allow for positions within the social division of labour which can be objectively contradictory. Thus, for example, the category of semi-autonomous employees (white collar technicians and skilled craftsmen) can be seen to occupy a contradictory location between the working class and the petty bourgeoisie.[18] Though they retain relatively high levels of control over the immediate labour process they do not constitute even small-scale capitalists. Managers and supervisors are likewise in an objectively contradictory location between the bourgeoisie and the proletariat — the political position they adopt will depend on the concrete historical situation. It is the class struggle, defined by the inherent contradiction of the two polar opposites — bourgeoisie and proletariat — which resolves this contradictory class location. In this process we must distinguish between *immediate* class interests (constituted within a given structure of social relations), and *fundamental* interests, which represent the 'objective' or potential class interests of these groups and which may call into question the very structure of the social relations themselves.[19] This distinction does not entail the same idealist vision as that of 'false consciousness', as though workers are simply mystified and require education to see their 'true' interests.

Finally, we must consider the relation between classes and politics. The great Italian Marxist, Antonio Gramsci, drew very strong links between political parties and classes — 'every party is only the nomenclature of a class'.[20] Political parties are seen by Gramsci as 'the expression and the most advanced element' of a particular social group.[21] In the analysis of politics in Latin America this could be a most fruitful guide to research, although one can too automatically equate a class with a party which appears to be articulating its interests. Barry Hindness has recently criticised Poulantzas for what amounts to an essentialist mode of political analysis along these lines. Against the appeal for a 'relative autonomy' of politics from the economic structure of society, Hindness argues bluntly that:

> *Either* we effectively reduce political and ideological phenomena to class interests determined elsewhere (basically the economy). . . .
> *Or* we must face up to the real autonomy of political and ideological phenomena and their irreducibility to manifestations of interests determined by the structure of the economy.[22]

Hindness utilises the women's movement to show that there are political forces not directly tied to economic class relations. This is true, and one must guard against economic reductionism and essentialism, but the either/or choice presented by Hindness is not quite convincing. Politics may be irreducible to economics but this hardly makes it totally autonomous — the task would seem to be to specify and articulate how its 'relative autonomy' (or 'dialectical interpenetration') operates in practice.

There have been several attempts recently to question the 'class reductionism' of classical Marxism. Laclau criticises a conception in which,

all ideological content has a clear class connotation and any contradiction can be reduced — through a more or less complicated system of mediations — to a class contradiction.[23]

Clearly, nationalism or feminism have no automatic 'class belongings' and in this sense the point is well taken. Laclau also distinguishes between the 'class struggle' — between workers and capitalists — and 'classes in struggle'.[24] These latter groupings occupy a common position in the relations of production — landlords, the petty bourgeoisie or the lumpenproletariat — but they are not necessarily in direct antagonism with another social class. As Urry notes, 'these classes-in-struggle are less directly structured by capitalist relations of production than are capitalists and workers.'[25] In a sense, they are not fundamental or essential classes under capitalism. There are other social groups — blacks, women, youth — which are not classes at all. Now, no one would try to reduce all conflict in capitalist society to the class struggle between capitalists and workers, but this does not mean that these other struggles are totally autonomous or independent. No class, or class fraction, operates in a vacuum, and its scope for action is limited by the fundmental class antagonisms and their effects. If one takes the women's or ecology movements, we see that they operate in a context set by the class struggle and they are cut through by class contradictions. Class reductionism is a serious danger, but indeterminacy is no answer. Even 'non-class' movements, not to mention say, peasant movements, are framed by the basic antagonism of capital and wage-labour.

If we can sum up this section, the most important point is the relational and dynamic understanding of class — the history of a class is the history of its reproduction under conditions set by the development of capitalist exploitation. Classes cannot be conceived in gradational terms, simply above or below other strata, but in terms of their relations with other classes. Class relations are defined primarily by the social relations of production but political or ideological criteria may be deployed to specify class boundaries. The critique of the 'proletariat as class/subject' conception cannot, in itself, resolve the objective/subjective aspect of class and the need for an adequate theory of class consciousness.[26] A purely subjective analysis of class is, however, insufficient — a basic starting point must be the objective structural determination of classes. Of course, as Wright notes:

> Marxism is not fundamentally a theory of class structure. It is above all a theory of class struggle and social change. The analysis of class structure is intended not as the end point of an investigation, but as the starting point.[27]

This gives us the constraints upon active intervention and human agency. The dynamic aspect of the Marxist theory of class must be stressed — classes are continuously made and remade through the effect of struggles. As Prezowrski puts it 'the process of class formation is a perpetual one: classes are continually organised disorganised and reorganised.'[28] This process is a historical one, and the critique of Lukac's historicism must not lead us to forget that history is essential to historical materialism.

The Marxist theory of class, as briefly discussed above, has often been rejected as a valid tool for an analysis of Third World social formations. For many years, writers on Africa, for example, consciously rejected the applicability of 'European' Marxist class theories to the reality of Africa. More recently, of course, class categories have been productively employed in critical social analysis of the Third World, although at times there has been a tendency to fit reality to the categories to 'prove' the validity of Marxism.[29] We sometimes operate with a simplified class schema drawn from the Communist Manifesto and then seek out elements which fit into the respective boxes. The starting point must be the concrete reality of the Third World with Marxist categories developed, modified or even rejected if necessary. The use of 'labels' can be quite sterile, as with the use of terms such as the lumpenbourgeoisie, the labour aristocracy, the national bourgeoisie, or the lumpenproletariat. A multiplication of pseudo-categories too often takes the place of detailed investigation of concrete reality. Our aim is to deploy the Marxist categories outlined above, bearing in mind the distinct features of the Third World and the different regions of which it is composed. As a starting point we can take Ian Roxborough's conclusion that 'the class structures of the Third World differ from those of the advanced nations in two principal ways: they are more complex, and the classes themselves are usually much weaker'.[30] The first characteristic is due mainly to the incomplete penetration of the capitalist mode of production and the second is related to the subordinate position imposed on Third World countries by the process of dependent reproduction.

Bourgeois Fractions

The starting point of any analysis of the bourgeoisie must be the different fractions of capital — banking, industrial, and commercial — of which the individual capitalist is but a personification. The dominant agrarian class is more difficult to classify as it is sometimes seen as a feudal landlord but more often as simply an agrarian capitalist fraction. A common image in modernisation studies, and also in orthodox Marxism in Latin America, was of an 'oligarchy' comprising the feudal landlords and the 'comprador' bourgeoisie, totally tied to imperialist interests. Against this was pitted a 'national' industrial bourgeoisie and the 'middle class' generally, which was oriented towards development goals and a radical agrarian reform. There are several misconceptions involved here which can be clarified only by examining the underlying historical debate.

As we mentioned in Chapter 1, the 1928 congress of the Third International marked a reorientation of Marxist thinking on the colonial and semi-colonial countries. Imperialism was seen, not as the dynamic unfolding of capitalist relations in the periphery, but rather as an element 'blocking' the development of the forces of production. One resolution went on to say that:

> where the ruling imperialism is in need of a social support in the
> colonies it first allies itself with the ruling strata of the previous social
> structure, the feudal landlords and the trading and money-lending
> bourgeoisie, against the majority of the people. Everywhere imperialism
> attempts to preserve and perpetuate all those pre-capitalist forms of
> exploitation (especially in the village) which serve as the basis for the
> existence of its reactionary allies. . . .[31]

Because of the foreign domination and 'the presence of strong survivals of
feudalism', the situation is defined as 'the stage of the bourgeois democratic
revolution'.[32] The comprador bourgeoisie involved in commercial relations
with the metropolis is uniformly anti-national, but 'the other parts of the
native bourgeoisie, especially those representing the interests of native industry,
support the national movement. . . .'[33] In this way the mythical figure of the
'progressive national bourgeoisie' came on to the scene — thwarted in its
nationalist developmentalist drive only by imperialism and the feudal survivals.
The working-class movement was oriented towards uncritical support for this
fraction (or those who should be it) from the 1930s onwards. In Latin
America, this conception was dominant until the 1960s when the Cuban
Revolution led to a radical rethinking of this question. A very different
understanding of the 'national bourgeoisie' emerges from the OLAS (Latin
American Solidarity Organisation) Conference in 1967:

> Latin America exists in conditions of convulsion, characterised by the
> presence of a weak bourgeoisie which, in indissoluble union with the
> landholders, constitutes the controlling oligarchy of our countries . . .
> It would be absurd to suppose that, under such conditions, the so-called
> Latin American bourgeoisie could develop political action independent
> of the oligarchies and imperialism in defence of the interests and
> aspirations of the nations.[34]

Social reality is obviously more complex than *either* of these counterposed
versions. We must, in the first instance, question the characterisation of the
agrarian ruling class as a 'feudal oligarchy'. This is, of course, a continuation
of the debate mentioned in Chapter 1 on whether agriculture in Latin America
was feudal or capitalist. We established that, historically, this was not so
clear-cut, with rather an uneven development which included non-capitalist
modes of production but was *combined* under the domination of an
international mercantile system. That the landowners even today display
'aristocratic' patterns of behaviour and consumption, that they practise a
paternalistic and patrimonial form of politics is secondary. The determinant
element is the integration within a world mercantilist and then capitalist
system. The 'extra-economic' coercion inflicted on the peasantry was a
function of this, and not the supposedly 'feudal' makeup of the landowners.[35]

Furthermore, some countries, such as Argentina and Uruguay, were characterised by wage labour relations from the start. Other countries saw the development of a capitalist agrarian bourgeoisie after the 1930 crisis, and certainly since the 1970s it has been an absolute anachronism to refer to a feudal or even semi-feudal oligarchy (see Chapter 6). The diverse forms of land tenure in Latin America do not constitute an insuperable barrier to the development of capitalism, as the simplistic calls for an agrarian reform as the solution for the expansion of the internal market lead some to believe.

Perhaps the most important criticism of the 'feudal' agriculture versus 'modern' industrialists scheme springs from the historical origins of the latter. Studies of the 'interlocking élites' in Chile, Argentina and Brazil at least, show conclusively that there is a considerable overlap between rural and industrial interests. In fact it makes more sense in this respect to talk simply of a single ruling class. In Chile, a study of the largest businessmen concluded that almost half were either landowners or were related to landowners.[36] In Argentina, the industrial bourgeoisie did not develop out of an artisan class but, from its inception, was rather tied to the landed interests. Industry emerged as a complementary sector to agriculture – flour-mills, meat-packing plants etc – and remained an integral part of *dependent* development. As Polit writes:

> both sectors, industrialists and landowners, are intertwined; the vague boundaries that separate them are attenuated through the investment of industrial profit in agriculture, converting the landowners into industrialists and the industrialists into landholders.[37]

Taking the 'industrial élite' as a whole, Cardoso concludes in one study that:

> the permeability of the traditional dominant classes and the special circumstances in which the industrialisation is taking place in Latin America, make it difficult, if not impossible, for industrialists and businessmen to play the same dynamic role that they have sometimes taken up elsewhere in the development of capitalism and the formation of an industrial society.[38]

In short, the industrial bourgeoisie in Latin America cannot, because of its structural position – integration with landed interests and domination by imperialism – aspire to a hegemonic role in the development process.

The above does not lead us necessarily to accept the conception of a 'lumpenbourgeoisie' or, as the Peruvian Marxist Mariátegui said in 1929, that:

> the Latin American bourgeoisie . . . is totally unwilling to consider the idea that a second struggle for Independence is necessary . . . the ruling class has no yearning for a greater . . . degree of national autonomy.[39]

Against the prevailing orthodoxy of the times this seems a healthy corrective, but there are problems here as with all the Cuban-influenced studies of the 1960s, which concluded that the 'national bourgeoisie' did not exist. In both there is a certain degree of confusion of capitalist development with national development. Certainly the industrial bourgeoisie has been subordinated firstly to the agrarian ruling class and then to the multinational corporations. Nevertheless, no one would deny that there is a powerful bourgeois class in the largest countries of Latin America today. The Mexican or Brazilian bourgeoisie has a degree of power comparable more to its counterparts in Spain or Italy than to those in Tanzania or Sudan. The term 'national bourgeoisie', in fact, conflates geographical location and political orientation. The indigenous bourgeoisie will pursue the development of the forces of production within its national boundaries in the manner it sees fit — through state intervention and associated with or in competition with international capital as circumstances demand. The close alliance with the transnationals today is not a 'sell-out' as some dependency writers pretend, but simply a rational development model in present circumstances. The notion of a 'progressive national bourgeoisie' should not be replaced by an equally caricaturised 'lumpenbourgeoisie'.

Clearly there are other fractions of the bourgeoisie outside the major agrarian and industrial sectors. In the 19th Century, under British domination, the most powerful capitalist interests in Latin America were the financial and commercial fractions. They played a vital intermediation role between the metropolis and the peripheral nations, running the import-export houses, the banks and the commercialisation circuit. In the enclave economies there were often important mining fractions linked to copper in Chile, tin in Bolivia, etc. The financial fraction of the bourgeoisie remained an important element into the 20th Century with the new model of dependency dominated by the USA. It is worth noting against the most simplistic dependency accounts, that these fractions of the bourgeoisie (along with the agrarian sector) could benefit immensely from the links with the metropolis. The fertility of the Pampas, and the differential rent which accrued, led to an immense flow of resources into Argentina between 1860 and 1930 out of all proportion to its productive structure.[40] The guano boom in Peru between 1840 and 1880 generated some 750 million pesos, of which the Peruvian state received nearly three-quarters. Saltpetre in Chile and cocoa in Ecuador led to similar super profits at the turn of the century (not to mention oil in Venezuela and other countries later). This, it might be added, entailed the transfer of surplus value produced by metropolitan workers to the Third World.[41] Of course, the export sector could also enter into sharp conflict with the metropolitan bourgeoisie over commercial issues — falling out amongst thieves no doubt — but nevertheless, this is far removed from the more simplistic notions of a 'comprador bourgeoisie'.

What unifies the diverse fractions of the bourgeoisie is the state, which, following Poulantzas, acts as the organiser of the bourgeoisie and disorganiser of the proletariat. The state is the site of ruling class compromise achieved under the hegemony of the dominant fraction. Some writers go further, and see the emergence of a 'state bourgeoisie' in some Third World countries, and a new 'bureaucratic' mode of production. Property is redefined from its juridical aspect to the notion of 'effective possession', and those in control of the important state apparatus in post-colonial Africa and present-day Brazil or Peru, for example, become a 'state bourgeoisie', which replaces the 'national bourgeoisie' as the demiurge of development.[42] The theoretical problems are immense – this bourgeoisie is not defined by the extraction and appropriation of surplus value, but through its *organisation* of the process of accumulation – but the debate reflects real changes. This thesis of growing 'state capitalism' in the Third World is essentially economistic (because it is based on the purely quantitative weight of the state sector *vis-à-vis* private capital) and it grossly overestimates the degree of relative autonomy exercised by the techno-bureaucracy in control of the state apparatus.[43] The state bourgeoisie can operate only within the limits set by the global needs of capital's reproduction (of which the state is only one element) and is unlikely to develop class interests at variance with those of the capitalist class as a whole.

We can now briefly recapitulate on the nature of the bourgeoisie in Latin America.[44] The earliest power bloc was formed by a semi-feudal agrarian oligarchy (producing for the external market but operating with non-capitalist relations of production) and a commercial or comprador bourgeoisie, which together constituted the 'agro-export oligarchy'. This model of domination entered into crisis in the 1930s and this led to a restricted but important process of industrialisation and the incorporation of the 'middle classes' into politics. An internal, industrial bourgeoisie arose which could act as a nationalist force under certain conditions (the populist regimes) but could also become a simple 'comprador' bourgeoisie subordinated to imperialism. The compromise state which arose after the 1930s, integrating the industrial bourgeoisie into the power bloc, in turn entered a crisis from the mid-1960s onwards. This was owing to the rise of a new, internationalised fraction of the bourgeoisie, which had become integrated into the international circuit of capital in a dynamic process of extended reproduction. The state is a site of class struggle between these fractions, but also it is an element of cohesion. As was true in Marx's time, the bourgeoisie often 'reigns but does not govern'. The state apparatus is variously dominated by a technocratic-bureaucratic element and the military institution, which are powerful 'social categories' defined primarily by their position in the political relations of society.

Petty Bourgeoisies

According to Marx, 'the petty bourgeoisie is composed of on-the-one-hand and on-the-other-hand. This is so in his economic interests and *therefore* in his politics ... He is a living contradiction.'[45] This 'living contradiction' will be examined in its traditional and modern variants, with some discussion of its political outlook.

Peasant owners of the means of production and labourers at one and the same time — such is the rural side of the petty bourgeoisie. They are exploited by capitalism through the market and yet they own the means of production (land). The peasantry was, for Marx, a strictly non-capitalist class in 'transition' to a capitalist form. It is, however, very debatable whether the peasantry has in fact undergone a process of 'dissolution' through the inexorable advance of capitalism. In his analysis of Mexico, Roger Bartra notes that:

> close to 60% of the population are totally lacking in land and living from wage-earning: a third more are in a situation of semi-proletariani- sation and pauperism. This amounts to 93.5% of the economically active population in the agricultural sector. It is possible to predict an even greater polarization of the class structure, in which the bourgeoisie (and the proletariat) will increase and the peasantry will be reduced.[46]

Other authors however suggest that the majority of the landless do have access to land through their family, or through sharecropping and tenant farming. Furthermore, even those who are strictly wage earners retain their peasant forms of communal existence. Capitalist penetration into agriculture does not necessarily separate the peasant from the means of production, but rather tends only towards the *formal* subordination of their labour to the process of capital valorisation.[47] That land is short does not mean that proletarianisation is necessarily occurring — the reality is more one of de-peasantisation (exclusive dependence on land is broken).

One line of interpretation is to see the peasantry as a distinct mode of production. This may be true if one takes mode of production to be simply the manner in which production takes place, but not as an abstract theoretical concept. Firstly, the peasant community is internally divided and this constant differentiation leads to hierarchies (see Chapter 6). One could, however, argue that inter-peasant inequality, and even exploitation, is secondary to the overall subordination of the countryside by the city. More effective, is the point that the peasantry cannot be a mode of production because they lack a relatively self-sufficient political and economic structure. That is to say, the most significant systems of exploitation and surplus appropriation are generally external.[48] Normally, the peasants are defined by the specific form of village community (i.e. culturally) or by their particular unit of production, the family-labour farm. Neither of these characteristics can lead us to the conclusion that there is a distinct mode of production, in so far as 'peasant' production has become subordinated to the laws of commodity production (i.e. capitalism). Judith Enew and her co-authors conclude correctly that there is no concept of:

> Peasant Mode of Production, there are only specific forms of agricultural production, worked and managed to a greater or lesser

degree by household units. The conditions of existence of such household units and their relations to other forms of production are specific
to the mode of production in which they exist. They are differentiated
by the social relations which form them and reproduce them.[49]

This approach is more in tune with Marx's conception of economic categories
from previous modes of production which acquire new and specific
characteristics under capitalism.

The urban petty bourgeoisie for its part is a broad catch-all category
covering teachers and traders, clerks and civil servants, prostitutes and
policemen, etc. There is a tendency towards proletarianisation in this group
too, although new layers constantly re-form, making it more a process of
simultaneous conservation/dissolution. In much the same way as the small-
scale production of the peasants, these sectors cannot withstand the advance
of capital. The market traders make way for the supermarket and the home
weavers drop out when the textile factory opens. But the small garage can
fit in quite nicely with the big car factory down the road. So the process
is contradictory. Capital clearly extracts a surplus from the peasant and the
urban petty-commodity producer through the control of commercialisation.
In this sense, the petty bourgeoisie is exploited by capital and has social
demands which are to some extent compatible with those of the proletariat:
labour intensive industrialisation to create more jobs and increased social
services to ameliorate the bad conditions many share with the proletariat.
But the petty bourgeoisie is, by virtue of its material position, individualistic
and seeks advance at the expense of its fellows rather than collective action.

If the traditional petty bourgeoisie is one of the major social sectors in
African countries, it is the 'modern' petty-bourgeoisie which is expanding
most rapidly in many countries of Latin America. This new petty bourgeoisie
is a product of monopoly capitalism – it embraces the non-productive wage
earners: teachers, office workers and professionals generally. So far we have
given this new and the traditional petty bourgeoisie only a negative definition
– belonging to neither the bourgeoisie nor the proletariat. Poulantzas, however,
refers to the political and ideological relations which are indispensable to define
the position of the petty bourgeoisie in the structural class determination.
These include, for the new petty bourgeoisie, their place in the division
between mental and manual labour, and in the relations of power and
authority.[50] Since the 1960s the new petty bourgeoisie has grown apace
with the extended reproduction of monopoly capitalism but they have not
all prospered subsequently. In Brazil, since the 'economic miracle' began
around 1968 this layer has become an important consumer of durable
consumer goods. In Argentina, on the other hand, this sector has suffered
from the concentrationist measures taken by successive military governments
since 1966. The modern petty bourgeoisie has been thoroughly proletarianised,
with teachers and state employees being in the forefront of trade union
militancy. This reinforces our point about the essential heterogeneity of the
petty bourgeoisie both economically and politically.

Orthodox modernisation theory made the 'middle class' the main agent of development in the Third World. During the 1960s, as one author writes:

> publications dealing with Latin America assume that a kind of progressive spirit is inherent in individual members of the middle class, and that spirit is usually defined in terms of development.[51]

The 'spirit of capitalism' in the Third World is a particularly stunted and subordinate variety and certainly did not lead to national autonomous development. Even more questionable, however, is the associated notion that 'the political ideal upheld by typical groups in the middle sectors was an elected civil government in contrast to the military regime originating in a coup d'etat'.[52] History has proved this statement to be simply wrong, to the extent that some authors refer to the 'middle class military coup'.[53] During the 1970s this faith in the middle class as a dynamic democratic force was displaced to the new petty bourgeoisie of salaried employees, of the state bureaucracy, managers, technicians, and so on. Certainly, under the 'new' military regimes of the 1970s, this techno-bureaucracy assumed an increasingly important role. In the largest countries of South America this is a well established force, but it is also increasing in importance in the smaller countries of Central America, though more subordinate to international capital there. Overall, though we must conclude, as do Jonas and Dixon, that:

> given the simultaneous weakening (and gradual disappearance) of any 'national bourgeoisie', oriented toward the domestic consumer market in Latin America, this new petty bourgeoisie, tied to international capital and the world market, is unlikely to present any nationalist/ anti-imperialist challenge.[54]

Can we really refer to the politics of the petty bourgeoisie at all? For Marx and Engels:

> The intermediate strata, the small industrialist, small merchant, the artisan, the peasant, all these fight against the bourgeoisie to safeguard their existence from ruin as intermediate strata. They are therefore not revolutionary, but conservative. Nay more, they are reactionary, for they try to roll back the wheel of history. If they are revolutionary, they are so in view of their impending transfer into the proletariat, they thus defend not their present but their future interests; they desert their own standpoint to place themselves at that of the proletariat.[55]

There is plenty of evidence regarding the revolutionary/conservative role of the peasantry in the Third World. The Algerian war for national independence provides a clear case. For Frantz Fanon, 'in the colonial countries the peasants alone are revolutionary, for they have nothing to lose and everything to gain.'[56] On the other hand, Ian Clegg writes that:

> neither the peasantry, nor the truly 'wretched' — the subproletariat — can be said to have played an objectively revolutionary role. . . . The peasantry were fighting for what they regarded as their inheritance: a heritage firmly rooted in the Arab, Berber and Islamic past. Their consciousness was rooted in the values and traditions of this past and their aim was its re-creation.[57]

Peasants have, of course, been the major social force in successive revolutions — one cannot imagine the Russian or Chinese revolutions without them. Clegg's estimate of their real motivations and the limits of their nationalist consciousness also seem irrefutable. Furthermore, Fanon was wrong in seeing the poorest peasant — 'outside the class system' he says — as the most easily mobilised. International experience shows rather that the poor peasantry is, at least initially, the least revolutionary sector, and that the middle peasants are in fact more likely to lead a militant upsurge.[58]

The new petty bourgeoisie — the non-productive wage earners — are more able to look to their 'future interests', as Marx says, because they are often heading towards proletarianisation. To take the example of Peronism in Argentina — the traditional petty bourgeoisie was the movement's main enemy in the 1940s but by the 1960s the 'new' fraction had become its most fervent supporters and the militants behind the armed struggle tendency. What happened in between was a decisive expansion of monopoly capitalism over traditional competitive capitalism, with a whole new layer of occupations formed. These white-collar sectors were the most rapidly unionising sector of the working class, and when their social and economic aspirations were not met, its most militant vanguard. In Peru the teachers union is led by militant Maoists and their strikes have been aggressively political; the bank workers likewise have forsaken their traditional attachment to bourgeois parties. As Alan Angell notes:

> a powerful reason impelling white collar workers into a leftist confederation like the CGTP was the feeling that their social position and salary levels had been reduced to the position of *capas medias pauperizadas* (pauperised middle layers).[59]

To conclude, one cannot speak of the petty bourgeoisie as a social class any more than 'middle class'; there are in fact several 'petty bourgeoisies' amongst the intermediate strata of modern capitalist society. Nor can one refer to the 'politics of the petty bourgeoisie' as such, which conflates the highly unionised teachers and the small conservative peasantry. At all points one must distinguish between the objective position of a class fraction in the relations of production and the position of that fraction in the concrete social and political struggles of the day. These may tend to transform or preserve the existing social relations. Above all, capitalist society, the Third World included, is dynamic, these relations, therefore, cannot be seen as immutable. The class structure is being constantly transformed as capital accumulation advances, so that we cannot deal with simplified notions of a conservative or modernising petty bourgeoisie nor simply see it as a 'transitional class', as Marx did, arguing that there was, inevitably, a tendency for it to disappear. We can see quite clearly how the peasantry and, for example, some of the urban professions are becoming proletarianised. This is, however, a contradictory process, because while some layers become subsumed under the wage-labour relation, others are expanding to become a substantial 'third market' for monopoly capitalism alongside the external market and the bourgeoisie.[60]

Working Classes

The working class or 'labouring poor' is, in fact, a vast mass of social categories with flexible boundaries ranging from the artisans and 'labour aristocrats' to the real 'wretched of the earth' or 'marginal' layers of the population. There is even some doubt that there is a 'proletariat' in the Marxist sense — Peter Lloyd asks in the first sentence of his recent book 'Is there, in the cities of the Third World, a proletariat?'[61]

The category of the self-employed dealt with above shades imperceptibly into the wage-earning class. A recent attempt to clarify the precise nature of the self-employed in the Third World shows that it includes artisans and outworkers with radically different degrees of control over the production process.[62] A sharp dichotomy between the self-employed and wage-labourers is clearly inadequate. The reality is one of artisans, outworkers and wage-labourers, linked together by a series of subcontracting relations with capitalist enterprises. Another study of 'self-employed' wastepaper pickers in Colombia shows how 'the garbage recycling business is characterised by a hierarchy of vertical links which extend from the factory to the garbage picker'.[63] There is a chain of exploitation from the multinational corporation through to the garbage picker in the streets below. The overall tendency is for the 'autonomous producers' to become proletarianised, although a few will obviously pass into the category of small capitalists. The tendency towards becoming wage-labourers does not prevent these workers maintaining many of the trappings of autonomy. It would, however, be ludicrous to consider this sector outside the labouring masses.

The question inevitably arises as to whether the most dynamic capitalist sectors will generate a 'labour aristocracy' bought off economically and politically by the relative privileges of having a well-paid job in countries with massive underemployment. The term 'labour aristocracy' was particularly current in Africa during the 1960s to describe a working class 'élite' which benefited from neo-colonialism and whose trade unions had become narrowly 'economistic'. Arrighi and Saul put forward the view that the better paid section of the labour force or

> the proletariat proper of tropical Africa . . . enjoy incomes three or
> more times higher than those of unskilled laborers and, together with
> the élites and sub-élites in bureaucratic employment in the civil service
> and expatriate concerns, constitute what we call the labor aristocracy
> of tropical Africa.[64]

A highly simplified linkage is made here between a class economic situation
and that class's political position. Furthermore, it tends to generalise from
particular situations to global theoretical statements.

The labour aristocracy thesis has since been thoroughly criticised,
including its earlier application by Engels and Lenin to British workers who
were supposedly corrupted by the gains of empire.[65] In African studies a
succession of empirical investigations show that the proletariat is not a part
of the 'élite' simply because it may earn relatively high monetary wages.
Peace shows how in Nigeria gains made in wages and salaries 'have repercussions
throughout the urban arena and promote economic and political
identifications between the labour force and the non-wage-earners'.[66] In
radical movements the non-proletarian forces will tend to follow the lead of
the organised working class if this class fraction can put forward demands
which articulate the needs of the labouring masses as a whole. Another
study, based on a detailed investigation of railway workers in Ghana,
concludes that the organised industrial working class represents the most
progressive political force now existing in African societies.[67] This does
not, of course, mean that Third World workers are inherently 'revolutionary'
in a simply reversed version of the labour aristocracy theory. Even where
economic differentiation leads to the emergence of a relatively privileged layer
of the working class (and this is by no means so widespread as once supposed)
this does not necessarily result in a conservative political position. The
development of monopoly capitalism has led to the creation of a 'modern'
working class with higher wages and usually more stability of employment
than the competitive sector. This sector has, however, tended to be in the
vanguard of the class struggle, articulating the most advanced anti-bureaucratic
demands and raising issues of workers control and so on. Economic
differentiation does not automatically lead to political fragmentation of the
working class, as our case study of Argentina and Brazil (Chapter 5) will
show. In fact 'labour aristocracy' is a term which, as Stedman Jones writes:

> has often been used as if it provided an explanation. But it would be
> more accurate to say that it pointed towards a vacant area where an
> explanation should be.[68]

The industrial working class in Latin America did not emerge fully formed
but through a long process of articulation with artisan sectors. In 1920, we
can see in Table 3.1, three-quarters of those employed in industry still worked

Table 3.1
Distribution of employment between artisan and industrial sectors in some Latin American countries (1925-1960) (%)

Country	1925		1940		1950		1960	
	Artisan	Manufacturing	Artisan	Manufacturing	Artisan	Manufacturing	Artisan	Manufacturing
Argentina	60	40	51	49	39	61	42	58
Brazil	68	32	51	49	48	52	44	56
Chile	71	29	52	48	51	49	46	54
Colombia	89	11	76	24	70	30	66	34
Mexico	70	30	50	50	45	55	36	64
Peru	94	6	84	16	71	28	62	38
Venezuela	86	14	56	44	53	47	40	60
Latin America	74	26	59	41	52	48	48	52

Source: Cardoso, F.H. (1969) *Sociologie du développement en Amérique Latine.*
Paris, Anthropos, pp.124-5.

in the artisan sector, and only a quarter in manufacturing as such. In Peru fully 94% of those employed in the secondary sector worked in the small workshops of the artisan sector. Even in Argentina, the country most thoroughly dominated by the capitalist mode of production, 60% of the industrial workers were artisans. By 1940 the artisan/manufacturing proportion was 59%:40% respectively; in 1950 it was 52%:48%, and only in 1960 did manufacturing gain the upper hand with 52% of employment as against 48% in the artisan sector. Even at that late stage Colombia still had 66% of artisan workers over the total. The basic conclusion is that it was not until the 1960s that manufacturing gained predominance over the artisan sector. The heterogeneity of the working class in these conditions is especially marked, and politically it placed obstacles in the way of unified working-class action. This 'impure' origin of the working class recalls the formative stages of the English working class, which, contrary to popular labour history, did not become a full fledged proletariat overnight. Samuel has shown how concurrent phases of capitalism − represented by hand and steam-powered technology − persisted into the Victorian era.[69] Manufacturing rested on a broad handicraft artisan sector, though this *uneven* development was also *combined* in so far as each fed off the other's achievements. In short, the development of capitalism, and mechanisation in particular, is a process and not an event.

At a certain stage of the world-wide accumulation of capital the more 'modern' face of capitalism becomes predominant. One way of approximating to this shift is by distinguishing a 'modern' sector, composed of white-collar and blue-collar workers, and a 'traditional' sector made up of the self-employed, family-employed and domestic employees (and their employers). In Table 3.2 we can see the results of this comparison within the labour market for a number of Latin American countries. This allows us to distinguish those countries in which the modern sector predominates, those in which it represents around half of the total and those in which it is still a minority. Purely for comparative purposes we have included data for some countries in Africa and Asia which show that Egypt falls into the intermediate category and Sri Lanka into the higher category of 'modern' employment, but other representative countries are still completely dominated by the 'traditional' sector. Clearly, there are still forces working towards the preservation of non-capitalist relations of production in the Third World as a whole. Nor can Sri Lankan tea plantation workers be classed as a 'free' proletariat. In Latin America, however, the dominant tendency seems to be towards an accelerated development of capitalist relations of production in terms of the proportion of wage and salary earners in the working population. Marx referred to two historical forms of labour development based on personal dependence and independence respectively. As Chattopadhyay concludes:

> in some countries of the Third World the 'second great form' of the development of 'human productivity' has reached significant proportions whereas in others, the 'first form' is still dominant.[70]

Table 3.2
Wage and Salary Earners in the Working Population of the Third World (%)

Latin America

High		Intermediate		Low	
Costa Rica (1973)	72	Nicaragua (1971)	56	Honduras (1963)	40
Argentina (1970)	71	Panama (1970)	55	Domincan Rep (1970)	38
Chile (1970)	64	Brazil (1970)	55	Colombia (1964)	37
Mexico (1970)	62	El Salvador (1971)	49	Paraguay (1962)	34
Venezuela (1961)	60	Guatemala (1973)	48		
Mean	66	Mean	53	Mean	37

Africa		*Asia*	
Egypt (1960)	49	Sri Lanka (1963)	60
Mozambique (1960)	30	Pakistan (1961)	20
Ghana (1960)	20	India (1961)	13
Tanzania (1962)	10	Thailand (1960)	12

Source: Buttari, J. (ed) (1979) *Employment and Labor Force in Latin
America Vol II*, ECIEL, p.459. For Asian and African examples
Chattopadhyay, P. (1980) Labour and development,
Labour Capital and Society, Vol.13 No.1:23.

This process of differentiation has also occurred in the rural areas with
the emergence of a substantial rural proletariat.[71] There has been a rural
proletariat on the banana, cotton, coffee and sugar plantations and on the
estancias since the turn of the century. Since the 1960s, however, the growth
of 'agri-business', by which agriculture has become just another branch of
capital, has accelerated the proletarianisation of the peasantry. There is now
a growing rural proletariat composed of landless peasants who have been
dispossessed by the expansion of a capitalist export-oriented agriculture. In
Brazil, the *boias frias* who were once sharecroppers or tenant farmers on the
big plantations now make up a six million strong force of agricultural day
labourers. Paid by piece rates, they are dependent on labour contractors,
which makes for erratic employment patterns. A more 'classical' rural
proletariat are the banana workers of Central America, who are employed all
the year round, receive relatively high wages and are even unionised. But
even there, the export-oriented sector, often dominated by multinationals,
turns to the traditional *minifundista* peasant for a cheap labour reserve. The
subsistence of these plots allows capital to pay a much lower wage to achieve
the reproduction of the labourer. It is notable that a 1979 wildcat strike by
sugar-cane workers in Pernambuco (Brazil) called for wage increases, improved
transport facilities *and* household plots for subsistence cultivation. The old
and the new thus coexist.
    Against the rather populist glorification of the peasantry and the

lumpenproletariat promoted by Fanon, it would be tempting to raise a pure 'Leninist' vision of a class-conscious proletariat doing battle directly with capital. If, however, the peasantry is not a class but a conceptual category embracing a multitude of different situations, so the category of 'worker' shades off into that of artisan, out-worker and even peasant. Proletarianisation may be the dominant tendency in some countries and in some periods, but one also notes a process of 're-peasantisation'. De Wind shows how Peruvian mineworkers regularly give up their wage-work (one-fifth leave every year) to return to their small-holding in the countryside or become traders and craftworkers.[72] There is thus a two-way flow between the working class and the other groupings of the labouring poor. If structural positions are fluid so also are ideologies. As the experience of the Algerian war of independence shows, the peasants may wage a fierce anti-colonial struggle but this does not necessarily lead to an anti-capitalist orientation. Whereas the workers pushed forward with a vigorous wave of factory occupations towards a system of self-management, the peasants were fighting for what they regarded as their inheritance. The petty bourgeoisie looks to the past for its inspiration. Workers, on the contrary, are, at least potentially, bearers of a superior co-operative mode of production which will lead to the abolition of classes.

Given the numerical minority of industrial workers in the 'underdeveloped' countries, Marxists since Lenin have developed the concept of a 'workers' and peasants' alliance'. This is not a formal political contract but is based on the material interpenetration of workers and peasants in the relations of production and their (limited) common interests. Certainly, as Ken Post notes for Algeria 'the main thrust of the revolution was generated by the articulation of interplay between workers and peasants. . . .'[73] Today, the concept of the 'mass alliance' goes beyond this rather instrumental pact to include all the various artisan and 'petty bourgeois' layers oppressed by capital.[74] Fragmentation within the labouring poor is matched by the objectively unifying effect of capital penetration, which tends to accentuate the linkages between sectors, especially during recessions. Nor are the barriers absolute between different sectors as we have seen, and most families will be spread across various occupations (miner, farmer, artisan, part-time factory worker, etc). Though capital tends to bring a whole range of 'intermediate strata' under its sway, unity is not automatic and is only created consciously. In a sense, the intermediate layers are the site of a class struggle between proletariat and bourgeoisie for their political allegiance.

Marginality

The question of 'marginality' merits a separate discussion because it has often been pointed out as the distinguishing factor of the Third World class structures. Outside most Third World cities there are conglomerations of tin or cardboard huts, often without water or electricity, known as 'shanty-towns'. Half the population of Lima, the capital of Peru, live in the *barriadas*. They are often seen as a 'marginal' sector because they appear to be outside the economic and political process. Their origins are usually a massive migration of peasants to the cities (expelled by the mechanisation of agriculture) where the expansion of industrial employment cannot keep pace with the rate of urbanisation.[75]

The origin of the term marginality lies in the work of the American sociologists Park and Stonequist, who developed a theory of the 'marginal man' to describe the Jewish community in the USA seen as between two social worlds.[76] In Latin America this term gained currency in the mid-1960s to describe the rise in land invasions on the outskirts of the cities by homeless people who built precarious houses there. Marginality was seen as a 'social problem' to do with housing, lack of employment and in many cases the psychology of the *marginales* themselves. One of the earlier attempts at a Marxist explanation of this phenomenon was carried out by José Nun.[77] In this account, Marx's discussion of the reserve army of labour created by capitalism was not seen as relevant to a situation dominated by monopoly capitalism and dependency. There was a 'marginal mass' thrown off by capital-intensive industrialisation which was not functional to capitalism as the reserve army had been. That something might be considered 'dysfunctional' to the working of capitalism is, of course, quite foreign to any Marxist understanding of this contradictory mode of production.

The Marxist discussion of marginality finds its most sophisticated expression in the work of the Peruvian writer Anibal Quijano.[78] He sees the marginalised labour force as a distinct new sector within the working population excluded from the hegemonic level of economic activity. The 'marginal pole' in the dependent capitalist economies is seen to consist of those occupations of minimal productivity, not linked to the direct production of goods, unskilled and, therefore, unstable. These marginalised workers do not even help to keep wages down in modern industry as the 'reserve army of labour' does in Marx's analysis, because they are not competing for the same jobs. This marginal employment is concentrated in the urban tertiary sector — small-scale trade, repair shops and above all personal services of every kind. Quijano virtually considers this a separate mode of production — the petty-commodity mode of production — or as some call it the 'informal sector'. The key error in Quijano's exposition is that he does not establish a relation of direct exploitation between the big bourgeoisie and this sector because 'surplus value', in the strict sense, is not extracted. But the bourgeoisie *requires* these casual workers — car washers, maids, cooks, and gardeners. This expanding service sector is an integral part of expanded capitalist reproduction at the periphery and in no way 'marginal'.

The 'marginal underclass' or sub-proletariat is not lacking in integration with the dominant capitalist mode of production. All the recent work on Brazil in particular, has made that abundantly clear.[79] In the first instance capital-intensive industrialisation has not proved so totally unable to absorb labour-power. Between 1950 and 1970 manufacturing employment grew by one and a half million jobs. The 'hypertrophied' tertiary sector many writers

complain of must be broken down into personal/social services and
production/distribution services. It is these latter services, directly tied to the
expansion of industry, which were growing fastest in the 1970s and are
the sign of a dynamic economy. Above all, the urban poor are in no way
'marginal' to the needs of capital, rather they are articulated within the overall
economic system. The industrialisation of São Paulo would simply not have
been possible without the exploitation of the services provided by its vast
labour-intensive tertiary sector. Small-scale transport and commercial
facilities are a boon to capital, especially when housing costs do not enter
into the cost of reproduction of the labour-power which provides it. The
'archaic' forms of production are reproduced by the cycle of capital
accumulation and help lower the overall costs of reproducing labour-power
by selling goods and services at low prices. Finally, the 'marginals' do operate
as a reserve army of labour in maintaining low wages because they are a
relatively available pool of labour to renew the largely 'unskilled' mass of
jobs in modern industry.

As to the politics of 'marginality', it is Fanon, once again, who gave rise
to a powerful myth:

> the *lumpen-proletariat* . . . is the sign of the irrevocable decay . . . at the
> heart of colonial domination. So the pimps, the hooligans, the
> unemployed and the petty criminals . . . throw themselves into the
> struggle for liberation like stout working men.[80]

Many in Latin America saw this social group as the revolutionary class *par
excellence* because it had nothing to lose. The reality has been more
contradictory. In many situations the shanty-town dwellers have supported
right-wing or populist politicians if they could 'deliver the goods'. In other
cases, most noticeably during the Popular Unity government in Chile
(1970–73) they were at the forefront of a movement for social change.
The *pobladores* in Chile were amongst the most radical sectors supporting
the government, and their demands went beyond their traditional ones
(housing in particular) to take up the revindications of the mass movement
as a whole. Their main slogan was 'our struggle is bigger than a house'.[81] If by
'marginality' one is referring to an isolation from the political process this
must be rejected. The only sense in which the term may be used is that this
sector is deprived of many of the benefits (such as they are) of capitalist
development in the Third World. But the peasantry are *not* a class, but rather
a heterogeneous and fluid category generated by the unfolding of monopoly
capitalism (in fact, in Chile, many of the *pobladores* were industrial workers).
Their political role will only be determined by their specific relationships
with other social classes, in particular the organised working class.

The concept of 'marginality' points to some of the underlying weaknesses
in modernisation and dependency theories alike. For the first it represents a
lack of economic and social assimilation into the urban/modern milieu, or in
the 'poverty of culture' variant it is attributed to psychological weaknesses in

the individual slum-dweller. For the dependency theorists 'marginality' sums up the stagnationist, exclusionary nature of monopoly capitalism which is incapable of generating employment. As we have seen, neither version explains the phenomenon at hand. The simplifications operated in this area have consequences for the analysis of other social sectors. For the modernisation theorists — operating with a simple traditional/modern and rural/urban dichotomy — the process of internal integration of the 1950s was a major focus. This was seen to lead to either a form of 'anomie' (social and psychological disorganisation) or the re-creation of the rural kinship network in the cities. For the few who made it into the factories, their recent rural origin was seen as a major factor. Patterns of identification, solidarity, organisation and class action were determined by the 'traditional' milieu from which they came.[82] From this derived the widespread view of a passive and conservative urban working class in Latin America, that neglected the powerful moulding factor of capitalism which, through exploitation, led to 'industrial habits' including class solidarity and resistance to the 'tyranny of the factory'.

With the popularisers of dependency the problem is a different one. Marginality is one of those pseudo-concepts which relate to concrete facts but do little to theorise them. In this it is similar to the notion of 'agrarian oligarchy', 'national bourgeoisie', 'lumpenbourgeoisie', 'labour aristocracy', etc. The reality of 'marginality' — primarily casual labour — existed in Victorian Britain.[83] But Dale Johnson could write in 1969 that in his work for 'the first time the concept of "marginal" has been combined with "underclass" '.[84] The development of capitalism had always produced regional inequalities, class inequalities and poverty alongside prosperity. The radical dependency writers thought it was a unique historical reality they were confronting and labelled it 'lumpen-development'. The bourgeoisie, which always proceeds in the manner it best sees fit to serve its interests, was berated for its 'anti-national' character because it turned towards the international arena rather than the internal market. The logic of this discourse is towards supporting a vague form of populism. This is made explicit in the marginality debate when Johnson refers to the rural and the new urban (marginal) *mass* involved in a struggle against the urban *classes* (as a whole). He cites approvingly the conclusion by Irving L. Horowitz that 'instead of the classical Marxist or European pattern of struggle between classes, a struggle between class and mass takes place'.[85]

Class Structure

We have said that Marxism is not primarily a theory of class structure but rather of class struggle, but it is still necessary to make the first clear and explicit as it is the starting point for any analysis of class movements and, indeed, for discussions of class strategy. A convenient way of summarising this Chapter is through the stylised representation of a 'typical' Third World

Figure 3.1
The Social Structure of a Third World Country

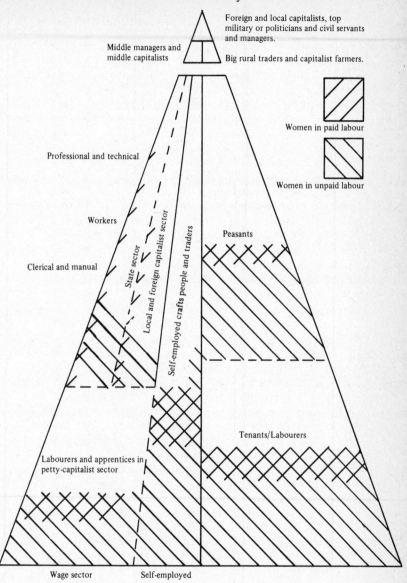

Source: Waterman, P. (1979), *The Labouring Poor in the Third World*. The Hague, Institute of Social Studies, p.18.

social structure in Figure 3.1. It should be made clear that no quantitative aspect pertains to the size of various parts of the triangle. Furthermore, this figure was devised by Peter Waterman as an illustration of African social structures and certain aspects would have to be modified to fit the Latin American situation. For example, the modern petty bourgeoisie would have a far greater role, in many countries the peasants would be less important, etc. Bearing that in mind we can examine the various sections of our simplified social structure figure.

At the top of the triangle we have the ruling class, divided into various fractions but united through the capitalist state. The upper ranges of the lower half of the triangle belong to the petty bourgeoisie — with diverse economic positions and a fluid political outlook. The vast mass of the population fall within the generic category of 'labouring poor'. In the cities workers are divided according to what capitalist sector they work in and by 'grades and trades'. The 'self-employed' or petty commodity production sector may merge into the petty bourgeoisie in its upper reaches but the vast majority form part of the labouring poor. In the rural areas the peasants (large, medium and small) coexist uneasily with the tenants and labourers. In every single sector, usually concentrated at the bottom of each category, are the women, doing paid or unpaid labour (see Chapter 4). Women are particularly important in the self-employed category, but everywhere their gender oppression is inextricably linked with class divisions.

Bearing in mind that the Third World is part of a global imperialist system, we should make some attempt to analyse the international class structure as a whole. This is obviously a risky undertaking, given the unreliability of statistics generally, and more specifically their comparability across nations. Samir Amin has however attempted the task as summarised in Table 3.3. Here again, Latin America must be distinguished from the overall 'peripheral areas' category. It is estimated that around half of the total Third World 'middle strata and bourgeoisie' and its income pertains to the Latin American countries. The area is also far more urbanised than the general picture may lead us to believe. Overall we can draw several conclusions from Table 3.3 regarding world income distribution by class. There is an international web of exploitation, with centre and periphery forming an integral whole (not two autonomous systems). The small metropolitan bourgeoisie (2% of total production) receives mainly half the total income generated by this system. The vast bulk of the world population — the peasantry (over 50%) — receive a miserable 6% of the total income. Unemployment, even in a period of capitalist recession, is at least double in the periphery than the centre. The working class or proletariat of the Third World receives a *relatively* higher wage than the peasantry — material basis of the 'labour aristocracy' thesis. The 'proletarianised petty bourgeoisie' covers the diverse reality of the artisans and merchants (petty commodity producers) and the growingly important white-collar workers who should perhaps be seen as part of the working class as such.

One conclusion we cannot accept simply on the basis of Table 3.3 is that

Table 3.3
Class Structure of the Imperialist System (1975)

	(1) Millions of active members	(2)* % of grand total	(3) Average income per active member ($)	(4) Aggregate income (billions of $)	(5)* % of grand total
A-Centres					
Peasantry	35	3%	4,300	150	6%
Working class					
'Inferior' category	50	4%	3,000	150	6%
'Superior' category	60	4%	4,500	270	10%
Proletarianized petty bourgeoisie	110	8%	5,200	570	21%
Middle strata & bourgeoisie	90	7%	12,000	1,080	40%
Unemployed	25	2%	–	–	–
Total A	*370*	*27%*	*6,000*	*2,220*	*83%*
B-Peripheral areas					
Peasantry					
Poor and exploited	600	44%	200	120	4%
Middle	150	11%	400	60	2%
Landowners & capitalists	50	4%	1,000	50	2%
Working class	50	4%	600	30	1%
Proletarianized petty bourgeoisie	80	6%	800	65	2%
Middle strata & bourgeoisie	20	1%	6,800	135	5%
Urban unemployed	50	4%	–	–	–
Total B	*1,000*	*73%*	*460*	*460*	*17%*
Grand total	**1,370**	**100%**	**1,950**	**2,680**	**100%**

* Discrepancies in percentages are due to rounding

Source: Amin, S. (1980) *Class and Nation*, New York, Monthly Review Press, p.15.

the working class of the advanced industrialised countries benefits directly from the exploitation of the Third World. The vast differential between the first group (27% of population and 83% of income) and the second (73% of population and only 17% of income) lays the objective basis for nationalism. It does not follow that the centre is composed of 'bourgeois nations' whose proletariat co-exploits the labouring masses of the Third World. Emmanuel, on the basis of his theory of unequal exchange, concludes that:

> from the moment when the sharing out of the product of international exploitation assumes an important, if not preponderant, place in what is at stake in the class struggle within the nation, this struggle ceases to be a genuine class struggle in the Marxist sense of the term, and becomes a settlement of accounts between partners around a jointly-owned cake.[86]

Samir Amin himself refers disparagingly to a 'pro-imperialist current within Marxism . . . limited to 4 percent of the exploited workers of the capitalist world [which] can no longer act as a subversive force'.[87] This Third Worldist position has a basis in fact in so far as the labour and socialist movements of the centre have not had a particularly good record on the question of imperialism. This does not, however, mean that the international solidarity of workers is a pipe-dream.

Increasingly, workers in the metropolitan countries are disciplined by the threat to relocate 'their' plants in the Third World. As production becomes internationalised so does the objective basis for international workers solidarity. There is a considerable tradition of joint action across plants in different countries on the part of European workers. Extension of this practice to the Third World is more recent but by no means negligible, and it is not uncommon for workers employed by a multinational in both the metropolitan and dependent countries to come together. Trade union imperialism — when metropolitan unions operate as labour ambassadors for imperialism — is of course not dead.[88] The tendency today is, however, towards international co-ordination at the level of the World Corporation Councils and, more importantly, at the level of the shop stewards' committee. More fundamentally, we must question Emmanuel's thesis that the proletariat of the centre shares in the exploitation of peasants and workers in the Third World. This would imply that they are no longer exploited and that their labour-power is no longer a source of surplus-value. In fact, in strict Marxist terms, workers of the centre are *more* exploited than those of the Third World — that is, the proportion of surplus labour to necessary labour is higher given the greater productivity there. This in no way denies the wretchedly low wages of the periphery but runs against an impressionistic argument that the central workers receive the 'crumbs' off the imperialist table, something that has been difficult, in fact, to demonstrate since it was first proposed by Engels. As Bettelheim argues against Emmanuel:

since it is not possible to speak of exploitation of the workers of the 'poor' countries by those of the 'rich' ones, it must be acknowledged that no fundamental contradiction sets the interests of the former against those of the latter.[90]

References

1. Lenin, V.I. (1971) *Selected Works* Vol.3. Moscow, Progress Publishers, p.231.
2. Marx, K. (1981) *Capital* Vol.3. London, Penguin Books, p.1025. For an elaboration of Marx's theory of class see Draper, H. (1978) *Karl Marx's Theory of Revolution. Volume II The Politics of Social Class.* New York, Monthly Review Press.
3. Ibid., p.1025.
4. Marx, K. (1974) *The First International and After*. London, Penguin Books, p.270.
5. Lukacs, G. (1971) *History and Class Consciousness*. London, Merlin Press, p.149.
6. Cutler, A., Hindness, B., Hirst, P., and Hussain, A. (1977) *Marx's 'Capital' and Capitalism Today*. London, Routledge and Kegan Paul, p.194.
7. On the Marxist theory of ideology see Larrain, J. (1979) *The Concept of Ideology*. London, Hutchinson; and Sumner, C. (1979) *Reading Ideologies*. London, Academic Press.
8. Poulantzas, N. (1975) *Classes in Contemporary Capitalism*. London, New Left Books, p.16.
9. Cutler, A. et al (1977) *Marx's Capital and Capitalism Today*, op.cit., p.197.
10. Althusser, L. and Balibar, E. (1970) *Reading Capital*. London, New Left Books, p.189.
11. For a critique of the concept of class in Poulantzas see Cardoso, F.H. (1973) Althusserianismo o Marxismo? A Propósito Del Concepto de Clases en Poulantzas. *Las Clases Sociales en América Latina.* (ed) R. Benitez Zenteno, Mexico, Siglo XXI, and more generally Clarke, S. (1977) Marxism, Sociology and Poulantzas' Theory of the State. *Capital and Class*, No.2:1-31.
12. Poulantzas, N. (1975) *Classes in Contemporary Capitalism*, op.cit., p.14.
13. Thompson, E.P. (1978) *The Poverty of Theory*. London, Merlin Press, pp.298-9.
14. Ibid., p.295.
15. Thompson, E.P. (1968) *The Making of the English Working Class*. London, Penguin Books, p.11.
16. Anderson, P. (1980) *Arguments Within English Marxism*. London, New

Left Books, p.33.

17. See Wright, E.O. (1978) *Class, Crisis and the State*. London, New Left Books. For a similar interpretation see Carcheddi, G. (1977) *On the Economic Identification of Social Classes*. London, Routledge & Kegan Paul.
18. Ibid., p.63.
19. Ibid., p.88.
20. Gramsci, A. (1971) *Selections from the Prison Notebooks*. London, Lawrence and Wishart, p.152.
21. Ibid., p.151.
22. Hindness, B. (1977) The concept of class in Marxist theory and Marxist politics. *Class, Hegemony and Party* (ed) J. Bloomfield. London, Lawrence and Wishart, p.104.
23. Laclau, E. (1977) *Politics and Ideology in Marxist Theory*. London, New Left Books, p.105.
24. Ibid.
25. Urry, J. (1981) *The Anatomy of Capitalist Societies*. London Macmillan, p.67. This book is a useful guide to the whole debate on economics, politics and class.
26. For some discussion of class and consciousness see Mann, M. (1973) *Consciousness and Action among the Western Working Class*. London, Macmillan; and Weber, H. (1975) *Marxisme et conscience de classe*. Paris, Union Générale d'Éditions.
27. Wright, E.O. (1980) Varieties of Marxist Conceptions of Class Structure. *Politics and Society*, Vol.9 No.3:365.
28. Przeworski, A. (1977) Proletariat into a Class: The Process of Class Formation from Karl Kautsky's The Class Struggle to Recent Controversies. *Politics and Society*, Vol.7 No.4:372.
29. See the discussion in Shivji, I. (1970) *Class Struggles in Tanzania*. London, Heineman; and Guerra, H. (1979) *Angola: Estrutura Económica e Classes Sociais*. Lisboa, União dos Escritores Angolanos.
30. Roxborough, I. (1979) *Theories of Underdevelopment*. London, Macmillan, p.72.
31. Degras, J. (1970) *The Communist International 1919–1963* Volume 2. Oxford, Oxford University Press, p.533.
32. Ibid., p.136.
33. Ibid., p.138.
34. OLAS General Declaration (1967) *International Socialist Review*. Vol.28 No.6, pp.52 and 57.
35. See the famous essay by Stavenhagen, R. (1968) Seven Fallacies about Latin America. *Latin America Reform or Revolution*, (ed) J. Petras and M. Zeitlin. New York, Fawcett Publications.
36. See Zeitlin, M. et al (1976) Class Segments: Agrarian Property and Political Leadership in the Capitalist Class of Chile.*American Sociological Review*, Vol.41 No.6.
37. Polit, G. (1968) The industrialists of Argentina. *Latin America: Reform*

or Revolution? op.cit., p.399. For the Brazilian case see Dean, W. (1969) *The Industrialisation of São Paulo, 1880-1945.* Austin, University of Texas Press.

38. Cardoso, F.H. (1967) The Industrial Elite. *Elites in Latin America,* (ed) S.M. Lipset and A. Solari. New York, Oxford University Press, p.113.

39. Mariátegui, J.C. (1977) Anti-imperialist perspective. *New Left Review,* No.70:67.

40. This is pursued in Laclau, E. (1969) Modos de producción, sistemas económicos y población excedente. Aproximación histórica a los casos Argentino y Chileno. *Revista Latinoamericana de Sociologia,* Vol.1 No.1.

41. An interpretation developed in Sorj, B. (1982) Reflexiones heréticas sobre el imperialismo y las economías de exportación en América Latina. *Estudos PECLA,* (Federal University of Minas Gerais, Brazil) Vol.1 No.1.

42. See for example Shivji, I. (1976) *Class Struggles in Tanzania,* op.cit.; and Petras, J. (1978) State Capitalism and the Third World. *Critical Perspectives on Imperialism and Social Class in the Third World.* J. Petras. New York, Monthly Review Press.

43. A critique developed by Hirata, H. (1979) Capitalisme d'Etat, bourgeoisie d'Etat et mode de production techno-bureaucratique. *Critiques l'Economie Politique,* No.16-17 (old series):6-41.

44. For a full historical discussion see the national studies in González Casanova, P. (ed) (1982) *América Latina: historia de medio siglo* 2 vols., Mexico, Siglio XXI.

45. Marx, K. and Engels, F. (1965) *Selected Correspondence.* Moscow, Progress Publishers, p.157.

46. Bartra, R. (1974) *Estructura agraria y clases sociales en Mexico.* Mexico, Ediciones Era, p.172.

47. See Paré, L. (1977) *El proletariado agrario en Mexico.* Mexico, Siglo XXI, and the excellent summary of these issues in Harris, R. (1978) Marxism and the agrarian question in Latin America. *Latin American Perspectives,* Vol.V No.4:2-26.

48. Shanin, T. (1979) Defining Peasants: Conceptualizations and Deconceptualizations. *Peasant Studies,* Vol.8 No.4. For a broad discussion of the peasant economy see Harriss, J. (ed) (1982) *Rural Development Theories of Peasant Economy and Rural Change.* London, Hutchinson.

49. Ennew, J., Hirst, P., and Tribe, K. (1977) 'Peasantry' as an Economic Category. *The Journal of Peasant Studies,* Vol.4 No.4:320.

50. Poulantzas, N. (1975) *Classes in Contemporary Capitalism* op.cit., p.208.

51. Ratinoff, L. (1967) The New Urban Groups: The Middle Classes. *Elites in Latin America* (ed) S.M. Lipset and A. Solari. New York, Oxford University Press, p.61.

52. Ibid., p.75.

53. See Nun, J. (1968) The middle class military coup. *Latin America:*

Reform or Revolution? op.cit.

54. Jonas, S. and Dixon, M. (1980) Proletarianization and class alliances in Latin America. *Processes of the World System*, (ed) T. Hopkins and I. Wallerstein. London, Sage Publications, p.237.
55. Marx, K. and Engels, F. (1973) *The Revolutions of 1848*. London, Penguin Books, p.77.
56. Fanon, F. (1969) *The Wretched of the Earth*. London, Penguin Books, p.47.
57. Clegg, I. (1971) *Workers and Self-Management in Algeria*. New York, Monthly Review Press, p.180.
58. See Alavi, H. (1965) Peasants and Revolution. *Socialist Register 1965*, pp.241–77.
59. Angell, A. (1980) *Peruvian Labour and the Military Government since 1968*. London, Institute of Latin American Studies, Working Papers No.3, p.19.
60. See the nature of this process in Tavares, M.C. and Serra, J. (1973) Beyond Stagnation: A Discussion on the Nature of Recent Developments in Brazil. *Latin America: From Dependence to Revolution*. (ed) J. Petras, New York; John Wiley & Sons.
61. Lloyd, P. (1982) *A Third World Proletariat?* London, Allen and Unwin, p.11.
62. McEwen Scott, A. (1979) Who are the self-employed? *Casual Work and Poverty in Third World Cities*, (eds) R. Bromley and C. Gerry. Chichester, John Wiley and Sons, p.115.
63. Bromley, R. (1979) Industry, and the 'Vultures' of Cali. *Casual Work and Poverty in Third World Cities*, op.cit., p.181.
64. Arrighi, G. and Saul, J. (1973) *Essays on the Political Economy of Africa*. New York, Monthly Review Press, pp.18–19.
65. See the broad survey in Gray, J. (1981) *The Aristocracy of Labour in Nineteenth-century Britain c 1850–1914*. London, Macmillan. On the African debate see Waterman, P. (1975) The Labor Aristocracy in Africa: Introduction to a debate. *Development and Change*, Vol.6 No.3.
66. Peace, A. (1975) The Lagos Proletariat: Labour Aristocrats or Populist Militants. *The Development of an African Working Class*, (eds) R. Sandbrook and R. Cohen. London, Longman, p.298.
67. Jeffries, R. (1978) *Class, Power and Ideology in Ghana: the Railwaymen of Sekondi*. Cambridge, Cambridge University Press.
68. Stedman Jones, G. (1975) Class Struggle in the Industrial Revolution. *New Left Review*, No.90:61.
69. Samuel, R. (1977) The Workshop of the World: Steam Power and Hand Technology in mid-Victorian Britain. *History Workshop*, No.3:6–72.
70. Chattopadhyay, P. (1980) Labour and Development. *Labour, Capital and Society*, Vol.13 No.1:22–3.
71. This paragraph draws on the very useful survey Agribusiness Targets Latin America (1970) in *NACLA Report on the Americas*, Vol.XII No.1.
72. de Wind, J. (1979) From Peasants to Miners: The Background to

Strikes in the Mines of Peru. *Peasants and Proletarians: the Struggles of Third World Workers*, (ed) R. Cohen, P. Gutkind and C. Brazier. London, Hutchinson and Co.

73. Post, K. (1979) The Alliance of Workers and Peasants: Some Problems Concerning the Articulation of Classes (Algeria and China). *Peasants and Proletarians*, op.cit., p.280.

74. This theme is developed in Waterman, P. (1981) Understanding Relations Amongst Labouring People in Peripheral Capitalist Societies. *Labour, Capital and Society*. Vol.14, No.1:88–108.

75. For a broad survey of urbanisation in Latin America see Roberts, B. (1978) *Cities of Peasants – The Political Economy of Urbanization in the Third World*. London, Edward Arnold.

76. See Park, R. (1928) Human Migration and the Marginal Man. *American Journal of Sociology*, Vol.XXXIII, No.6; and Stonequist, E. (1935) The Problem of the Marginal Man. *American Journal of Sociology*, Vol.XLI No.1. The classic Latin American text in this tradition is Germani, G. (1980) *Marginality*. New Brunswick, Transaction.

77. Nun, J. (1969) Superpoblación relativa, ejército industrial de reserva y masa marginal. *Revista Latinoamericana de Sociologia*, (Buenos Aires, Argentina). Vol.1 No.2.

78. Quijano, A. (1980) The marginal role of the economy and the marginalised labour force. *The Articulation of Modes of Production*, (ed) H. Wolpe. London, Routledge and Kegan Paul, pp.254–88.

79. See Kowarick, L. (1979) Capitalism and urban marginality in Brazil. *Casual Work and Poverty in Third World Cities*, op.cit.

80. Fanon, F. (1969) *The Wretched of the Earth*. op.cit., p.103.

81. See Threlfall, M. (1976) Shantytown dwellers and People's Power. *Allende's Chile* (ed) P. O'Brien, New York, Praeger Publishers.

82. This theme is developed in Jelin, E. (1979) Orientaciones e Ideologías obreras en América Latina. *Fuerza de Trabajo y Movimientos Laborales en América Latina*, (ed) R. Katzman and S.L. Reyna. Mexico, El Colegio de Mexico.

83. See the study of the 'casual poor' in Britain in Stedman Jones, G. (1976) *Outcast London – A Study in the Relationship Between Classes in Victorian Britain*. London, Penguin Books.

84. Johnson, D. (1972) On Oppressed Classes. *Dependence and Underdevelopment – Latin America's Political Economy*, J. Cockcroft, A. Gunder Frank and D. Johnson. New York, Anchor Books, p.274.

85. Ibid., p.278.

86. Emmanuel, A. (1970) The Delusions of Internationalism. *Monthly Review*, Vol.XXII, No.2, p.18.

87. Amin, S. (1980) *Class and Nation*. New York, Monthly Review Press, p.166.

88. See the exposé in Thompson, D. and Larson, D. (1978) *Where were you, brother? An account of Trade Union imperialism*. London, War on Want. On the Latin American case see Scott, J. (1978) *Yankee Unions, Go*

Home! How the AFL helped the US build an empire in Latin America. Vancouver, New Star Books.

89. See the examples given in Somavia, J., Trajtenberg, R. and Valdés, J.G. (eds) (1979) *Movimiento Sindical y Empresas Transnacionales.* Mexico, Editorial Nueva Imagen.

90. Bettelheim, C. (1970) Economic Inequalities Between Nations and International Solidarity. *Monthly Review*, Vol.XXXII, No.2, p.23. For a full empirical critique of the 'labour aristocracy' thesis see Szymanski, A. (1981) *The Logic of Imperialism.* New York, Praeger, pp.465-91.

4. Beyond Class: Women in Latin America

> The worker is the slave of capitalist society, the female
> worker is the slave of that slave. . . . None so fitted to break
> the chains as they who wear them, none so well equipped
> to decide what is a fetter. In its march towards freedom
> the working class must . . . cheer all the louder if in its
> hatred of thraldom and passion for freedom the women's
> army forges ahead of the militant army of Labour.
>
> James Connolly[1]

The Irish socialist James Connolly's uncompromising feminism of 1913 is
probably more relevant to Latin America than the work of Clara Zetkin and
others in Germany because he was dealing with a largely rural society. Women
in Gaelic Ireland, prior to the English conquest, held an important economic
and political position. Later, the combined impact of imperialism, landlordism
and Catholicism served to subjugate women almost totally. Connolly shows
how women on the land became 'slaves to their own family who were in turn
slaves to all the social parasites of a landlord and *gombeen* (money lender)
ridden community.'[2] In this situation he stated clearly that only women
could achieve the tasks of women's emancipation and that they could not be
held back until the labour movement advanced. The quotation above ends on
another note: 'But whosoever carries the outworks of the citadel of oppression
the working class alone can raze it to the ground.'[3] The implication of this
is that the definitive or total liberation of women can be achieved only when
labour overthrows capitalism and constructs a society where oppression and
exploitation no longer exist.

Non-Class Cleavages

One of the favourite liberal criticisms of Marxism is that it cannot deal with
'non-class' cleavages in society. The obsession with class conflict has
supposedly blinded Marxism to other forms of oppression and struggle. Thus,
according to Frank Parkin in his 'bourgeois critique', Marxist class theory:

cannot account properly for those complexities that arise when racial, religious, ethnic and sexual divisions run at a tangent to formal class divisions.[4]

It is debatable whether orthodox political theory can better *explain* these divisions (except in their own terms) and relate them to the class structure of modern capitalism. The fundamental point is, however, that Marxism *has*, until recent years, seriously neglected social divisions not based on property, be they national, ethnic or gender based. Preoccupation with economic determination, even if 'in the last instance', and a type of 'productivism' which places all emphasis on the industrial working class as the focus of resistance to capitalism lie at the root of this problem. Feminists have pointed out quite correctly that Marxist categories are 'gender-blind' as Black militants have earlier tackled Marxism's inability to deal coherently and consistently with racial oppression. This type of critique is of a quite different nature from that of orthodox political science with its emphasis on 'pluralism' and, in fact, some of these critics accept the methodological strength of Marxism.

Even during the radical 1960s the prevailing opinion amongst North American Marxists was that racism could be reduced to a class question. As Genovese explains that view:

> as an oppressed proletariat, the blacks had class interests identical to those of the white working class and a clear duty to join with their white brothers in bringing down the capitalist system: 'Black and white, unite and fight'.[5]

That slogan summed up the limits of economistic Marxism. As Black consciousness and Black power movements forced the white left out of their complacency, so did the women's movement in the 1970s. It was gradually accepted that Marxist analysis could not simply reduce all forms of 'non-class' oppressions to capitalist exploitation. White male dominance was seen to cut across classes and was not the sole prerogative of the bourgeoisie. Even then there was a tendency to see gender and race as divisions cleverly fomented by capital to divide the working class. This neglects the material bases of non-economic oppression and assumes that working-class unity is somehow natural, whereas in fact it is always (and only partially) constructed. As one recent account explains: 'work relations construct not only class relations and class consciousness but simultaneously gender relations and gender consciousness.'[6] Without neglecting its specificity much the same could be said of race.

In Latin America the earliest and most brutal 'non-class' exploitation was that inflicted on the indigenous peoples by the Spanish conquest. The highly developed civilisations of the Incas (covering what is today Peru, Bolivia and Ecuador) and the Mayas (covering Mexico and Guatemala) were subverted by the conquest and their people incorporated into the colonial economy as virtual slaves. They had their land stolen, their language was suppressed and they were usually barred from the most elementary civil rights. When capitalism needed to expand its frontiers, the Indians were simply eliminated. This happened in Argentina, in 1878, when President Roca's 'Conquest of the Desert' massacred the Indians of the Pampas to make way for the latifundia, in Ecuador in the 1940s when oil was discovered, and most notably in Brazil's Amazon region until the present day. There are still, however, some 30 million Indians in Latin America, of whom most live on the land as labourers or poor peasants, though growing numbers are moving to the slums around the cities.[7] There are two main responses to the 'problem'. The first is the *indigenismo* movement, promoted by the Mexican and Bolivian revolutions with the aim of assimilating the Amerindians into capitalist society.[8] More recently the Peruvian military regime has adopted a similar policy, which amounts to a paternalistic social work type policy though it has encouraged the native languages. The other tradition, which traces back to the Tupac Amaru rebellion of the 1780's saw the Peruvian Quechua peasant revolt of the 1960s and today's massive incorporation of the indigenous peoples into Guatemala's guerrilla movements.

The tradition of active Indian resistance to bourgeois 'civilisation' raises the question of whether we are dealing with national oppression. The Peruvian Marxist José Carlos Mariátegui developed a remarkable analysis in 1929 which concluded that Indian oppression was essentially a result of the semi-feudal land system and the precapitalist labour bondage. In short, the 'Indian question' was seen as part of the 'agrarian question'.[9] This was certainly an advance on the moralistic and romantic analysis of the *Indigenista* tradition, but it probably underestimated the relevance of the racial question to Latin America and even the extent to which the Amerindians constitute legitimate nations with a consequent right to self-determination.

The second major minority grouping in Latin America — the Blacks — are descendants of the slaves brought from Africa to work on the plantations and as artisans in the cities. Both liberals and early Marxists argued that racism in South America was less severe than in North America. There were, of course, serious differences between the two situations — in 1860 for example only 11% of the total Black population in the United States were freedmen, compared to 38% in Cuba and over 70% in Brazil at the same time.[10] One explanation is that the more rigid class relations of Latin America were sufficient to impose 'peaceful' race relations and absorption was a better tactic than the Ku Klux Klan. The Latin American Communist parties of the 1920s also maintained that 'the Black in Latin America does not suffer the same scorn as in the United States', and more specifically: 'the situation of Blacks in Brazil is not such that our party would be required to organise particular campaigns for their rights with special slogans.'[11] However, the legal abolition of slavery, as in the United States, changed the form of oppression but it did not end it. Racist oppression is an integral part of Brazil's class structure with readily ascertained discrimination in jobs, housing, social services and education.[12] For the first time since the 1930s a movement against racial discrimination has recently been formed in Brazil. There, and elsewhere in Central America and the Andean countries, the national oppression of Blacks is emerging as an important political issue.

In Latin America today there is a complex intersection of racial, national and indigenous oppression, not forgetting the position of migrant workers. Integration into bourgeois society means, essentially, proletarianisation and we must stress, as do Bollinger and Lund, that 'quite apart from the spectre of racial oppression, many Indians consider assimilation through proletarianisation to be a form of cultural genocide'.[13] It is quite right to stress, as did Mariátegui, that there is a social and economic basis to this oppression but one cannot simply dissolve the specificity of this oppression into a 'class issue'. For example, racism in Cuba has declined sharply since the revolution, but problems remain. In Nicaragua, the revolutionary Sandinista government has had serious difficulties in dealing with the Miskito tribe.[13] This can only confirm that oppression of minorities does not simply fade away with the proletarian revolution.

Dual Exploitation of Women

Working women are doubly exploited through the social and the sexual division of labour. If women are exploited by capital *and* men then it is necessary to develop a theory of patriarchy to complement the Marxist analysis of capitalism. Heidi Hartmann defines patriarchy as

> a set of social relations between men, which have a material base and which, though hierarchical, establish or create interdependence and solidarity among men that enable them to dominate women. Though patriarchy is hierarchical and men of different classes, races, or ethnic groups have different places in the patriarchy, they also are united in their shared relationship of dominance over their women; they are dependent on each other to maintain that domination.[14]

The patriarchal oppression of women is held to exist prior to and to operate independently of capitalist exploitation. At one extreme the class position of women is defined by their common position within a domestic mode of production and the patriarchal mode of exploitation. Christine Delphy thus focuses on the power relationship between husband and wives and concludes that 'whatever the nature of women's tasks, their relations of production are the same'.[15]

There are several shortcomings in the commonly accepted theory of patriarchy. At one level it is a historical generalisation from the quite specific non-capitalist peasant societies in which the father ('patriarch') ruled over the women of the family *and* the younger men. If we take, instead, an ideological version of patriarchy (i.e., akin to racism) there are also problems. One example is Juliet Mitchell who claims 'we are dealing with two autonomous areas, the economic mode of capitalism and the ideological mode of patriarchy'.[16] This strict demarcation of the economic and ideological levels of society cannot explain the links between the two. Racial and sexual divisions cannot be reduced to property relations, but they do not necessarily create new relations of production and cannot, therefore, constitute criteria for class boundaries in their own right. Non-class divisions are still articulated within a given class system, in which different forms of exploitation and oppression coexist. The 'ideological mode of patriarchy' can only be relatively autonomous from its socio-economic base, it is never totally divorced from it. In conclusion we can agree with Michéle Barrett that patriarchy:

> is redolent of a universal and trans-historical oppression . . . [which] . . . invoke[s] a generality of male domination without being able to specify historical limits, changes or differences.[17]

Another key element in conceptualising the position of women is that of the 'sexual division of labour'. In some Marxist accounts this is taken as given, as part of a general biological tendency to see gender divisions as natural ones. In his discussion of the family, for example, Engels fails to really integrate the sexual division of labour, which is surprising given the importance he attaches to the division of labour in human development. For Engels:

> Division of labour was a pure and simple outgrowth of nature; it existed only between the two sexes. . . . Each was master in his or her field of activity: the man in the forest, the women in the house. Each owned the tools which he or she made and used: the men, the weapons and the hunting and fishing tackle; the women the household goods and utensils.[18]

Feminist analysis rejects the 'natural' basis of the sexual division of labour. As Mackintosh points out:

> only in a society where men and women constitute unequal genders is there any reason why gender should be an important organising principle of the social division of labour, with the exception of the physical process of child bearing.[19]

Clearly, then, the sexual division of labour is socially constructed and its terms are constantly ratified in the patriarchal mould. Because women are defined primarily in terms of housework, men are generally paid a 'family wage' i.e., sufficient to reproduce the model nuclear family. For this reason, when married women are drawn into the labour force they are generally paid lower wages than would be needed to reproduce the labour-power of a male worker. During periods of labour shortage, such as in wartime, married and unmarried women are pressed into the labour force often with the express purpose of 'deskilling' the labour process.[20] Unskilled female labour is driven to take over skilled occupations, with the consequent resistance of the pre-existing skilled workers who see the 'rate for the job' being undercut, When industries expand women are taken on but during periods of recession the resultant 'shake out' invariably sees women leave first. Though one must stress the growing incorporation of women into the labour force as capitalism develops, the overriding feature of the economic position of women is that they are at one and the same time wage-labourers and domestic workers. The result is a complex and contradictory form of dual consciousness.

A vital element in the sexual division of labour is the work women perform in the home. The recent debate on domestic labour has helped to clarify the role of this work in the capitalist mode of production.[21] The first basic position is that:

> domestic work — child-care, cooking, laundering, cleaning and so on — functions in capitalist society as a whole to produce those use-values which are necessary to the life of the individual. . . . It is concrete labour which lies outside the capitalist production process and therefore cannot produce value or surplus-value.[22]

At the other extreme is the position of Dalla Costa and James, for whom the home is the very essence of the 'social factory'.[23] Work in the house produces, therefore, not only use-values but the commodity labour power and consequently surplus value. It is thus seen as productive in the strict Marxist sense — i.e., productive of surplus-value. Taken separately, both positions seem unsatisfactory, the first in somehow downgrading the importance of domestic labour to capitalism and the second in stretching the terms of capitalism to embrace a non-capitalist domain. Domestic labour can, alternatively, be seen as a subordinate form of production within capitalism which is *essential* to its survival (ideologically as much as economically) but only *indirectly* productive through its reproduction of labour-power.[24] Undoubtedly domestic work provides a source of unpaid surplus labour to capital and drives up profits, and the housewife forms part of the reserve army of labour which helps keep wages low. It would, however, be wrong to reduce this debate to the economic level — i.e., usefulness to capital — neglecting the fundamental ideological role of the family unit.

The overarching term in the conceptualising of women's position in society is that of 'reproduction'. Human reproduction is, of course, an essential element in the process of social reproduction, but we should not confuse the two terms. In the first sense women have been subordinated by men since the lineage mode of production in which the elders control the domestic community to the modern doctor's control over women's fertility.[25] At another level women intervene in the reproduction of the labour force as we saw above. Women not only create the future workers for capitalism but continually maintain and service those workers throughout their life. The family is the site of socialisation of the young worker into the norms of capitalism and into the expected place s/he will occupy in the division of labour. The role of women, in both senses of the word reproduction, is essential to the broader social reproduction of society and their constituent relations of production.[26] The concept of reproduction has helped us move beyond the earlier 'productivist' bias of Marxism. The labour-capital relation may still be seen as the essential element of capitalism, but now so-called 'reproduction issues' are also brought to the fore. By challenging the economism of orthodox Marxism, feminist theory has directed our attention to the broader social, psychological, political and ideological aspects of oppression which ensure the stable reproduction of the capitalist mode of production.

We can now sum up this section which develops a basic framework for the understanding of the dual exploitation of women as the prime example of non-class cleavages in society. The concept of patriarchy helps us to break out of the class-reductionism of most versions of Marxism. However, it has to be specified historically otherwise it becomes a rather vague category. The social division of labour is cut across by a sexual division of labour – though some women obviously exploit men, men as a whole benefit from the subordination of women. The concept of reproduction takes us beyond an economistic productivist Marxism and poses new political horizons. One must not, however, conflate the biological and social aspects of reproduction if we are to conceptualise the position of women correctly. As with racism, patriarchy is an ideology but also a set of social relations with a *material* basis. As Hartmann writes, 'racial hierarchies, like gender hierarchies, are aspects of our social organisation, of how people are produced and reproduced.'[27] The specific oppression of women or national minorities cannot be collapsed into a simple class analysis. It does not follow that we are dealing with a 'battle of the sexes' detached from the class struggle. Clearly, the reductionism of a sex-blind class theory cannot be adequately replaced by the indeterminacy of a pure patriarchy analysis which ignores the precise form in which gender divisions have been entrenched in the capitalist division of labour.

Women and Work

Classical Marxism maintained that women's entry into the labour market was the precondition for their liberation. Thus for Engels, 'the first premise for the emancipation of women is the reintroduction of the entire female sex into public industry', and this will mean that 'the last remnants of male domination in the proletarian home have lost all foundation'.[28] There is a similar perspective in the early study by Esther Boserup on *Women's Role in Economic Development* which was very much within the modernisation theory perspective.[29] The main problem was seen as the lack of women's participation in the development process as equal partners with men. Capitalism may well break down certain forms of oppression of women but it will only lead to the recomposition of subordination in new forms. Marxism and modernisation theory alike stressed the determinant role of non-domestic production and did not address the root of patriarchal relations — the household. Thus, Marx could say that:

> The maintenance of and reproduction of the working class remains a necessary condition for the reproduction of capital. But the capitalist may safely leave this to the worker's drives for self-preservation and propagation.[30]

As we saw above, more recent Marxist analysis recognises the primary role played by domestic labour in the reproduction of the male worker. Modernisation theory remains wedded to its traditional approach which does not question the socio-economic system itself, only the lack of equal participation by women within it.

Women in Latin America suffer from this dual exploitation by capital and by men, but aggravated by the particular conditions of dependent development. This is manifested in the accentuated male chauvinism of 'machismo' which is the acute ideological expression of this domination. When the Spanish conquest began, the indigenous people of America were, on the whole, in a period of transition to patriarchy. This was consolidated in the colonial period as indigenous women lost many of the rights held under the old communities. Formal political independence, gained in the first decades of the 19th Century, did not change the subordinate position of women enforced by colonialism and sanctified by the powerful Catholic church. As the 20th Century began, the patriarchal system maintained most women firmly within the home. There was, nevertheless, a growing participation of women in economic activities such as artisanal work and the growing textile workshops. The 'putting out' system of the early factories also exploited women's work in the home, for pitiful wages. In the countryside, women worked on their husband's land or as wage-workers at harvest time.

It is difficult to generalise about the economic position of women in Latin America today but some broad points can be made. The majority of Latin American women (slightly less than three-quarters) are restricted to work in the home, carrying out unpaid labour. Another sector works without pay usually on the farms or in the small workshops owned by members of the family. Yet others are 'self-employed' — the seamstresses, hairdressers, food makers, and so on — with a minimum income. Women in wage work (perhaps a fifth of the total) are employed in the factories, commerce, offices and public services. There are then the professional women (teachers, nurses, etc) and the bourgeois women, who may own factories or farms. The percentage of women in manufacturing has generally decreased over the last decades, although those in the professional, clerical and sales categories have risen considerably. A general phenomenon in the Third World, as yet only partially noticeable in Latin America, is the increase of women's employment in the so-called 'world market factories' of which electronics in the Far East is only one example. Here, low wages are the result of women's secondary status in the labour market, and the supposed 'nimble fingers' of women make for big profits. At the other end of the scale is the vast mass of peasant women engaged in subsistence agriculture, tending animals and growing food, so that the male proletariat can be paid a lower price for his labour-power by the employers in the cities. We will now examine some of these groups in more detail.

As we saw in Chapter 2, the multinational corporations have in recent decades begun to relocate the most labour-intensive and low-skill parts of the labour process in the Third World. The most extreme example of the 'global assembly line' in Latin America is the *maquiladoras* in Mexico – electronic or apparel assembly plants which are either subsidiaries or sub-contractors to US corporations. Around three-quarters or more of the workers in these plants are women because they 'are willing to accept lower pay' and, as one personnel manager explains: 'girls are educated to obey at home. It is easier to get their confidence. They are loyal to the company.'[31] Though only a small proportion of the overall female labour force (1% in Mexico) this is a highly concentrated sector with a disproportionate economic and political weight. The women in these plants are certainly superexploited but one cannot neglect this 'progressive' side. The effects on patriarchal relations are less clear-cut because though some values are changed (by the very fact of women going out to work) traditional values are usually reassembled around new figures, such as the boss. In this situation, as one recent study of Mexico concludes:

> women workers are trapped both by traditional suspicions about their participation in the world outside of home and family, and by corporate programs designed to reinforce the submissive 'feminine' behaviour that they have been taught all their lives.[32]

The study of Fröbel, Heinrichs and Kreye shows how the new international division of labour creates working conditions in the Third World characterised by an extremely high intensity of labour, social insecurity, shift work and inadequate provisions for safety at work. The US 'world market factories' located in Mexico report 25% higher labour productivity there than in their electronics plants at home, 30% higher in the apparel plants and even higher in other sectors.[33] Female workers provide much of this extra surplus owing to the fact that their wages are anything from a quarter to more than half less than those paid to male workers. In spite of the low wages, employees must be single, childless, 17 to 25 years old, with at least six years of formal education.[34] Apart from manual dexterity trials a pregnancy test is mandatory. It is, of course, unemployment which facilitates this type of behaviour. When the young women are 'burnt out' by the intensity and conditions of work they are simply replaced. There is here a dialectic of capital and gender relations, as Elson and Pearson explain:

123

Women are considered not only to have naturally nimble fingers, but also to be more docile and willing to accept tough work discipline, and naturally less inclined to join trade unions, than men; and to be naturally more suited to tedious, repetitive, monotonous work. Their lower wages are attributed to their secondary status in the labour market which is seen as a natural consequence of their capacity to bear children.[35]

Peasant women suffer a more 'traditional' burden, which is of course no more 'natural' than that of the workers in the *maquiladoras* or runaway shops on the Mexican border. Women on the land are likely to be involved centrally in the marketing of agrarian produce and artisanal or agricultural work on top of the domestic work. A study of peasant women in Ecuador states that:

> in practice the impoverished peasant women of the Sierra have to cope with a double work-load, productive work as well as housework. Even so, their importance in production, currently as well as in the past, means that they are not as devalued, oppressed and dominated as ordinary housewives.[36]

This statement should not be misunderstood, because peasant women *are*, of course, oppressed but they are also able to link this oppression with class exploitation. The account by Domitila Barrios of women in the tin mines of Bolivia shows the resources of solidarity and the possibility of class action there.[37] Obviously, the family is the central unit of production amongst peasants, and women play a primary economic role in that sense. But this does not mean that the sexual division of labour is any less rigid, or that oppressive patriarchal values are not predominant. The reproductive activities of women in this area are never seriously considered, and this patriarchal domination is reinforced by the values of rural society.

The development of capitalism in the countryside and the consequent differentiation of the peasantry does lead to changes in the position of women, but not necessarily improvements. Carmen Deere has carried out an interesting empirical study of the changing social relations of production amongst Peruvian peasant women.[38] Women rural workers were amongst the last to rid themselves of servile obligations on the *hacienda*, but it did lead to a decrease in the absolute exploitation of women. Clearly,

> for the women that are proletarianised with the development of capitalism, the form of exploitation changes, but continues, as the value which they produce in the production process is appropriated by the nascent capitalist class.[39]

As capitalist competition increases, the women on the small-holdings are again forced to take on more agricultural jobs as the men seek work outside to supplement the declining rural income. Paradoxically, Deere concludes that in the small-holdings women's status and self-esteem have increased significantly, but not on the co-operatives. The main point to emerge is that the sexual division of labour is not immutable and it will vary in time as the overall relations of production are transformed.

Apart from agriculture, the other main area of female employment is the services sector, where around half the women employed are in domestic service.[40] Only nominally covered by labour legislation, and rarely organised in trade unions, this sector is grossly overexploited. Women migrate in their thousands to the cities in search of work and almost inevitably end up working as maids and cooks in the homes of the middle class. Minimum wages, social security, holiday and working hours stipulations are flouted with impunity. To move out of domestic service is rare if not impossible, and in any case it would be into factory work rather than clerical jobs. Another area where working-class women are employed in significant numbers is petty commodity production or cottage industries. Though classified as part of the industrial sector these jobs are really part of the 'informal sector' in terms of stability, wages and the privatised nature of work there.

To theorise the position of housewives and peasants within capitalism one author, Bennholdt-Thomsen, has recently distinguished subsistence reproduction from extended reproduction or accumulation.[41] One could also add the cottage industries to this subsistence sector. Workers in the home, craftworkers and peasants are not exploited directly by capital though their work serves the overall accumulation of capital. Where Marx distinguishes between formal subsumption of labour to capital (based on extraction of surplus value and characteristic of manufacturing) and real subsumption (based on extraction of relative surplus value under factory production) this author adds the category of 'marginal subsumption'. This 'indicates that these workers and their work take diverse forms, and that their work is valorised by capital, although they themselves are responsible for their subsistence.'[42] Marginal in this sense cannot be taken to mean isolation or lack of importance. In fact the primary role of women in this sector is quite literally essential to the continued reproduction of capital.

We can now turn to the overall evolution of women's participation in the Latin American economy. Table 4.1 shows us the participation rates of active age females by age group in 1950 and 1970. At the two extremes — under 19 years of age and over 65 — we find a marked decline in the rate of participation but in all the bands in between an increase which is most noticeable is the 20–24 years age group. These are the women most likely to enter the new 'world factory' plants, and significantly, the rate of increase is most notice-ably in such countries as Mexico and Brazil. In short, there is a positive and significant association between product per capita and participation rates for women in particular.[43] As one economist notes:

> economic development could be expected to lead to relative increases in
> female participation rates since development tends to bring about a

Table 4.1
Participation Rates of Active Age Females (in years) in Latin America by Age Group (1950-1970)

	15-19	*20-24*	*25-44*	*45-54*	*55-64*
1950	24%	24%	20%	18%	16%
1970	21%	27%	21%	19%	14%

Source: J. Buttari, (ed.) (1979) *Employment and Labor Force in Latin America*. Vol.II. Washington, ECIEL, p.488.

widening of the differential between the marginal productivities of work within and outside the house (reflected in respective remunerations).[44]

Essentially, an hour of work in the home given the more complex and co-operative division of labour.

If we now turn to the current situation as shown in Table 4.2, we can see the percentage of women in the 'economically active population' (a suspect term because it neglects domestic labour) as a proportion of the total and the

Table 4.2
Women in the 'economically active population' of Latin America (1978)

	as % of total population	as % of female population
Argentina	25	19
Brazil	31	24
Colombia	26	15
Costa Rica	19	12
Cuba	18	11
Chile	23	13
Dominican Republic	28	16
Ecuador	17	10
El Salvador	29	22
Guatemala	14	8
Haiti	47	49
Mexico	22	12
Nicaragua	22	12
Panama	26	18
Paraguay	21	14
Peru	21	12
Uruguay	25	19
Venezuela	28	17

Source: Latin American ed Caribbean Women's Collective (1980) *Slaves of Slaves*. London. Zed Press, p.180.

female population for each country. Compared to other Third World areas the labour participation rates of women in Latin America are low; although there are enormous variations across countries. There is also an important expansionary trend which will see the female work force rise from about 23 million in 1975 to over 55 million by the year 2000 for Latin America as a whole.[45] With urbanisation and industrialisation the formal economic role of women will increase dramatically. As one study notes 'recent partial analyses suggest that female urban labor force growth is even higher than had been projected.'[46] This prognosis seems to be totally contradicted by a recent Latin American women's collective conclusion that, 'the idea that increased industrialisation necessarily results in greater participation in the economically active population by women is clearly erroneous'.[47] One side of the equation is that women's participation in the industrial sector has not increased significantly — in Brazil, male employment in that sector doubled between 1950 and 1970 whereas the percentage of women employed remained at 10%. The big expansion of women's participation has occurred in the services sector, which at one extreme means domestic services where, certainly, the position of women in the labour market remains weak. At the other extreme:

> élite, well-educated women in Latin America have been entering the labor force in greater numbers, particularly in white-collar employment, while the employment picture for working-class women has remained stagnant or even declines.[48]

This serves to remind us that patriarchal domination notwithstanding, class division and struggle persists across women.

Women and Politics

As a group, women in Latin America, as elsewhere, are neither conservative nor revolutionary. The image of the conservative Latin American women guided by the ideology of *Marianismo* (based on the virtues of the Virgin Mary) cannot be replaced by an equally simplistic vision of the woman guerrilla with gun in hand. As elsewhere, much of the women's political activity has been 'hidden from history'.[49] It remains a fact that women as a whole have had an only limited history of political activity in Latin America. The suffragette movement, for example, was very late in developing and then only sporadically and unevenly effective. Elsa Chaney argues that in Peru, for example, women received the vote in 1955 'without any notable agitation for suffrage on their part' arguing furthermore that, 'throughout recent Latin American political history women in the electorate *as a group* have almost always proved to be a conservatizing force.'[50] This may be an over-generalisation but Table 4.3, which shows the date when women's suffrage was introduced in each country, illustrates how late women, generally, began to vote, and that there is no evident pattern to its introduction. In Argentina and

Table 4.3
Women's Suffrage in Latin America

Country	Year of Introduction
Ecuador	1929
Brazil	1932
Uruguay	1932
Cuba	1934
El Salvador	1939
Dominican Republic	1942
Guatemala	1945
Panama	1945
Venezuela	1946
Argentina	1947
Chile	1949
Costa Rica	1949
Haiti	1950
Bolivia	1952
Mexico	1953
Honduras	1955
Nicaragua	1955
Peru	1955
Colombia	1957
Paraguay	1961

Source: Latin American and Caribbean Women's Collective (1980) *Slaves of Slaves. The College of Latin American Women*. London. Zed Press, p.178.

Bolivia it coincides with their respective nationalist revolutions, but in Mexico it arrived only 53 years after the revolution. The radical democratic revolutionaries of Mexico apparently believed that women would oppose the secularisation of the state.

   In those countries where the suffragist movement did play a considerable role in winning the vote it was largely middle-class based. These women were in a different social world to their working-class sisters who played an active role in the anarchist and the trade union movements. The social and political rights claimed by the first remained totally separate from the bitter fight against economic exploitation waged by the latter. As Mirta Hinault writes in relation to Argentina, the two currents of women's combativeness 'did not fuse in a common front of struggle against patriarchy, because on every occasion the identification of the women with the social class to which the men of the family belonged prevailed'.[51] There was no real consciousness of the unity of women as an oppressed group with common problems, which also recognised the exploitation of capitalist society. A woman doctor from Argentina took the following message to the 1899 International Women's Congress:

> When we have a National Women's Council in our own country, it will be clear for all to see that, in Argentina, women are the main pillars of our religion, the vanguard of social purity, refined manners, elegance and domestic happiness, and that they can, at the same time, carry out many good works.[52]

While this social class were carrying out their 'good works' the women artisans of the anarchist movement were fighting for a living wage and being killed by the police during political demonstrations.

In Argentina women were really integrated into political life for the first time with the emergence of the Peronist national-popular movement in the 1940s.[53] With relatively early industrialisation, women had already been largely incorporated into the labour force, especially in the textile industry. Already in 1944 Perón, as Minister for Labour, had declared that women should be protected by labour legislation and were entitled to equal pay. When he became President in 1946 he moved towards the political integration of women to match their growing role in social production. Already the Peronist movement had put forward 24 women deputies and senators in the 1951 parliamentary elections, all of whom were elected. Within the movement itself, a separate women's party was set up in 1949, which was to play a dynamic part in the nationalist movement. From those days to the present women have played a major role within the revolutionary nationalist movements in the 1970s, the Montoneros integrated women into their structures at all levels, including the leadership. In the union struggles and general strikes women have played a primary role in the plants themselves and in the wider community.

All this is not to say that Peronism's relations with women were without contradictions. This tension can best be seen in the figure of Eva Perón, wife of General Perón and a militant leader of the Peronist movement in her own right.[54] When Perón was nearly driven from power in 1945 it was 'Evita', together with trade union leaders, who helped the massive demonstration of 17 October which brought him back triumphantly. Until her premature death in 1952 she was the driving force behind Perón's attempt to capture the trade unions and organise the masses. Since her death she has become the figurehead of the most radical wing of the movement. Yet, ultimately, she owed her power to Perón and stressed constantly her total devotion and subordination to this patriarchal populist figure. On the one hand, she could state that 'just as only the workers could wage their own struggle for liberation, so too could only women be the salvation of women'.[55] On the other hand, she could tell the Women's Peronist Party that they 'could only aspire to the honour of placing themselves at the orders of the leader and struggle till the last breath for his work and for him'.[56] Perón had brought women on to the political scene for reasons of expediency. Evita, in spite of her contradictions, showed that a more radical course was possible.

Since the 1976 military coup which displaced the renewal of Peronist government (see Chapter 10) the army and church have launched a full scale assault to drive women back into the home. The 'struggle against subversion' means also the return to 'Christian and family' values which had been threatened by 'atheistic Marxism'. As one woman who entered the country shortly after the coup describes:

> Given the tight governmental control exercised over the mass media, the purveyors of the images of women as mothers and guardians of political and Christian values have a virtual monopoly over the attention of Argentine women.[57]

The economic recession is also pushing women out of waged employment and back to their traditional domain.

The Popular Unity government in Chile (1970–73) saw a frustrated attempt at a peaceful transition to socialism. This experience has already been dissected in detail, but the contradictory role of women during this period is still of immense relevance.[58] From 1971 onwards the women of the middle class became a fundamental piece in the right's carefully orchestrated campaign against the Allende government. There was a precedent for this in the marches for 'March of the Family with God for Liberty' which the Brazilian bourgeoisie organised to 'soften up' public opinion prior to the 1964 military coup. In Chile, the campaign took a more secular tone centred on the alleged mismanagement of the economy by the socialist government. Regular 'marches of the empty pots' took middle-class women to the streets, while at home they hoarded food, thus creating a black market. From this relatively 'apolitical' basis the right-wing women went on to tackle the Marxist menace head-on in the realm of education and ideology generally. The power of this reactionary Women's Movement was demonstrated when they achieved the downfall of the one remaining constitutional general who stood in the path of a *coup d'etat*. After the coup, the new military rulers of Chile regularly payed homage to the women of the bourgeoisie, but naturally enough, the general position of women took several steps backward.

The left-wing parties of the Popular Unity coalition also tried to mobilise women during this period. One of the most remarkable movements was the drive to organise committees for the distribution of goods in the working-class districts and to control prices. Women were the prime movers of this campaign. Professional women were also to be found serving the health and educational needs of the shanty towns. In general, this period saw a massive political mobilisation of women in the factories and in the fields. The position of women in legal and economic terms improved dramatically as a result of the reformist measures taken by the government. Yet, essentially, the left was less successful than the right in mobilising women. As Andreas notes:

> The left was slow to encourage women to organise as an independent force in Chile both before and during the Unidad Popular. Political

parties wanted to keep careful control of women's activities, and even within the Marxist-Leninist left (as distinct from the legalistic parties in control of the UP), giving political power to women as women was seen by many as a divisionary and possibly reactionary move.[59]

In short, 'feminism' was seen as part of bourgeois politics. President Allende's references to women were invariably paternalistic and usually referred to them as the *compañeras* of left-wing men. By refusing to take up the specific oppression of women, the left in Chile seriously divided the popular camp. Rather than being 'divisionary' this type of orientation would have brought even more women behind the popular government.

Clearly, a feminist movement cannot prosper in the present repressive conditions of Chile, Argentina or Uruguay. There have been developments in this direction, however, in countries such as Brazil and Mexico, which are not only highly industrialised but allow the minimal political conditions necessary for political mobilisation. The early suffrage movement in Brazil had been relatively successful compared to other Latin American countries. Feminism was a small radical current in the late 19th Century but it later broadened out to appeal to middle-class women. The result, as Hahner's recent study shows, was that:

> Neither radical in their goals nor militant in their tactics, the women who led the successful twentieth-century suffrage campaign wished some of the rights exercised by men of their own class. They did not want to revolutionise society and restructure the family.[60]

A similar type of division has been manifest in the modern women's movement, which really blossomed after 1975 when the Brazilian dictatorship began a policy of *abertura* – a gradual and controlled political decompression. 1975 was the United Nations International Women's Year and the officially sponsored activity around it helped spawn a number of women's groups. One of these, the Brazilian Women's Centre, composed largely of professionals has, as Schmink reports:

> increased knowledge of and political awareness about many issues including those related to reproduction and sexuality, education, reform of the Civil Code and of labour laws, provision for day care, and recognition of women's contribution to popular art and culture.[61]

As the opposition towards the military regime intensified, so the women's groups began to feel the tension between an autonomous feminist orientation and the insertion of women's struggles within the broader democratic movement. Working-class women were raising feminist demands in the unions, particularly during the big strikes of 1978 and 1979 (see Chapter 5). Neighbourhood committees and Housewives' Associations also brought women into an intense round of political activity. Naturally there are divisions:

131

in general, working class women are far from assuming most feminist goals, while the feminist groups are prone to impose their own conceptions of priorities for working class women.[62]

While in principle all feminist groups give priority to the problems of working-class and peasant women, their priorities are bound to be different. For professional educated women, often with other women to look after their children, are a world apart from the women in the slums around the big cities without the most basic human amenities. Not surprisingly, the 1980 São Paulo Women's Congress led to a major split in the movement. For example, as Schmink mentions in her extremely useful report,

> women from the peripheral neighbourhoods complained about the apparent egotism of the students, who were in their opinion overly concerned with individualistic issues of sexual pleasure and abortion.[63]

In Mexico there is a particularly strong tradition of autonomous women's organisations which goes back to the revolution of 1910–17. In 1915, a women's congress had put forward a platform in advance of those of European and US suffragists, which included equal pay, union rights and birth control demands. The contemporary women's movement was formed in the aftermath of the 1968 students' revolt. The early groups were mainly middle-class consciousness-raising movements patterned on contemporaneous US developments. Later, the Movement for the Liberation of Women was formed with a socialist-feminist orientation which has achieved considerable success, publishing a magazine with a circulation of 10,000. By 1979 this Movement had succeeded in forming a Women's Front which drew in the main left-wing parties and the combative trade unions. This front has maintained the principle of the self-organisation of women but within a framework of a class struggle orientation. As one of their leaders stated:

> The name 'women's liberation movement' does not imply that it pretends only to liberate women, or that women must oppose themselves to men, but that they must start with their own interests, uniting with all other oppressed sectors which are also seeking a revolutionary change for all.[64]

This type of movement seems to be setting a pattern which breaks equally with the traditional paternalism of the left regarding the 'women's question', and the attempt by the radical feminists to sidestep the class struggle.

This raises the question of whether the structures, programmes and tactics of the European and North American women's movements can be applied directly to Latin America. Most groups now recognise that this would lead to a movement isolated from the broad working-class and peasant masses. The basic right to divorce takes on a different meaning in countries where up to half the women live in exploitative 'free' unions. The demand for 'equal pay for equal work' does not mean the same in a highly industrialised context as in a subsistence economy. The essential demands of the women's movement on contraception and abortion take on a different light where imperialist agencies practise the forced sterilization of Indian women. The Mexican magazine *Fem* proposes a way out:

> It is not enough to struggle for voluntary maternity — i.e. access to contraceptives and abortion — but also against the forced sterilization and birth control adopted by many governments due to North American pressure. It is not enough to fight for such services as daycare centers, laundromats, etc., but also for such basic community provisions as water, electricity, housing and medical and sanitation services. The issue of the double day takes on another dimension here as well: the demand for wages for housework is inappropriate as long as the broader struggle remains focused on issues of high unemployment, exploitation of the heads of household and starvation wages. Women should have the right not to work under such existing conditions. Finally, it is not enough to fight against the consumerism of one group in society, but against the impoverishment of the majority, and the impossibility of their being able to consume anything at all.[65]

The vanguard of women in struggle today are undoubtedly the women fighters who made up one third or more of the Sandinista army which overthrew the Somoza dictatorship in Nicaragua, and those who are now taking up arms in El Salvador and Guatemala.[66] This renews a tradition which goes back to the wars of independence, the Mexican, Bolivian and Cuban revolutions, and countless land invasions and factory takeovers in the years since. It is the particularly acute class struggle in Latin America and the high stakes (sometimes survival itself) which make a specifically feminist struggle appear secondary. But, women in Latin America regardless of class are a severely oppressed group. There have been several cases in recent years in Brazil in which the courts absolved men of the murder of women on the grounds that male 'honour' had been offended by the latter's adultery. In many countries women cannot travel out of the country with their children without the father's permission. In 1956, the women of Puerto Rico were used as unwitting guinea pigs for the first tests on the contraceptive pill. As one account recalls:

> during these experiments, which involved hormonal vaccines and intra-uterine coils as well as pills, the women patients were given no protection against side effects, and some of them died.[67]

In these conditions women's specific demands are not a 'luxury' but a precondition for the active involvement of women in the movement for social change.

Women and Socialism

A Marxist analysis of women must obviously confront the question of whether socialism has led to the emancipation of women. The first and most obvious point is that the transition to socialism has occurred in societies — Russia, China, Vietnam, Cuba, etc — with a relatively low level of development of the productive forces (see Chapter 11). This has meant that the new post-revolutionary society has been unable to start from a position of 'socialisation of plenty' such as the early Marxists had hoped for. This means that the overriding aim of economic development often leads to a secondary position for the 'revolution within the revolution' of women's liberation.

We should bear in mind the earlier distinction between the role of women in production and reproduction. The development exigencies of these new states has created a demand for the incorporation of women into the labour force. However, as Elisabeth Croll notes on the basis of a study of the Soviet Union, China, Cuba and Tanzania, 'the emphasis on attracting women into the collective waged labor force has outweighed the concern for redefining women's reproductive and domestic roles'.[68] In fact, the rural areas in particular reveal an intensification of women's work, as work on the state farms is added to subsistence and domestic activities. The sexual division of labour is hardly affected at all in this area. The early Marxist belief that incorporation into social production was a panacea for women is clearly belied by this experience.

The position of women has changed beyond recognition in the post-capitalist societies and one can agree with Molyneux that 'judged by the goals they have set themselves, they have achieved a great deal'.[69] The point is that these goals may have been limited and insufficient to achieve a full emancipation of women. There has been an overwhelming economistic bias which has given priority to the development of the *forces* of production at the expense of fundamental changes in the social *relations* of production. Where attention has been placed on ideological factors which perpetuate the subjugation of women, as in China and Cuba, this has often detracted attention from possible material changes. It is no use complaining about *machismo* and then have a criterion of 'women's work' only marginally different from that of capitalist societies. At the heart of this problem is the lack of change in the domestic situation of women due as Molyneux concludes, to:

> the failure to re-define men's roles in a manner comparable to the re-definition of women's roles — so that even the latter become not so much a re-definition as the addition of a new role (participation in the labour force) into an almost completely unreconstructed older one (mother and housewife).[70]

The role of the family has not been fundamentally questioned and the allegedly 'natural' division of labour between men and women remains essentially untouched. In the pages which follow we shall trace some of the fundamental changes in the position of women in Cuba since the revolution, and their limits.

Women in pre-revolutionary Cuba were really the 'slaves of slaves' that Connolly described. Havana, the capital, was a holiday city for rich American tourists and their needs were served by 12,000 prostitutes.[71] Among the beggars who teemed the streets of the city were some 25,000 women. There were also 70,000 women employed as domestic servants in the homes of the rich and the middle class. Apart from a few women employed in administration and in the textile, tobacco and food industries, the rest of Cuban women (85%) were housewives. Before the revolution women comprised less than 10% of the labour force, now they comprise more than 30%. In 1958, only one in every 100 women over the age of 25 had university education. By the mid-1970s women represented half the students studying science and pedagogy at the universities, and one-third of those reading medical science and economics. This is obviously vital, because education is the key to entry into the labour force at all levels. Whereas, before, women were defined legally in terms of their relationships to men, now, women's equal rights in all domains are enshrined in the Constitution. Socially, the oppressive weight of the Catholic church has been considerably eased. In 1958, there were 2,500 divorces, whereas in 1970 there were 25,000. An unwanted social relationship was no longer maintained because of economic dependence on a male breadwinner.

As a result of an increasing labour shortage during the 1970s there was a systematic incorporation of peasant women into the waged agricultural labour force.[72] In the cities too, women were progressively drawn into the labour force, particularly after the 1969-70 season when hundreds of thousands of women participated as volunteers in a countrywide mobilisation. The aim in subsequent years was to eventually draw all women into socially productive work outside the home. There was, however, also a heavy drop-out rate, partly because of the old patriarchal stereotypes of the role of women but also because of the intolerable weight the 'double shift' of home and outside work imposed on women. During the period from 1969 to 1974, 700,000 women were recruited into the labour force, but at the end of this period the net gain was only 200,000. Half a million women had, therefore, joined and left waged employment in those five years. The women who remain in the formal labour force are concentrated in certain sectors of the economy such as the traditional nurturing and service roles. They are less likely than men to hold management posts and one can assume that 'women's work' is generally classified as less skilled and, therefore, less well paid. The few women engineers, architects and astronauts, who feature as 'heroines of labour' and so on, are obviously the exception to the rule given this overall picture.

Marxism in general, and Fidel Castro in particular, have stressed that women must be fully incorporated into political life under socialism. There is, of course, a pragmatic element in this in so far as women who are not isolated in the home are less susceptible to such counter-revolutionary manoeuvres as happened in Chile. Women are most active politically at the local level — the Committees for the Defence of the Revolution have a 50% female membership. The youth movement of the Communist Party has a 30% women's membership, but in the Party itself the proportion of women falls to 13%. At the leadership level the proportion of women becomes progressively lower. During 1974 a trial run for the national assembly elections was held in Matanzas province. Only 7.6% of the candidates put forward were women and only 3% of those actually elected were women. A subsequent survey showed that there was considerable male resistance to women occupying political leadership positions and that the material obstacles in their way (e.g. responsibilities for the home) were formidable. One could assume that the Cuban Women's Federation would promote the independent organisation of women and their specific demands. In spite of its mass membership, however — from 10,000 in 1960 to more than two million in 1975 — this organisation is really designed to take the party's line to women rather than to act as an autonomous organisation. Its role is undoubtedly positive, but it is rarely critical of the leadership.

In the wake of widespread female withdrawal from the labour force the party leadership carried out an intensive study of its causes. The reasons listed by the investigation were 1) women's inability to cope with family chores; 2) lack of services to lighten family chores; 3) women's lack of motivation to work; 4) poor working conditions; 5) lack of understanding of women's specific problems on the part of the administration, and 6) misconceptions of the role of women in socialist society.[73] Several measures were taken in an attempt to overcome this rather diverse list of 'problems', but which centred around working women's 'second shift' in the home. The *Plan Jaba* (shopping bag) gave working women preferential treatment in the grocery stores, and the availability of day care centres and launderettes was increased. Within the constraints of economic underdevelopment there was a considerable move towards the socialisation of child care and of housework. The problem is that while some women are being freed to enter social production, other women (never men) are reproducing traditional sex roles as nursery workers. One critical feminist review of these measures concludes that:

> as women continue to bear the overwhelming burden of the remaining (household) chores, the fact that they may now go to the head of the grocery line hardly solves the problem. As long as the notion holds that the state is freeing *women* from this work rather than *people*, those tasks that remain uncollectivized inevitably rest in women's hands and on their shoulders.[74]

Undoubtedly, the most radical measure taken to even up the sexual division of labour was the Family Code adopted in 1975. This is certainly a revolutionary document, and Cuba is clearly the socialist country that has gone furthest in questioning the nature of the relationship between women and men. One of its central articles declared that men have an equal duty with women in the upbringing of children and in the household tasks. The Code is based on the assumption that women and men should have equal opportunity to develop their full potential for their own and society's good. The self-image of men and women did begin to change with these measures. It was, nevertheless, still common for the Party militant to offer to do the washing so long as his wife hung it out to dry, so that the neighbours would not hear of it. Women could appeal to the mass organisations if men in their households did not share in domestic tasks but, not surprisingly, there have been few cases actually taken to court which, in theory, is possible. The Women's Equality document calls on men to 'take up their domestic responsibilities with the care of children' but it is posed in terms of 'all the family' being called upon to 'help the women'. In this basic acceptance of the sexual division of labour, and in its uncritical support of the traditional nuclear family, the new laws represent only a partial break with patriarchal domination.

The Cuban leadership has been constantly educating Cuban men on the question of *machismo* and even though the wolf-whistle is still common the violence of rape is not. Women are not used to sell cars and advertisements for cosmetics do not deface the walls of the city. There is, however, still a certain biological determinism in Castro's speeches on women, such as when he called for 'proletarian courtesy' because: 'It is true with women, and must be so with women because they are physically weaker and because they have tasks and functions and human responsibilities that the man does not have.'[77] Such determination of social roles through assumed biological characteristics is bound to have its effects in the world of work and politics. One cannot, however, adopt an abstract model of what 'socialist woman' should be. A remarkable oral history of Cuban women shows the wide diversity of motivation and aspirations amongst women. For many poor women who had to work out of sheer economic necessity in the old society 'liberation' meant simply a release from work outside the home, taking care of their own homes and having time to spend with their children.[78] It would be rather presumptuous to say simply that these women had 'a misconception of the role of women in socialist society'.

Beyond Economism

We return now to our starting point, which was the relative inability of Marxism to come to grips theoretically and politically with issues which did not immediately reduce to the 'class struggle' between workers and capitalists in the factory. Recently there have been serious moves to take Marxism 'beyond economism'. In this we are only renewing a plea by Lenin that the revolutionary ideal was not the trade union secretary:

but *the tribune of the people*, who is able to react to every manifestation of tyranny and oppression, no matter where it appears, no matter what stratum or class of the people it affects . . .[79]

The subsequent history of the Russian Revolution was to bury this subversive thought of Lenin's, and it is really the women's movement which has brought these issues to the fore again.

The women's movement asserted in practice the right of autonomous social movements which would not be subordinated to political parties. Unity of the working class can be attained only through recognition of the diverse, particular interests which coexist within it — women/men, black/whit young/old, skilled/unskilled, etc — and not by administrative fiat. Capital was no longer reduced to the 'factory' as the emphasis on 'social capital' and the 'social factory' shifted attention to reproduction of society as a whole. The reproduction of the working class takes place in the home, the school and in the community. In this new situation, workers were beginning to question the wage relation itself, the question of hierarchies, and authority the conditions of work and not only the size of the pay packet. Radical women's movements directed attention to issues concerned with the 'quality of life' under late capitalism. Women questioned the traditions of the trade union movement on such issues as the 'family wage' and their general neglect of women workers. They also questioned the orthodox image of the Leninist party for its inability to channel the immense well of frustration created by capitalism.

These types of issues were systematically raised by Sheila Rowbotham and the co-authors of *Beyond the Fragments*.[80] New ways of organising were posed by the women's movement which broke with the traditions of hierarchy and leadership. The concept of 'prefigurative political forms' was advanced to describe attempts within the present to build the future society. How could a trade union or revolutionary party organised along (capitalist) competitive and hierarchical lines be the instrument of the transition to socialism? These questions are at first glance far removed from the reality of the class struggle in Latin America. Military dictatorships will not permit 'consciousness-raising' groups to meet or allow agitation for 'wages for housework'. Guerrilla organisations fighting for their survival cannot afford the luxury of putting into practice 'the personal is political' slogan. Nor can the essence of Leninism — a centralised combat organisation — be rejected simply as *machismo*. There is a point at which this defensiveness becomes regressive. For example, some sectors of the Latin American left reject the women's movement as 'imperialist ideology', and some actually stress the values of *machismo* because the 'US left' opposes it. The left in Chile failed to recognise that women actually had specific problems demanding specific solutions. Women's oppression simply cannot be subsumed under an abstract 'class struggle', and the fight against it suspended until the 'struggle for socialism' is successful.

Helen Safa recently posed the issue pertinently in the course of a discussion on working class women in Puerto Rico:

Viewing class consciousness from a feminist perspective permits one to question whether the narrow focus on work roles is even appropriate for men in the Latin American working class.[81]

Because of the lack of stable employment prospects for men as much as women Safa proposes the community as a more appropriate locale than the factory for the development of class consciousness. This in a sense is obvious, and various urban explosions in recent years have cut across traditional boundaries and embraced the working class communities as a whole. The more profound significance of this position is that all the issues raised by the women's movement have a more than sectoral significance and are also relevant to men. It certainly means in the most immediate terms that women will not be mobilised for progressive social change until labour and socialist organisations make the fight against the sexual division of labour (at work, at home and in the community) a definite priority.

That patriarchal relations persist under socialism should be evident from our brief look at Cuba. Heidi Hartmann poses the issues most clearly:

> Women should not trust men to 'liberate' them 'after the revolution', in part because there is no reason to think they would know how; in part because there is no necessity for them to do so; in fact their immediate self-interest lies in our continued oppression . . .[82]

The first reason has been proven correct by history, the second is only partly true. Certainly immediate male self-interest dictates the continued subordination of women, but the long term aims of socialism, even for men, are impossible against the interests of half the population. That Castro is one of the most prominent advocates of women's rights in Cuba is due not only to conviction, but to recognition of this fundamental truth. Hartmann goes on to show how women have learnt through the sexual division of labour, the significance of human interdependence and needs such as nurturance, sharing and growth. That is why, as she rightly says, 'while men have long struggled *against* capital, women know what to struggle *for*'.[83] Questions surrounding the nature of future society, once raised by the young Marx and dismissed by subsequent Marxists as 'utopian' can now come to the fore again, revitalised by the contribution of today's socialist feminism.

References

1. Connolly, J. (1949) *Labour in Ireland*. Dublin, Irish Transport and General Workers' Union, pp.292, 299.
2. Ibid., p.292.
3. Ibid., p.299.
4. Parkin, F. (1979) *Marxism and class theory: a bourgeois critique*.

London, Tavistock Publications, p.4.

5. Genovese, E. (1971) *In Red and Black*. New York, Vintage Books, p.55

6. CSE Sex and Class Group (1982) Sex and Class, *Capital and Class*, No.1 86.

7. For a brief factual report see O'Shaughnessy, H. (1973) *What Future for the Amerindians of South America*. London, Minority Rights Group Report No.15.

8. For a critique of *indigenismo* see Diaz-Palanco, H. (1982) Indigenismo, Populism and Marxism, *Latin American Perspectives*, Vol.IX No.2: 42–61.

9. See Mariátegui, J.C. (1971) *Seven Essays on Peruvian Reality*. Austin, University of Texas Press.

10. Klein, H. (1973) Slavery in Latin America, *Problems in Latin American History*, (ed) J. Tulchin. New York, Harper and Row, p.210.

11. Quoted in Bollinger, W. and Lund, D. (1982) Minority Oppression: Forward Analyses that Clarify and Strategies that Liberate, *Latin American Perspectives*, Vol.IX No.2, p.12.

12. Ibid., p.15.

13. See Bourgois, P. (1982) Class, Ethnicity and the State Among the Miskitu Amerindians of Northeastern Nicaragua, *Nicaragua in Revolution*, (ed) T. Walker. New York, Prager Publishers.

14. Hartmann, H. (1979) The Unhappy Marriage of Marxism and Feminism towards a more progressive union, *Capital and Class*, No.2, p.11.

15. Delphy, C. (1977) *The Main Enemy*. London, Women's Research and Resources Centre, p.31.

16. Mitchell, J. (1975) *Psychoanalysis and Feminism*. London, Penguin Books, p.412.

17. Barrett, M. (1980) *Women's Oppression Today – Problems in Marxist Feminist Analysis*. London, New Left Books, p.14. See also the various articles in Eisenstein, Z. (ed.) (1979) *Capitalist Patriarchy and the Case for Socialist Feminism* New York, Monthly Review Press; and Jansen-Jurreit, M. (1982) *Sexism: The Male Monopoly of History and Theory*. London, Pluto Press.

18. Engels, F. (1970) The Origin of the Family, Private Property and the State, *Selected Works*, Marx and Engels. London, Lawrence and Wishart p.567.

19. Mackintosh, M. (1981) The Sexual Division of Labour and the Subordination of Women, *Of Marriage and the Market: women's subordination in international perspective*, (ed.) K. Young, C. Wolkowi and R. McCullagh. London, CSE Books, p.3.

20. See Beechey, V. (1977) Some Notes on Female Wage Labour in Capita Production, *Capital and Class*, No.3:45–66.

21. For a general survey of the debate see Molyneux, M. (1979) Beyond the Domestic Labour Debate. *New Left Review*, No.116:3–28.

22. Adamson, O., Brown, C., Harrison, J. and Price, J. (1976) Women's Oppression Under Capitalism. *Revolutionary Communist*, No.5:8.

23. Dalla Costa, M. and James, S. (1972) *The Power of Women and the Subversion of the Community*. Bristol, Falling Wall Press.
24. See Gardiner, J. (1975) Women's Domestic Labour, *New Left Review*, No.89:47–58.
25. For a critical analysis of Meillasoux's work which takes up this question see O'Laughlin, B. (1977) Production and Reproduction. Meillasoux's Femmes, Greniers et Capitaux. *Critique of Anthropology*, Vol.2 No.8:3–32.
26. For a full analysis see the seminal article by Edholm, F., Harris, O. and Young, K. (1977) Conceptualising Women. *Critique of Anthropology*, Vol.3 No.9–10:101–30. Also, O'Brien, M. (1981) *The Politics of Reproduction*. London, Routledge.
27. Hartmann, H. (1979) The Unhappy Marriage of Marxism and Feminism, op.cit., p.13.
28. Engels, F. (1970) The Origin of the Family, Private Property and the State, op.cit., p.501.
29. Boserup, E. (1970) *Women's Role in Economic Development*. London, Allen and Unwin. For a critical review of this work see Benería, L. and Sen, G. (1981) Accumulation, Reproduction and Women's Role in Economic Development. *Signs: Journal of Women in Culture and Society*, Vol.7 No.2:279–98.
30. Marx, K. (1976) *Capital* Vol.1. London, Penguin Books, p.718.
31. Cited in Latin American Women — One Myth Many Realities (1980). *NACLA Report on the Americas*, Vol.XIV No.5:13.
32. Ibid., p.16.
33. Frobel, F., Heinrichs, J. and Kreye, O. (1981) *The New International Division of Labour*. Cambridge, Cambridge University Press, p.356.
34. Latin American Women — One Myth, Many Realities (1980), op.cit., p.15.
35. Elson, D. and Pearson, R. (1981) The Subordination of Women and the Internationalisation of Factory Production. *Of Marriage and the Market*, op.cit., p.149.
36. Latin American and Caribbean Women's Collective. (1980) *Slaves of Slaves — the Challenge of Latin American Women*. London, Zed Press, p.108.
37. Barrios de Chungara, D. (1978) *Let Me Speak! Testimony of Domitila, a woman of the Bolivian mines*. London, Stage 1. For further direct testimonies, see Bronstein, A. (1982) *The Triple Struggle, Latin American Peasant Women*. London WOW Campaign Ltd.
38. Deere, C.D. (1977) Changing Social Relations of Production and Peruvian Peasant Women's Work, *Latin American Perspectives*, Vol.IV No.1/2. See also Deere, C.D. and Leon de Led, M. (1981) Peasant Production, Proletarianization, and the Sexual Division of Labor in the Andes. *Signs: Journal of Women in Culture and Society*, Vol.7 No.2: 338–60.
40. Souza, J.F.A. de (1980) Paid Domestic Service in Brazil. *Latin American Perspectives*, Vol.VII No.1:35–63.

41. Bennholdt-Thomsen, V. (1981) Subsistence Production and Extended Reproduction, *Of Marriage and the Market*, op.cit.
42. Ibid.
43. Buttari, J. (ed.) (1979) *Employment and Labor Force in Latin America*. Washington, Organisation of American States, p.495.
44. Ibid., p.495.
45. Inter-American Development Bank (1981), *Economic and Social Progress in Latin America 1980–81*. Washington D.C., Inter-American Development Bank, p.128.
46. Ibid., p.131.
47. Latin American and Caribbean Women's Collective (1981) *Slaves of Slaves*, op.cit., p.182.
48. Safa, H.I. (1977) The Changing Composition of the Female Labor Force in Latin America. *Latin American Perspectives*, Vol.IV No.4:133.
49. See Rowbotham, S. (1973) *Hidden from History. 300 Years of Women's Oppression and the Fight Against it*. London, Pluto Press.
50. Chaney, E. (1979) *Supermadre: Women in Politics in Latin America*. Austin, The University of Texas Press, pp.68-9.
51. Hinault, M. (1976) Las mas pobres. Realidad económica y social de las trabajadoras en Argentina, Buenos Aires. Cited in Vitale, L. (1977) *La Formacion Social Latinoamericana (1930–1978)*. Barcelona, Editorial Fontamara, p.117. For a full discussion of working women in Argentina see Gil, E. (1970) *La Mujer en el Mundo del Trabajo*. Buenos Aires, Ed Libera.
52. Cited in Latin American and Caribbean Women's Collective (1980) *Slaves of Slaves*, op.cit., p.29.
53. See Hollander, N. (1974) Si Evita Viviera. *Latin American Perspectives*, Vol.1 No.3:42–57; and Hollander, N. (1977) Women Workers and the Class Struggle: The Case of Argentina. *Latin American Perspectives*, Vol.IV No.1/2:180-93.
54. Most of the English biographies of Eva Perón are of the 'Woman with the Whip' or stage-musical variety, whereas in Argentina they are largely mythological. One reasonable recent title is Llorca, C. (1980) *Llamadme Evita*. Barcelona, Editorial Planeta.
55. Cited in Hollander, N. (1977) Women Workers and The Class Struggle: The Case of Argentina, op.cit., p.188.
56. Cited in Llorca, C. (1980) *Llamadme Evita*, op.cit., p.119.
57. Marini, A.M. (1977) Women in Contemporary Argentina, *Latin American Perspectives*, Vol.IV No.4:119.
58. See in particular Matellart, M. (1980) Chile: The Feminine Version of the Coup D'Etat; *Sex and Class in Latin America*, (ed) J. Nash and H.I. Safa. New York, J.F. Bergin Publishers; also, Crummett, M.A. (1977) El Poder Femenino: The Mobilization of Women Against Socialism in Chile. *Latin American Perspectives*, Vol.IV No.4:103-113.
59. Andreas, C. (1977) The Chilean Woman; Reform, Reaction and Resistance. *Latin American Perspectives*, Vol.IV No.4:124.

60. Hahner, J.E. (1980) Feminism, Women's Rights, and the Suffrage Movement in Brazil, 1850-1932. *Latin American Research Review*, Vol.XV No.1:103. See also the classic study of Brazilian women in Saffioti, H.B. (1978) *Women in Class Society*. New York, Monthly Review Press.

61. Schmink, M. (1981) Women in Brazilian *Abertura* Politics. *Signs: Journal of Women in Culture and Society*, Vol.7 No.11:117.

62. Ibid., p.124.

63. Ibid., p.126.

64. Cited in Latin American Women: One Myth — Many Realities (1980) NACLA, op.cit., p.24.

65. Ibid., p.23.

66. See for example Randall, M. (1982) *Sandino's Daughters: Testimonies of Nicaraguan Women in Struggle*. London, Zed Press.

67. Latin American and Caribbean Women's Collective (1980) *Slaves of Slaves*, op.cit., p.140.

68. Croll, E. (1981) Women in Rural Production and Reproduction in the Soviet Union, China, Cuba and Tanzania. *Signs: Journal of Women in Culture and Society*, Vol.7 No.2:398.

69. Molyneux, M. (1981) Women in Socialist Societies: Problems in Theory and Practice. *Of Marriage and the Market*, op.cit., p.197.

70. Ibid., p.197-8.

71. The data for this paragraph are drawn from Cole, J.B. (1980) Women in Cuba: The Revolution Within the Revolution. *Comparative Perspectives of Third World Women — The Impact of Race, Sex and Class*, (ed) B. Lindsay. New York, Praeger Publishers.

72. For a systematic account see Murray, N. (1979) Socialism and Feminism: Women and the Cuban Revolution. *Feminist Review*, Nos. 2 and 3. Most of the factual data in this and the next paragraph is from this article.

73. Cited in King, M. (1977) Cuba's attack on women's second shift; 1974-1976. *Latin American Perspectives*, Vol.IV No.1/2:108.

74. Bengelsdorf, C. and Hageman, A. (1979) Emerging from underdevelopment: women and work in Cuba. *Capitalist Patriarchy and the case for Socialist Feminism*, op.cit., p.288.

75. On the Family Code see King, M. (1977) Cuba's attack on women's second shift, 1974-1976. op.cit., and Cockburn, C. (1979) Women and Family in Cuba, *Cuba: The Second Decade*. London, Writers and Readers Publishing Cooperative.

76. Cited in Cockburn, C. (1979) Women and Family in Cuba, op.cit., p.160.

77. Cited in Bengelsdorf, C. and Hageman, A. (1979) Emerging from underdevelopment: Women and work in Cuba, op.cit., p.282.

78. Lewis, O., Lewis, R. and Rigdon, S. (1977) *Four Women — Living the Revolution — An Oral History of Contemporary Cuba*. Urbana, University of Illinois Press, p.XV. For a different view of Cuban women see Randall, M. (1974) *Cuban Women Now*. Toronto, The Women's Press.

79. Lenin, V.I. (1970) What is to be Done? *Selected Works* Vol.1, Moscow, Progress Publishers, p.183.
80. Rowbotham, S., Segal, L. and Wainwright, H. (1980) *Beyond the Fragments — Feminism and the Making of Socialism*. London, Merlin Press.
81. Safa, H.I. (1980) Class Consciousness Among Working Class Women in Latin America; Puerto Rico, *Sex and Class in Latin America*, op.cit., p.83.
82. Hartmann, H. (1979) The Unhappy Marriage of Marxism and Feminism, op.cit., p.24.
83. Ibid.

5. Urban Social Movements: Labour in Argentina and Brazil

> Labour is the source of all wealth, the political economists assert . . . But it is even infinitely more than this. It is the prime basic condition for all human existence, and this to such an extent that, in a sense, we have to say that labour created man himself.
>
> F. Engels[1]

In recent years there has been an increased level of interest in Third World urban labour movements, even giving rise to a distinct field known as the 'new international labour studies'. This chapter begins with a brief discussion of some of the major methodological issues raised by this literature. Having set the scene we move on to a comparative study of the labour movements in Argentina and Brazil through their various phases from their origins to the present. On that basis we then examine some of the major comparative aspects, and the weight that can be attributed to the labour movement's trajectory in each country's political history. We see how in its historically evolving relationship with capital and the state labour becomes a working *class* with distinct forms of organisation and levels of class consciousness. This movement then reacts back on the society which spawned it, setting limits to its course in accordance with its objective strength and social combativness. We seek an understanding of what a working class 'is', not in stratification studies or opinion surveys but rather in the way it struggles historically to assert its own interests and objectives.

New International Labour Studies

The capitalist *production* process is at the same time a process of *reproduction* of the capital-relation itself, that is the capitalist and the wage-labourer. The process of accumulation requires the constant creation of wage-labourers to realise and increase the available capital. As labour produces capital so does capital 'produce' labour, or as Marx summarises: 'the *growth of capital* and the *increase in the proletariat* appear therefore, as interconnected — if opposed — *products* of the same process'.[2] As we have

145

seen, this reproduction on a steadily more massive scale leads to the concentration and centralisation of capital. The exploitation of workers is also intensified 'but with this there also grows the revolt of the working class, a class constantly trained, united and organised by the very mechanism of the capitalist process of production.'[3] For Marx, of course, it was not the most oppressed class which was the most revolutionary – the proletariat, by virtue of its position in the relations of production, is involved in an increasingly *socialised* work process which conflicts with the still *private* appropriation of surplus. This places the proletariat in direct conflict with capital and in a position to implement a new co-operative mode of production when capitalism is overthrown.

This classical Marxist perspective finds some support in the history of Third World labour in spite of the Fanonist claim that the working class in those areas is a small, relatively privileged élite. Since the mid-1970s the Black working class in South Africa has been at the forefront of a series of important strikes and the struggle for political rights. David Hemson surveys the role of Black trade unionism there and concludes that 'the urban section of the black proletariat constitutes the vanguard of the working class in South Africa'.[4] In Mexico likewise, a recent study concludes that 'the industrial proletariat is already, in Mexico, the natural representative of the bloc of the oppressed'.[5] Within the working class itself we find that it is workers in the most dynamic (and therefore usually better paid) sectors who are the most militant. In Peru, for example, the modern sector of the manufacturing economy is clearly associated with support for radical trade unions. As Howarth argues:

> the crucial reason is the nature of the labour process in which the industrial park workers found themselves. The unity arising out of the cumulative experience of the workers in this highly capitalised, high technology industrial park provided the base for the construction of the FTPIA (an 'ultra-left' federation) as the radical response to the policies of the CGTP [the main union federation].[6]

Comparative studies of revolutions from Russia to Cuba have shown that a major role was played by the urban working class.[7] The most recent experience of the Nicaraguan revolution in 1979 showed that the urban insurrection was a vital component of Third World revolutions and that the working class is still the key social force in the implementation of post-revolutionary reforms.[8] The question now arises as to how one can best study the Third World labour movements.

On the basis of dissatisfaction with traditional labour history, and influenced by recent trends in social history, 'new international labour studies' has emerged in recent years. Work on Africa and Latin America had gradually begun to point in this direction, at least since the mid-1970s. Robin Cohen has recently tried to systematically define this area of study.[9] He notes in the first place that it is distinct from industrial relations or trade union studies or the 'technicist' labour studies associated with the International Labour Office publications. Perhaps more questionably, he maintains that it cannot be conceived as an extension of 'labour history', although he concludes that the new developments could be encompassed by a broader framework of labour history less reliant on documentation (as against oral evidence) and more international in character. As to its 'objects of analysis', Cohen has identified a number of areas with which this new field is concerned: proletarianisation and class formation; workers struggles in the capitalist periphery; the urban poor; labour migration, and the role of working women in the Third World are just some of their themes. Some of these themes have certainly been neglected in the past — the labouring poor, migration and women — while others, such as the process of formation of the working class, have perhaps been overly influenced by the British example (e.g. F. Engels 'The Conditions of the Working Class in England' and E.P. Thompson 'The Making of the English Working Class'). So, the change in emphasis towards issues hitherto considered 'marginal' can only be welcomed.

There is, however, a lingering doubt regarding the apparent 'downgrading' of some traditional concerns, such as the development of trade unions (which need not be a dry institutional type study) and the more directly political issues debated by Third World labour students themselves: the role of labour in the anti-imperialist struggle, organs of dual power in the revolutionary process, etc., in short, all the major issues debated by the international worker's movement since 1917. Trade unions, for example, are still as Engels called them 'the real class organizations' of the proletariat. Peter Waterman has also stressed the continuing importance of organised labour in the Third World — 'unions remain the typical and universal organisation of the workers, the one that they cannot do without and through which they both discover and impose themselves on society.'[10]

Having said that, I think it is correct that we should begin to examine the *diversity* of class consciousness and forms of class action in the Third World. It is also true that many of the concerns of European and North American social historians of labour — oral history, the sexual division of labour, even perhaps the quantitative study of strikes — could fruitfully be extended to the Third World. In fact, I think it is quite wrong to have 'Third World studies' isolated as a distinctive area of study. As Richard Hyman notes in his contribution to a volume on *Strikes in the Third World*:

> it is important to insist that any special features of 'third world strikes' are significant not so much in indicating distinctive characteristics of this group of countries but rather in exemplifying *general* tendencies in the inter relationships between workers, their organizations, their employers and the state . . .[11]

In Latin America there has recently been a similar debate on the appropriate methods to study the labour movement. The standard text in this area is

Hobart Spalding's *Organized Labor in Latin America* which isolates three main variables which have influenced the evolution of labour: 1) changes in the world economy and decisions by metropolitan governments, 2) the relation between the international and local ruling classes and their composition; and 3) the composition, structure and historical formation of the working class.[12] In practice, however, Spalding seems to accord explanatory privilege to the first two elements, so that he has rightly been questioned on his 'dependency approach'. Eugene Sofer for example claims that:

> Spalding's conceptual framework, precisely because of its emphasis on that variant of dependency theory which emphasizes the international dimension, significantly underestimates the ability of Latin American workers to participate actively in shaping their own destinies.[13]

This is particularly true for those authors such as Spalding who emphasise the machinations of the North American trade unions in Latin American affairs. 'Trade union imperialism' certainly exists, but it has hardly been a determining influence in the evolution of the Latin American labour movement. Workers in Latin America, as elsewhere, are not passive recipients of capitalist or state decisions, they are rather active agents of social change.

It is always easier to offer critiques than to advance a coherent alternative. Sofer does say that we should attempt 'to write the history of the working class from the bottom up . . . of the working class as a whole rather than merely the history of trade unions or political parties. . . .'[14] Other critics have pointed to the need to extend oral history and the factory study to Latin American labour history — 'letting workers speak for themselves'.[15] This is quite correct as far as it goes, but there is a danger of falsely counterposing the global 'dependency' studies (which have pointed correctly to parallel processes in different countries, for example, under populism) and the 'new' social history's emphasis on working class culture. Two recent studies on Bolivia do, in fact, illustrate the strengths and weaknesses of the new alternatives. June Nash in *We Eat the Mines and the Mines Eat Us* carries out a remarkable study of Bolivian tin miners and their families, based largely on interviews.[16] This constitutes a major contribution to the study of class consciousness amongst Third World workers, but it is much weaker in its attempts to relate this to the important revolutionary role of the miners in Bolivia's political history. Guillermo Lora's history of the Bolivian labour movement is, on the other hand, a first hand account by a trade union and political leader.[17] Here we have the opposite problem of a passionate political history of the labour movement but with no real 'feel' of working-class culture which is brought out so well by the less politicised social historians.

The approach to be followed in our study of labour in Argentina and Brazil breaks with that of static dependency which reduces each country's history to its global situation of subordination. Clearly, dependent development followed different paths in each country, and class alliances were forged in a distinctive pattern. Above all, labour forged its *own* history — within these structural limits — and this we must study in its own internal dynamic. Charles Bergquist has attempted to chart a way out of the false dilemma of 'either we have the new social history of the working class or we have the institutional history of labor in dependent capitalist society.'[18] Such a synthesis would show how some dependent social formations have seen the development of an autonomous working-class culture and independent working-class organisations, whereas others have not. It would incorporate the concerns and methods of the new working-class history while avoiding its reactionary (i.e., antiquarian) element. Above all:

> such an approach would perceive the central role of labor — whether because of its strength and independence or because of its weakness and subordination — in determining the direction of the evolution of national history.[19]

The basic proposition which informs this study is that the comparative social weight, degree of organisation, and level of militancy of the working class in each country are major determinants of their respective political histories. These variations, in turn, can be understood only in terms of the specific historical formation of the labour movement in each case. Our analysis begins with an economic/structural outline of the classes considered and then moves on to a political/historical periodisation of the two social movements. This approach rejects any artificial separation between the mode of production and politics/ideology. One can say that the mode of production (dependent capitalism in this case) actually requires specific political/ideological characteristics of its labour force at each stage of its historical development. Our concern, though, is more the 'logic of class struggle' than the 'logic of capital' in this case.

Rise of the Labour Movement

It is essential to set the structural determinants of labour before entering into its history. The first essential point is to situate the position of the working class within the overall class structure. This we can see in Table 5.1 which shows that in Argentina nearly three-quarters of the 'economically active population' is subject to the capital/wage-labour relation, compared to around half in Brazil. The proportion of self-employed is considerably higher in Brazil than in Argentina, whereas in Argentina there is a higher percentage of employers than in Brazil. Argentina emerges as more thoroughly proletarianised, with a much smaller petty commodity production sector, but with a much more substantial medium-sized bourgeoisie than Brazil. In Table 5.2 we examine the internal structure of the labour force which shows that the percentage of non-manual workers has risen in both countries between 1960 and 1970. In Argentina, the much greater weight of the modern petty bourgeoisie and the 'new' working class is reflected in a proportion of

Table 5.1
Employment Categories (Argentina and Brazil)

	1960 (%)	
	Argentina	*Brazil*
Self-employed	12.1	35.1
Employers	12.4	1.8
Wage Labour	69.9	48.0
Others	5.6	15.1
Wage labour/employers	5.6	26.7

Source: M. Murmis, (1974) *Tipos de capitalismo y estructura de clases.*
Buenos Aires, La Rosa Blindada, pp.14–15.

Table 5.2
Manual and non-manual workers (Argentina and Brazil)

Total economically	*Argentina*		*Brazil*	
active population	*1960*	*1970*	*1960*	*1970*
Non-manual workers (1)	28.9%	32.3%	15.1%	19.4%
Manual workers (2)	71.1%	67.7%	84.9%	80.6%
(1/2)	40.6%	47.7%	17.8%	24.1%

Source: H. Muñoz and O. Oliveira (1979) Algunas controversias sobre la
fuerza de trabajo en América Latina. *Fuerza de trabajo y movimientos
laborales en América Latina*. (ed.) R. Katzman and J.L. Reynas.
Mexico, El Colegio de Mexico.

Table 5.3
Unionisation in Argentina and Brazil

	Trade Union Members (A)	*Economically active population (B)*	*Unionization Rate (A/B)*
Argentina	2,532,000 (1964)	7,524,463 (1960)	33.6%
Brazil	1,952,752 (1974)	29,557,224 (1970)	6.6%

Source: Zapata, F. (1979) Las organizaciones sindicales, *Fuerza de trabajo y
movimientos laborales en América Latina*. (eds) R. Katzman and
J.L. Reyna. Mexico, El Colegio de Mexico.

non-manual to manual workers nearly double that of Brazil. Finally, Table 5.3 shows the relative importance of trade union organisation in both countries. Brazilian unionisation rates are distinctly low (though they increased in the 1970s) whereas that of Argentina compares favourably with Italy (34.7%), the USA (23.4%) or France (15.2%). The potential strength of labour in Argentina is clearly greater, given the lack of a massive non-capitalist sector which might act as a reserve army of labour, and the level of objective and subjective organisation making for a homogeneous working class.

The formative period of the Latin American labour movement is sometimes referred to as the 'heroic period', which accurately describes the isolated and persecuted early labour organisers. As elsewhere, the working class of Argentina and Brazil emerged out of the artisan groups formed in the colonial period. With the tremendous spurt of European immigration towards the end of the 19th Century, and the emergence of the first industries, a proletariat, as such, emerged. The dominant ideology in this early period was anarcho-syndicalism which corresponded with the individualist consciousness of the early artisan. The anarchist strand, brought over to Latin America by prominent Italian and Spanish activists, was particularly appropriate to the oligarchic state with its incapacity to meet popular demands through incorporation. Labour organisation progressed from the early mutual-aid societies in the 1850s and 1860s to the first rudimentary trade unions. The printers of Buenos Aires are credited with the earliest union organisation which began life as a mutualist society in 1857 and, by 1878, had won a shorter working day after a 30 day strike. In this period, the vanguard of the labour movement corresponded closely to the leading sectors of the economy — the printers, tailors, bakers, etc. This was a militant minority unionism, highly politicised but drawing together an as yet small working class, based largely on workshops, and the transport sector.

The labour movement in Argentina was already the strongest in the continent by the early 1900s. At this juncture there were some 23,000 factories and workshops employing around 170,000 workers, half of these in the capital, Buenos Aires. Strikes increased considerably in number, with over 1,000 in Buenos Aires alone between 1907 and 1913. Political organisation of the working class proceeded apace — apart from the various strands of anarchism and syndicalism, the Socialist Party began to grow in strength especially in electoral terms. The First World War led to a considerable expansion of the textile and food industries as integration with the world economy faded. This growing working class engaged in a growing number of strikes: in 1916 there were 80 strikes (with 24,321 workers involved), by 1919 there were 367 strikes (with 308,976 workers involved). By this stage the petty-bourgeois based Radical Party was in power, but it was no less repressive towards labour than the landed oligarchy. In December 1918 a small metal-workers' strike for better wages and working conditions began. The employers dubbed it a 'rebellion' and called in the police who acted alongside the right-wing armed gangs of 'patriots'. As the workers were shot down in the streets, a vast movement of solidarity spread across the city and a semi-insurrectionary general strike began. Those days of January 1919 went down in history as the Semana Trágica (Tragic Week) and thousands of dead workers marked the coming of age of the Argentine labour movement.[20]

The Brazilian labour movement emerged somewhat later owing to the particular economic development pattern in that country — slavery was abolished only in 1889. By the beginning of the 20th Century there were 3,000 industrial establishments — mainly in textiles and food — employing some 150,000 workers. The First World War acted effectively as a protectionist barrier, and industrialisation accelerated considerably — by 1920 there were 13,500 'factories' with nearly 300,000 workers. In the post-war period trade union organisation advanced rapidly. A general strike in São Paulo in 1917 was followed by general strikes both there and in Rio de Janeiro in 1919. According to Spalding, 'these strikes collapsed in the face of forceful government measures, poor planning, and internal divisions among workers.'[21] Though weak and divided politically, the labour movement in Brazil was becoming a potential power, as in Argentina. Anarchism was particularly strong in Brazil, but the failure of these strikes and the impact of the Russian Revolution of 1917 led to the emergence of the Communist Party in 1921. In Brazil this had emerged out of anarchist circles, but in Argentina the Communist Party was formed in 1918 out of a split in the Socialist Party. One way or another a powerful new movement had emerged which would have an important effect on the subsequent history of labour in both countries.

The international crisis of 1929 marked a watershed in the history of the two working-class movements. It promoted the process known as import-substitution industrialisation, greatly increasing the weight of labour in the class structure. In Argentina, in 1930, a military coup displaced the Radical government, beginning the era known as the *Década Infame* (Infamous Decade) because of widespread electoral fraud and the virtual demise of bourgeois democracy. The labour movement was gaining in strength — in 1930 the CGT (*Confederación General de Trabajadores*) union federation brought together the various political tendencies — but it proved too weak to oppose the military intervention. This was to be a period of bitter splits and a disunited labour movement under heavy pressure from the state and capital alike.[22] The Communist Party was to become an effective union organiser, coming to lead the building workers union which, after that of the railway workers, was the largest in the country. The militant building workers strike of 1935 was the highpoint of communist influence, but also the date of its fateful turn towards the 'popular front' ideology. This was to subordinate the struggle of the working class to the quest for 'progressive' bourgeois allies, which from then on remained the overriding concern of the CP.

The rise of Peronism is still a subject of fierce debate. One interpretation stresses the factor of internal migration which brought thousands of workers in from the provinces to seek work in Buenos Aires. With their 'traditional' mentality they were easily captivated by the 'populist' and paternalistic rhetoric of Perón who was Minister of Labour in the new military government which came to power in 1943. Gino Germani is the sociologist who has put forward this view most clearly: for him Peronism is fundamentally 'a consequence of a rapid *displacement* of a great mass of population and its subsequent rapid *mobilization* which did not find an appropriate political expression in the pre-existing party and trade union structures.'[23] Emphasis is placed on the lack of trade union experience of the 'new' immigrants in comparison with the earlier European migration flow. Their 'political virginity' ostensibly made them easy prey for the 'charismatic' Perón. Other authors have pointed to the importance of the pre-existing labour movement in the rise of Peronism. Miguel Murmis and Juan Carlos Portantiero in particular have shown that the old socialist and syndicalist union leadership supported the rise of Perón because his measures corresponded with their reformist orientation: 'rather than stress the internal divisions of the working class, start with its opposite: the unity of the class, as a social sector subjected to a process of capitalist accumulation without income distribution.'[24]

Labour set the parameters of the Peronist coalition from the moment it was formed and throughout its history. One event, above all others, symbolises the rise of the Peronist working class – the 17 October 1945. On this date, the working class mobilised because Perón had been dismissed as Vice-President, but also to maintain and consolidate its social and economic gains. Some authors have attributed this massive mobilization to Perón's dynamic wife Evita, others have seem it as purely spontaneous. In fact, it was more of an organised political mobilisation by the whole labour movement (including the traditional leadership) to defend *its* interests. This was not just the 'new' working class of the meat-packing houses (the *frigoríficos*) displacing the old 'labour aristocracy' of the railway workers and so on, but a united mobilisation which brought the working class squarely on to the political scene.[25]

In Brazil, the year 1930 saw a rather different military coup, which brought Getulio Vargas to power, based on a disparate coalition of social groups which displaced the previously dominant coffee bourgeoisie. As in Argentina, a vigorous process of industrialisation led to the development of 'mass unionism' based on the new leading sectors such as textiles, transport workers and so on.[26] In 1935, the Communist Party launched an ill-fated insurrection and in its aftermath Vargas was able to 'incorporate' the working class in more favourable conditions than in Argentina. Whereas in Argentina it was the workers movement as much as Perón which 'made' Peronism, in Brazil labour was in a more demoralised and subordinate state. After 1935 workers were weaned from the previously dominant communist and anarchist trade unions and a new corporatist union structure was set up. Most of the institutional characteristics of the Brazilian labour movement were shaped during the Estado Nôvo (1937–45). As Timothy Harding notes:

> with the coming of the Estado Nôvo in 1937, all radical and independent labour leadership was suppressed, and unions were carefully regimented

into a corporatist system. An elaborate structure of labour legislation enveloped union activities, denying the right to strike and converting the unions into government agencies.[27]

The main characteristics of this corporatist structure can be summarised as follows:

1) the state retains for itself the right to guarantee certain minimal rights of labour related to the work situation etc. rather than allowing an unmediated conflict between capital and labour, with the explicit aim of conciliation;
2) a labour justice system was set up, which became a key element in the cushioning of the class struggle and took the employer/employee conflict away from the work place channelling the struggle into the confines of the state apparatus itself;
3) a pyramidal type of union structure was established, with the explicit prohibition of trade union organisation in the work place and horizontal bodies which could co-ordinate unions and federations through a centralised trade union structure;
4) a social security system was set up, which corresponds to the tendency of the state towards social intervention and, at the same time, reinforced the mass base of the populist movements.[28]

Nothing resembling the union-based *Partido Laborista* (Labour Party) in Argentina, which flourished briefly before Perón stifled it, could emerge in this context, where statist ideology reigned supreme.

Until 1945, Vargas had not moved decisively towards the political mobilisation of labour, but as the corporatist Estado Nôvo gave way to a restricted democracy this was to change. The unions launched a series of strikes in an attempt to regain the living standards lost during the Second World War period. Vargas carried out a series of measures to gain labour support, and in return the Communist Party helped dampen the strike wave which it labelled reactionary. Vargas was beginning to forge the ideology of *tribalhismo* (labourism) which stressed the conciliation of classes rather than class struggle, and the mediating role of the state between labour and capital. However, Vargas was displaced from power in 1946 and it was not until 1950, when he returned to the presidency, that Brazilian 'populism' really began. The 1945–46 period was thus the first attempt to forge a Peronist type coalition in Brazil. Francisco Weffort concludes that:

> the official trade union structure . . . had to wait for the effort of the left, in particular the Brazilian Communist Party, to conquer some real efficiency as an instrument for mobilisation and control of the working class.[29]

In this way, the CP was a vital ingredient in the genesis of populist politics in Brazil which, in the period following, were to subordinate labour to nationalism

So, it is not — as many authors maintain — just a question of the 'backward-ness' of the Brazilian working class in this period, but the particular policies of its leadership which led to populism.

Labour and Nationalism

In the post-Second World War period nationalist regimes consolidated a simultaneous mobilisation/containment of the working class. As we saw in Chapter 2, this was the period in which industrial capital gradually became the main axis of capital accumulation in the larger Latin American countries. Octavio Ianni correctly relates this economic shift with the politics of populism when he notes that 'it is a form of political organisation of the relations of production in a period of expansion of the forces of production and the internal market.'[30] Populism was the form in which the nationalist regimes incorporated the growing working class produced by the new expansive phase of accumulation. It did this, as Ianni says, in a way which 'depoliticizes social classes, through politicizing the alliance and harmony between classes.'[31] The trade unions are a key element in controlling labour and they become virtual state institutions. Certainly the unions retain their functions of bargaining for an increased share for labour in the distribution of the social product, but they operate within the logic of the capital relation. On the other hand, favourable political conditions allowed for a considerable amount of political bargaining by the unions, and a series of strike actions brought the working class to the centre of the political stage.

In Argentina, Perón's period in power from 1946–55 led to a series of impressive economic and political gains by the working class. Perón consolidated his ideological grip over the masses at a time (prior to the Korean War) when economic conditions allowed for considerable concessions to labour. Perón's main strategy in relation to labour involved a complete renewal of its leadership so that it would become dependent on state patronage. Pre-existing Socialist, Syndicalist or Communist labour leaders either fell in with the new situation or were displaced. Some thought they could maintain the independence of the trade unions within the wider national movements. These illusions were shattered as Perón replaced any leader with an independent power base who might threaten his own position. With a totally submissive labour bureaucracy the element of mobilisation began to lose importance. As one trade union leader reflected:

> the unions built the working class houses, its clinics, its holiday camps, its sports fields, and negotiated its wages and conditions of work. What could the labour movement aspire to that Perón could not grant it?[32]

The other element in Perón's strategy was the organisation of the working class so that it could become a more powerful counter to the traditional oligarchy. Union membership increased from a half million in 1941 to one and a half million in 1947, to over three million in 1950.[33] The consolidation of the industrial trade unions, and the extension of the union movement to the provinces, was also the work of labour militants not only the functionaries of the Ministry of Labour. The most important element in this organisation drive was the form it took. Each factory section elected delegates on the basis of a political slate; they, in turn, elected a plant committee known as the *comisión interna*. These bodies could become virtual 'workers' parliaments' in periods of upheaval and they helped maintain a level of basic organisation during repressive phases.[34] The economic and social gains of this period also led to a more intangible break by workers with traditional society and its ideology. This was summed up by the phrase 'the dignity of labour', coined by Perón but of wider relevance.

Perón was driven from power by a military conspiracy in 1955 and his failure to organise a workers' militia, as his more radical supporters suggested, meant that working-class protest was swiftly silenced. The period known as the Peronist resistance, which now began, was to culminate in the return of Perón in 1973. The military authorities had 'intervened' the unions – that is replaced the elected leadership by an appointed figure – so the main task was their recovery. This was gradually accomplished by a process of mass mobilisation which threw up a new union leadership based on the *comisiones internas*. This phase culminated with the 1959 strike and local insurrection over the proposed privatisation of the Lisandro de la Torre meat-packing plant. The union federation, the CGT, launched the *Plan de Lucha* (Struggle Plan) in 1963 which, in 1964, led to a massive wave of factory occupations across the country.[35]

The movement was, however, beginning to lose impetus – days lost through strikes declined from 10 million in 1959 to 268,000 in 1962. This demobilisation led to a gradual loss of working-class control over the shop-floor through the *comisiones* as employers launched a rationalisation drive.[36] This also helped consolidate a new labour bureaucracy epitomised by the metal-workers leader, Augusto Vandor. The basic contradiction of Vandor was his bureaucratic, gangster-like hold over the labour movement on the one hand, and his stress on the unity of the movement against capital and the state on the other.[37] The unity and strength of the working class was a necessary bargaining element for the labour bureaucracy. In this sense the 1964 factory occupations were the high point of Vandor's power, because they were an impressive but tightly controlled mobilisation.

In this phase of labour demobilisation a new military coup in 1966 closed a phase of civilian government which had alternated with military ones since 1955. The labour policy of the new regime was intensely repressive, and the movement eventually responded with the 1969 insurrection, known as the Cordobazo, which opened up a new phase. We shall examine this in more detail in the next section which deals with labour under the dictatorships. We need say now only that it led to a new period of Peronist rule which began in 1973 when Perón returned from exile.

The return of Peronism to state power was marked by an upsurge of workers struggles similar to that which had taken place during the early years of the first Peronist administration. The Peronism of the 1970s was not, however, in a position to 'deliver the goods' as in the 1940s, and a fierce internal struggle began within the Peronist movement. The trade union bureaucracy acted as the power behind the throne, especially after Perón died in 1974 and the right-wing course of the government was accentuated. The period since the Cordobazo had, however, been marked by an intense politicisation of the labour movement, or at least significant parts of it. A series of strikes in the provinces culminated with the 1975 Villa Constitución strike, which was the first large scale response to the government's offensive. By mid-1975 discontent among the union membership was widespread and a general strike materialised in mid-July to enforce wage increases to match the rising rate of inflation. Significantly, this mobilisation was organised by inter-factory co-ordinating committees (the *coordinadoras*) which raised the threat of a rank and file mobilisation outside the control of the labour bureaucracy.[38] As the government descended into administrative chaos with guerrilla activity intensifying, sections of the working class were beginning to break with Peronism. This social break, however, was not consolidated in an alternative political leadership which could confront the inevitable military coup which came in 1976 (see Chapter 9).

In Brazil, the nationalist economics and populist social programme of Vargas came to a close in 1954 when he committed suicide, apparently under pressure from conservative interests. The working class had, however, already begun to assert its growing social weight. A watershed on this process was the São Paulo general strike of 1953 which mobilised engineers, glassworkers and typographers in a fierce struggle which effectively regained the right to strike.[39] There were further big strikes in the mid-1950s, culminating in the 1957 São Paulo state wide strike which boosted the trade union co-ordinating body known as the *Pacto de Unidade Intersindical* (Interunion Unity Pact) which was an attempt to make up for the lack of a central labour organisation. During the early 1960s there were several general strikes against the effects of inflation. There was also a concerted campaign for a central union body, which led to the short lived CGT (General Labour Confederation) of 1962. State employees who only recently had gained the right to strike, were an important element in this wave of strikes. Another important sector was that of the transport workers and the rail and dock workers. Hegemony within the labour movement was maintained by a coalition of nationalist and communist forces, which largely refused to create a grass roots labour organisation in the work place capable of escaping state control. Taken as a whole, the 1954–64 period of successive populist governments was one of broad labour mobilisation, but under general ideological and organisational control by the state.[40]

A key element in the actual implementation of the corporatist union structure was a particular type of 'organising cadre' which were promoted by the Ministry of Labour with the aim of controlling the unions. Known as the

157

pelegos they fulfilled functions akin to those of a trade union official, and were to become the lynch-pin of the collaborationist union structure. These cadre helped fulfil the dual purpose of the union structure, that is, on the one hand, to maintain the proletariat in submissive passivity (accentuated by the paternalist relations in the work place itself) and on the other, to develop the mass base of the populist governments which dependend on popular support for political survival. From the mid-1950s onwards the *pelegos* were consistently displaced from the leadership of the larger, more militant unions, being replaced by a new organising cadre which was beginning to consolidate itself by 1964. This new layer, composed primarily of the factory delegates and organised in factory committees, was potentially a new leadership for the workers movement. They began to play an important role in the development of class consciousness and the recovery of the labour movement from the *pelegos*. Some idea of the extent to which this phenomena was occurring can be gained from a 1960 survey of São Paulo textile workers which found that of 30 firms 11 had factory delegates and seven had factory committees.[41] Considering the degree of persecution to which these delegates were subjected this survey is certainly an underestimate, and one can, furthermore, assume that the massive wave of strikes in the period 1960-64 led to an increasing importance of this new organising cadre.

The period 1961-64 was critical for the labour movement, highlighting both its innate strength and its grave political weaknesses. According to Harding's definitive study of organised labour in Brazil there was, in this period, a general radicalisation of the mass movement and, additionally, the populist manipulation of labour broke down to a certain extent in the face of mass radical pressure and demands. The focus of the union leadership, after a series of economic strikes in late 1961, was the struggle for the return of full presidential powers to Goulart. During these events Goulart had to use his full authority to have strikes called off before specifically working-class demands could be won. By 1963, however, 'political' strikes were increasingly directed against Goulart, such as the massive mobilisation of the state railway workers, the CGT opposition forces, the Students Union and others, which prevented Goulart from establishing a state of seige during the crisis provoked by the Brasilia Sergeants Revolt.[42] General strikes were called to demand changed in Goulart's cabinet and also to oppose the *Plano Trienal* (three year plan) of 1963. In fact, the working class was effectively exercising a 'right of veto' on crucial questions in the political arena.

What was perhaps the most fundamental characteristic of the Brazilian labour movement at that stage was that the particular history and structure of the trade unions left them without any real roots in the factories. In the first place this was due to rulings in the CLT labour laws, but at the same time the whole evolution of the trade union movement since that time did nothing to alter the situation. This lack of organic structures in the work place, and the predominance of populist relationships between the leaders and the masses in demonstration and assemblies etc., can be seen as a major cause of the near total collapse of the workers' movement in the face of the military uprising in 1964. According to Angela de Almeida and Michael Löwy:

> for these reasons, the military dictatorship was easily able to decapitate the labour movement by persecution of the top labour leadership. The base was totally formless, without any organic structure at the factory level to react to a rapid deterioration of purchasing power and the loss of all means of expression. Even had the former labour leadership wished to do so, it would have been very difficult, lacking a rank and file structure, to mobilise the workers under the clandestine situation to which they were reduced. The labour movement, losing its top leadership, found itself completely atomised and unstructured.[43]

Labour and Dictatorship

The 1964 military coup in Brazil launched a new 'modernising' dictatorship which was to profoundly restructure the relations with labour (see Chapter 7). Its counterpart in Argentina in 1966 had a similar project to restructure capitalism, but it was frustrated by a powerful alliance of the workers and popular movements. These new regimes were attempts to consolidate at the level of political hegemony the predominance which monopoly capital had attained at the level of accumulation. The Kubitschek regime in Brazil and the Frondizi government in Argentina had, in the early 1960s, accelerated the concentration and centralisation of capital under the influx of a wave of international investment. This 'new' working class of the car plants and the modern engineering works began to expand alongside the more traditional proletariat of the textile and food factories launched in the post-war industrialisation drive. The Brazilian working class expanded massively during the 1968–73 period of accelerated capital accumulation (see Chapter 7) and became the protagonist of a series of important strikes after 1978. The import of this new phenomena is still being analysed today but it undoubtedly marks a new pattern of independent working class politics in Brazil.[44] Argentina, meanwhile, fell under military rule again in 1976, although labour resistance eventually made this regime unstable too, as it had done after 1966.

The Onganía government, which came to power in Argentina in 1966, set out to break the 'pendulum' in political life there which had seen civilian and military regimes come and go since 1955. This time, economic and political relations would be radically restructured to attain a stable corporatist system. However, 'rationalisation' inevitably provoked opposition from Argentina's sizeable medium and small bourgeoisie. This centred around the provincial towns, which were particularly hard hit by these plans. It was in one of these, Córdoba, that an unprecedented urban insurrection exploded in 1969, bringing workers and students on to the streets with the support of middle-class snipers at their apartment windows.[45] Contrary to its mythology, this action was carefully planned by the combative union leadership of the car workers and power workers in particular. Workers who had been in retreat since the defeat of the Buenos Aires port workers' strike in 1966 now took to the streets in their thousands. The labour movement was the axis of a number of local uprisings across the country which peaked with a new Cordobazo in 1971.

The labour bureaucracy began to collaborate discreetly with the military authorities to achieve a return to civilian rule in 1973. The growth of militant rank and file currents amongst the working class, and even the organisation of a radical alternative CGT to the official union central, threatened their grip over the masses. The military state, for its part, was concerned that opposition to the regime might coalesce into a serious political alternative. There was no choice but to allow a return of Perón which led to the 1973-76 Peronist revival mentioned in the previous section. The point to stress here is that the labour movement — in alliance with broad sectors of the middle class and even the bourgeois opposition — was able to block a cohesive ruling class project. This was not a socialist movement but a nationalist-populist one, so the alternative posed was not formally anti-capitalist. But in conditions of dependent reproduction this was objectively a threat to continued bourgeois rule. It was this inherent insecurity which led to a new military intervention in 1976.

The 1976 coup was even more decisive and far-reaching in its effects with regards to labour than its predecessors of 1955 and 1966. Wages were cut by half, unemployment escalated rapidly, and union rights were cancelled. The significant point about this economic and social repression was that the labour bureaucracy was relatively unscathed. The need for a collaborationist labour bureaucracy to act as a buffer in the class conflict was as urgent as ever. The working class retained a considerable residual of organisation and combativeness which would threaten to burst out in new Cordobazos, but this time on a national scale. Government efforts centred around breaking up the old unified CGT union centre and creating in its place a professional business unionism along North American lines. When the union leadership perceived that opposition currents were organising, they achieved government support to neutralise these 'alien structures'. If the working class in Argentina had been weaker, sheer repression would have been sufficient. In the circumstances, a long range plan was required to reduce the size and homogeneity of the working class (through deindustrialisation) along with a complicated set of confrontations and alliances with the union leadership to achieve a stable 'a-political' labour movement.

Rank and file resistance began the day after the coup and has persisted until today, even though under very difficult conditions. During 1976 and 1977 resistance took a mainly diffuse character with go-slows, work-to-rules and discreet sabotage. This molecular process of recovery culminated in spectacular strikes by the power workers and dock and rail workers. The accumulation of forces continued in 1978 and by April 1979 the first 24 hour general strike was called. From then on there were strikes in virtually every industrial sector and a new general strike in 1981. In May 1982, on the eve of the Malvinas repossession by the military government, the unions were launching a new phase of organised resistance akin to the *Plan de Lucha* of a decade earlier. Though a new Cordobazo has not materialised in Argentina the continuous resistance of the labour movement prevented the consolidation of the regime and led indirectly to the Malvinas adventure with all its far-reaching effects.

The history of Brazilian labour after the military coup in 1964 followed a rather different course from that of Argentina. In the wake of the coup, a whole layer of trade union militants and leaders were arrested, thus effectively paralysing the movement. Wages were cut by half within a few years and the right to strike was effectively banned. The long years of subordination to the state and a vague nationalist ideology now left workers disoriented. There were no organic structures in the labour movement comparable to the *comisiones* in Argentina, which could maintain the cohesion of the working class during the period of repression which began. There were, however, two strikes in 1968 which were a sign of things to come. In April, a largely spontaneous strike was launched in Contagem (a suburb of Belo Horizonte) led by the *Oposicão Sindical* (Union Opposition) which culminated in the occupation of the Belgo-Mineira plant. Shortly after, there was another factory occupation in São Paulo's Osasco suburb which spread to other plants before it was broken up by the repression. A certain degree of working-class independence was emerging, but the basic point is that there were no major strikes in Brazil between 1968 and 1978.[46] This provided a crucial breathing-space for the gestation and consolidation of Brazil's 'economic miracle'.

The period from 1974 to 1977 was one of organic molecular changes within the trade unions, with a noticeable increase in the level of internal union life. A number of strikes in late 1977 signalled a qualitative change in the relations between labour and the military state.[47] The cost of living indexes had been falsified by the government, and the metal-workers began a campaign to recover the lost wages. In May 1978 the Saab Scania factory went on strike and the movement spread throughout the motor industry, largely organised by an in-plant leadership. In the four months following the original strike 250 firms employing 280,000 workers went on strike for higher wages. There was another round of strikes by the metal workers in November 1978 and again in March 1979. Between March and August of 1979 there were 1.2 million workers on strike and 14.3 million days 'lost' (for capital). Picketing appeared for the first time since 1964, and shop-floor delegates were elected in most of the big plants. The major characteristic of these strikes was, in fact, the advanced form of organisation practised along the lines of a general strike committee, with frequent struggles cutting across occupational lines, and with massive street demonstrations. Early in 1980, the 12,000 dockers in Santos came out on strike against the recommendations of the *pelego* union leadership, and in spite of the fact that the port was declared a 'national security' area. In April, some 300,000 metal-workers of São Paulo's industrial belt struck over wages, but also, quite significantly, for a 40-hour week and the right to elect shop stewards. After a month the strikers were driven back to work by hunger and repression after their militant leaders were arrested. In spite of this partial defeat a new phase in Brazil's labour history had begun.

Two main lines of interpretation arise over the underlying significance of these strikes. For Tavares de Almeida they were due fundamentally to structural contradictions between the 'new' proletariat of the dynamic industrial sectors and the old corporatist union structures.[48] The main demands raised — wage adjustments in accordance with increases in productivity, collective bargaining at plant level, and recognition of union organisation at plant level — were those of a potential labour aristocracy according to this view. John Humphrey on the other hand has argued that:

> far from adopting the 'apolitical business unionism' that Almeida predicted, the auto workers had become involved in a militant struggle against both the employers and the State . . . [They] are more likely to play the role of class vanguard in Brazil than that of labour aristocracy.[49]

I think this latter position is correct in the short term, but there will, logically, be a tendency by the more enlightened employers to accommodate the most 'advanced' sectors along 'business unionism' lines at the expense of the majority. The workers in the monopoly sector would thus become a relatively privileged layer in comparison with those in the competitive sector, not to mention those in agriculture, the artisans and others. Whether this sector is absorbed and institutionalised depends, of course, not only on conditions in the factory but also on the overall process of class struggle.

We have stressed how the type of organisation at the base represented by the *comisiones* in Argentina was a great source of strength there. It is not surprising, therefore, that when the labour movement in Brazil burst on to the scene in the late 1970s similar forms of organisation were adopted. In the course of the 1979 metal-workers strike, some 200 factory committees were formed in São Paulo alone, although they did not stabilise. After the defeat of the strike the number fell to 50 of which only ten were recognised by management. The *Oposicão Sindical* (Union opposition) movement had encouraged the development of factory commissions since at least 1973, although at that stage they were really groupings of militants and not representative workers' organisations. Their view was that 'the workers' commissions are the place of unity of all the workers who are prepared to organise and fight for their interests, even the most immediate ones'.[50] This movement was, however, a very small vanguard, and its influence outside the metal workers was small. More traditional sectors of the working class, such as the transport workers, continued to organise along orthodox trade union lines. The spectre of 'parallel unionism' raised by the *Oposicão Sindical* was opposed by even the most militant of the new union leaders. Thus 'Lula' the famous leader of the metal workers could say that 'in my view, the factory commissions inside of a free labour-union movement would have to remain subordinate to a broad coordination by the union'.[51] Whatever the result of this dispute, the old corporative style unions have suffered a crippling blow by this wave of worker mobilisations.

In 1979 the São Paulo metal workers union sponsored the formation of a workers' party on the grounds that 'history has shown us that the best instrument the workers can use to pursue the struggle is their own party'.[52] Thus the *Partido dos Trabalhadores* (Workers' Party) was born — the first class-based workers party in Brazil. Only the faint memory of the *Partido Laborista* (Labour Party) which flourished briefly in Argentina before the rise of Perón existed as a precedent. The demand for organisational autonomy from the state within the trade unions was now matched by a clear call for class independence of the proletariat in politics. Lula, its first leader, said that the workers did not want another multi-class 'populist' party but one 'without bosses, without foremen and without sell outs, a party that would fight to defend the economic and democratic rights of the workers and for socialism'.[53] Their immediate aims were to take advantage of the liberal *abertura* (opening) in Brazilian politics to demand a free and sovereign constituent assembly. Furthermore, they called for the dismantling of the repressive apparatus and the construction of a United Workers Federation. Not surprisingly, this movement developed close links with the free trade union Solidarity in Poland. The essence of proletarian democracy leads to similar patterns of insurgency in a Third World dictatorship and in a bureaucratic state socialist regime.

Comparative Aspects

We can now turn to compare and contrast the Brazilian and Argentine experiences starting with their respective national movements. Peronismo and Varguismo share many characteristics, and their functional role in the process of dependent capitalist accumulation — incorporation of the working class — is quite similar.[54] Where they differ radically, to an extent which is still having its effects today, is the way in which the working class was incorporated into the national popular movement. In Brazil, the working class was incorporated directly into the state apparatus through the Ministry of Labour, of which the trade unions were mere appendages. The unions were organised from above as part of a corporatist project where the element of class mobilisation was largely absent. In Argentina, the path Perón took to the working class went *through* the trade unions which were a critical element in mediating between the class and the nationalist movement. Furthermore, though ultimately Peronism was to hold back the class by tying it to a bourgeois political project, it also served historically to give organisational, political and social cohesion to the workers' movement.

Another difference is the respective role of the Communist Party in each case. Both parties had achieved a very significant weight in the labour movement in the period leading up to the 'populist' state. In Argentina, the Comintern (Communist International) perspective that the Second World War was a struggle between 'democracy' and 'fascism' was to have particularly disastrous results.[55] Between 1943 and 1946 the CP was to become totally isolated from the working class because it categorised Perón as 'fascist' and allied itself with the most reactionary sectors of Argentine society against him, and by extension against the labour movement. They thus performed a vital service to populism by discrediting Marxism amongst the workers movement for many years to come. The Brazilian CP (PCB) on the other hand, which began to see Vargas as an ally against fascism after 1943, achieved its legalisation in a deal concluded in 1945.[56] The PCB even polemicised with its counterpart in Argentina over its negative attitude towards Perón. As we saw above, CP backing was crucial in winning working-class support for populism, and this was to be even more marked in later phases. In a way, Vargas had to go through the CP to reach the labour movement, whereas Perón was able to reach out directly when its so-called Marxist leadership had committed political suicide. So, both parties were thoroughly subject to the dictates of the Comintern with all its twists and turns, but whereas one applied this astutely under the completely national and petty bourgeois leadership of Luis Carlos Prestes, the other was totally divorced from national reality.

Two related questions will be considered next: the labour bureaucracy and the labour aristocracy. Referring to Robert Michel's famous 'iron law of oligarchy' on the bureaucratisation of labour organisations, Richard Hyman has recently pointed out that 'who says organisation says firstly discipline, secondly routinisation. This virtual truism is less dramatic than Michels' dictum yet at the same time perhaps more fateful'.[57] This dual nature of organisation is illustrated by the case of Vandor, the union boss in Argentina who could intimidate and kill opponents yet, at the same time, it was under his leadership that the metal-workers union developed a vast network of union delegates and factory committees. Another example is the statement by a Brazilian union leader after the 1979 strikes that:

> in spite of it being harder to carry on a strike for 20 or 30 days, it is easier than everybody in 13,000 or even 200 factories striking for 5 minutes at the same time.[58]

The importance of centralised organisation (and inevitably bureaucracy) can be seen when we recall that Vandor could reputedly organise a general strike by telephone.

The debate in Argentina around the trade union bureaucracy has centred on the individual corruption and 'class betrayal' of the labour leaders. Other authors, such as Portantiero, have maintained that:

> the union bureaucracy expressed an intermediate layer, though numerically very powerful, of industrial development and the working

class 'common sense' which accompanied it. In this layer, its
representativity was unquestionable . . . .[59]

In a sense this is correct, because the political space occupied by the labour
bureaucracy is space ceded by a demobilised working class; nor is a mythical
rank and file the only source of militancy. However, it ignores the tremendous
vitality and periodic anti-bureaucratic struggles of the Argentine working
class. Especially after the Cordobazo of 1969 a series of *clasista* (class
struggle) unions sprang up, particularly in the motor industry and other
dynamic sectors.[60] Until they were defeated by military intervention these
unions set an example of active democracy and permanent mobilisation. In
comparison with the Brazilian *pelego*, the union bureaucracy in Argentina
has been more representative. One was simply a state functionary appended
to the labour market, whereas the other acted as a broker for labour-power
in the labour market with all the contradictions that entailed. The current
upsurge of labour in Brazil is tending to displace the old *pelego* figure, but
whether this will simply lead to a renovated, more dynamic bureaucracy, or
the emergence of solid rank and file organisation is not clear.

The 'labour aristocracy' debate is, in many ways, a false problem, because
economic class determination can never lead automatically to a given political
position. The real question is that of the heterogeneity or homogeneity of
the working class. In Argentina, a differential of 71% in the wages of skilled
and unskilled factory workers in the 1935-39 period was reduced to 26%
by 1950-54 and eventually reached only 13% in 1965. As to the differential
between workers in the 'traditional' and the 'dynamic' sectors this seems to
have widened between 1958 and 1966, but since then the gap has narrowed.
In fact, the 2.6% wage increase in the 'dynamic' sector between 1964-66 and
1967-72 is less than the overall 3.6% increase in industry registered over the
same period. As two Argentine economists note 'the second is a consequence
of the first: when a privilege is extended massively it ceases to be a privilege
and becomes a conquest of the labour movement.'[61] In Brazil, we note that
average real earnings in the 'high-wage' sector grew almost three times more
than those in the 'low-wage' sector in the period from 1966 to 1971; and in
large firms it grew almost twice as fast as those in small firms.[62] Nevertheless,
here too there is evidence which suggests that the position of the 'new'
working class, in the car factories for example, is by no means especially
privileged. As John Humphrey argues:

> the evidence from the auto industry suggests that workers there share
> many of the problems faced by the working class in general — stagnant
> or declining real wages, bad working conditions, excessive pressure of
> work, insecurity in employment, etc — and that their higher-than-
> average wages do not constitute the basis for a general situation of
> privilege.[63]

In conclusion, the greater homogeneity of the working class in Argentina has been a source of strength. The powerful metal workers' union negotiates relatively high wages for its members *across* industry from the giant car plant to the small workshop. This type of mechanism, and the political homogeneity of the class through Peronism, creates a movement less susceptible to splits and divisions. Since the 1976 military coup in Argentina all this has changed, with the active encouragement of wage differentials by the new economic authorities. In Brazil, the tendency will be towards creating a 'labour aristocracy' unless this is prevented by constructing the *political* unity of the working class from the São Paulo car workers through to the more 'traditional' sector.

We can now turn to the most significant difference between the two working classes which is the degree of internal organisation. A labour *movement* is more than just the organs of self-defence achieved by combination in trade unions. It is a whole series of intermeshing networks, economic, political and social, which prevent the natural tendency towards the atomisation of labour under capitalism and turn it into a movement. A social phenomenon like this can become thoroughly routinist and even conservative, as the British labour movement shows. When workers are part of a social movement, however, they are in a different position from that of other workers who are just election fodder for bourgeois parties. When workers organise in the work place they begin to think and act collectively and can become a social movement. When this movement passes through long years of clandestinity, confronts repressive military regimes and structures a broad nationalist movement, as in Argentina, it accumulates an immense wealth of experience. It is only within its own movement that the class builds up its confidence, exchanges experiences and elaborates its class perspectives. In the case of Brazil, it is difficult to actually speak of a labour movement as such. That is, there has not been the degree of unity, cohesion and organisation necessary for the crystallization of a basic class consciousness. Whether or not this will emerge from the recent upsurge of labour activity is still an open question.

In Argentina there has always been a distinction between the formal organised labour movement and an informal or 'real' movement. James Petras has recently developed this analysis, referring to a 'political class' composed of trade union and political leaders, intellectuals and others belonging to formal organisations, and a 'rank and file' working class.[64] Powerful informal bonds go out from the factory to the working-class areas, passing through the family networks. An extraordinary level of class solidarity and organisation and a distinctive working-class culture has resulted from this, which has been the mainspring for labour resistance to dictatorship. As Petras notes:

> the 'rank and file' working class has its own social, political and familial networks around which it organises a good part of its life . . . there is a common subculture that unites the working class independently of the formal organisation, which embraces kinship, neighbourhood, work place, and social clubs.[65]

The main element which has allowed the labour movement in Argentina to survive successive military governments is its grass-roots organisation. The *comisiones internas* (factory committees) have, on occasion, become bureaucratised, but in moments of upsurge they have become militant organs for the self-organisation of the class. The military know this, and in 1976 some 10,000 of the 100,000 shop stewards in industry were killed or imprisoned. The *comisiones* have been forced in many instances to become clandestine, but what is clearly evident is that they have maintained the capacity to resist under the most brutal military regime ever to rule in Argentina.

The point of our comparative analysis was more than just an aid to drawing out general features and specific developments of the two labour movements. We started with the proposition that labour is a key factor in the political history of both countries. One certainly cannot abstract from the very different levels of capital accumulation, in short the distinct history and structure of capitalism in both countries. Having said that, there is considerable support for our position that the respective position of labour (determined primarily by the degree of internal organisation) was a key difference between the histories of Brazil and Argentina after 1964 and 1966 respectively. When Roberto Campos (chief architect of the Brazilian 'economic miracle') was asked what would have happened if an uprising similar to the Cordobazo had occurred in Brazil he replied that 'an episode like that would have ruined everything'. For his part, the head of Argentina's industrialists was asked why the Brazilian 'model' had not been applied there and he responded: 'The Argentine trade unions are too strong; they would resist. There might be a civil war and we don't know who would win, how it would come out'.[66] On both sides key representatives of capital recognised the major role played by labour in facilitating or blocking certain capitalist strategies. This certainly lends weight to our own historical account.

Another study which supports this conclusion is Skidmore's detailed comparative analysis of 'economic stabilisation' programmes in Argentina and Brazil, which leads him to conclude that:

> variation in the character of the labour movement (which may in turn be attributable to the level of economic development) is the most important single variable in explaining the success or failure of stabilization programs.[67]

There is no space to reiterate here the conclusions of each historical section. The culmination of these partial arguments would be the following: the history of the labour movement is inseparable from the development of capitalist accumulation, and one must constantly bear in mind the rhythms and ruptures of this process. However, labour does not simply exist in relation to capital as labour-power, but rather it has its own history as a labour movement with its unique and complex internal development. Further, if there is one element that is absolutely critical in determining the weight of the labour movement in the class struggle it is the degree and extent of its internal organisation as a class 'for itself', and not only as against capital. If, as we maintain, the capital/wage-labour relation is the fundamental basis of capitalism its history must be the key to an understanding of bourgeois society. Our analysis cannot substitute for a full consideration of *all* the social forces at work during the periods we consider, but it must be the starting point.

References

1. Engels, F. (1970) The part played by labour in the transition from ape to man. *Selected Works*, Marx and Engels. Moscow. Progress Publishers, p.354.
2. Marx, K. (1976) *Capital* Vol 1. London, Penguin Books, p.1062.
3. Ibid., p.929.
4. Hemson, D. (1978) Trade Unionism and the struggle for liberation in South Africa. *Capital and Class*, No.6:2.
5. Alvarez, A. and Sandoval, E. (1976) Industrial Development and the Working Class in Mexico. *The Situation of the Working Class in Latin America*. Latin American Research Unit Studies No 1, Toronto, p.7.
6. Quoted in Angell, A. (1980) *Peruvian Labour and the Military Government since 1968*. University of London, Institute of Latin American Studies, Working Paper No.3, p.ii.
7. See Petras, J. (1981) Socialist Revolutions and their Class components. *Class, State and Power in the Third World*, J. Petras. London, Zed Press.
8. See Black, G. (1981) *Triumph of the People: The Sandinista Revolution in Nicaragua*. London, Zed Press.
9. Cohen, R. (1980) *The 'New' International Labour Studies:A Definition*. Montreal, Centre for Developing-Area Studies, McGill University, Working Paper Series No.27.
10. Waterman, P. (1977) Workers in the Third World. *Monthly Review*, Vol.29 No.4:58.
11. Hyman, R. (1979) Third World Strikes in International Perspective. *Development and Change – A Special Issue on Strikes in the Third World*, (ed) P. Waterman, Vol.10 No.2:326.
12. Spalding, H. (1977) *Organized Labor in Latin America – Historical Case Studies of Urban Workers in Dependent Societies*. New York, Harper and Row, p.ix.
13. Sofer, E. (1980) Recent Trends in Latin American Labor Historiography. *Latin American Research Review*, Vol.XV No.1:170.
14. Ibid., p.168.
15. See Winn, P. (1980) Oral History and the Factory Study: New Approaches to Labor Historiography. *Latin American Research Review*. Vol.XV No.1.

16. Nash, J. (1979) *We Eat The Mines and The Mines Eat Us – Dependency and Exploitation in Bolivian Tin Mines*. New York, Columbia University Press.
17. Lora, G. (1977) *A History of the Bolivian Labour Movement*. Cambridge, Cambridge University Press.
18. Bergquist, C. (1981) What is Being Done? Some Recent Studies in the Urban Working Class and Organized Labor in Latin America. *Latin American Research Review*, Vol.XVI No.2:205.
19. Ibid., p.211.
20. See Rock, D. (1975) *Politics in Argentina 1890–1930*. Cambridge, Cambridge University Press.
21. Spalding, H. (1977) *Organized Labor in Latin America*, op.cit., p.52.
22. On this phase see Tamarin, D. (1977) *The Argentine Labor Movement in an Age of Transition, 1830–1945*. University of Washington, Ph.D dissertation.
23. Germani, G. (1973) El surgimiento del peronismo: el rol de los obreros y de los migrantes internos. *Desarollo Económico*, No.51:486.
24. Murmis, M. and Portantiero, J.C. (1974) *Estudios sobre los origenes del peronismo 1*. Mexico, Siglo XXI, p.76.
25. On labour and the rise of Perón, see Little, W. (1975) The Popular Origins of Peronism. *Argentina in the Twentieth Century*. London, Duckworth.
26. The best overall history of Brazilian labour is Harding, T. (1973) *The political history of organised labor in Brazil*. Stanford University, Ph.D dissertation.
27. Ibid., p.16.
28. Tavares, M.H. (1975) O Sindicato no Brasil: Novos Problemas, Velhas Estructuras. *Debate e Critica*, (São Paulo, Brazil) No.6:35–6.
29. Weffort, F. (1973) Origens do sindicalismo populista no Brasil (A conjuntura do após-guerra). *Estuados CEBRAP*, (São Paulo, Brazil) No.4:71.
30. Ianni, O. (1975) *A Formacão do Estado Populista*. Rio de Janeiro, Ed Civilização Brasileira, p.135.
31. Ibid., p.115.
32. Gazzera, M. (1970) Nosotros Los Dirigentes. *Peronismo: autocritica y perspectivas*. M. Gazzera and N. Ceresole. Buenos Aires, Ed Descartes, p.42.
33. See Doyon, L. (1975) El crecimento sindical bajo el peronismo. *Desarollo Económico*, (Buenos Aires, Argentina) No.57.
34. For a general discussion of factory commissions see Gilly, A. (1978) Los consejos de fabrica: Argentina, Bolivia, Italia. *Coyoacán* (Mexico) No.5.
35. See Bourdé, G. (1978) La CGT Argentine en 1964. *Le Mouvement Social*, (Paris) No.103.
36. For a full account see James, D. (1981) Rationalisation and Working Class Response: the Context and Limits of Factory Floor Activity in

Argentina. *Journal of Latin American Studies*, Vol.13 Part 2:375–402.

37. For a discussion of *Vandorismo* see James, D. (1978) Power and politics in Peronist trade unions. *Journal of Interamerican Studies and World Affairs*, Vol.20 No.1.

38. On the 1973-76 phase generally see Jelin, E. (1979) Labour conflicts under the second Peronist Regime, Argentina 1973-76. *Development and Change*, Vol.10 No.2.

39. On this strike see Moises, J.A. (1978) *Greve de Massa e Crise Política (Estudo da Greve dos 300 Mil em São Paulo – 1953/54)*. São Paulo, Editora Polis.

40. For an overview of strikes in this period see Harding, T. (1973) The politics of labor and dependency in Brazil – an historical approach. *International Socialist Review*, Vol.33 No.7.

41. Rodrigues, S.A. (1968) *Sindicato e desenvolvimento*. São Paulo, Difusão Europeia do Livro, p.148.

42. A detailed account of the 1960-64 strikes can be found in Erickson, K. (1977) *The Brazilian Corporative state and working class politics*. Berkeley, University of California Press. Chapter 6.

43. Mendes de Almeida, A. and Lowy, M. (1976) Union structure and labor organizations incontemporary Brazil. *Latin American Perspectives*, Vol.III No.1:108.

44. For a preliminary discussion see Moises, J.A. (1979) Current issues in the labor movement in Brazil. *Latin American Perspectives*, Vol.VI No.4:51-70. Also special issue of *Cadernos do CEAS* (Bahia, Brazil) No.70 (1980) on the 1979 strikes.

45. On the Cordobazo see particularly Delich, F. (1974) *Crisis y protesa social, Córdoba 1969-1973*. Buenos Aires, Siglo XXI. and Balve, B. et al. (1973) *Lucha de calles, lucha de clases (Córdoba 1971-1969)*. Buenos Aires, Ed Rosa Blindada.

46. For an excellent study of these two strikes see Weffort, F. (1972) Participação e conflito industrial: Contagem e Osasco 1968. *Cadernos CEBRAP* (São Paulo, Brazil) No.5.

47. On the build up to the strikes see Mendes de Almeida and Lowy, M. (1976) Union Structure and labour organizations in contemporary Brazil, op.cit. On subsequent events see Green, J. (1979) Liberalization on trial: the workers' movement. *NACLA Report on the Americas* May/June.

48. Tavares, M.H. (1975) O Sindicato no Brasil. Novos Problemas, Velhas Estruturas, op.cit., pp.68-70.

49. Humphrey, J. (1980/81) Labour Use and Labour Control in the Brazilian Automobile Industry. *Capital and Class*, No.12:56. See also, Humphrey, J. (1979) Auto workers and the working class in Brazil. *Latin American Perspectives*, Vol.VI No.4:71-89.

50. *Ante-Projecto de Programa de Oposicão Sindical de São Paulo*, cited Vigevani, T. (1980) Del golpe militar (1964) a las comisiones de fábrica (1979). *Coyoacán*, (Mexico) No.7/8:76.

51. Interview with Luis Inacio Da Silva (Lula). *Latin American Perspectives*, Vol.VI No.4:96.
52. Cited in Green, J. (1979) Liberalization on trial, op.cit., p.24.
53. Cited in *Intercontinental Press*, 5 November 1979, p.1080.
54. For a broad ranging comparison of the two movements see Spalding, H. (1977) *Organized Labor in Latin America*, op.cit., Chapter 4, Labor and Populism:Argentina and Brazil.
55. On the Comintern's influence in Latin America see Munck, R. (1984). *Revolutionary Trends in Latin America*, Centre for Developing-Area Studies, McGill University (Montreal).
56. There is an excellent history of the Brazilian CP: Chilcote, R. (1973) *The Brazilian Communist Party: conflict and integration*. New York, Oxford University Press.
57. Hyman, R. (1979) The Politics of Workplace Trade Unionism: solvent tendencies and some problems of theory. *Capital and Class*, No.8:60.
58. Cited in Antunes, R. (ed) (1980) Pur un Novo Sindicalismo. *Cadernos de Debate*, (São Paulo, Brazil) No.7:56.
59. Portantiero, J.C. (1977) Economía y política en la crisis Argentina: 1958-1973. *Revista Mexicana de Socilogia*, Vol.XXXIX:555. This line of argument is expanded in Ducatenzeiler, D. (1980) *Syndicats et politique en Argentine 1955-1973* Montréal, Les Presses de l'Université de montréal.
60. For a case study of the militant power workers' union in Córdoba see Roldan, M.I. (1978) *Sindicatos y protesta social en la Argentina (1969-1974).* Amsterdam, CEDLA.
61. Data from Gerchunoff, P. and Llach, J. (1978) El nuevo caracter del capitalismo en la Argentina. *Desarollo Económico*, (Buenos Aires, Argentina) Vol.15 No.60:634.
62. Data from Mericle, K.S. (1975) *Conflict regulations in the Brazilian industrial relations system*. University of Wisconsin, Ph.D dissertation, pp.275-6.
63. Humphrey, J. (1979) Auto workers and the working class in Brazil, op.cit., p.72.
64. Petras, J. (1981) Terror and the Hydra: The Resurgence of the Argentine working class. *Class, State and Power in the Third World*. J. Petras, London, Zed Press, p.259.
65. Ibid., p.259. For a full discussion of these family networks see Ramos, S. (1981) Las relaciones de parentesco y de ayuda mutua en los sectores populares urbanos. *Estudios CEDES*, (Buenos Aires, Argentina) Vol.4 No.1.
66. Ibid., p.255.
67. Skidmore, T. (1977) The politics of economic stabilization in post war Latin America. *Authoritarianism and Corporatism in Latin America*, (ed) J. Malloy, Pittsburgh, University of Pittsburgh Press, p.178.

6. Rural Social Movements: Peasants in Chile

> The very position of the small farmers in modern society
> inevitably transforms them into petty bourgeois. They are
> eternally vacillating between the wage workers and the
> capitalists. . . . Only an independent organisation of the
> wage workers, which conducts a consistent class struggle,
> can wrest the peasantry from the influence of the
> bourgeoisie and explain to them the absolute helplessness
> of the position of the small producers in capitalist society.
>
> V.I. Lenin[1]

Lenin's analysis of the Russian peasantry was obviously more complex than
this quote would lead us to believe, but the general point is relevant to our
analysis — the peasantry are torn between the bourgeoisie and proletariat.
They do not have an independent class position and, in practice, follow one o
other of the fundamental classes. Our concern in this chapter will be to move
beyond this simple dichotomy and illustrate the general Marxist position on
the agrarian question through a discussion of land reform and peasant
movements in Chile. The analysis begins with an examination of the relation
between capital and the land, developing some of the key theoretical concept
Next, we turn to the class structure of the countryside — the different strata
of the peasantry and the landlord system. The next two sections discuss
agrarian reforms and peasant movements in general and in relation to Chile.
Finally, we turn to the prospects for rural social movements in the movement
in terms of objective trends towards agri-business and a displacement of the
traditional terms of reference of agrarian reform.

Capital and Land

The first obvious point to discuss in relation to the 'agrarian question' is
whether it pertains to capitalism or to a precapitalist mode of production.
When Marx begins his discussion of ground rent he says:

> We assume . . . that agriculture just like manufacturing, is dominated by

the capitalist mode of production, i.e. that rural production is pursued by capitalists, who are distinguished from other capitalists, first of all, simply by the element in which their capital and the wage-labour that it sets in motion are invested.[2]

The intervention of capital in agriculture transforms landed property into its image, whether it be feudal landed property or small peasant agriculture. For Marx the farmer produces wheat simply in the same way that the manufacturer produces cloth. One must question though whether ground rent is a 'purely' capitalist relation. For Pierre-Philippe Rey, on the contrary, ground rent is a *non* capitalist relation of production which can also operate as a capitalist relation of distribution.[3] In the relation of production the peasant is opposed to the landlord, and as a relation of distribution it serves to redistribute surplus between the landowners and the capitalist class. It is a precapitalist relation of production because the source of rent is not the global social surplus-value but value created directly in a dependent relation of exploitation. Of course, the landlord may also hire 'free' labour to work seasonally on his land with whom a directly capitalist relation of exploitation obtains.

Historically, there have been several different 'paths' of capitalist development in agriculture. Marx showed how this process unfolded in England's 'classical' transition from feudalism to capitalism. In this variant the poorer peasants were separated from their means of production (land) thus being forced to work for the new capitalist tenant farmers (the yeomen) who paid a rent to the landowners. Lenin's study of the development of capitalism in Russia pointed to two other major forms of transition: the Prussian or Junker road and the American or Farmer road.[4] In the first variant the feudal landlord becomes a capitalist entrepreneur in a process of 'conservative modernisation', which leaves the landowners in a dominant political position. In the second variant, the absence or violent elimination of the feudal landowning class leads to the proliferation of small farmers who become a petty bourgeoisie. The 'farmer' road is more progressive according to Lenin because:

> if capitalist development proceeds along this course it should develop infinitely more broadly, more freely and more rapidly as the result of the tremendous growth of the home market. . . .[5]

In Latin America only exceptional situations, such as the Mexican revolution or, more briefly, during the land reforms in Peru and Chile, did this path predominate. A weak peasantry and the predominance of the latifundia have generally led to some variant of the 'Prussian' transition to agrarian capitalism. As Kay notes:

> by controlling most of the agricultural resources and by exercising strong political influence landlords are able to ensure that the transition progresses according to their interests.[6]

Open proletarianisation and social differentiation of the peasantry along the North American pattern has, therefore, not been dominant.

It would be wrong to think that the historical experience of Latin American agriculture can be reduced to these few theoretical paths of development. Teresa Meade has developed an interesting analysis of how Brazilian agrarian development has diverged from both the English and the Prussian roads.[7] Primitive accumulation in Brazil was conditioned by its subordinate position in the international division of labour. Whereas in both European variants the dissolution of precapitalist forms of production proceeded more or less rapidly in Brazil, according to Meade, 'pre-capitalist forms of production were restructured and conserved . . . as it was increasingly integrated into world capitalist relations'.[8] De Janvry also mentions the 'merchant road', which is particularly important in Colombia where urban merchant capital is involved in modern medium-sized farms.[9] In Argentina there was an open frontier, as in North America, but the 'farmer' road did not develop because the ruling colonial élite was able to establish a monopoly over land. This does not mean that the 'Prussian' variant automatically applies, because agriculture from the beginning was based on proletarian not feudal labour forms. The immigrants to the New World in the 19th Century were not able to establish themselves as independent farmers as in North America, because the land had already been distributed in huge latifundia. Rather they became *chacareros*, paying rent to the landowners often in the form of a share of the crop. By the 1960s many of these smallholders had become owners of land themselves, accounting for nearly half of the agrarian production in the Pampas. There was, thus, a particular variant of the 'Prussian' form of agrarian development.[10]

The genesis of capitalist ground-rent is clearly not a unilinear simple process under conditions of dependent capitalist development. According to Marx the simplest form of ground-rent is *labour rent* 'where the direct producer devotes one part of the week, . . . to land that is in practice his own, and works the other days of the week for the landlord or his estate without reward.'[11] Unpaid surplus labour here takes the form of rent rather than profit. Another form that ground-rent can take is *rent in kind*, which is a variation in form only, in so far as surplus labour is performed 'freely' on the immediate producers own land rather than by direct compulsion on the landlords demesne. Marx notes that 'the transformation of labour rent into rent in kind in no way changes the nature of ground-rent, economically speaking.'[12] Finally, with *money rent* the immediate producer pays the landowner the price of the product instead of the product itself. The tradition-based relation between the landowner and his dependent peasants becomes a contractual relationship enshrined in law and based purely on monetary considerations. This is a higher stage of agrarian development which is completed only in the dominant economies. As Marx notes:

> the transformation of rent in kind into money rent that takes place at first sporadically, then on a more or less national scale, presupposes an

already more significant development of trade, urban industry, commodity production in general and therefore monetary circulation.[13]

In the dominated economies the particularly acute form of uneven development has meant that this process has been sporadic and partial only, at least until recent decades.

In industry, the development of monopolies leads to super-profits, and with landed property, which constitutes a form of monopoly, this surplus profit takes the form of *absolute ground rent*. Even the worst placed land perceives this ground rent, given private property of land by a landlord class. On the other hand a *differential rent* obtains when differences in fertility, location or capitalisation lead to acquiring a surplus profit due to productivity differences. As Kautsky says in his classic treatise on the agrarian question:

> To summarise, differential rent results from the capitalist character of production, not from the private ownership of land. Absolute rent results from private ownership of land and from the opposition of interests that obtain between the landowner and society as a whole.[14]

There are serious problems involved in Marx's concept of absolute ground rent, at the most basic level because this super-profit is based on the relative scarcity of agrarian produce on the market, which may or may *not* lead to the worst land selling its produce above the price of production.[15] The concept of differential rent is of much greater interest and one which aids our understanding of situations where dependent countries perceive a surplus profit from their monopoly (or simply strong position) in certain raw materials.

Argentina was integrated into the world economy as a producer of agrarian and livestock produce, for which it possessed certain natural advantages, particularly in the fertile Pampas zone. Producing for the world market in highly competitive conditions placed the landowning class of Argentina in a key position, at least for the period from 1860 to 1930. According to Ernesto Laclau 'the monopoly over land and the extremely high differential rent proceeding from the great fertility of the Pampas plains united to consolidate the at once capitalist and dependent structure of the Argentine economy.'[16] Laclau stresses the central importance of ground rent in Argentina's economic development based on the international differential rent derived from the low costs of production in the country and the strong demand for raw materials on the international market. Surplus value generated by European workers thus went into the construction of Buenos Aires city and port in this period alongside the super-exploitation of local workers. It is not surprising in this situation that the incipient industrialists would not threaten or subordinate the agrarian interests to their hegemony as in the original transition to capitalism. The concept of differential rent can, therefore, be used to explain situations such as copper in Chile, guano in Peru, coffee in

Brazil or, of course, oil in the Middle East where dependent Third World economies undoubtedly benefit from their integration into the world capitalist economy. However, whether it is British imperialism as in Argentina or American imperialism in Chile, the internationally dominant powers, through their control of the local economy, may recoup some of the differential rent. Much of what remains is dissipated by the local élite in conspicuous consumption.

Peasants and Landlords

In this section we move towards a more concrete characterisation of the agrarian economy, based on a combination of the landlord (or demesne) and the peasant economic systems. We are concerned here with the major forms of farm enterprises in Latin America and the resulting class structure. We will then focus on the formation of the *hacienda* system and the rural class structure in Chile from its formation until 1964 when the period of agrarian reform begins.

It is necessary first of all to present some definitions, because the terms 'peasant' and 'landlord' are notoriously imprecise. As Morner notes, ' "Landlord" is in fact far from being a homogeneous concept. It covers highly traditional *haciendas* as well as modernizing agricultural entrepreneurs with a strong commercial orientation.'[17] It is hardly, therefore, an analytical tool but a rather broad descriptive term we are dealing with. Likewise, Morner points out that:

> 'Peasant' appears to be even more ambivalent and vague a concept . . . there are those settled *within* large estates on a sharecropper or labour-tenant basis . . .[and] . . . those who are settled *outside* the estates but are periodically drawn upon as a source of seasonal or part-time labour.[18]

We will refer to 'peasants' as a broad rural social grouping characterised by subsistence production and production for the market which is appropriated by a dominant social class. It is necessary to relate now the different 'landlord' and 'peasant' types who coexist in conflict in the rural universe.

In Figure 6.1 we present a simplified typology of farm enterprises in Latin America and the social classes which predominate in each. In the non-capitalist or 'semi feudal' mode of production in de Janvry's terminology, there are two main forms of farm enterprise: the precapitalist estate and internal (to the estate) subsistence farms. The first is operated by the hegemonic landed élite and employs extra-economic coercion (labour services) to extract a surplus from the peasantry. The peasants and sharecroppers use family labour to work on land which is paid for in kind or cash. Both these economies tend to disappear with the development of capitalism. As capitalism develops along Lenin's 'Junker' or 'Prussian' road the precapitalist estate is converted into a large-scale capitalist enterprise. The 'Peasant' or 'Merchant' road to

Figure 6.1
Social Classes and types of Farm Enterprise in Latin America

Modes of production	Social classes	Types of farm enterprises	Control of the state	Status on labor market	Forms of labor payment	Dynamic status as capitalism develops
Semifeudal	Traditional landed elite	Precapitalist estates	Hegemonic as landed elite	Users of bonded labor	Paid in land usufruct, kind, and cash	Disappearing
	Internal peasants and sharecroppers	Internal subsistence farms	No	Bonded semi-proletarians	Paid in land usufruct, kind, and cash	
	Capitalist landed elite	Capitalist estates	Hegemonic as landed elite	Employers	Paid in cash	Emerging in junker roads
	Farmers: rural bourgeoisie	Commercial farms	Shared with non-agricultural bourgeoisie	Employers	Paid in cash	Emerging in peasant and merchant roads
Capitalist	Upper peasants: rural petty bourgeoisie	Family Farms	No	Small employers of self-sufficient	Paid in cash and labor exchange	Emerging and differentiating
	Lower peasants: semi proletarians	External sub-family farms	No	Semi-proletarians	Paid in cash	Emerging rapidly
	Rural proletariat	Landless workers	No	Proletarians	Paid in cash	Emerging slowly

Source: Adapted from A. de Janvry (1981) *The Agrarian Question and Reformism in Latin America*. Baltimore, The Johns Hopkins University Press, p.110.

capitalism results in a class of farmers which is the rural bourgeoisie proper operating commercial farms. Both sets of employers use proletarianised labour which is paid for in cash ('free' wage labour). The rural petty bourgeoisie is not very numerous in Latin America (except for such places as the Santa Fé region in Argentina and the Mexican *ejido* or reformed sector). The semi-proletarian small peasants eke out an insufficient living from their plots of land which must be supplemented by wage labour of different forms. Finally, landless workers constitute the rural proletariat which, in distinction to the above grouping, is emerging only slowly in Latin America. As de Janvry notes, each social class is defined by the mode of production, the social relations of production (forms of labour payment) their respective status on the labour market, and the degree of control they exercise over the state.[19]

The social relations of production in the rural areas are obviously of vital interest to any Marxist understanding of the situation. For that reason we will briefly enumerate the major forms of labour relations in Latin America. The enslavement of the indigenous peoples, and later of Africans was the first and most naked labour relation. A more discreet form of slavery was the Spanish *encomienda*, whereby colonialists were granted lordship rights over native settlements from which they could demand a labour tribute. This was displaced, as Pearse shows, when 'the lands passed steadily into Spanish hands [and] the natives were forced to become predial dependents of the Spaniards in the classic manner.'[20] Now, in Pearse's words, 'the *repartimiento* or *mita* . . . functioned to effect a periodic transfer of labour from the native settlements to the mining, agricultural and public works enterprises of the Spaniards.'[21] Where there was a labour shortage, such as in Argentina and Uruguay, the post-colonial period was characterised by European immigration, which came as wage labour. Elsewhere, different forms of labour-duty such as *debt-peonage* evolved. This meant that a peasant was pressed into debt and then forced to work it off for the landlord. As Pearse notes:

> debt-peonage was a device based on trickery and class connivance and used for mobilising the repressive apparatus of the state to capture and hold in bondage individual labourers.[22]

Alongside this, *service-tenure* flourished, whereby the (internal) peasant received usufruct rights to land in exchange for agricultural or other services for the landowner. The transition towards full proletarianisation proceeded slowly and unevenly, with extra-economic coercion persisting into the 1960s in most of the countries of Latin America.

By focusing on the development of the Chilean *hacienda* system we will see in more detail how relations of production in Latin America have developed from the time of the Conquest until the 1960s. A bitter war against the Araucanian people cleared land for the Spanish conquerors who were awarded *mercedes de tierra* (land grants) for their services. By the 17th Century gold was no longer available and cattle production had become profitable. The native settlements were systematically taken over by the commercial and other capitalists of the cities who built up the *hacienda* system of the Central Valley and stabilised their influence over the rural areas. Towards the end of the 17th Century an increased demand for wheat from other parts of South America led to a demand for more labour on the *haciendas*. The institution of *inquilinaje* or service tenure thus became widespread. The *inquilino* worked on the landlords estate in exchange for a plot of land and payment in kind — for example, wood, and the right to graze his animals on the estate. This was not a feudal relation (free mobility of labour existed) nor a purely capitalist relation of production (the wage relation did not predominate). As time went by the wage element was to increase. For the time being — that is the second half of the 19th Century — labour services were actually tightened as demand for agricultural produce on the world market increased. Arnold Bauer notes how

> during the years following 1860, the institution of *inquilinaje* was extended and by 1930 had hardened into a conservative symbiosis with the hacienda system that was not shaken until recent years.[23]

It is interesting to note the parallels of this process with that in Eastern Europe known as the 'second serfdom' of the 16th Century, when increased international demand led to a consolidation of landlord rule. Kay notes 'the similar effects wheat exports had on the consolidation of the large landed estate system (manorial or hacienda) and the political power of the landlords' in both Eastern Europe and Chile'.[24] The *inquilinos*, however, were not serfs in the full feudal sense and there were sufficient reserves of labour in Chile to take up tenancies or carry out seasonal work without extra-economic coercion. Bauer has described how the *inquilinaje* system was tightened up under the impact of a growing market — whereas previously the *inquilino* had to provide one *peon obligado* (bonded worker) to work on the estate after 1850, he had to provide two or even three full-time workers.[25] As McBride wrote in the 1930s, the *inquilino* worked on the *hacienda* '240 days a year, from sunrise to sunset, nearly 10 hours in the winter and more than 12 hours in the summer'.[26] Oppression was sharpened through the debt contracted in the *hacienda* store (the *pulperia*) which was generally owned by the landlord. The landlord was also often the local judge and his political influence was immense, and most *inquilinos* voted according to his orders.

This was the era of the oligarchic state in Chile, which was dominated by the mining, commercial and agrarian fractions of the bourgeoisie. A more capitalist type of agriculture had developed through colonisation in the southern provinces, but the agrarian oligarchy of the central valley retained its pre-eminent political position, based in part on the differential rent it received due to higher fertility in that area. As Roxborough and his co-authors note:

> from Independence until 1920, this small elite retained all the essentials

of power within the new nation-state, using its control over the armed forces to suppress occasional challenges to its rule from landowners further south and mine-owners in the northern desert . . . .[27]

This hegemonic class fraction was, however, highly dependent on the international market, and this was disrupted by the First World War and then the international recession of 1929.

Around 1930 this model of agrarian development entered into crisis, and agriculture basically stagnated from then until the agrarian reform era of the mid 1960s. The increased urban demand for food (as internal migration to the cities and industrialisation accelerated) could not be met by an archaic rural social structure. There was a tendency towards proletarianisation best represented by the decline of the *inquilinos* who, comprising 21% of the rural population in 1935 fell to only 6% in 1965. The land under cultivation now ceased to expand and increases in productivity could be obtained only through mechanisation, greater use of fertilisers and so on, and, of course, a transformation in the labour relations. But this was to undermine the social and economic cohesion of the *hacienda* system and was one of the underlying causes for post-1964 agrarian reforms. As Kay explains:

> the landlord enterprise managed to dominate the *hacienda* system by modernising and expanding its economy and effectively proletarianising the internal peasant enterprise. But, as the landlord no longer allocated tenencies or offered stable employment he gradually lost his source of legitimacy and paternalistic control over peasants.[28]

The effect this had on the political organisation of the peasantry will be examined shortly, for the moment we need to study the process of proletarianisation more carefully.

The decline of the *inquilino* system did not lead to an automatic rise of a 'pure' agricultural proletariat. Two figures emerged to provide the labour previously obtained from the *inquilino*. On the one hand the *voluntarios* (volunteers) who lived on the estate (usually with the *inquilino*) and who worked freely as and when required by the landlord. They were paid a wage and a food ration. The other type of labourer was the *afuerino* (outsider) who came from outside the estate (they were small-holders or migrant labourers) to provide work at harvest time, and then more regularly. A rural proletariat as such developed only in the wheat or cattle *haciendas* and the vineyards of the central zone, and on the sheep farms of the southernmost provinces. Even then, the percentage of agricultural labourers was lower than that of *inquilinos medieros* (sharecroppers) and the *minifundista* smallholders. The proletarianisation of the external *minifundista* peasantry was as sharp as that of his internal counterpart. Kay notes how 'the fragmentation of the external *minifundia* drove more peasants into the seasonal labour market, thus depressing wages.'[29] Proletarianisation was never complete however, because even the *voluntarios* retained a small plot of land to produce some basic subsistence goods.

Was it a feudal or a capitalist system of agriculture which prevailed in Chile after 1930? According to the supporters of the feudalism thesis, the main reason for the stagnation of agriculture since the 1930s was its 'feudal' character, which ignores all the transformations that had occurred since the colonial period. The political effect of this thesis was to restrict the struggle in the countryside to bourgeois-democratic demands. At the other extreme for Gunder Frank:

> The well-known failure of agriculture to supply needed food supplies, dramatized in the case of Chile by the switch from exporting to importing basic foodstuffs, is due not so much to the lack of capitalist or market penetration of a supposedly archaic or feudal countryside as it is to agriculture's incorporation in the monopolistic metropolis-satellite structure of the national and world capitalist system.[30]

If land is held idle as a means of speculation, or to avoid taxes, this does not reflect a 'feudal' mentality. Frank is ubdoubtedly right to reject the thesis that agriculture represented a rigid feudal barrier to the penetration of capitalism. Where he is totally wrong is in making integration into the market the hallmark of capitalism and thus refers to Chilean agrarian relations as capitalist since the 16th Century. The system of *inquilinaje* represented a non-capitalist relation of production, and it was not until the 1950s that wages became more important than payment in kind in that relation. We have already seen how the *inquilino* declined after 1930, as landlords found cultivation of the land more profitable than the labour rents. Kay shows how, since 1930, the landlords were engaged in a significant transformation in the technical and social relations of production on their estates, to such an extent that they became simply capitalist agricultural entrepreneurs. His conclusion is 'that during this period [1930 to 1964] landlords had *almost* completed the transformation of their estates into capitalist enterprises'.[31] The caveat is due to the persistence of *inquilino* labour and *medieros* (sharecroppers) on some estates. This would seem a more satisfactory response to the rather sterile counterposition of 'feudalism' and 'capitalism'.

Politically, the period from 1930 to 1964 saw the gradual decline of the agrarian oligarchy as industrialisation advanced. The state was able to divert a proportion of the significant mining revenue towards industry, thus avoiding a frontal clash between the agrarian and industrial sectors. By the mid-1960s, the industrial bourgeoisie in alliance with foreign capital had become the dominant sector. For economic (insufficient supply of foodstuffs to the city) and political (growing rural class struggle) reasons it began to move against the traditional agrarian sector. It is important to note, however, that it did this in alliance with the new agricultural bourgeoisie, which was just as interested in a more complete capitalist transformation of Chilean agriculture.

We turn finally to the class structure in Chile's agrarian sector, which resulted from the development of capitalism since the 1930s. Table 6.1 based

Table 6.1
Agrarian Class Structure in Chile (1966)

Sector	No	%	Income distribution
Latifundistas	12,737	2	36.7
Rich peasants (permanently hire outside labour)	42,980	7	15.4
Middle peasants (occasionally hire outside labour)	141,477	21	12.7
Minifunistas	132,021	20	
Foremen and Custodians	45,971	7	
Inquilinos (semi-proletarian tenants)	82,367	12	35.2
Medieros (Sharecroppers)	26,861	4	
Afuerinos and voluntarios (wage workers outside and inside the farm)	179,778	27	

Source: Steenland, K. (1974) Rural Strategy under Allende. *Latin American Perspectives*, Vol.1 No.4, pp.132–3.

on a 1966 survey by CIDA (Inter-American Committee of Agrarian Development) provides the basic information. The *latifundistas* or landowning oligarchy, represented scarcely 2% of the rural population, yet they received over one-third of the total income. The rich peasants, or rural bourgeoisie, who were based on the exploitation of hired wage-labour were 7% of the population and received 15% of the total income. The middle peasants, or rural petty-bourgeoisie, who were based on family labour but occasionally hired outside labour were 21% of the population but their share of the income was only 12%. Finally, the *minifundistas* (semi-proletarian small-holders) together with the *inquilinos* (internal peasants), *medieros* (share-croppers) and *afuerino* and *voluntario* wage-workers made up the remaining three-quarters of the rural population, but accounted for only one-third of income. Thus, an uneven distribution of land resulted in a highly unequal distribution of income in the Chilean countryside. This, with small variations, was the general pattern in Latin America prior to the agrarian reforms which are the subject of the next sub-section.[32] It was not only an economically inefficient system but one which produced dangerous tensions for the continued stability of capitalist rule. The agrarian reforms were to be an attempt to preempt a radical resolution of the agrarian question.

Agrarian Reform

Partly as a response to the Cuban revolution, the United States began to promote a policy of agrarian reform in Latin America during the mid-1960s. The intention was to defuse any potential agrarian radicalism which could provide a social base for the guerrilla movements. The left, for its part, supported agrarian reform, often on the basis that the dominant relations of production in the countryside were 'feudal' and, therefore, a transition to capitalism was still pending. The Alliance for Progress was formed in 1961 and in its Charter it declared that:

> programs of comprehensive agrarian reform leading to the effective transformation, where required, of unjust structures and systems of land tenure and use, with a view to replacing *latifundia* and dwarf holdings by an equitable system of land tenure. . . .[33]

The left in Latin America developed a similar reformist project, best articulated in the Chilean Popular Unity programme of 1969. It said that:

> The big landowner is exclusively to blame for the Chilean's lack of food. He is responsible for the backward conditions and for the poverty which characterises the Chilean countryside. . . . These problems have not been resolved by the inadequate land reform of the Christian Democrat government. Only the struggle of the peasant with the support of the entire people can solve these problems.[34]

This was effectively a more radical agrarian reform being posed than that of the Alliance for Progress, but its basic assumptions were similar. The aim was to eradicate the supposedly irrational aspects of *latifundista* agriculture and promote a 'farmer' road to agrarian capitalism.

It is necessary to specify what we actually mean by 'agrarian reform' which has been used in widely differing senses by different sectors.[35] First, it should be clear that an agrarian reform, even if it goes to the extent of nationalising all land, is a *bourgeois* measure, in so far as it does not threaten the capitalist mode of production. The decisive question is what happens to ground rent. In some cases the ex-*latifundistas* transform ground rent into industry, as happened in Peru after the 1968 reformist military agrarian reform. The proponents of agrarian reform argue that it will effect a redistribution of wealth and political power. Usually, however, this is carried out *within* the power bloc (i.e., between fractions of the ruling class) and it would be exceptional for the peasant beneficiaries of agrarian reform actually to join the power bloc. The usual criterion for judging the success of an agrarian reform is the increase in productivity of agrarian produce, but then the question arises as to whom this benefits. Certainly these measures can become radical only if they are inserted within a global project of transforming capitalist society. One last point to consider is whether agrarian reforms are carried out by a *weak* ruling class bowing to peasant pressure or a *strong* ruling class moving to transform the countryside to the benefit of capitalism. This is a fundamental point in assessing the significance of particular agrarian reform experiences.

On this basis we can now build a typology of agrarian reforms in Latin America using the very useful breakdown by Alain de Janvry in Figure 6.2. It shows the way pre-capitalist estates, capitalist estates and commercial farms are affected by agrarian reforms in terms of Lenin's 'roads' to capitalism. We see that Chilean agriculture has gone through three different reforms – one pre-capitalist redistributive (1962–67), a second which was a transition to farmer agriculture (1967–73), and finally, a regressive shift from farmer to junker agriculture since 1973. In Mexico, the first phase of the revolution carried out the redistribution of pre-capitalist estates (1917–34) and later, under the Cárdenas presidency (1934–40), a transition to farmer agriculture followed. There are, of course, alternative typologies of agrarian reform but, as de Janvry correctly notes, 'none of these typologies uses the concept of mode of production (transitions) or social class structure and control of the state (shifts among roads of development)'.[36] These alternative conceptions basically narrow down to a 'modernising' version – pre-capitalist redistributive and transition to junker – and a 'reformist' one – transition to farmer, junker to farmer, and farmer redistributive. Then, the Cuban agrarian reform becomes simply a 'radical' agrarian reform, which is hardly sufficient to describe a transition to socialism. This schema is an improvement on this but it still oversimplifies, as when the Christian Democrat and Popular Unity agrarian reforms in Chile are classified equally as 'transition to farmer', in spite of the radically different political context. It is to the Chilean experience that we now turn to put some historical flesh on this rather abstract typology.

The Allessandri government launched a very timid agrarian reform in 1962, but its results were extremely partial only. More decisive measures were taken by the Christian Democrat government which came to power in Chile in 1964. It was seen by many as a showcase of the Alliance for Progress project of a 'revolution in liberty' in Latin America, which would thwart possible repetitions of the Cuban (real) revolution. The agrarian reform legislation introduced by this government in 1967 had the dual aim of modernising the agrarian structure and building up a base of political support for the Christian Democrats amongst the peasantry. In the first instance it authorised the government to expropriate properties of over 80 'basic irrigated hectares' (a standardised measure on the basis of one hectare in the very fertile Maipo Valley). Repayment to the landowner would vary according to how effectively the land had been cultivated. In fact, though the terms for land repayment were not always favourable, farm machinery, livestock and buildings were paid for in full. The beneficiaries of the reform were organised in *asentamientos* (settlements) which were managed jointly with CORA (Agrarian Reform Corporation). As Castillo and Lehman explain:

the 1967 Reform Law envisaged an ultimately individualist model,

Figure 6.2
Typology of Land Reform in Latin America

Land tenure	*Precapitalist estates and reform sector*	*Capitalist estates and reform sector*	*Commercial farms and reform sector*
Pre-capitalist estates	Pre-cap Redistributive Mexico, 1917–34 Chile, 1962–67 Colombia, 1961–67	Transition to Junker Colombia, 1968– Ecuador, 1964– Bolivia, 1952– Peru, 1964–69 Venezuela, 1959–	Transition to Farmer Mexico, 1934–40 Chile, 1967–73 Guatemala, 1952–54
Capitalist estates	Transition from Junker	Junker Redistributive Costa Rica, 1963– Shift from Farmer to Junker Chile, 1973–	Shift from Junker to Farmer Peru, 1969–75
Commercial farms	Transition from Farmer Guatemala, 1954–		Farmer Redistributive Mexico, 1940– Dominican Republic, 1963–

Source: Adapted from de Janvry, A. (1981) *The Agrarian Question and Reformism in Latin America*. Baltimore, the Johns Hopkins University Press, p.205.

> providing for collective organisation only during a transitional period
> and subsequently only if the beneficiaries so desired.[37]

The Frei government's rhetoric was not really matched by the actual
results of agrarian reform. In fact, less than one-third of the *latifundios* were
expropriated, and even then the landowner could choose a 'reserve' of prime
land under 80 hectares to operate himself. The *asentamientos*, which emerged
in the reformed sector, benefited some sectors of the peasants, but the
voluntarios (on farm wage workers) had only limited rights and the *afuerinos*
(seasonal wage labourers) none at all. There was a distinct tendency for the
new *asentados* to become simply another landlord in their relation with the
landless peasants. Finally, the *asentados* retained their private plots, to which
they usually dedicated considerably more attention than to the co-operative
enterprise. Perhaps, however, just as important as the failures of this period is
the fact that it legitimised agrarian reform and made it easier for the Popular
Unity government to attempt more radical measures. Cristobal Kay provides
a useful summary of this phase of agrarian reform in Chile:

> the Christian Democrats had the clear intention of forming a privileged
> group of peasants, the asentados, who, with the subdivision of
> asentamientos would eventually become a rural petty bourgeoisie,
> spreading the peasant mode of production in the countryside, acting as
> a buffer for the social tensions resulting from the conflicts between the
> rural bourgeoisie and the agrarian proletariat, and opposing more
> radical land reform.[38]

This attempt at co-optation was only partially successful because it unleashed
class conflicts in the countryside which would continue into the next more
radical phase.

When President Allende came to power in 1970 his government was
committed to radicalising the agrarian reform of the Christian Democrats,
but under the terms of the 1967 law, because he lacked the parliamentary
majority to pass a new law.[39] Nevertheless, the provisions of that law were
stretched to the maximum and expropriations proceeded rapidly. On the last
day of 1970 the government expropriated the first *latifundio* — 530,000
hectares in Tierra del Fuego — which was the biggest in the world. In Table
6.2 we see the extent to which the rural structure was transformed between
1965 and 1972. In 1965 estates over 80 hectares represented over half the
total hectarage but in 1972 they were reduced to under 3%. The reformed
sector held no land in 1965 but over one third of the total in 1972. The
agrarian bourgeoisie retreated to the farms between 20 and 80 hectares. On
the other hand the *minifundistas* holding less than five hectares and the
middle peasants holding between five and 20 hectares did not increase their
share of the land. From when it came to power in 1970 to mid-1972 the
Allende government expropriated 3,282 *latifundios* equivalent to
approximately 442,000 basic irrigated hectares. Many *latifundistas*' escaped

the reform, however, by subdividing their holdings during the Christian Democratic period. Of the 90,000 beneficiaries of the agrarian reform, two-thirds gained their rights to land under the Allende government. In fact this government expropriated twice as many holdings in its first one and a half years in office than the Christian Democrats had done in its six years in office. The changes were not only quantitative as we shall now see.

The *asentamientos* clearly failed to meet the criteria for a socialist transformation of the countryside, but at first Popular Unity did not advance an alternative. The CERA (Agrarian Reform Centre) was then formed to initiate a collectivist mode of agricultural production, joining together expropriated *latifundios* in order to make more rational use of the infrastructure. They also aimed at drawing in the wage labourers to establish a more egalitarian structure. However, the differences from the *asentamientos* were not always clear, peasant resistance was considerable and, as Steenland concludes, 'the existing CERA's were in most cases exactly like the asentamientos, with the exception that they were not to be divided after the period of three to five years'.[40] Another form promoted in some areas was the CEPRO (Production Centre) which were straightforward state farms encouraged by the more radical components of the Popular Unity coalition. Here, collective work predominated over the individual plot of land, but this form remained quite marginal (mainly applying to agro-industrial enterprises). Peasant resistance to both CERAs and CEPROs — which should not, however, be generalised to the whole rural population — led to the formation of the *comite campesino* (peasant committee) in other areas. These were designed to smooth over the worst features of the *asentamiento* and draw in the seasonal labourers by agreement with the settled workers.

Table 6.2
Land Distribution in Chile (1965–72)

Farms by Basic Irrigated Hectares	1965		1972	
	% farms	% hectareage	% farms	% hectareage
Less than 5 (minifundistas)	81.4	9.7	79.3	9.7
5/20 (middle peasants)	11.5	12.7	11.3	13.0
20/40	3.0	9.5	3.3	11.6
40/60	1.3	7.1	2.5	14.5
60/80	0.8	5.7	1.6	12.8
More than 80	2.0	55.3	0.1	2.9
Reformed sector	0	0	1.9	35.5

Source: Steenland, K. (1974) Rural Strategy under Allende. *Latin American Perspectives*, Vol.1 No.4, pp.132–3.

The most radical aspect of land reform was when peasants took it upon themselves to seize the landlords' estate without waiting for governmental approval. The *tomas* (land seizures) were a remarkable feature of this period – in 1967 there were nine such seizures; in 1968, 26; in 1969, 148 seizures; in 1970, 456, and in 1971, 1,278 seizures.[41] These were in response to the failures of the agrarian reform to comprehensively draw in the whole rural working population. They occurred on a massive scale in the southern provinces where the indigenous Mapuches began to reclaim their hereditary land rights by simply moving the fences at night (often alongside militants of the far left). The Mapuches had represented three quarters of the rural population of Cautín province and yet they owned less than one quarter of the land. The *tomas* broke the rather artificial 80 hectare limit on expropriations, often taking over the modern farms of the agrarian bourgeoisie. Thus they were challenging the official policy of restricting the rural class struggle to the 'feudal' *latifundio*. This radical outflanking of the official land reform process had a considerable political effect and forced some of the Popular Unity parties to support the *tomas*, albeit belatedly.

There were, in conclusion, several limitations to the agrarian reform carried out by Allende's government. One of the most general problems was the different meanings which could be attached to the aim of 'ending the *latifundio*'. For the Communist Party and its allies this meant limiting the targets of the agrarian reform to the 'feudal' sector. After that, the main task was seen as winning the 'battle for production' by increasing rural productivity. This, logically enough, meant not alienating the agrarian bourgeoisie and the middle peasants. For the left of the Socialist Party and particularly the extra-parliamentary MIR (Movement of the Revolutionary Left) this was seen as a demobilising strategy. It was considered to be more important to intensify the rural class struggle and destroy agrarian capitalism as a whole, even if producion was disrupted in doing so. The first strategy focused on production and the second on the question of power as primary in the transition to socialism – in practice neither was fully resolved. For Steenland, Popular Unity:

> pushed a traditional progressive land reform to its ultimate consequences, always within the context of capitalism. Such a land reform increased the class consciousness and the combativity of the peasantry, and opened up the possibility of radicalizing the land reform into a socialist one, through the stressing of collective forms of exploitation and the creation of dual power in the countryside.[42]

We shall shortly examine the nature of the class struggle in the rural areas, but first we must turn to the effects of the counter-revolutionary victory of 1973 on the agrarian structure.

When the Allende government was violently overthrown by a military coup in 1973 it was inevitable that the new regime would try to set the clock back in the countryside as much as everywhere else in Chilean society. Farms in the reformed sector were systematically returned to their former owners or divided up and sold to individuals. By 1979 somewhat less than one-third of the land expropriated in the agrarian reform from 1965 to 1973 had been returned to its former owners. In the remaining *asentamientos* the more 'deserving' peasants received titles to private plots whereas the more 'subversive' elements were weeded out in an atmosphere of military terror. By mid-1979 the process of land assignment was basically completed, with 36,746 peasants having been allocated an average of 10 standard hectares each. The massive privatisation of the reformed sector does not mean that the military have returned to the status quo ante. As Kay notes:

> a new agrarian structure is emerging as a result of the counter-reform and the process of capitalist socio-economic differentiation. Nevertheless the *latifundio* has so far not been reconstituted.[43]

The main beneficiaries of the Junta's agrarian policy have been not the remains of the old oligarchy but the agrarian bourgeoisie with their modernised farms producing fruit and vegetables for export. The middle farmer fostered by the Christian Democrats, survived the Allende period intact, and was now to flourish under the militarist-monetarist regime.

The privatising drive of the military regime extended to the state marketing agency and the subsidised state farm machinery enterprises. Technical assistance and economic support to smallholders declined. All in all, its economic effects were disastrous if measured in terms of the supposed function of agriculture to produce cheap and plentiful foodstuffs for the city. Kay reports that wheat production in 1976 was just over half that of 1971, and only equivalent to that of the 1920s when the population was half the size of what it is today.[44] One reason why this is acceptable to the regime is that the urban working-class wages are so depressed that food consumption has declined dramatically. For the peasants, the increased cost of inputs and consumption has driven many into debt, reproducing the old institution of debt-peonage. As Winn points out:

> the rural counter-revolution is recreating (and with a vengeance) the very social problem which the agrarian reform had been intended to resolve – and politically alienating the peasantry in the process.[45]

Even the peasantry who supported the anti-Allende opposition now suffer the consequences of the military rural policy. The picture today, following Castillo and Lehman, is of a 'reformed' agrarian structure:

> in which an impoverished small-scale production sector coexists not with large *latifundia* but with medium-scale farms which use capital intensively and produce for export or for the upper income groups.[46]

Peasant Movements

As we saw in Chapter 3, peasants are neither revolutionary nor conservative as such. We will now try to establish a more positive typology of peasant behaviour on the basis of a study of the Chilean peasant movement, particularly during the Popular Unity period (1970–73). Some more general points will be made first.

The attempts by Hamza Alavi and Eric Wolf to distinguish between the political behaviour of the various layers of the peasantry are an advance on simplified assumptions of peasant revolutions.[47] Clearly, each revolutionary situation where the rural population has played a role – from Russia to China, Mexico to Cuba – different categories will have responded to *particular* situations. In other words, it is not an abstract 'desire for land' which motivates an undifferentiated peasantry. In his book *Agrarian Revolution* Jeffrey Paige has provided a useful analysis of how peasant protest results from different agrarian systems.[48] Protest will occur when rural productivity can be increased only by sharper exploitation, as in the *hacienda* system or in sharecropping. Furthermore, protest movements require some form of favourable conditions to organise, be it a reformist government or the presence of a broad anti-colonial movement. Most interestingly, Paige relates the type of protest movement and its aims to the dominant agrarian structure. So, whereas the *hacienda* system is most likely to produce a peasant revolt, the plantation (a more mechanised commercial enterprise) will lead to a reformist labour movement. The migratory labour estate typical of parts of Central America, with its encroachment on community lands, will typically lead to a revolutionary nationalist movement if conditions are right.

Though one should not generalise in this way too much, the underlying primary cause of peasant revolt is the disruption caused by the advance of capitalism into the countryside. Paige's work lends support to this thesis which had earlier been advanced by Wolf for whom peasants rebel 'where the social dislocations produced by the market go unchecked, [and] the crisis of power also deranges the networks which link the peasant population to the larger society . . .'[49] The spread and diffusion of capitalism typically produces an ecological crisis, as commercialisation threatens the traditional peasant access to natural resources. Capitalism is also revolutionary because it loosens some of the traditional bonds which subject the peasantry and replace them with the impersonal bonds of the market place. Barrington Moore's broad historical sweep of peasants and revolutions similarly concludes that:

> where the peasants have revolted, there are indications that new and capitalist methods of pumping the economic surplus out of the peasantry had been added while the traditional ones lingered on or were even intensified.[50]

This would seem to support the thesis of uneven and combined development, mentioned in an earlier chapter, which lies at the root of capitalist expansion in the periphery. For this diffuse peasant revolt to become a revolution it is, of course, necessary that alliances be established with other forces in society, in the modern era the industrial working class.

In the study of Latin American peasant movements there have always been simplifications deriving particularly from a heroic vision of Zapata's peasant army of the Mexican revolution and a misreading of the Cuban revolution. As Roxborough notes correctly:

> some of the causes of the Mexican Revolution may have been agrarian, and in the course of the revolution the peasantry may have been mobilised as never before, but it was in its innermost nature not a peasant revolution but a bourgeois revolution.[51]

The peasant armies of Emiliano Zapata and Pancho Villa played an indispensable role in the revolution, but they did not on their own determine its dynamic or outcome.[52] In Cuba, some histories of the revolution have tended to romanticise the role of the peasantry when, in fact, Castro's Rebel Army was more dependent on the *urban* resistance network for logistical support and supplies. Some of the rural groups who supported Castro were not really peasants at all, but rather a rural proletariat, as with the sugar cane workers. That it carried out a radical land reform does not make the Cuban revolution a 'peasant war' in any real sense.[53] Another area in which simplifications occur is on the 'revolutionary potential of the peasants' type of discussion. Huizer rightly points out that:

> there is not a characteristic and generalised 'peasant mentality' that is basically different from the mentality of other people. Peasants are 'apathetic' or 'organisable' according to circumstance, which, in the rural areas of Latin America, is determined by the prevailing 'culture' of repression.[54]

Aníbal Quijano provides a typology of peasant movements in Latin America which, though firmly dated in the 1960s, is a useful general framework.[55] There are several types of 'pre-political' peasant organisations, such as social banditry, racial and messianic movements. Sometimes social banditry merges into a more political movement, as in the long years of *la violencia* in Colombia after 1948. Racial-based revolts, such as those of the Indian serfs in Bolivia prior to the 1952 Revolution, paved the way for more organic social changes. Progressively these movements are replaced by more directly political peasant organisations. Quijano distinguishes the 'reformist-agrarianism' movements 'which seek partially to reform the social order, and propose the elimination of a few of the most oppressive effects of the existing power structure.'[56] These only rarely threaten the fundamentals of the agrarian social structure, although in practice they may become radicalised (i.e., 'revolutionary reformism'). This happens especially when the movement is repressed by the state, as with the *ligas camponesas* (peasant leagues) in

Brazil, and the rural union movement of La Convención in Peru in the early 1960s.[57] Finally, revolutionary agrarianism calls for a fundamental restructuring of the power structure as it affects the peasantry. One of the most far reaching examples, apart from Cuba of course, was the peasant based revolution of 1952 in Bolivia rooted in an alliance with the radical miners.[58] On this basis we turn our attention to the Chilean case, which will illustrate some of the broader problems of conceptualisation outlined above.

The first rural workers strike in Chile exploded in 1912 in the province of Magallanes in the south of the country.[59] Intense exploitation, low wages, arbitrary dismissals and various kinds of personal abuse by the landlords drove the rural workers to unionise. Particularly after the First World War, the Chilean Workers Federation (FOCH) spread its influence from the city to the countryside. The collaboration of the urban and mining proletariat helped forge an early worker-peasant alliance in Chile. One of the most militant early actions of the peasant movement was the 1934 Ranquil revolt. With their primitive carbines, hatchets and knives, over 1,000 peasants took on the troops. In 1935, the National League for the Defence of Poor Peasants was formed by sharecroppers, small holders, agricultural workers and *inquilinos*. It demanded a reduction of land rent, an end to evictions and an improvement of peasant housing. Reflecting the evolution of national politics the rural movements had its ups and downs, but it gained steadily in strength up to the 1960s. In fact, the post-1964 agrarian reforms cannot be understood outside the context of this steady pattern of rural insurgency. As Emilo Zapata one of the leaders of the Ranquil rising was to say many years later — 'The Agrarian Reform is not Frei's but is a product of the years of struggle and the suffering they imposed on us'.[60]

In a later period, under the Christian Democrat government, there was a flourishing peasant movement again. Frei hoped to create an alliance between a peasantry unionised from above and the urban bourgeoisie he represented. By promising land distribution, the Christian Democrats effectively gained wide support amongst the peasantry. Whereas in 1964 there were only a few thousand rural workers organised in 19 unions, by 1969 there were 394 unions covering 103,644 workers.[61] Mobilisations began to go further than the official guidelines which sought to contain them within a corporatist framework. The rise of the peasant movement culminated in the 1969 first ever national agrarian strike. At this stage the rural class struggle was probably in advance of that in the cities, in terms of the breadth of its organisation and the militancy of its methods. Strikes in the countryside were rising constantly and the first *tomas* (land seizures) took place. The effect on peasant consciousness was considerable. Ecological analysis of voting data from the 1958 and 1964 elections suggests a positive relationship between areas with a high proportion of agricultural wage labour and a high proportion of votes for the Socialist-Communist coalition.[62] Overall, these years demonstrated an upsurge in class solidarity and commitment to collective struggle in the countryside.[63] This class consciousness was to deepen under the Popular Unity government as part of the overall upheaval of society in those years.

There is no one factor to account for agrarian radicalism in Chile, but one interesting hypothesis is that peasants were radicalised through contact with the miners and urban workers generally. This certainly is an international pattern, with the children of peasants migrating to the cities of work and returning with new ideas. A rural group particularly susceptible to this type of influence was the *afuerinos*, the seasonal wage labourers. As Petras reports in his study:

> the contact many have with industrial workers, especially with miners, who have long been the center of Chilean working-class organisation, gives the afuerinos a taste of unions, of class conflict rather than submissiveness, of the possibilities inherent in class organisation, and provides them with different explanations of social reality than the inquilinos.[64]

A major weakness of the Popular Unity period was that the government did not tap the militancy of this sector. The 250,000 *afuerinos* (a third of the active rural population) were never organically incorporated into the process of social change and political mobilisation. This was due, no doubt, to the fact that their revindications — stable employment and access to land — conflicted with the self-imposed limitations of the Popular Unity rural strategy. These aims of the *afuerinos* could threaten the stability of a government, which restricted its offensive to the *latifundista* and not the whole agrarian bourgeoisie. When *afuerinos* were present in the land seizures they were soon reminded of their 'outsider' status when the 'inside' workers had achieved their aims. Thus the radical potential of this stratum was dissipated.

When Allende came to power in 1970 the countryside was in turmoil. The socialist coalition moved rapidly to consolidate its position amongst the rural population. Previously, two-thirds of the unionised rural workers were in organisations controlled by the Christian Democrats and one third had left-wing leaderships. Now the proportions were reversed, as the more radicalised Christian Democratic sectors passed over to the left. Even Jacques Chonchol, who had been Minister of Agriculture under Frei, joined one of the left-wing parties and held the same position in Allende's government.[65] By the end of their period in office the Popular Unity leftist coalition had more than doubled the number of unionised workers, which by then organised most of the *voluntarios* and *inquilinos*, around a third of the *minifundistas* and only a few of the *afuerinos*. Strikes continued to escalate after 1970, and, as Kay notes:

> although the aims of these strikes still revolved around the solution of labor and economic problems, they increasingly became an expression of peasant solidarity.[66]

The renaissance of agrarian unionism, since its legalisation in 1967, took place on a clearly proletarian basis. The aims of the movement reflected the accelerated proletarianisation of the countryside in that they stress wages, conditions of work, and the enforcement of social legislation. Struggles *against* proletarianisation – to recover personal land plots and rights of pasture – were rarer, even though they could be an effective means to combat pauperisation, given the decline of real monetary wages.[67]

The main form taken by the peasant movement locally was that of the *consejos campesinos* (peasant councils), which never really took on the functions of a dual power in the countryside. Their role was more that of an intermediary between the government and the peasants on technical matters. In the more militant areas the *consejos* were created as a product of rank and file participation, and not simply by decree. Even so, they were not marked by a great deal of success, partly from a lack of official support and partly because they had no clear political functions. Essentially, as Castells writes, 'the "Consejos campesinos" are not elements for an alliance of the exploited peasantry, nor organs of a popular power. . . .'[68] They neither constituted alternatives to bourgeois state power – only parts of the government were in the hands of the working-class parties – nor did they resolve the fatal divisions within the peasantry. Even a rural organiser who was sympathetic to the government said later that 'the PU [Popular Unity] leadership saw the councils as spokesmen for government policy – as a means of participation, yes, but within the dominant strategy of gradualism. . . .'[69] Without real power the *consejos* inevitably stagnated and reproduced all the divisions between wage-labourers, sharecroppers and the reformed sector small holders. When the objective situation was moving towards a civil war in the countryside the *consejos* were unable to articulate a strong peasant power to take on the role of rural soviets.

The reformed sector of Chilean agriculture did not provide the most radical vanguard to the peasant movement as some had expected. Most of the studies show that conservatism set in very rapidly after the agrarian reform. Kyle Steenland's perceptive account of one of the most militant groups, the Mapuches, concludes that:

> They were militant when it came time to take land away from those who had exploited them. They were conservative, however, when it came to their own land on the reservations . . . generations of poverty had bred revolutionaries, but the dependence on scarce land for subsistence had bred conservatives – with the same people.[70]

Other sectors were more consistently militant. Brian Loveman's historical study shows how the periodic crises in the nitrate fields brought waves of unemployed workers back to the countryside.[71] The hegemony of landlord authority was increasingly contested by these workers with urban/trade union experience. This occurred to such an extent that in the 1970s landowners actually refused to employ ex-nitrate workers, even during the harvest season. The significant proletarianisation which occurred in the rural areas between 1930 and 1960 – both 'internal' (the *inquilinos* becoming effectively wage labourers) and 'external' (through the breaking of the *minifundia*) – provided the motive force for rural insurgency in the mid-1960s. This would appear to fit in with the general conclusion earlier that the advance of capitalism creates the social forces which will oppose it.

It is not idle speculation to assess the chances of an alternative rural strategy during this period. As the general political crisis sharpened in mid-1972 the Communist Party held that with the 'end of the latifundios' the more serious and difficult problem remained – 'to organise the new agriculture with the central objective of increasing agrarian production'.[72] Against this the extra-parliamentary MIR (and some sectors of Popular Unity) urged the rapid expropriation of the rural bourgeoisie, reducing the land limit to 40 hectares, and the expropriated landlord's right to a 'reserve' alongside the animals and farm machinery, and the granting of more powers to the *Consejos Comunales*.[73] Essentially, this strategy maintained that the key question was the transformation of the relations of production in the countryside, and not the increase in the forces of production, as the Communist Party insisted. Changing peasant consciousness was more important than meeting production targets. This was not necessarily utopian. As one of the more leftist rural activists recalls:

> The growth of *campesino* consciousness in this period was impressive. They were sharply aware of the question of power. Following the first bosses strike [October 1972], they regularized their contacts with the urban workers and industrial cordons [dual power bodies]. Many distribution arrangements developed in the strike were maintained. The two sectors held regular consultations, political as well as practical.[74]

The potential for a solid worker-peasant alliance must surely have existed in this type of situation. Its development could have led to intensified popular mobilisation and popular power.

Prospects

According to de Janvry:

> Today, precapitalist estates with rent in labor services have, for all practical purposes, disappeared in Latin America. Those with rent in kind remain important only in some Central American countries and in parts of Brazil, but even there they represent fundamentally capitalist social relations.[75]

This final section will illustrate this proposition with a brief look at the present trend towards 'agribusiness' – agriculture as simply another branch of capitalism. Capital has gradually brought agriculture under its sway but this does not mean that the 'agrarian question' is resolved, only that its form has now changed.

The changes in Latin America since the 1960s have been far-reaching. One element in this is the so-called Green Revolution, which entailed the use of improved seed, more fertiliser and modern production methods. As Burbach and Flynn report, 'Between 1965 and 1975, fertiliser consumption more than tripled and the number of tractors increased by roughly 75 percent.'[76] This advance was concentrated in a few countries — Mexico, Brazil, Argentina and Colombia — and then only particular regions within them. Though uneven, the shift towards agribusiness has fundamentally changed the social patterns of Latin American agriculture. The methods of 'scientific management' were transferred from the factory to the farm, which now became a capitalist enterprise like any other. Wage labour became absolutely predominant. An agrarian bourgeoisie has as its counterpart an agrarian proletariat. As capitalist agriculture destroyed small scale subsistence plots — in much the same way as monopoly capital absorbs its competitors industry — so the mass of dispossessed peasants becoming casual labourers increased. Seen in this context, agrarian reform is not necessarily inimical to capitalist interests. Rather, it effects a rationalisation of the agrarian class structure and permits the flourishing of a dynamic agrarian capitalism.

The new agribusiness is often tightly integrated into urban/industrial society. As Burbach and Flynn note:

> agribusiness in the third world means an integrated food system that extends from factory to consumer — from food production to the manufacture of farm implements and pesticides to food processing and food marketing.[77]

Agriculture is now 'rationalised' along capitalist lines, it is integrated into the capital circuit, but it is also internationalised. For the main actors in this new phase are large multinational corporations which dominate the world food industry. One of these agribusiness giants is the Del Monte Corporation, which is the biggest producer of tinned fruits and vegetables in the world, with plantations in every continent of the Third World.[78] In the grain trade, dominated by five huge companies, one of these, Cargill, is particularly adept at controlling production from the fields to the market place:

> they control local grain elevators, storage bins, railroad cars, shipping barges, and port elevators; they operate charter companies and control shipping to every part of the world; and in scores of countries they own port facilities and processing plants.[79]

Agrarian modernisation has now become an effective alternative to agrarian reform. During the 1950s and 1960s agrarian reform was necessary to create a land market and to free the peasantry from their traditional bonds to the land.

By the 1970s international capital had become the dominant element in Latin American agriculture which moved towards the concentration of production. Peasant agriculture was not necessarily destroyed, because it could be profitably subordinated to the big concerns. Furthermore, subsistence production could bear part of the costs of the reproduction of rural wage-labour. Given the undesirable political consequences of proletarianisation in a context of high unemployment, international financial organisations such as the World Bank and the Inter-American Bank have promoted efforts to strengthen 'small-scale farming'. These projects aim at maintaining (or creating) a class of small farmers serving the internal market and acting as a buffer in the rural class struggle. This is effectively a selective modernisation of part of the peasantry, which can then act in a subcontracting relation with agribusiness. As Sergio Cajarville explains:

> agribusiness provides peasants with credits, technical assistance and supervision. In exchange, they ensure crops at low costs and the reimbursement of credits (by way of their production outputs).[80]

This system is a perfect illustration of how capital reproduces non-capitalist relations of production to its advantage. The peasant bears all the risks, works longer hours and boosts the productivity of international capital's investments in agriculture.

One area where a type of 'wildcat capitalism' has gone furthest in its predatory march into the rural areas is the Amazon region of Brazil.[81] The super-exploitation of labour, and the extraction of absolute surplus value here rule supreme. The agrarian expansion of this area is based on the penetration of national and international capital from the dynamic industrialised South-East of the country. In this process, as Cardoso and Muller write, 'exploitation and progress, semi-servitude and big capitalism, violence and economic growth are not separated as water from oil, rather they fuse to allow the expansion of the frontier. . . .'[82] The state provides the necessary infrastructure — such as the Transamazonian highway — and subsidises the expansion of private capital. As in the process of 'primitive accumulation', violence is the midwife of this new cycle of expansion into the Amazon region. The naked repression of the indigenous peoples — sometimes by the very state agencies charged with their protection — is the most well-known aspect. But it also affects every pioneer who takes seriously the government's aim of 'opening up' the Amazon. After the arduous task of clearing the jungle they are often moved out by the big business consortiums who naturally have the support of the law-enforcement agencies. As the Estado de São Paulo reported in 1975:

> After ten years, the results of the policy of colonization are extremely disappointing, if not for the colonisers with greater resources, at least for the great majority of the people involved in this process: the peasants expelled from their land of origin, and the natives of Amazonia virtually

transformed into a colonialized people.[83]

The beneficiaries of this wildcat capitalist expansion are, of course, the monopoly capitalists — national as much as foreign. In spite of the legal limit of 3,000 hectares for properties, the huge *latifundia* prosper — an American, Daniel Ludwig, bought one and a half million hectares in the area in 1962. Volkswagen owns a 140,000 hectare 'farm', King's Ranch has 100,000 hectares, etc. Alongside the traditional *fazendeiros* (landowners) of the South-East, many of the transnationals, such as Goodyear, Nestlé, Mitsubishi, Swift, etc have moved into the profitable cattle raising business there. These often sell their produce directly to markets in Europe or the USA. For the workers on these agro-industrial enterprises semi-servile labour relations are the rule, except for a few paternalistic 'showcases'. Even President Medici was reportedly shocked when he visited Ludwig's Jari complex in 1973 (this was bought by government and private Brazilian interests in 1982) and saw the working, housing and sanitary conditions of the workers there. A 'social plan' was hurriedly elaborated to alleviate the 'regime of semi-slavery' which his government had, of course, created the conditions for. The notorious subcontracting system, the lack of work contracts, the control over labour mobility, all make for a reproduction of non-capitalist relations of production at the very frontier of monopoly capital's expansion.

Today, the centre of gravity of the class struggle in Latin America has shifted decisively from the countryside to the city. Its future course will depend primarily on the evolution of the labour movements in the urban conurbations of Brazil, Mexico, Argentina, Colombia, Venezuela, Chile, Peru, and even, also in Central America. This in no way means that the 'agrarian question' has now been resolved by capitalism and that the specific oppression of the rural population can be simply subsumed under the general anti-capitalist struggle. What can no longer be posed realistically is an alliance between workers and industrial capitalists to vanquish the 'feudal' *latifundia*. The industrial and agrarian faces of capitalism can simply not be opposed in this simplistic manner, regardless of the competition which exists between these two sectors. The experience of Chile under Allende shows that the prime axis of the class struggle is in the cities, pitting the capitalist class against a growingly assertive proletariat. But the failure to achieve a successful agrarian policy — that is in economic *and* political terms — played a not insignificant role in crystallising a counter-revolutionary class alliance.[85] The Chilean peasantry did vacillate between the wage workers and the capitalists, as Lenin described in the opening quotation of this chapter. The popular government was not able to resolve this vacillation by demonstrating that an independent working class organisation waging a consistent class struggle could pose a realistic long term alternative for the peasantry. The terms on which *this* alliance can be posed in the future will displace previous debates from the populist period on alliances with the 'national bourgeoisie'.

References

1. Lenin, V.I. (1936) *Selected Works 12 – Theory of the Agrarian Question.* London, Lawrence and Wishart, pp.296-7.
2. Marx, K. (1981) *Capital* Vol.3. London, Penguin, p.751.
3. Rey, P.P. (1973) *Les Alliances de Classes.* Paris, Maspero, p.20.
4. See Lenin, V.I. (1964) *The Development of Capitalism in Russia.* Moscow, Progress Publishers. For a broad discussion of the various 'paths', see Goodman, D. & Redclift, M. (1981) *From Peasant to Proletariat: Capitalist Development and Agrarian Transitions.* Oxford, Basil Blackwell.
5. Lenin, V.I. (1936) *Selected Works 3.* London, Lawrence and Wishart, p.280.
6. Kay, C. (1981) Political Economy, Class Alliances and Agrarian Change in Chile. *The Journal of Peasant Studies*, Vol.8 No.4:486.
7. Meade, T. (1978) The Transition to Capitalism in Brazil: Notes on a Third Road. *Latin American Perspectives*, Vol.V No.3.
8. Ibid., p.15.
9. Janvry, A. de (1981) *The Agrarian Question and Reformism in Latin America.* Baltimore, The Johns Hopkins Press, p.109.
10. See Flichman, G. (1977) *La renta del suelo y el desarollo agrario argentino.* Mexico, Siglo XXI.
11. Marx, K. (1981) *Capital* Vol.3, p.925.
12. Ibid., p.930.
13. Ibid., p.932.
14. Banaji, J. (1980) Summary of selected parts of Kantsky's *The Agrarian Question. The Articulation of Modes of Production*, (ed) H. Wolpe. London, Routledge and Kegan Paul, p.64.
15. See the discussion in Amin, S. and Vergopoulos, K. (1974) *La Question Paysanne et le Capitalisme.* Paris, Anthropos.
16. Laclau, E. (1969) Modos de produccion, sistemas económicos y población excedente. Aproximación histórica a los casos argentino y chileno. *Revista Latinoamericana de Sociologia* (Buenos Aires, Argentina) Vol.1, No.2:293.
17. Morner, M. (1977) 'Landlords and 'peasants' and the outer world during the national period. *Land and labour in Latin America*, (ed) K. Duncan and I. Rutledge, Cambridge, Cambridge University Press, p.456.
18. Ibid., p.457.
19. Janvry, A. de (1981) op.cit., p.110.
20. Pearse, A. (1975) *The Latin American Peasant.* London, Frank Cass, p.21.
21. Ibid.
22. Ibid., p.32.
23. Bauer, A. (1975) *Chilean Rural Society from the Spanish Conquest to 1930.* Cambridge, Cambridge University Press, p.159.
24. Kay, C. (1981) op.cit., p.491.

25. Bauer, A. (1975) *Chilean Rural Society*, p.159.

26. McBride, G. (1935) *Chile, su tierra y su gente*. Santiago, Ed Universitaria, cited in Vitale, L. (1980) *Interpretación Marxista de la Historia de Chile. De semicolonia inglesa a semicolonia norteamericana*. Barcelona, Ed Fontamara, p.60.

27. Roxborough, I., O'Brien, P. and Roddick, J. (1977) *Chile: The State and Revolution*. London, Macmillan, p.5.

28. Kay, C. (1977) The development of the Chilean *hacienda* system, 1850-1973. *Land and Labour in Latin America*, p.123.

29. Ibid., p.120-1.

30. Frank, A.G. (1971) *Capitalism and Underdevelopment in Latin America*, p.123.

31. Kay, C. (1981) Political Economy, Class Alliances, and Agrarian Change in Chile, op.cit., p.495.

32. For more general discussions of the land tenure system in Latin America see Barraclough, S. (ed) (1973) *Agrarian Structure in Latin America*, Lexington, Mass., Lexington Books; Feder, E. (1971) *The Rape of the Peasantry*. New York, Anchor Books; and Lindquist, S. (1979) *Land and Power in Latin America*. London, Penguin.

33. Cited in Petras, J. and La Porte, R. (1973) *Cultivating Revolution – The United States and Agrarian Reform in Latin America*. New York, Vintage Books, p.381.

34. Allende, S. (1973) *Chile's Road to Socialism*. London, Penguin Books, p.28.

35. I draw here on Gutelman, M. (1974) *Structures et Réformes Agraires*. Paris, Maspero; for a broader analysis of agrarian reform in Latin America see Stavenhagen, R. (ed) (1970) *Agrarian Problems and Peasant Movements in Latin America*. New York, Anchor Books; and Griffin, K. (1975) *The Political Economy of Agrarian Change*. London, Macmillan.

36. Janvry, A. de (1981) op.cit., p.211.

37. Castillo, L. and Lehman, D. (1982) Chile's Three Agrarian Reforms: The Inheritors. *Bulletin of Latin American Research*, Vol.1 No.2:28. For an overview of the Christian Democrat agrarian reform see Kaufman, R. (1972) *The Politics of Land Reform in Chile, 1950-1970*. Cambridge, Mass., Harvard University Press.

38. Kay, C. (1976) Agrarian Reform and The Transition to Socialism. *Allende's Chile* (ed) P. O'Brien. New York, Praeger, p.81.

39. One of the best discussions of the Allende agrarian reform is contained in *Sociedad y Desarollo* No.3, 1972. Also Barraclough, S. (1974) *Diagnóstico de la Reforma Agraria Chilena*. Mexico, Siglo XXI.

40. Steenland, K. (1974) Rural Strategy Under Allende. *Latin American Perspectives*, Vol.1 No.2:137.

41. Kay, C. (1976) op.cit., p.84.

42. Steenland, K. (1974) op.cit., p.143.

43. Kay, C. (1981) Political Economy . . ., op.cit., p.508. The data above is

drawn from this article.

44. Ibid., p.509.

45. Winn, P. (1974) The Economic Consequences of the Chilean Counter-Revolution: An Interim Assessment. *Latin American Perspectives*, Vol.1 No.2:99.

46. Castillo, L. and Lehman, D. (1982) Chile's Three Agrarian Reforms, op.cit., p.40.

47. Alavi, H. (1965) Peasants and Revolution. *Socialist Register 1965*; and Wolf, E. (1971) *Peasant Wars in the Twenthieth Century*. London, Faber and Faber.

48. Paige, J. (1975) *Agrarian Revolutions*. New York, Free Press.

49. Wolf, E. (1971) op.cit., p.285.

50. Moore, B. (1969) *Social Origins of Dictatorship and Democracy*. London, Penguin, p.473.

51. Roxborough, I. (1979) *Theories of Underdevelopment*. London, Macmillan, p.92.

52. See in particular, Womack, J. (1969) *Zapata and the Mexican Revolution*. London, Penguin Books.

53. See amongst others O'Connor, J. (1970) *The Origins of Socialism in Cuba*. Ithaca, Cornell University Press.

54. Huizer, G. (1973) *Peasant Rebellion in Latin America*. London, Penguin, p.11. See also Landsberger, H. (ed) (1969) *Latin American Peasant Movements*. Ithaca, Cornell University Press.

55. Quijano, P. (1967) Contemporary Peasant Movements. *Elites in Latin America*. New York, Oxford University Press.

56. Ibid., p.308.

57. See Pearse, A. (1975) *The Latin American Peasant*. Ch IV: Peasants and Revolution in Latin America.

58. See Julião, F. (1972) *Cambão — The Yoke. The Hidden Face of Brazil*. London, Penguin.

59. This historical sketch draws on Vitale, L. (1980) *Interpretación Marxista de la Historia de Chile*.

60. Quoted in Loveman, B. (1976) *Struggle in the Countryside Politics and Rural Labor in Chile, 1919–1973*. Bloomington, Indiana University Press, p.133.

61. The basic text on rural unions is Loveman, B. (1976) op.cit.

62. Petras, J. and Zeitlin, M. (1970) Agrarian Radicalism in Chile. *Agrarian Problems and Peasant Movements in Latin America*, (ed) R. Stavenhagen pp.503–31.

63. For differing discussions see Bossert, T.J. (1980) The Agrarian Reform and Peasant Political Consciousness in Chile. *Latin American Perspectives*, Vol.VII No.4:6–28 and Chinchilla, N. and Sternberg, M. (1974) The Agrarian Reform and Campesino Consciousness. *Latin American Perspectives*, Vol.1 No.2:106–28.

64. Petras, J. (1970) *Politics and Social Forces in Chilean Development*. Berkeley, University of California Press, p.264.

65. See the very useful analysis by Chonchol, J. (1970) Poder y Reforma Agraria en la Experiencia Chilena. *Chile Hoy* A. Pinto et al. Santiago, Siglo XXI.

66. Kay, C. (1976) Agrarian reform . . . op.cit., p.84.

67. Castex, P. (1977) *'Voie chilienne' au socialisme et luttes paysannes.* Paris, Maspero, p.175.

68. Castells, M. (1974) *La lucha de clases en Chile*. Buenos Aires, Siglo XXI, p.355.

69. Interviewed in Henfrey, C. and Sorj, B. (1977) *Chilean Voices – Activists describe their Experiences of the Popular Unity Period.* Brighton, Harvester Press, pp.92–3.

70. Steenland, K. (1977) *Agrarian Reform under Allende: Peasant Revolt in the South.* Albuquerque, University of New Mexico Press, p.139.

71. Loveman, B. (1976) *Struggle in the Countryside* . . . op.cit., p.191.

72. Cited in Castells, M. (1974) *La lucha de clases en Chile*. p.358.

73. Ibid., p.357.

74. Interviewed in Henfrey, C. and Sorj, B. (1977) *Chilean Voices*, p.120.

75. Janvry, A. de (1981) *The Agrarian Question*, op.cit., p.221.

76. Burbach, R. and Flynn, P. (1980) *Agribusiness in the Americas*, New York, Monthly Review Press/NACLA, p.84.

77. Ibid., p.12.

78. Ibid., p.165.

79. Ibid., p.221–2.

80. Cajarville, S. (1980) New Trends in the Agrarian Development of Latin America: Modernization against Agrarian Reforms. UNITAR International Conference, New Delhi, p.30.

81. For a broad overview of the 'frontier question' in Brazil see Foweraker, J. (1981) *The Struggle for Land: A Political Economy of the Pioneer Frontier in Brazil from 1930 to the Present Day.* New York, Cambridge University Press.

82. Cardoso, F.H. and Muller, G. (1977) *Amazônia: Expansão do Capitalismo*, São Paulo, Editora Brasiliense, p.9. For an indictment of the repression of the indigenous peoples see Davis, S. (1977) *Victims of the Miracle, Development and the Indians of Brazil*. Cambridge, Cambridge University Press.

83. Ibid., p.50.

84. Ibid., p.161. Subsequent data same source. See also Moran, E. (1981) *Developing the Amazon*. Bloomington, Indiana University Press.

85. For a critical overview of the 'agrarian question' and the transition to socialism in Chile, see the above cited work of Kay, Castells, Castex. Also Santana, R. (1975) Réforme Agraire et Alliances de Classes sous le Gouvernement de l'Unité Populaire. *Les Temps Modernes* No.342: 744–60; and Roxborough, I. (1980) Class conflict in the Chilean countryside. *Classes, Class Conflict, and the State*, (ed) M. Zeitlin, Cambridge, Mass., Winthrop Publishers.

PART III
Politics

7. State and Capital: Brazil 1930–80

> The state in its turn strove to force the development of
> social differentiation of a primitive economic foundation.
> Furthermore, the very need for forcing, caused by the
> weakness of the social-economic formations, made it natural
> that the state in its efforts as guardian should have tried to
> use its preponderant power to accelerate the country's
> natural economic development. New branches of handicraft,
> machinery, factories, big industry, capital, were, so to say,
> artificially grafted on the natural economic stem. Capitalism
> seemed to be an offspring of the state.
>
> Leon Trotsky[1]

The aim of this chapter is to examine the relationship between the state and
development as exemplified by Brazil over the last 50 years, focusing on
periods of crisis and transition. Our emphasis is on the intervention of the
state in the process of capital accumulation. The specific state forms which
are derived from the accumulation process — for example, corporatist,
populist, dictatorial modes of political domination — are considered only
in so far as is relevant to our main object of analysis. The study proceeds
from the abstract to the concrete as follows: 1) we explore the general
theoretical determinants of state intervention; 2) the specificity of the
dependent capitalist state is examined; and 3) we proceed to our study of
capital and state in the Brazilian social formation and its periodization. Then
our concrete study (guided by our preliminary theoretical outline) allows us
to reflect back on the general relationship between state, capital and crisis.
On this basis we draw some tentative conclusions.

State, Capital and Crisis

The state must be seen as an essential component of the capitalist relations
of production which is subject to the law of value, and whose intervention is
determined by the dynamic of the capital accumulation process. Its basic
function is to provide the general conditions for the reproduction of the

wage-labour/capital relation which is at the heart of bourgeois society. According to·Engels, 'the modern state, no matter what its form, is essentially a capitalist machine, the state of the capitalists, *the ideal personification of the total national capital.*[2] The state not only reproduces capitalist social relations but it also regulates the competition between individual capitals in the interests of capital as a whole. The anarchy of a 'pure' capitalism must be overcome through the particularisation of the state which becomes 'a separate entity, beside and outside civil society'.[3] Study of the state, as an organisation of political class dominance, must be based on the derivation of the 'state form' from the contradictions of bourgeois society.[4] The Bolshevik theorist of law, Evgeny Pashukanis, pointed out that 'to the extent that society represents a market, the machinery of state is actually manifested as an impersonal collective will, as the rule of law and so on'.[5] However:

> class society is not only a market where autonomous owners of commodities meet, but is at the same time the battlefield of a bitter class war, where the machinery of state represents a very powerful weapon.[6]

At this stage one could point to the 'relative autonomy' of the capitalist state and accuse the preceding analysis of 'economism'. Nicos Poulantzas, for example, states that the 'characteristic autonomy of the economic and the political' is such that it 'permits us to constitute the political into an autonomous and specific object of science.'[7] This, however, tends to obscure the commodity fetishism characteristic of capitalism which makes the state appear as a 'thing', rather than a particular historical form of the capitalist social relation. John Holloway and Sol Picciotto aptly point out that:

> the autonomisation of the state is, like all forms of fetishism, both reality and illusion . . . [it] forms part of, and is a necessity for the accumulation of capital, involves not only the necessity of separate political institutions, but also a constant class practice involving the structural and ideological separation and fetishisation of economics and politics and of the private and the public.[8]

In conclusion, there is no contradiction between: 1) an understanding that the intervention of the state is guided by the 'requirements of capital'; and 2) a recognition of the necessary particularisation of the state as a discrete form of the capital relation.

We turn now to the major functions performed by the state in capitalist society. Simplifying somewhat, these can be reduced to the following: 1) the provision of the general material conditions of production necessary for capital; 2) regulating the conflict between labour and capital through co-optation and repression; 3) safeguarding the existence and expansion of total national capital on the capitalist world market.[9] Taking these in reverse order, we can say that point 3 is often assumed non-operative when dealing with those social formations dominated by imperialism. Following the analysis of the first two chapters we must reject any conception based on the 'sell-out' assumption, that is, that 'betraying' their own interests the dependent bourgeoisie will commit economic suicide. The role of the state in containment of wage-labour will be a constant thread running through our concrete analysis so we will not deal with it here. It is point 1 we need to expand on at present.

The capitalist state must provide the basic 'infrastructure' necessary for the reproduction of 'capital in general', even though these tasks may be unprofitable from the point of view of individual capitals. In analysing the 'general conditions of production' such as roads, canals, etc. Marx concluded that:

> there are works and investments which may be necessary without being productive in the capitalist sense, i.e., without the realisation of *surplus labour* contained in them through circulation, through exchange, as *surplus value*.[10]

More specifically:

> All *general, communal* conditions of production — so long as their production cannot yet be accomplished by capital as such and under its conditions — are therefore paid for out of a part of the country's revenue — out of the government's treasury — and the workers do not appear as productive workers, even though they increase the productive force of capital.[11]

It is now established that state investment tends to be unproductive in Marx's sense and represents a drain on surplus value for the total social capital. Furthermore, Marxists have traditionally maintained that, as Altvater says 'if the state acts as a capitalist then this can be explained only through the particular history and particular conditions of a country'.[12]

The 'state capitalist' tradition of Marxism tends to recognise that the state *can* be a productive capitalist under whose direct domain surplus-value is produced. Colin Barker argues along these lines, pointing out that 'the obvious case [of the state as productive capitalist] is the nationalised industry sector in western capitalism, within which wage-labour is combined with state-owned means of production. . . .'[13] A full-blown state capitalist analysis, however, presents many problems, not least of which is its inability to specify the nature of a mode of production which is neither capitalist nor socialist. More specifically, it tends to ignore the Marxist understanding of capitalism as inevitably based on competition between individual capitals. Capital can exist only in the form of different capitals, otherwise there is no compulsion to accumulate. Having said that, we wish to retain the theoretical possibility of a 'productive state sector', whose origins, tendencies and contradictions can be uncovered only by historical analysis. It is worth noting at this stage how Marxism conceives the question of state ownership of the means of production. For Engels:

> the more [the state] proceeds to the taking over of the productive forces, the more does it actually become the *national capitalist*, the more citizens does it exploit. The workers remain wage-workers — proletarians. The capitalist relation is not done away with. It is rather brought to a head.[14]

Against the ultimately reformist 'state capitalist' view (which assumes that the anarchy of capitalist production can be overcome) we do not see state intervention as overcoming the operation of the law of value, but rather, as *internalizing* the contradictions of the capital accumulation process. That is to say, a 'state capital' is, on the one hand, a particular, individual capital seeking to reproduce itself through the extraction and realisation of surplus value in competition with other capitals; and on the other hand, it is part of the collective state capital serving the interests of capital as a whole and, especially when a 'public service', taking account of interests other than its own reproduction.

Finally, we must outline briefly the determinants of state intervention in production. The framework is set by Marx's 'law of the tendency of the rate of profit to fall'.[15] At its simplest this results from capital's endless pursuit of surplus value ($S \div V$), which leads to the replacement of labour (variable capital: v) by machinery (constant capital: c), expressed in a growing organic composition of capital ($C \div V$). It follows, that given a constant rate of surplus value, the average rate of profit ($S \div C + V$) must fall as the organic composition of capital is driven up. For Marx:

> the progressive tendency for the general rate of profit to fall is thus simply *the expression, peculiar to the capitalist mode of production,* of the progressive development of the social productivity of labour.[16]

Clearly, there are several opposing, counterparting tendencies which tend to counteract this trend, amongst them a drive to cheapen the elements of constant capital, which slows the rise in the organic composition of capital. State intervention is also functional in this sense, in so far as it tends to take over operations involving a high organic composition of capital (and low rates of profit) which are thus withdrawn from the process of equalisation of the rate of profit, ensuring the maintenance of adequate average profit levels. In a general sense, the state activity in production is highly functional for private capital as it can provide cheap inputs. Its function in relation to Marx's 'law' just outlined is to mobilise the counter-tendencies which prevent the falling rate of profit from becoming a secular tendency.

The concept of capitalism is inseparable from that of crisis, and the state has a key role to play in 'crisis-management'. As Andrew Gamble and Peter Walton note:

the objective basis for the interventionist role of the State in modern capitalist economies is to perform more smoothly the task once crudely effected by the business cycle. Put another way, it ensures that one or more of the counteracting influences to the decline in the rate of profit do in fact assert themselves.[17]

State intervention in the production process, as the business cycle, answers the need for capitalist restructuring and regeneration, as the inherent contradictions of capital accumulation are played out. As some capital units are 'subsidised' as we saw above, at other times, certain capital units must be 'rationalised'. In conclusion, the state is a powerful (but not omnipotent) agent for the resolution of the barriers in the way of the self expansion of capital.

Dependent Capitalist State

Brazil is, of course, a dependent or dominated social formation and the laws of motion of capitalism are consequently modified. Here, Marx pointed to the development of imperialism when he noted that 'the tendency to create the world market is directly given in the concept of capital itself. Every limit appears as a barrier to be overcome'.[18] Extending this point, Lenin developed the theory of imperialism in the course of which he examined the 'transitional forms of state dependence' which resulted from the struggle of the great powers for the economic and political division of the world. More specifically, and quoting Argentina as an example, Lenin referred to 'the diverse forms of dependent countries which, politically, are formally independent but in fact, are enmeshed in the web of financial and diplomatic dependence, typical of this epoch.'[19] So, referring back to Chapter 1 for a full discussion of imperialism, we will use Lenin's concept of dependence as a starting point to account for Brazil's dominated position in the imperialist chain.

The debate concerning the specificity of the dependent capitalist state has centred recently around the conception of its 'increased relative autonomy'. Hamza Alavi, in his analysis of the post-colonial state has, in particular, stressed this aspect.[20] I believe this concept is rather ambiguous, as pointed out earlier. It is used in the absence of a specified relation, but in the belief that there is some sort of *causal* link. Our approach is rather to trace the contradictory relations of capital accumulation and the manner in which these contradictions are resolved historically. The 'relative autonomy' of the dependent state, for example in periods of imperialist crisis, must be established for each historical conjuncture in relation to the class struggle, and not assumed as a theoretical a priori.

At a more specific level, Alavi has pointed to the particular interventionist role of the dependent capitalist state. He sees the state apparatus taking on a new and relatively autonomous economic role, with a direct appropriation of a large part of the economic surplus, which is then deployed bureaucratically to promote 'economic development'.[21] More recently, Ziemann and Lanzendorfer have referred to the development in the periphery of 'the intervention state in permanence'.[22] In their view, the permanent economic crisis in these countries forces the state, (through a 'functional imperative') to carry out a constant intervention in the economic process. But:

> the state of crisis is neither alleviated nor overcome by this, at most it may be shifted to another level. The consequence is to aggravate the social contradictions and conflicts, to increase the imbalance, which inevitably encourages wider state intervention and this can only be based on a paternalistic regime of military—bureaucratic—techno-cratic type.[23]

This analysis is rather formalistic and not a little catastrophic, but it points to a crucial element — the relation between economic crisis and the form of political regime. The general point, from these authors and Alavi, that we wish to retain, is the idea of a particular type of interventionist role which the dependent capitalist state must play.

As we have seen in Chapter 1, 'dependence' can become a convenient *deus ex machina* (as in the theatre of Antiquity where a god often comes down to resolve in a flash the problem at hand) which explains anything and everything in the colonial and semi-colonial world. At its extreme one has the 'metropolis-satellite' analogy, where the latter by definition can only play 'follow the leader'. Two quite representative authors, Hein and Stenzel, affirm, for example, that:

> the state in underdeveloped capitalist societies is primarily an agent for transmitting the global dynamics of the international division of labour to the national level and of reproducing the internal class and political power structure according to these dynamics.[24]

More explicitly, they analyse the 'metropolitan bourgeoisie' as an 'external ruling class [which] more or less determines which fraction of the internal bourgeoisie dominates in domestic affairs [and] consequently breaks up any internal 'bloc au pouvoir'. . . .[25] The effects of this Manichean type of analysis have led to a symmetrical reaction in the opposite direction, which lays stress on the *internal* dynamic of capital accumulation in the dependent social formation. Thus, the Brazilian economist Maria de Conceção Tavares maintains that:

> commerce and the flow of foreign capital do not exogenously determine the dynamic of accumulation, they are just articulated with it and *modify it from within*, accentuating the internal shifts that are taking place in the productive structure, and in the historical pattern of accumulation.[26]

Debate can be falsely polarized over the primacy of 'internal' or 'external' factors in determining the course of capital accumulation in the oppressed nation-states. For my part, I believe the economic intervention of the dependent capitalist state must be posed *simultaneously* in terms of both the internationalisation of capital in its various phases, and of the internal process of capital accumulation and class struggle. Only on the basis of historical analysis of given conjunctures can we determine the specific causality of 'internal' and 'external' factors. We now turn to our concrete analysis of Brazil.

Oligarchic State

The abolition of slavery in Brazil in 1888 opened the way for the emergence of the capital/wage-labour relation in the Centre-South coffee producing area. As Teresa Meade points out:

> a combination of pre-capitalist and capitalist modes of production replaced the slave system in the countryside of the coffee producing regions but co-existed with the emergence of capitalist production in urban areas.[27]

The uneven development of Brazilian capitalism was expressed in an extension and hardening of non-capitalist relations of production, in the largely sugar, and later cotton, producing North-East. The bourgeois character of the Brazilian state derived from its relation with the imperialist powers, rather than from a fully developed internal capitalist system. This state was controlled mainly by the coffee interests, and the foreign dominated mercantile capital.

The coffee sector was the real motor of capital accumulation during this phase – between 1889 and the First World War Brazilian exports expanded two and a half times, with the coffee exports from the port of Santos being quadrupled. It was also through coffee that the Brazilian economy was integrated into the world capitalist market, and its overwhelming reliance on this product made it extremely susceptible to crises in the imperialist system. Britain, then the dominant imperialist power, controlled a large part of Brazilian trade and established the 'classic' dependent pattern of exporting its manufactured goods to Brazil and importing Brazil's agrarian produce, through a system of unequal exchange. It is generally accepted, as one author puts it, that:

> classical dependence restricted the possibility of industrial growth because it created such a poor domestic market. Dependence also made industrialisation difficult because it left a large part of the surplus from the booming primary exports in the hands of the British.[28]

The first part of the argument smacks of underconsumptionism, (which posits the restricted consumption of the masses as the barrier to capitalist expansion rather than the internal contractions of the mode of production itself), and we would have to explore the basis for this in the realm of production, but the overall assessment holds good. Industrialisation, in so far as it did take place, occurred in the pores of the old system, and was completely subordinated to the agrarian economy. Thus food, drink, clothes and textile production emerged, linked to the various agrarian sectors, and not integrated amongst themselves.

The First World War was to be a point of rupture in this situation. Britain's undisputed hegemony in the imperialist system was shattered, and the United States emerged as its most threatening rival. United States imperialism did not fundamentally contest Britain's financial hold over Brazil, but directed its investment to productive areas, such as plantations and mining. On the other hand, the effects of the World War on Brazil's productive structure was to encourage diversification and industrialisation, as the links with the imperialist system were temporarily broken. These changes were to mature in the period leading up to the Great Depression which was to constitute the decisive break in the system of 'classical' dependence. The role of the state during this phase was far from negligible, and one cannot accept Werner Baer's conclusion that it 'was relatively non-interventionist in economic matters'.[29] The state organised the relations of production to ensure the reproduction of the 'factors of production' necessary for the agro-export based economy.[30] This involved a role in financial intermediation and the promotion of public works, such as the transport network linking the productive sectors to the ports. The state was also to become the key element in the vital coffee support programmes. The fluctuations in world prices of previous export commodities had been absorbed fairly passively by the Brazilian economy. The critical dependence on coffee however, necessitated a system of state-managed price support and production control programmes. This system resulted in the 'socialisation of losses' in periods of downturn, with a return to 'privatisation of profits' in the upswing. State intervention however, could not prevent a growing crisis of over-production in the coffee sector which was the inevitable product of the 1920s 'golden period'. Thus the mainspring of the Brazilian economy was heading for a crisis even before the Great Depression was to hit Brazil.

By 1922, the coffee valorisation process had become one of 'permanent defence' resulting in big increases of production regardless of the falling prices on the world market. The international economic depression, begun in 1929, was to complete the irreversible decline of coffee, with its price in 1931 falling to one third of what it had been over 1925–29. As the hegemony of the coffee bourgeoisie was shattered, so the state system of 'oligarchic compromise' entered into crisis. This had maintained a political balance between the regional sub-systems generated by the export oriented economy, centred around the São Paulo and Minas Gerais oligarchies. This balance was broken now and the regional oligarchies not linked to coffee, supported by the middle class and with the diffuse presence of the popular masses, launched the 1930 'Revolution' which brought Getulio Vargas to power.

The agrarian sector did not lose its economic predominance in 1930 but rather its leading political role. Thus, the role of the coffee bourgeoisie as the hegemonic bourgeois class fraction was drawn into question but it still retained a preponderant economic role. In fact, many of the post-1930 measures which promoted industrialisation were designed in the first instance to protect the coffee sector — 'unconscious Keynesianism' as Celso Furtado says.[31] The 1930 events have somewhat mechanically been seen as Brazil's 'bourgeois-democratic revolution'. It certainly did open up a new stage in the development of capitalism in that country, but Boris Fausto, amongst others, has shown conclusively that the industrial bourgeoisie as such played no significant role in the 'revolution' so it can hardly be seen as a classical bourgeois revolution.[32] Fausto shows that the measures favouring industriali-sation were not adopted 'consciously'. In other words, there was no 'classical' opposition of industrial bourgeoisie-feudal oligarchy and certainly no 'revolutionary' middle class. Be that as it may, 1930 certainly *does* mark the end of one cycle, based on agrarian-export hegemony, and the beginning of a new phase, centred around the urban-industrial axis.

Considering this turn in terms of the dialectic between 'internal' and 'external' factors we must assess to what extent it resulted from a gradual accumulation of internal contradictions, or whether it was precipitated by the international capitalist crisis. Boris Fausto points out that:

> the crisis did not produce the revolution as a sort of short-circuit in a fully functional system, and it is even possible to speculate on the fall of the Republica Velha, independently of it. But, the contradictions of the coffee economy, and of the institutions which consolidated its predominance, gained a new dimension.[33]

It would seem that the crisis of the world capitalist economy acted as a catalyst for changes already taking place internally, and that 'external' factors were clearly 'overdeterminant' with respect to the 1930 reorientation of the Brazilian economy. Pierre Salama on the other hand prioritises the articulation between nation-states:

> the crisis of 1929, by its duration and scope, and the modification of the articulation between states which results from this, allows the development of the industrialising potential of the export economy from around 1933–4.[34]

In the new phase which now begins, the state is to play a crucial role, as it does in the transitional process itself.

Bonapartist State

As we mentioned above, industrialisation accelerated in 1933; from 1933 to 1939, industrial production grew at 11.2% per annum. Also, of the 49,418 establishments accounted for in the 1940 Industrial Census, 34,691 had been formed since 1930. Significantly, 56.4% of the firms surveyed in 1940 employed less than five workers. The industrialisation of the 1930s occurred under adverse conditions of foreign commerce, with the international depression limiting Brazil's capacity to import industrial equipment. As industrialisation was becoming the axis of capital accumulation, so too government policy moved towards a decisive centralisation of the state, overcoming the previous regionalism, and consolidating an internal market. The political form adopted, after a transitional period, was the 'corporatist' Estado Nôvo (1937–45) dominated by the figure of Getulio Vargas. Corporatism, following Panitch, is a political structure 'which integrates organized socio-economic producer groups through a system of representation and cooperative mutual interaction at the leadership level and social control at mass level.'[35] One of the most important aspects of the state's intervention during this period was in relation to the working class. A prominent politician, Antonio Carlos, said in 1930: 'We must make the Revolution before the people do it.' With the acceleration of industrialisation in the 1930s and the concomitant growth of an industrial working class (which grew from 84,000 in 1920 to a quarter of a million in 1940 and half a million in 1950) the 'labour question' became a priority for the bourgeois state. A whole series of mechanisms carried out the incorporation of the unions into the bourgeois state apparatus (see Chapter 5) whose effects have weighed like a millstone around the neck of the working class ever since. In this way the capital/wage-labour relation came directly under the aegis of the state, moulded into a class-collaborationist structure and subordinated to nationalist ideology. This has rightly been called a policy of 'preemptive co-optation'.

The economic intervention of the state also took on a new increased dimension after 1930. In the 1930s the government took over control of various commodities, such as salt, sugar, maté, pinewood, etc., through state cartels known as *autarquias*. In its initial stages state intervention was clearly directed towards promoting private capital accumulation. As Baer outlines:

> the use of exchange controls, of 'autarquias', and the creation in 1937 of the Carteira de Credito Agricola e Industrial of the Banco do Brasil to provide longer-term credits to industrial establishments point in this direction.[36]

During the 1940s, state intervention accelerated and began to acquire a dynamic of its own. After long negotiations with the United States, the National Steel Company was set up in 1941 by the state, with an integrated steel mill built at Volta Redonda, which began production in 1947. In 1941 the important mining company *Companhia Vale do Rio Doce* was also

214

established and in 1943 the motor company *Fábrica Nacional de Motores* was set up. The crucial extension of the state's role, however, occurred in the 1950s. In 1952 the National Economic Development Bank (BNDE) was created to furnish long-term credits for industrialisation. In Baer's words 'the BNDE was established to provide the finance for the recommended growth and modernization program of the country's infrastructure.'[37] Then, in 1953, the state petroleum monopoly, *Petrobrás*, was established after a fierce nationalist campaign in its favour.

It is important now to provide an overall understanding of the state's role in this phase of 'conservative modernisation'. The whole Vargas era can be usefully understood as a unified historical sequence analogous to that described by the Italian Marxist, Antonio Gramsci, as a 'passive revolution'.[38] This entails a whole series of molecular transformations which progressively modify the previous composition of class forces and thus become the matrix for further changes. In Brazil this meant internalizing the relations of dependence and establishing a new articulation of the state with imperialism. It is, furthermore, in Gramsci's terms, a situation where the progressive class cannot advance openly (as in France after 1815) resulting in a simultaneous revolution/restoration. In Brazil, this resulted in the failure of the industrial bourgeoisie to seize political power, and led to the 1937 'compromise' between itself and the old dominant agrarian sectors. Finally, the concept points to the critical role of the state in generating an accumulation process — it is a case in Gramsci's words of 'a state which, even though it had limitations as a power, "led" the group, [ie., the bourgeoisie] which should have been "leading" '. Effectively, Brazil in the 1930s was a case where, 'a State replaces the local social groups in leading a struggle for renewal'.[39] Furthermore, as also analysed by Leon Trotsky for the backward conditions of 18th Century Russia, the state played a generating role in the formation of classes and class alliances. The state in Brazil during this period played a role analogous to that of the Absolutist state in 17th Century Western Europe — it accomplished certain functions in the primitive accumulation of capital necessary for the triumph of the capitalist mode of production, but without a radical rupture with the old order, that is, within the limits set by the feudal framework.

We must now set the scene for a new phase of capital accumulation which emerged in the 1950s. The Estado Nôvo, set up by Vargas in 1937, was losing its corporatist character even before it fell in 1945. A new mode of political domination was emerging, known in Brazilian political history as the 'populist' state, which was consolidated by Vargas when he returned to power through elections in 1950. Populism in reality expressed a contradictory unity of nationalism, developmentalism and populism in the restricted sense. The first element focused on the nation-state as the point of conciliation of the various social classes; the second promoted the idea of a 'drive for development' ambiguously posed between 'autonomous' and 'dependent' development, but always capitalist; and the last element referred to the surface phenomena of these political regimes, including their personalisation of power in the 'charismatic' leader, etc.[40] Most important for our concerns in this chapter, a key element running through populist discourse is a 'statist' ideology, resulting in a general fetishism of the state, which was accorded an autonomous accumulation potential removed from the contradictions of the capitalist mode of production.

In this period the capital accumulation process in Brazil acquired its own endogenous dynamic.[41] The process of accumulation between 1933–55 has been called one of restricted industrialisation, because the technical and financial bases of accumulation were insufficient for the implantation of a production goods industry (Department I) necessary for a nationally determined process of industrial development. This horizontal pattern of capital accumulation gave way after 1955 to a new mode based on a block of highly complementary investments carried out between 1956 and 1961, which completely transformed the structure of the productive system. This has been referred to as a process of 'heavy industrialisation' because it resulted in the accelerated growth of the production goods sector. In a more speculative vein I believe that this transition involved a move from the 'formal' to the 'real' subordination of labour, from the extraction of absolute surplus value towards relative surplus value, and from industries based on a low to a high organic composition of capital. It would be wrong to conclude that 'capitalism' began only in the 1950s, but in terms of the domination of 'large-scale industry', as against manufacture, it is certainly correct.

We must now assess the contribution of the state sector to this accelerated growth period between 1955 and 1959. Government participation in fixed capital formation more than doubled between 1947–60 (with a steep rise after 1956) and if we include mixed government enterprises we find that its share approached 50% in 1960. It is this important state sector which laid the infrastructure for the boom of the Kubitschek period (1956–60). The state was to become a fundamental element in the 'great leap forward' promoted by Kubitschek's *Plano de Metas* (Target Plan) whose avowed aim was to advance Brazil 'fifty years in five'. During this cyclical acceleration there was a wave of state investments, directed mainly to the transport-energy sector and to the steel and petroleum sectors. This development of public enterprises in Brazil has been related historically to: 1) the existence of industrial sectors which are not profitable (or require a long period for maturing), but which are necessary for the expansion of industry as a whole; 2) conditions where the amount of initial capital outlay can be met only by the state or foreign capital; 3) the expression of nationalist or military/ strategic policies; 4) the need to stimulate new levels of expansion in the downswing of an economic cycle. However, given that the Great Depression and then the war precluded imperialist capital from investing in such countries as Brazil during this period, Vargas's decision to carry out an ambitious programme of heavy investments was not in itself sufficient to establish a firm internal circuit of capital accumulation. The role of the imperialist countries was important in, for example, the development of a steel sector, which materialised only because the United States of America granted the indispensable external finance and equipment, in exchange for

Brazil's commitment to the war effort.[42] Likewise, the development of *Petrobrás* dragged on until 1954, and the plans for a chemical industry turned sour owing to the lack of the necessary advanced technology. The overall dynamic of state intervention in this period is clearly summarised by Francisco de Oliveira:

> We see the emergence and the extension of state functions in the years up to the mid-fifties; regulation of the price of labour power, investment in the infrastructure, imposition of the *'confisco cambial'* [government expropriation of foreign-exchange earnings] on coffee to redistribute its profits among the other capitalist fractions, reduction of the cost of capital through exchange subsidies for the import of industrial equipment, expansion of credit and investment in production (e.g. Volta Redonda and Petrobrás). In all these ways, the state continuously transferred resources to industry, which became the centre of the economic system. Both the left and the right saw a form of socialism in this 'statism', without ever asking themselves the old question — who benefits from all this.[43]

The state, however, was not the only expanding sector in this period. There had been a reorientation of foreign (particularly United States) investment in the second half of the 1950s towards the dependent nations. After the Second World War this had been oriented primarily towards the reconstruction of European capitalism, but now Latin America was to suffer a real 'foreign takeover'. Table 7.1 shows the direct evolution of foreign investment in Brazil by country of origin between 1914 and 1972. This investment is more dispersed than the more simplistic analysis of 'Yankee imperialism' would lead us to believe. Peter Evans concludes correctly from this historical evolution that 'the result of dispersion is to give the Brazilian state increased manoeuver room'.[44] We must note that this wave of imperialist investment was directed primarily towards the most dynamic sectors of the economy such as cars, chemicals and petro-chemicals, machinery and heavy electrical sectors, etc. If we examine the absolute figures for direct foreign investment in Brazil we find that in 1954 it was $52 million, in 1955, 79 million, then 139 in 1956, 128 in 1958 and so on. Again, 1956 emerges as a year of reorientation and acceleration of capital accumulation in Brazil. In her overall assessment of this phase Tavares concludes that 'the intervention of the state, in particular, its own potential for internal accumulation had necessarily to expand and *precede* the new form of articulation with international capital'.[45] Certainly it was the decisive intervention of the state which laid the basis for the mode of 'associated-dependent' development which followed, but one must not ignore the changes in the imperialist system which led to increased investment in the Third World. We find that the historical rhythm of the creation of state firms coincides with the development of imperialist investment. It is, however, very difficult to assess a priority for either internal or external factors in this process. What is clear is the profound organic complementarity between these

Table 7.1
Origins of Foreign Investment in Brazil (1914-1972)

	1914 (%)	1930 (%)	1950 (%)	1959 (%)	1972 (%)
North American	4	25	71	56	46
(U.S.)	(4)	(21)	(48)	(38)	(37)
(Canadian)	–	(4)	(23)	(18)	(9)
European	96	72	25	36	42
(British)	(51)	(53)	(17)	(7)	(8)
(French)	(33)	(8)	(3)	(5)	(5)
(German)	–	–	–	(9)	(11)
(Other)	(12)	(11)	(5)	(15)	(18)
Other	–	3	4	8	12
(Japanese)	–	(1)	–	(2)	(6)
Total	*100*	*100*	*100*	*100*	*100*

Source: P. Evans, (1979) *Dependent Development*. Princeton, Princeton
University Press, p.82.

sectors as illustrated in Figure 7.1.

As we noted in our introduction, the 'relative autonomy' of the dependent states in situations such as that of the Depression can be explained only *concretely*. It is precisely in terms of the emerging 'Bonapartist' state in this period that we can understand this phenomenon. Discussing the Cárdenas regime in Mexico, Trotsky posed the question as follows:

> In the industrially backward countries foreign capital plays a decisive role. Hence the relative weakness of the national bourgeoisie in relation to the national proletariat. This creates special conditions of state power. The government veers between foreign and domestic capital, between the weak national bourgeoisie and the relatively powerful proletariat. This gives the government a Bonapartist character of a distinctive character. It raises itself, so to speak, above classes. Actually, it can govern either by making itself the instrument of foreign capitalism and holding the proletariat in the chains of a police dictatorship, or by manoeuvring with the proletariat and even going as far as to make concessions to it, thus gaining the possibility of a certain freedom toward the foreign capitalists.[46]

This seems to me a more fruitful way of establishing the 'relative autonomy' of the Brazilian state, than the usual tendency to attribute it to the structural heterogeneity of the ruling class, which ostensibly prevents it establishing a clear-cut hegemony. Francisco Weffort tends to pose the question in this way, even referring to a permanent crisis of hegemony since 1930.[47] In a similar

Figure 7.1
Sectoral Distribution of Foreign and State Capital in Brazil

Foreign Capital	State
	Domestic Market
Transportation equipment	Land & sea transportation program
Mechanical equipment	Steel industry
Electrical equipment	Federal construction
	Electric energy program
	Communication systems
Chemical	Petroleum and its derivatives
Financial Services	Public utilities services
	Foreign Market (exports)
Cattle	Coffee (policies relating to)
Vegetable and mineral extraction	Iron minerals
Industrial surplus	

Source: Tavares, M.C. and Serra, J. (1978) Beyond stagnation: a discussion
of recent developments in Brazil. *Latin America: from dependence
to revolution*, (ed) J. Petras, New York, John Wiley & Co, p.78.

way, Alavi sees this heterogeneity of the 'power bloc' as the reason for the
'relative autonomy' of the post colonial state. Bonapartism is, on the other
hand, related to the *specific* situation of the dependent state, particularly
in the changed political circumstances following the 1929 world crisis, which
led to the gradual decay of the structures of domination established in the
'classical' imperialist epoch. I refer to a Bonapartist *state* form for the whole
period from 1937 to 1964, even though political *regimes* varied from
'corporatist' to the very distinct variants of 'populism'. Clearly, we are dealing
with concepts at a different level of abstraction. In a similar way, one must
distinguish between 'state intervention' and 'government expenditure'.

To round off our analysis of this period we must refer briefly to the
agrarian sector which was only displaced in 1956 from its predominance over
industry in terms of value added. As the capital relation became consolidated
in the Centre-South the regional division of labour within the country was
redefined. The North-East in particular provided a large reserve army of
labour with massive migrations to the industrial areas helping to maintain
the cost of reproduction of labour-power at very low levels. Likewise, food
production in the agrarian sector (often produced under non-capitalist
relations of production) allowed for a reduction of the wage levels of the
industrial workers. The agrarian sector plays a crucial role in reproducing the
conditions of capitalist expansion, to such an extent that it can be said to
play the role of 'primitive accumulation of capital' as outlined by Marx,
except in a structural sense, and not only in the genesis of capitalism. Clearly

the 'agrarian question' is inseparable from the 'regional question' in Brazil. Overall, as Oliveira outlines:

> at the moment when the expansion of the capitalist system in Brazil has its locus in the Southern 'region' dominated by São Paulo, the cycle of capitalist expansion takes the *spatial* form of destruction of the regional economies, or the 'regions'. This dialectical movement *destroys to concentrate*, and absorbs the surplus from the other 'regions' to centralize capital.[48]

Military State

A preliminary phase of an economic crisis opened up in 1960 with a slowing of accumulation in certain key industries. The central axis of the expansive phase of 1956–59 – namely inter-industrial demand – gradually gave way. The slump in leading industrial sectors, based on an accelerated reproduction of capital, affected the whole industrial sector. Then, in 1963, the crisis became sharper as the intense class struggle drew into question the very reproduction of the capitalist relations of production. The deterioration in the conditions of production of surplus-value was manifested in the violent acceleration of inflation during this phase. The exacerbation of labour struggles sharpened the deterioration of profitability and led to a further contraction of capital investment. A 'peaceful' transition to a new mode of political domination was made impossible by the increased activity of the masses. The bourgeoisie as a whole, when it saw the capital-wage labour relation itself threatened, threw its weight behind the military coup. Its undoubted beneficiaries were however the 'internationalised' or 'dynamic' fractions of the bourgeoisie, which had been consolidating their position since 1956. This fraction, supported by an ambitious military and civilian technocracy, moved in 1964 to seize political power directly and consolidate its hegemony within the power bloc, so as to sanction and deepen its economic dominance.[49] In Chapter 5 we have already discussed the development of the class struggle during this period. At this point, we need only reiterate that there was a growing radicalisation in the early 1960s amongst students, labour, the peasantry and even within the armed forces. General strikes were able to impose a virtual labour veto over crucial questions in the political arena. It was these struggles that transformed an 'economic' crisis into a pre-revolutionary situation. Certainly, this situation confirms the Marxist position that:

> the crisis (i.e., the periodic crisis of capitalism) is neither an economic nor a political crisis: it is a crisis of the capital relation, a crisis made inevitable by the inherent contradictions of that relation.[50]

The state is a critical element in the development of this crisis. Basically, the accumulation functions of the state came into contradiction with its

functions of legitimation. The nationalist component of the populist
ideological system had become highly contradictory as it stimulated a mass
movement which developed bourgeois nationalism to its most radical
consequence: an anti-imperialism with an objectively anti-capitalist dynamic.
Conversely, the coercive measures required by the accumulation process
were not forthcoming from the late populist state, which was itself riven by
class contradictions. Oliveira neatly summarises the crisis thus:

> the 'debacle' of populism is nothing other than the dissolution of the
> ambiguity of the State, determined by the movement of centralization
> of capital. This dissolution naturally reveals its hidden face to the
> subordinated classes, principally to the urban working class: the State is
> now producer of surplus-value, and from this it follows that its oppressive
> and repressive character can no longer be masked.[51]

The crisis of Brazilian capitalism in 1964 was fundamentally a crisis of the
dependent capitalist state whose nature and real functions could no longer
be hidden behind the traditional 'statist' ideology.

The broader implications of 1964 as a transition point must briefly be
considered in conclusion.[52] The 'pact' between industrial and agrarian
interests established in 1937 increasingly wavered after the death of Vargas
in 1954. The consolidation of the industrial sector in the years that followed
established the clear cut hegemony of industrial capital which was 'ratified'
by the 1964 coup. More specifically, the model of highly concentrated
capital accumulation, based on foreign capital and an 'internationalised'
fraction of the national capitalist class, had become incompatible with the
Bonapartist mode of political domination. It was a situation of asymmetry or
dislocation where the economic rearticulation of society proceeded more
rapidly than the political.

The 1964 coup constituted a decisive defeat for Brazilian labour, and the
new state moved rapidly to reconstitute the ailing profit rates of capital.
It did this through some of those measures which can counteract the falling
tendency of the rate of profit. In the first instance it led to a bid to increase
the exploitation of labour through the lengthening of the working day and
the increased extraction of absolute surplus value. The main element in this
bid to recompose the rate of profit was the reduction of real minimum wages
by 55% between 1961 and 1973, where as per capita product rose by 58%
over the same period. The 12-hour working day became the norm and 15- and
16-hour days were to become far from rare. The social effects were devastating
– in the industrial centre of São Paulo the infant mortality rate passed from
62.9 (deaths per 1000 live births) in 1960, to 69.4 in 1964, 84.0 in 1970 to
93.0 in 1973.[53] The overall changes in income distribution, shown in Table
7.2, provide a useful summary of the real effects of the 'economic miracle'
launched by the post-military dictatorships.

Once the balance of forces was shifted decisively in favour of capital,
the natural functions of the capitalist crisis began to work themselves out.

This entailed a sharpening of competition in which (mainly foreign) monopoly capital units predominated. Thus, the natural effects of concentration and centralisation to overcome the economic slump took the form of 'denationalisation'. This process was encouraged by the regime's policy of 'positive insolvency', which consisted in abruptly cutting off government credits to firms which failed to show an 'adequate' level of productivity. This capitalist rationalisation saw the bankruptcies in São Paulo rise from 838 in 1963 to 3,689 in 1967. The overall industrial concentration between 1960 and 1969 was as follows: small firms (less than 10 employees) declined from 91,000 to 16,000 over this period and the proportion of workers they employed declined from 18% to 3%; on the other hand, large firms (more than 250 workers) increased from 900 to 1,600 over the same period, and their percentage of employment rose from 38% to 53%.[54] These figures are, in themselves, eloquent testimony of the process of capital concentration which occurred in these years.

In conclusion, the basis for the 'economic miracle' of 1968–74 was laid by the cyclical downturn of 1962–67, which led to a violent restructuring of the economy. The basic pre-condition for this cyclical upturn over the period 1968–74, was the enormous increase in the rate of exploitation ensured by the military regimes which followed the 1964 coup. This qualitative shift in the relationship between capital and labour was accompanied by a strong process of capital concentration, which drove smaller and weaker capital units to inevitable bankruptcy. There was a sharp turn towards the world market in this period which, together with the marked increase in imperialist investment after 1968, resulted in a partial and sectoral integration of the Brazilian economy into the international circuit of expanded capital reproduction. Between 1964 and 1974 Brazil's participation in world trade more than doubled, and the share of manufactured exports in the total quantum increased by 20%.

Table 7.2
Distribution of Income in Brazil (1960–1976)

Percentage of working population	*1960*		*1970*		*1976*
	% of total income	*Per capita income in U$*	*% of total income*	*Per capita income in U$*	*% of total income*
Top 1%	11.7	3,242	17.8	6,644	39
Next 4%	15.6	1,081	18.5	1,726	39
Next 15%	27.2	502	26.9	669	28
Next 30%	27.8	257	23.9	287	21.2
Bottom 50%	17.7	98	13.7	102	11.8
Total 100%	*100*	*227*	*100*	*373*	*100*

Source: P. Faucher, (1981) *Le Brésil des militaires.* Montréal, Presses de l'Université de Montréal, p.80.

As to the role of the state in the process of capital accumulation, the military regimes after 1964 insisted that it constituted a brake on private enterprise. This desire for liberal orthodoxy would seem to be related more to pleasing the International Monetary Fund and obtaining 'international confidence' than to the reality of the process. What many have seen as a paradox or an irony is that since 1964 the role of the state has been increased by governments which were ideologically *privatist*. Guillermo O'Donnell clarifies this with an interesting analysis of how 'statism' develops as an alternative for the 'bureaucratic-authoritarian' state if the level of threat from the working class is low and the 'normalising' economic project of this type of state is effective fairly rapidly.[55] Brazil would seem to have been particularly successful in promoting an increased role for the state while maintaining the alliance with the international bourgeoisie.

It is important to establish the precise nature of the 'associated-dependent' model of capital accumulation as it was 'deepened' in the post-1964 period. If we examine the changes in ownership among the 300 largest capital units between 1966 and 1974, shown in Table 7.3, we can see the comparative evolution of what is known as the *tri-pé* (tripod) model. There is a steady decline in the weight of foreign capital, likewise with private national capital, although that has stabilized, but significantly the role of the state nearly doubles between 1966 and 1974.

In 1974, 19 out of the largest 20, and 45 out of the largest 100 Brazilian corporations were state owned. Furthermore, some 60% of all investment during the 1967-73 'boom' was carried out by the state. The growth rate of state corporations was high enough to increase their share in the total profits of the largest 100 corporations from 54% in 1968 to 63% in 1974.[56] The profitability achieved by the state sector in this period is important, as it was one of the main aims of the post-1974 economic policies. This process of financial *saneamento* (clearing up) and organisational modernisation of the state firms also led to their segmentation and sectoralization. Today, this means that the productive state sector lacks the financial autonomy necessary to lead the process of economic recovery as there is no organic articulation

Table 7.3
Distribution of Net Assets of 300 Largest Corporations in Brazil (1966-1974)

Manufacturing and Petroleum

	1966	1972	1974
State Enterprise	17%	30%	32%
Private Brazilian firms	36%	28%	28%
Multinational Corporations	47%	42%	40%

Source: W. Baer, et al. (1976) On State Capitalism in Brazil. *InterAmerican Economic Affairs*, Vol.30 No.3, p.80.

between the state firms which act virtually as isolated oligopolies. It is important to note that 'statization' was not a one-way process: in 1968 the state vehicle factory (*Fábrica Nacional de Motores*) was turned over to private capital, and in 1976, after extensive debate, the state petroleum monopoly, *Petrobrás*, signed contracts with imperialist firms for oil exploration.

Crisis

Towards 1974 the Brazilian 'economic model' entered a period of crisis partly as a result of the world recession, but also owing to its own internal contradictions.

The continued investment of the state meant that for a few years the effects of the international recession were not felt as sharply and immediately as in 1929–30. The military government since then has been faced with the task of reorienting the economy in the context of an unfavourable international situation, growing popular unrest over the continued depression of purchasing power and a major debate on the role of the state in 1975–76 which we will now examine. The *tri-pé* model mentioned earlier, which was an association of imperialist state and private national capitals, had achieved a certain stability in the period following 1964.[57] One condition for its success was, however, favourable international conditions and, with these rapidly disappearing, tension began to build up. As perceived by national capital units it was a problem of 'statization'. One lucid bourgeois representative, Roberto Campos, who was Planning Minister after 1964, even maintained that 'Great Britain is a crypto-capitalist country, with socialist rhetoric, and Brazil a crypto-socialist country, with capitalist rhetoric'.[58] Beneath the rhetoric of the statization debate and the accusations that 'totalitarianism' would be the sorry result of this process (what have the dictatorships since 1964 been if not totalitarian?) lies a real conflict.

The national economic plan of 1974 had suggested a certain rearticulation of the economy that would have given the state productive sector a considerable dynamic potential, the political implications of which were exaggerated by the self-appointed guardians of the 'national bourgeoisie'. It could, however, be advanced that though the bourgeoisie may suffer from 'false consciousness' on occasions, in this case the very real contradictions of state intervention in the process of production (outlined in our introduction) were being perceived, in however distorted a fashion, by the bourgeoisie. Whatever the case, the crucial point in this reorientation of the economy is neither the dilemma between 'statism' or 'state capitalism' and private enterprise, as the heated debates in the economic press might lead us to believe, nor between nationalism and further integration into the world capitalist economy.[59] The key aspect, is rather the need to carry out the rearticulation of the economy after the end of the substitution of consumer-durable goods cycle, and to lay the basis for a new level of capital accumulation capable of substituting for the import of 'capital' goods and guaranteeing the provision of basic industrial inputs such as steel and energy sources, for example, hydro-electric power. In fact, there was a threefold rise in the national production of 'capital' goods between 1973 and 1977, and whereas in 1974 there was only one manufacturer of heavy machinery by 1978 there were 21, of which nearly half were under national control. This reorientation of private and state investment toward Department I and the production of fixed capital was clearly expressed in the economic plan for 1975–79. This did not, however, particularly help the automobile industry, whose unsold stock was mounting and whose growth was declining sharply. Those sectors which no longer occupied top priority – the auto industry, consumer goods export, the speculative financial sector, etc. – perceived these changes as an attack and ignored the objective situation of the market. In those years this led to an increasing level of conflict among the various sectors of the bourgeoisie, and added to President Geisel's difficulties in maintaining hegemony within the ruling bloc. If, during the upswing, everyone spoke of 'big power Brazil', the talk during the downturn was of conspiracies, statism and government errors. Thus, in spite of the fact that the government's policies were a step forward for capitalism as a whole, and could lay the basis for a renewed and intensified accumulation of capital, some bourgeois sectors, such as those based in São Paulo, opposed these policies.

In analysing the political debate in Brazil around the nature of the economic crisis, we must confront the simplifications involved when one identifies state intervention in the economy as either the central cause of the crisis, or as its means of resolution. Taking up the arguments developed by these two opposed currents, we can see that the economic action of the state does not result simply from the intentions of a 'state bourgeoisie', or some other hegemonic fraction of the dominant classes. Rather, it is determined fundamentally by the movement of capital as a whole which, for each historical movement, fixes the limits and the various forms of state intervention. In this sense, the activity of the Brazilian state can be explained fundamentally as a necessary form of the restructuring of capital defined by the nature of the economic crisis. According to F.H. Cardoso, the state began to intervene more forcefully in the economy precisely when it was faced by the world economic crisis. It took on further powers to regulate economic activities and began to make its support for private firms conditional on the adherence to the import substitution programme designed to alleviate the balance of payments deficit.[60]

Advocates of 'statization' in the 1970s portrayed the state, and more specifically the state productive sector, as a potential ally of the working class in a bid to re-create the illusions of pre-1964 populist ideology. Effectively, during the whole populist period (but particularly during the Kubitschek period, precisely when imperialism moved in) there was an increased fetishi-zation of the state, expressed in a type of 'state nationalism'. The particular autonomy of the dependent state in Brazil was thus concretised in a 'statist' ideology. The specific dislocation between state and economy pushed the state into its role as arbiter of the 'national interest'. In 1974, in a period of economic and political crisis, the state again began assuming that role, even to the extent of acting against certain fractions of capital. There was an increasing tendency for analysis of this question to focus on surface developments to the detriment of a scientific understanding of the underlying processes. Thus, Evans spoke of 'the new role of the state' leading to the formation of a 'state bourgeoisie' (supposedly the core of the ruling class in Brazil). His conclusion that 'capitalist development in Brazil has required some redefinition of what is meant by capitalism'[61] is not one our analysis would bear out, if by that we mean that some 'intermediate' economic system is emerging, which is no longer shaped by the laws of motion of capital.

To what extent can we say that 'state capitalism' now exists in Brazil? There is a series of writers who to a greater or lesser degree maintain that since 1964 a 'state bourgeoisie' has emerged in Brazil, based on productive investment.[62] The work of Bresser Pereira and C.E. Martins suggests that there is a 'mixed' mode of production in Brazil, with an increasingly autonomous 'techno-bureaucracy' having become the new ruling class.[63] The 'state bourgeoisie' poses the alternative of a mode of production based on production goods (Department I) where the state firms have a decisive weight. According to Martins, 'the new functions taken on by the state apparatus are new to the extent that they are, in reality, *direct functions* of capital.'[64] For Cardoso, similarly:

> these social agents [the 'state bourgeoisie'] are not simple bureaucrats nor do they simply implement the 'public good'. They function sociologically, as the 'office holders of capital', for they support the accumulation of capital in the state enterprises.[65]

In the first place, this approach that characterises capital accumulation in Brazil as 'state capitalism' neglects that its dynamic axis since the mid-1950s has been the consumer-durable goods sector where international private capital predominates. The much vaunted project of 'import substitution' of capital goods and heavy inputs of the 1974 economic plan proved to be economically unrealisable.[66] More fundamentally, these conceptions distort the fundamentals of the capitalist mode of production. The capitalist is no longer defined by the extraction and appropriation of surplus value in the process of accumulation, but rather the 'state bourgeoisie' simply *organises* the process of exploitation. The state bureaucracy operates within limits set by the overall needs of extended capitalist reproduction. The rise of state capital is, therefore, a source for the valorisation of *private* capital and not a competing mode of production.

Turning now to the situation in 1979 (marked by the succession of General Figueiredo to the Presidency) we add a few elements which allow us to situate the 1980s in the light of the preceding analysis. An informed economic analysis suggested that the period 1979–85 would see a shift in broad priorities towards agriculture. Changes in the industrial sector 'will be directed towards a reduction in both the public and foreign private-enterprise components, with a corresponding rise in participation by domestic private firms.'[67] This would seem to confirm our analysis that the 'industrial bourgeoisie' is far from dead. Another development was on the 'statization' front. In early 1979 there were suggestions, from 'key economic figures' in the new regime, of selling state companies to the private sector. This could include up to nine subsidiaries of the state mining concern, *Companhía Vale do Rio Doce* (CVRD) and several from the giant *Petrobrás* oil company. But when a CVRD subsidiary, *Valefertil* (which produces fertilizers) was put up for sale recently, a São Paulo capital spokesperson commented: 'It is utopian to contemplate the sale of the low-profit state-controlled fertiliser companies to the local private sector.'[68] Finally it was bought by *Petrobrás*! What sets the limit to any reorientation in the future, is the hold of imperialism on the Brazilian economy through the massive foreign debt which totalled $40 billion for 1978, with interest and amortisation payments totalling $8 billion. This, of course, is in the context of a renewed slump in the world capitalist economy as a whole.

By 1980, the economic and political crisis in Brazil had reached serious proportions. The widespread strikes of 1979 continued and threatened the overall corporatist subordination of labour operated in the 1940s. Since it came to power in March 1979, the Figueiredo administration had accelerated the political *abertura* process begun under President Geisel. An amnesty for political exiles was declared, and political 'normalisation' was pursued. The international rise of oil prices in 1979–80, and the high interest rates of the world capital markets, acted to aggravate the endogenous crisis of capital accumulation. This was manifested in an increase in the rate of inflation up to 120% and the steep rise of the foreign debt to nearly $95 billion in 1983. Unemployment began to be felt even in the industrial heartland of the South-East, as industrial output fell by nearly 10% in 1981. Transnational investment declined — whereas in 1973 outflows of capital represented 20% of inflows, by 1979 they represented over 80%.[69] At the end of 1980 Volkswagen announced a loss in Brazil, an unprecedented event in their history there.[70] The international recession meant that exports declined and the internal market was still severely depressed as a result of anti-inflationary measures. Cheap labour costs are no longer taken for granted and the restrictions in money supply and bank credit have thwarted capitalist expansion. Not surprisingly, the 'triple alliance' is not as secure as it once was, with each element striving to maintain its own advantages.

In conclusion, there are a number of points which emerge from our analysis:

1) The laws of motion of dependent capitalism dictate an increased intervention of the state in the economy in conditions where economic or political crises lead to a modification in the articulation between nation-states. The 'over-determining' role of the world economic system is mediated by the internal process of capital accumulation, which has its own relatively autonomous dynamic. This autonomy is accentuated during periods of recession for the

world capitalist system, and makes imperative the intervention of the state to reorganise the conditions of production.

2) The particular dynamics of the dependent capitalist economy do not abstract it, however, from the general laws of capitalist development, nor from the inherent contradictions of increased state intervention. The dependent state sector is not 'beyond' the contradictions of capitalism, but is rather an integral element in the contradictory self-expansion process of capital. Nor is state intervention a voluntarist process and the state a mere 'object', above classes and the class struggle. This formalism would endow the state with a near absolute degree of autonomy in carrying out a national development strategy.

3) The basic difference between state intervention in the imperialist nations and dependent social formations such as Brazil, is that in the latter it arose as a precondition for the development of monopoly capital, rather than as a result of its development and contradictions. State intervention does not result from the process of over-accumulation and crisis characteristic of advanced capitalism, but rather from a 'scarcity of capital' or the incapacity of private capital to lay the basis for the expanded reproduction of peripheral capitalism. The extensive role of the state in Russia's early industrialisation process is continued in these countries, where the bourgeoisie is even weaker in the face of imperialism and its 'own' working class. I would suggest that the development of a productive state sector — neither removed from the laws of capitalism nor a 'state capitalism' — is not, in fact, exceptional in dependent social formations, given the congenital weakness of the national bourgeoisie.

4) Further, we must note that, whereas in Latin America the state reached high levels of participation in the economy (20-25%) at a time when roughly half, and in some cases two-thirds, of the labour force still depended on the primary sector in the more developed capitalist countries, this level of state participation in the economy was reached only when the primary sector accounted for less than a fifth of total employment; or, as in the case of Britain, one twentieth. In general, we can refer to an incomplete penetration of capitalist relations of production and a relatively tardy achievement of domination by the capital/labour relation in the dependent social formations.

5) We must reject a linear model of increased state intervention in the dependent social formations based on the historical pattern of Europe or the USA owing to the reasons mentioned in the last point. But it is also necessary to take into account the fundamentally different *political* matrix of state intervention in the dominated nations. We have seen how the laws of motion of capitalism impose themselves in a dependent social formation, but we cannot conceive of capital-in-general generating political forms in abstraction from the concrete unfolding of the class struggle. Thus, the relation between capital and state in Brazil, Algeria or Peru cannot be simply *deduced* but, rather, must be related to their distinct patterns of capital accumulation and the very different history of the class struggle in each country. The study of

Third World societies entails precisely this elaboration of the concrete political path taken by the dependent capital accumulation process in each country.

References

1. Trotsky, L. (1971) *The Permanent Revolution*. London, New Park Publications, p.173.
2. Engels, F. (1969) *Anti-Dühring*. London, Lawrence and Wishart, p.330 (emphasis added).
3. Marx, K. and Engels, F. (1970) *The German Ideology*. London, Lawrence and Wishart, p.80.
4. The debate on 'state derivation' is pursued in Holloway, J. and Picciotto, S. (eds) (1978) *State and Capital*. London, Edward Arnold.
5. Pashukanis, E.B. (1978) *Law and Marxism*. London, Ink Links, p.143.
6. Ibid., p.149.
7. Poulantzas, N. (1973) *Political Power and Social Classes*. London, New Left Books, p.29.
8. Holloway, S. and Picciotto, S. (1977) Capital, Crisis and the State. *Capital and Class* No.2:80.
9. Adapted from Altvater, E. (1973) Notes on some problems of state intervention.*Kapitalstate* No.1:100.
10. Marx, K. (1973) *Grundrisse*. London, Penguin, p.531.
11. Ibid., p.533.
12. Altvater, E. (1973) Notes on some problems of state intervention. p.108.
13. Barker, C. (1978) The state as capital. *International Socialism*. Series 2 No.1:27.
14. Engels, F. (1969) *Anti-Dühring*, p.330-1 (emphasis added).
15. For an introduction to this 'law' and the Marxist economic terminology which follows see Fine, B.L. (1975) *Marx's Capital*. London, Macmillan; or Mandel, E. (1970) *An Introduction to Marxist Economic Theory*. New York, Pathfinder Press.
16. Marx, K. (1981) *Capital* Vol 3. London, Penguin, p.319.
17. Gamble, A. and Walton, P. (1973) The British state and the inflation crisis. *CSE Bulletin*, Autumn, p.8.
18. Marx, K. (1973) *Grundrisse*, p.408.
19. Lenin, V.I. (1970) *Selected Works* Vol.1, p.734.
20. Alavi, H. (1972) The state in post-colonial societies. *New Left Review* No.74. See also Hamilton, N. (1981) State autonomy and dependent capitalism in Latin America. *British Journal of Sociology*, Vol.32 No.2: 305-29, and Bamat, T. (1977) Relative State Autonomy and Capitalism in Brazil and Peru. *The Insurgent Sociologist*, Vol.VII No.2:74-84.
21. Ibid., p.62.
22. Ziemann, W. and Lanzendorfer, M. (1977) The state in peripheral societies. *Socialist Register 1977*. For other attempts to develop a theory

of the peripheral state see Evers, T. (1981) *El Estado en la Periferia Capitalista*. Mexico, Siglo XXI, and Mathias, G. and Salama, P. (1983) *L'État sur développé. Des métropoles au tiers monde*. Paris, Maspero.

23.   Ibid., p.164.

24.   Hein, W. and Stenzel, K. (1973) The capitalist state and underdevelopment in Latin America — the case of Venezuela. *Kapitalistate* No.2:40.

25.   Ibid., p.35.

26.   Tavares, M.C. (1976) Acumulação de capital e industrialização no Brasil. Ph.D dissertation, Federal University of Rio de Janeiro, p.119.

27.   Meade, T. (1978) The transition to capitalism in Brazil: notes on a third road. *Latin American Perspectives*, Vol.V No.3:17.

28.   Evans, P. (1976) Continuities and contradictions in the evolution of Brazilian dependence. *Latin American Perspectives*, Vol.III No.2:33.

29.   Baer, W. et al. (1973) The changing role of the State in the Brazilian economy. *World Development*, Vol.1 No.2:23.

30.   On the formative period of the state in Latin America see Ozlak, O. (1981) The historical formation of the state in Latin America. *Latin American Research Review*, Vol.XVI No.2:3–32, Arnaud, P. (1981) *Estado y Capitalismo en América Latina*. Mexico, Siglo XXI, and on Brazil specifically, Uricochea, F. (1981) *The Patrimonial Foundations of the Brazilian Bureaucratic State*. Berkeley, University of California Press.

31.   Furtado, C. (1968) *The Economic Growth of Brazil*. Berkeley, University of California Press, p.212.

32.   Fausto, B. (1972) *A Revolução de 1930*. São Paulo, Editora Brasiliense.

33.   Ibid., p.97.

34.   Salama, P. (1976) El estado y las crisis en América Latina. *Ideología y Sociedad*, No.17–18:83.

35.   Panitch, L. (1979) Recent theorizations of corporatism. *British Journal of Sociology*, Vol.31 No.2:173. See also the discussion in O'Donnell (1977) Corporatism and the Questions of the State *Authoritarianism and Corporatism in Latin America*, (ed) J. Malloy, Pittsburgh, University of Pittsburgh Press.

36.   Baer, W. et al. (1973) The changing role of the State in the Brazilian Economy, p.25.

37.   Ibid., p.26.

38.   See Gramsci, A. (1971) *Selections from the Prison Notebooks*. London, Lawrence and Wishart, pp.105–20.

39.   Ibid., p.105.

40.   Perhaps one of the best historical treatments of 'populism' is Ianni, O. (1975) *A Formação do Estado Populista Na America Latina*. Rio de Janeiro, Edidora Civilização Brasileira. For an extended theoretical discussion of the concept see Laclau, E. (1977) *Politics and Ideology in Marxist Theory*. London, New Left Books, Ch.4: Towards a theory of populism.

41.   This is the interpretation of Tavares, M.C. (1976) *Acumulação de capital*.

42.   See the extended discussion of this issue and the role of the state in economic development generally in Martins, L. (1976) *Pouvoir et développement économique – formation et évolution des structures politiques au Brésil*. Paris, Anthropos.
43.   Oliveira, F. (1975) A economía brasileira: critica a razão dualista. *Seleções CEBRAP* No.1, p.14.
44.   Evans, P. (1972) Continuities and contradictions, p.47.
45.   Tavares (1976) *Acumulação de capital*, p.128.
46.   Trotsky, L. (1974) *Writings (1938-39)*. New York, Pathfinder Press, p.326.
47.   See Weffort, F. (1970) El Populismo en la politica brasileña. *Brasil Hoy* (ed) C. Furtado. Mexico, Siglo XXI.
48.   Oliveira, F. (1978) *Elegia para una re (li) gião*. São Paulo, Paz e Terra, p.75-6.
49.   The historical context of the coup is described well by Skidmore, T. (1967) *Politics in Brazil, 1930-1964 – An Experiment in Democracy*. New York, Oxford University Press.
50.   Holloway, S. and Picciotto, S. (1977) Capital, Crisis and the State, p.92.
51.   Oliveira, F. (1975) A economía brasileira, p.103.
52.   On the importance of 1964 see Fernandes, A. (1974) Le passage à un nouveau mode d'accumulation au Brésil: les racines de la crise de 1964. *Critiques de l'Économie Politique* No 16-17. On the subsequent evolution of capital accumulation see Faucher, F. (1981) *Le Brésil des militaires*. Montreal, Presses de l'Université de Montréal.
53.   This super-exploitation is documented in Arroyo, R. (1976) Relative and Absolute Pauperization of the Brazilian Proletariat in the Last Decade, Latin American Research Unit Studies No.1.
54.   From Industrial Census 1960 and 1970. On 'denationalization' as a whole see Bandeira, M. (1975) *Carteis e Desnacionalização*. Rio de Janeiro, Ed. Civilização Brasileira.
55.   See O'Donnell (1979) Tensions in the Bureaucratic-Authoritarian State and the Question of Democracy. *The New Authoritarianism in Latin America*, (ed) D. Collier, Princeton, New Jersey, Princeton University Press.
56.   See Mantega, G. (1976) O estado e o capital estrangeiro no Brasil. *Revista Mexicana de Sociología*, Vol.XXXVIII No.4.
57.   On the *tri-pé* see, fundamentally, Evans (1979) *Dependent Development – The Alliance of Multinational, State, and Local Capital in Brazil*. Princeton, New Jersey, Princeton University Press.
58.   *Visão* (3 Oct, 1977). Campos was Ambassador in Britain hence his interest in British labourism.
59.   On the 'statization' debate see Fernandes, A. (1975) Internationalisation et crise du capitalisme brésilien. *Critiques de l'Économie Politique* No.22; and the collection Martins, C.E. (1977) *Estado e capitalismo no Brasil*. São Paulo, Ed. HUCITEC-CEBRAP.
60.   Cardoso, F.H. (1976) Estatização e autoritarismo esclarecido. *Estudos CEBRAP*, No.15:16.

61. Evans (1977) Multinationals, state-owned corporations and the transformation of imperialism: a Brazilian case study. *Economic Development and Cultural Change*, Vol.26:63–4.

62. For a guide to the Latin American debate see Fox, J. (1980) Has Brazil Moved Towards State Capitalism? *Latin American Perspectives*, Vol.VII No.1:64–70; and for a broader survey of the theoretical issues, Perez Sainz, J.P. (1980) Towards a conceptualisation of state capitalism in the periphery. *The Insurgent Sociologist*, Vol.IX No.4:59–68.

63. See Bresser Pereira, (1977) *Estado e subdesenvolvimento industrializado*. São Paulo, Ed. Brasiliense and Martins, C.E. (1977) *Capitalismo de estado e modelo político no Brasil*. Rio de Janeiro, Graal. For a critique see Hirata, H. (1977) Capitalisme d'État, bourgeoisie d'État et mode de production techno-bureaucratique. *Critiques de l'Économie Politique* No.6 (new series).

64. Martins, C.E. (1977) *Capitalismo de estado*, p.24.

65. Cardoso, F.H. and Faletto, E. (1979) *Dependency and Development in Latin America*. Berkeley, University of California Press, p.210.

66. On this, see the review of recent economic problems in Tavares, M.C. (1980) La dinámica ciclica de la industrialización reciente del Brasil. *El Trimestre Económico*, Vol.XLVII No.185:3–47. For a good review of Brazilian economic debates see Mantega, G. and Moraes, M. (1980). A Critique of Brazilian Political Economy. *Capital and Class*, No.10.

67. Cunningham, S. (1979) Brazil — Recent Trends in Industrial Development. *BOLSA Review*, Vol.13 No.4:212.

68. Latin American Economic Report (9 February, 1979).

69. Brazil's Shaky Alliance. *South*, September 1981.

70. Ibid.

8. Comprador Regimes: Central America

> In economically backward and semi-colonial China the
> landlord class and the comprador class are wholly
> appendages of the international bourgeoisie, depending
> upon imperialism for their survival and growth. These
> classes represent the most backward and reactionary
> relations of production in China and hinder the develop-
> ment of her productive forces ... [They] always side
> with imperialism and constitute an extreme counter-
> revolutionary group.
>
> Mao Tse Tung[1]

The term 'comprador' is of Portuguese derivation and literally means 'buyer'.
It was used in 19th Century China to describe the local commercial agents of
foreign companies and was later expanded to encompass all sectors of the
bourgeoisie associated directly with foreign capital. We will use the term
'comprador regime' to describe a political system, typical of Central America,
where the main axis of power is determined by subordination to imperialism.
The first two sections examine the economies characterised by foreign
production 'enclaves' and the more modern variants of 'export platforms'.
The analysis then shifts to the political level where we examine the most
blatant personalist states, such as those of Anastazio Somoza in Nicaragua
and Rafael Trujillo in the Dominican Republic. These regimes were regularly
supported by imperialist interventions on which our brief analysis only
touches the tip of the iceberg. Finally, the 'comprador regimes' of Central
America have, in the last decade, proved to be the 'weak link' of the
imperialist chain in Latin America. We thus examine the basis for this
revolutionary crisis and its prospects.

Enclave Economies

Whereas in some countries of Latin America the principal productive sector
was in national hands in others this sector was simply a foreign 'enclave'
upon the national territory. This occurred because, in a sense, the development

of capitalism in these countries took place without a bourgeois revolution. In the mid-19th Century the formation of the nation-state was intimately linked to the development of an export crop — coffee — in Costa Rica and Guatemala and, towards the end of the century, in El Salvador and Nicaragua. In Honduras, first mining and then bananas constituted the main export sector. This subordination to the international economy was consolidated in the 20th Century and as Torres-Rivas notes 'by the '30's, the Central American republics were no more than agrarian appendices to the central economies'.[2] Foreign capital penetrated these territories without fundamentally altering the pre-capitalist social and economic structure of society. Alliances were established with the large landowners and the commercial bourgeoisie giving rise to the 'feudal-imperialist' alliance referred to by Mao and others. A local clientele class arose, which owed its position directly to the foreign 'enclave' to which it remained subordinate. It serviced the 'enclave', and its interests were, therefore, not 'national' but linked to this foreign outpost on their territory. This was the 'comprador' bourgeoisie defined economically and politically by its dependent relationship with imperialism.

The enclave economies were predominantly agricultural, (plantations and mines were their main form) with only a small derivative local industry. As Julio Cotler writes:

> since the purpose of the enclaves was to extract primary products which were inexpensive in relation to those which could otherwise be obtained in the home market of the metropole, they did not encourage the industrial development of the enclave country, organizing it instead as a monocultural producer of primary products.[3]

The enclave companies themselves often tended to produce the food required by their workers, so that even local agriculture was not stimulated. Otherwise they could rely on subsistence agriculture to bear part of the cost of reproduction of 'their' labour-power. The enclave companies not only controlled the primary-goods sector but also the whole financial and commercial circuit required for their realisation. Rail and sea transport, import-export houses, financial institutions, the ports, all depended on the dominant enclave sector. In this way, a whole web of local client classes was created whose interests coincided with those of the imperialist outpost. This local élite was defined more politically than in accordance with its economic functions. As Cardoso and Faletto explain:

> the economic weakness of national groups of power obliged these groups to maintain a more exclusive form of domination, because they could remain in power only through their connection with the enclave sector, which depended on their ability to keep an internal order that would ensure the supply of labor and natural resources needed by the enclave for economic exploitation.[4]

One of the clearest cases of a foreign 'enclave' economy was the operation of United Fruit, which owned nearly one million acres of land in Honduras and Guatemala. Eduardo Galeano writes how:

> the United Fruit Company swallowed up its competitors in the production and sale of bananas and became Central America's top latifundista, while its affiliates cornered rail and sea transport. It took over ports and set up its own customs and police. The dollar in effect became the national currency of Central America.[5]

This one company had become a state within a state, and the derogatory 'banana republic' expression was coined. Economic control was almost exclusive – railroads linked the plantations to the ports rather than serving as means of communication: taxes and import duties were only nominal for the company, and finally, its workers were forced to buy their goods in company-owned shops so that even this outlay was recouped. This, of course, had its political reflection in an ability to ensure that favourable Presidents only would be nominated. In Honduras, the competition between United Fruit and the rival Cuyamel Fruit Company was even built up into a civil war in 1923 such was the political weight of its affairs. In 1972 United Fruit eventually sold out to Del Monte in Guatemala, after exploiting the natural resources and labour force of the country for many decades. Although with a lower economic and political profile, Del Monte continues the old traditions of United Fruit but with a more 'rational' operation attuned closer to the late 20th Century.[6]

Rather than continue with a general discussion of Central America as a whole we should turn now to a number of individual countries, and first Guatemala. The starting point was the remarkably advanced society and economy of the Mayas. As Susanne Jonas remarks:

> *underdevelopment* as we know it today did not exist in Guatemala prior to 1524 [date of the Spanish conquest], but is the direct outcome of the conquest and integration of Guatemala into an expanding world capitalism.[7]

The colonial period, from 1524 until nominal political independence in 1821, laid the basis for Guatemala's subsequent status of 'comprador capitalism'. Indian labour was used to provide the dye *añil* (indigo), and later cochineal which was the lynchpin of the colonial economy. This production was not geared to an internal market – domination by subsistence production – but the foreign (European, later US) market. The link between the local and the international economy, was the merchant who was the predecessor of the 'comprador bourgeoisie'. As Jonas writes 'more than any other class, they personified the integration of the dependent capitalist economy into an international system designed to meet the needs of the ascendant European bourgeoisie.'[8] In the period after independence, fully 90% of all imports

235

came from Britain and the local merchants became local agents for British finance capital as the country became subordinated to the pound sterling empire.

In 1871 the Liberal 'revolution' helped consolidate the local oligarchy on the basis of the nascent coffee economy. This shift coincided with a decline of British imperialism in the area and the gradual rise of the USA, which was to make Central America its own 'backyard'. The nation-state thus emerges, out of the civil war following the independence struggles, as part of an export-based economy, subject to every shift in the international capitalist economy. The production of coffee led to a transformation of the country's social and economic structure. The coffee *hacienda* became the axis of this renewed social formation as the pre-capitalist barriers to free access to land — state and church — were removed. The agrarian oligarchy was becoming an agrarian bourgeoisie as non-capitalist relations of production became clearly subordinate to the capitalist mode of production. Jonas notes how:

> from the very outset, coffee growing, processing and trade had been largely financed by foreign (mainly German) interests: particularly during crises in coffee prices, Guatemalan producers were often forced to sell out to their creditors.[9]

By 1930, foreign interests controlled around one-third of the land under cultivation, but their weight was even greater than that in so far as their average holdings were 25 times larger than the national average. From the beginning of the 20th Century the economic life of the country was to be dominated by the already mentioned United Fruit Company with its banana-railroad empire.

The other countries of Central America followed diverse economic paths, but all within the broad 'enclave' economy framework. Costa Rica, in particular, was to evolve a distinct social and economic structure owing to the different pattern of colonization. This was based on independent, small property, founded on family farming, and with the virtual absence of an indigenous population. This meant that something approximating the 'farmer' road to capitalism, rather then the more usual 'landlord' path, could prosper here. As Torres-Rivas notes 'the colonial economy and politics did not provide in Costa Rica either the large landowners and parasitical bureaucracy nor the secular power that the church had in other countries.'[10] It is, of cours a myth that social equality therefore prevailed as differentiation between classes progressed. The latifundio did not prosper and few properties surpasse 600 hectares, but the concentration of property outside of land was inevitable. Unlike in its neighbouring countries, the distinct historical pattern of capitalist development in Costa Rica led to a certain degree of political stability and semi-democracy in the 20th Century.

Guatemala, Costa Rica and El Salvador were all integrated into the world economy on the basis of coffee production. Economic growth was based on the relations of production characteristic of the colonial period which were now reinforced — the indigenous *mandamiento* taking the place of the colonial *repartimiento* in enforcing regular labour duties on the *haciendas* and plantations.[11] The liberal 'revolutions' did, however, consolidate an essentially *capitalist* state, thus completing the tasks of the anti-colonial revolts. In other countries, notably Honduras and Nicaragua, the liberal reforms were incomplete, and incorporation into the world market occurred considerably later. This is significant, as Torres-Rivas explains, because:

> where there was not the formation of a primary goods mercantile export system, turned towards the international capitalist economy whose dynamic makes internal factors socially and politically decisive, internal cohesion was weak, and the articulation of regional dominant groups was difficult.[12]

Effectively, in these countries, a centralised state authority was slow to emerge, and several attempts to reform the outmoded colonial structures were frustrated. Regional family groupings, based on patrimony could not compensate for the lack of a stable bourgeois state. This prevented even the minimal bargaining with imperialism which the other 'comprador' regimes could carry out. This pattern persisted until the Second World War.

Panama is in a category of its own, in so far as its integration into the world economy did not occur through the productive sector but rather at the level of circulation through the Panama Canal. Though part of Colombian territory, this did not deter the US interests which needed the canal for commercial and strategic reasons. A Panamanian independence movement was encouraged which came to power in 1903 and immediately leased the Canal Zone to the US in 'perpetuity' (only really renegotiated recently). When it was completed, in 1914, the Canal helped consolidate and maintain a system characterised by:

> an extraordinarily open economy, hypertrophy of the tertiary sector, foreign control of the most dynamic sectors, relegation of the local bourgeoisie, and regional disarticulation[13]

as one author writes.

Cuba, geographically, is part of the Caribbean, but its economic position was similar to that of the Central American republics. Pre-revolutionary Cuba was dominated by the sugar economy, and the sugar-mills absorbed land and labour alike.[14] A 'sugarocracy' made its fortune on Cuba's dependent development based on the crop, but the mass of the population was reduced to poverty. The United States intervened in Cuba towards the end of the 19th Century as an independence movement against Spain was on the verge of victory. The notorious Platt Amendment thereafter maintained Cuba in a neo-colonial relation with the USA. North American interests had already moved from control of sugar exports to establish their interests in the production and transport spheres, and within a few years they owned one quarter of all the land. As Bray and Harding write:

> Representatives of American sugar interests became the leading figures
> in Cuban political life . . . American groups built twenty-seven new mills
> in the first twenty years of the republic, and these processed about half
> of the Cuban sugar production.[15]

Concentration led to an increase of this proportion, reaching three-quarters
of total sugar production on the eve of the 1929 slump. The nature of this
mono-crop export economy was notoriously unstable, with the immensely
prosperous (for some) 'Dance of the Millions' during the First World War
followed by the collapse of prices in 1920 and many bankruptcies. This led
to the sale of sugar fields and mills to Cuban nationals, although US interests
retained around one third of the best land until the 1959 revolution. From
the 1929 slump onwards, Cuban agriculture was basically stagnant, which in
no small part contributed to the 1959 revolution.

United States's domination of the local economy was not restricted to
the sugar sector. McEwan notes how:

> during the 1920s, US investments extended into other areas of the
> Cuban economy: a large share of electric utilities, the telephone system
> and the principal port facilities of Havana were in US hands by the
> late 1920s; the railway system of Cuba was dominated by US concerns
> . . .; and US banks held $100 million of Cuban government debt (not
> to mention private debt).[16]

Fully one-quarter of all direct US investment in Latin America during this
period went to Cuba. Trade agreements favourable to US interests helped
complete the economic stranglehold on Cuba. The sugar quota established by
the US government for Cuba could vary from year to year, with disastrous
effects for the local economy. In this overall situation of extreme dependency,
not surprisingly, Cuban capitalists did not enter into competition with US
interests but rather established themselves in a complementary and subsidiary
position. The Cuban bourgeoisie was, in fact, practically integrated structurally
into the network of imperialism. Sugar, however, required capitalist forms of
labour relations and was more technologically advanced than coffee. The
upsurge of the sugar-mill absorbed the small tobacco growing peasant and the
small urban artisan and forged a proletariat which was seriously to threaten
the stability of the system alongside its urban counterpart. The Revolution of
1933 was, in this sense, a direct portent of what was to come in 1959, but the
system was unable to modernise itself to any significant extent and thereby
absorb the proletarian threat through incorporation.

Export Platforms

The notorious *Yunai* (as United Fruit was known locally) no longer rules
supreme in Central America — other forms of exploitation have taken over.
The international recession of the 1930s precipitated the previous agro-export
model into crisis, though industrialisation did not seriously change the pattern
of accumulation until the 1950s. The 1929 slump led to the collapse of the
internal market in Central America, a situation which lasted until after the
Second World War. The coffee bourgeoisie was no longer the undisputed
leader of the hegemonic bloc, and new social forces committed to
diversification of the economy and industrialisation began to emerge. The
process of import-substitution industrialisation began in the late 1950s,
considerably later than in the rest of Latin America but following the same
pattern. One element in this was the reorientation of US investment away
from primary goods to the manufacturing sector. Direct investment from the
USA in Central America increased from US$173 million in 1943 to US$389
million in 1959. Foreign control over the industrial sector maintained the
pattern of dependent development characteristic of the earlier phase.[17]
Nor did industrialisation result from a crisis in the export sector — coffee
production has tripled since 1948 and banana production has doubled.
Furthermore, as Torres-Rivas mentions:

> the five most important farm products have contributed almost 70
> percent of the exports in Central America, a percentage that has been
> virtually constant for the past fifteen years.[18]

Thus diversification and industrialisation took place only within certain
restricted limits.

The process of industrialisation of the 1960s is inseparable from the
formation of the Central American Common Market in 1960. Though the
United Nations Economic Commission for Latin America had intended to
promote an element of regional planning, US influence (in the shape of
US$100 million in 'aid') meant that, in practice, the Common Market was
formed simply as a mechanism to promote free trade in the area. The
advantages for the transnational corporations were obvious, because a more
sizeable regional internal market was now opened up. A largely foreign-led
wave of industrialisation resulted in industry's contribution to the region's
Gross National Product rising from 13% in 1960 to 18% in 1970. Jenny
Pearce notes how:

> in addition to the traditional industries such as tobacco, textiles and
> clothing there was an expansion of new intermediate industries such as
> pulp and paper, chemicals, fertilizers, cosmetics, plastics, oil refining
> and pharmaceuticals.[19]

There was not, however, a proportionate increase in employment, as most of the new investment was capital-intensive and thus the traditional problem of under- and unemployment persisted. Rural unemployment for the region as a whole was 44% in 1975. At another level, the Common Market was a short term success only because the machinery and technology required by the new assembly plants led to a doubling of the region's balance of payments deficit between 1963 and 1968. By the mid 1970s the foreign debt represented 47% of the Gross Industrial Product in Nicaragua, 42% in Costa Rica, and 'only' 18% in El Salvador.[20]

The Common Market suffered a serious setback with the so-called 'football war' in 1969 between El Salvador and Honduras, which led to the withdrawal of the latter.[21] Behind the superficial causal events of the war there was an accumulation of uneven development over nearly a decade. Guatemala had developed into a major supplier of goods for the region as a whole, and El Salvador followed closely behind. Nicaragua, Honduras and Costa Rica, on the other hand, all had a substantial trade deficit. The first group of countries had established a substantial manufacturing base producing consumer goods for the regional market which undercut the pre-existing artisan economies. They also possessed an at least partially integrated internal market and were able to move into a profitable relation with international monopoly capital. In the build-up to the 1969 war, the numerous farmers from El Salvador in Honduras returned to that already over-populated country with its high concentration of landownership.[22] This accumulated social tensions in El Salvador and the withdrawal of Honduras meant a reduction of the captive market for the country's industrial products. During the 1970s the commercial exchange within the Central American region declined substantially, coinciding with the international capitalist recession of the mid 1970s. The effect of the international slump was more severe than in the 1930s as these countries were now integrated, not only through commerce, but also through a thorough internationalisation of the productive structures and internal market.

The 1970s generally were a period of economic recession in Central America after the boom years of the 1960s. Throughout the decade Costa Rica, Nicaragua and El Salvador experienced negative growth rates, as in 1981, did Guatemala. A recent economic report concludes that 'the prospects of the Central American economies for 1981, both individually and as a system of integration, are very unfavourable.'[23] Effectively, El Salvador experienced a massive flight of capital owing to the political crisis, and even relatively stable Costa Rica faced a larger scale fiscal and monetary crisis. By the end of the decade, the cost of servicing the foreign debt of Central America as a whole had increased more than seven times. Even the agricultural sector had become stagnant after the boom of the 1960s and early 1970s. The growing cost of imported capital goods necessary for the new industrial sector, the increasing cost of international loans and of oil, led to a rapidly spiralling rate of inflation. The underlying cause was the rejection of an alternative model for the Common Market which would have stressed state intervention and regional planning. Instead, multinational capital and the small local élite were the sole beneficiaries of a process of capitalist expansion with inbuilt contradictions. As Torres-Rivas writes:

> The processes of economic integration are processes of economic
> growth. Abandoned to the so-called laws of the market, to the
> anarchic reign of private interests, [so that] the results could not be
> different from those that are presently observed.[24]

   The agrarian structure was to be profoundly affected by the 'modernisation'
drive of the 1960s. Alongside the traditional goods, such as coffee and
bananas, there was a growing importance for cotton and beef. Cotton
cultivation and other cash crops involved rural relations of production.
Seasonal wage-labour also became increasingly important as the agrarian
'revolution' advanced. Even in the coffee sector there was an intense process
of reorganisation and modernisation of the productive structures, with the
coffee barons moving into the industrial and financial sectors as well. The
modernisation of agrarian capitalism went furthest in Costa Rica, whereas in
Guatemala and El Salvador the concentration of landholding set limits on
the emergence of a modern agro-export bourgeoisie. The international banana
producers have adapted to the growing tide of nationalism in the area by
establishing relationships with medium sized 'associate producers' who now
supply over half of their fruit. At the other end of the scale the crisis of the
minifundio — due to concentration of land and basic demographic pressures
— has removed one of the safety valves for the large mass of seasonally
unemployed rural workers. It is a case, as Anthony Winson writes, of:

> a growing surplus population of the poorest peasant farmers, unable to
> get onto the land, while the possibilities of augmenting their meager
> subsistence by labor in commercial agriculture is becoming less and less
> a viable economic alternative because of the changing structure of
> production in the latter.[25]

Certainly, the growing social contradictions in the countryside would become
a key element in the revolutionary crisis of the 1970s.
   In Guatemala we can see clearly the results of this process of conservative
modernisation. The 1954 counter-revolution, in a similar way to the 1971
liberal reform, achieved an expansion of the power bloc, without
fundamentally altering the conditions of class domination. The cotton
growers and industrialists who had sprung up in the economic diversification
of the 1950s now behaved as a 'modernized descendant of the old coffee
oligarchy'.[26] There was a growing interpenetration of élites — landowners
investing in industrial processing and industrialists buying up *fincas* in the
countryside. This was a real process of class recomposition which reinforced
the multisectoral nature of the Guatemalan bourgeoisie. The industrialists
certainly did not have a global modernising project for society, and the
traditional agrarian landholding patterns remained virtually untouched. This
entailed a severe concentration of economic and political power with the

total exclusion of popular sectors. Lacking an internal power base, foreign
support was, therefore, indispensable. Jonas concludes that, 'owing its
domestic dominance to economic, political, and military support from abroad,
the Guatemalan bourgeoisie "belongs" more organically to the international
bourgeoisie than to Guatemalan society.'[27] This clientelist status of the local
bourgeoisie does not, of course, preclude the development of inter-bourgeois
contradictions, particularly on the regional level, as when the Common
Market entered into crisis.

The Common Market was potentially of great benefit to the Guatemalan
'comprador' bourgeoisie. Industrialisation and integration went hand in hand
during the 1960s. The major participant in this process was, however, foreign
capital; in 1968 more than 62% of all major manufacturing plants were in
foreign hands. Neither was this industrialisation creating more jobs; industry's
contribution to Gross Domestic Product rose from 10% in 1950 to 14% in
1970, but industrial employment remained stagnant. Clearly, industrialisation
is not an organic process promoting an integrated development of Guatemalan
society. This does not mean in any real sense that 'Guatemalan industrialisation
is artificial' as Jonas concludes.[28] The truth is, that the very success of
Guatemala in the process of regional integration was based on the success of
the bourgeoisie in maintaining the working class in subordination. Torres-
Rivas says that:

> Paradoxically, the country that has the most important trade returns
> in its favor, Guatemala, is the one that has the highest unemployment
> and the most unequal distribution of income; nor is it coincidental that
> Guatemala is the country with the most anti-union violence.[29]

Effectively, behind the regional imbalance accentuated by the Common
Market lies the much more fundamental social imbalance, which has also
been aggravated by the process of conservative modernisation.

Puerto Rico is probably the most extreme case of dependent capitalist
development along the 'export platform' guidelines, and represents the 'best'
that can be hoped for if current policies are maintained in Central America.[30]
It constitutes a model presented to the rest of the Third World by the United
States. In fact 'Operation Bootstrap', implemented in Puerto Rico after the
Second World War as the Cold War began, was at least partly an inspiration
for the Alliance for Progress. This scheme was essentially a tax-holiday
programme designed to attract labour-intensive industry to the island to soak
up the large number of unemployed. In terms of employment this was hardly
a success, and a large migration to the USA began – 250,000 people left the
island between 1945 and 1953, and 500,000 between 1954 and 1964. In
terms of foreign penetration of local industry it was successful – between
1948 and 1968 foreign control of manufacturing increased from 22% to 77%.
Towards the mid 1960s, as emigration to the USA slowed down and the only
partial success in breaking out of the previous sugar and tobacco based
economy became evident, there was a shift towards investment in heavy

industry, particularly petrochemicals. In a way this model of dependent development is a modernised version of the 'enclave' economy, because Puerto Rico now serves mainly as an 'export platform' for North American multinational firms. This pattern is becoming increasingly important and nearly all the countries of Central America have developed 'free trade zones' and 'world factories' along the lines of Hong Kong and other countries of South East Asia.[31]

The Puerto Rican 'miracle' clearly did not result in improved conditions for the mass of the population, in fact it was premised on low wages. In 1970, 88% of the workforce received less than the Department of Health's calculated minimum family wage. It was, however, immensely profitable for US capital; whereas direct investment in Puerto Rico represented 5% of total US foreign investment, it produced 10% of total profit. Dependency is almost complete, with all raw materials, food and manufactured products coming from the USA. José Villamil writes that:

> Puerto Rico represents in many ways the most extreme example of the dependent growth model . . .; high rates of growth of production with very unequal distribution of its benefits; the definition of the role of the state in terms of providing support for foreign investment; an active and economically important local bourgeoisie, but a dependent one; denationalization of the economy; marginalization of a large proportion of the population and growing external indebtedness.[32]

Even the high growth rates declined in the mid 1970s as this highly integrated economy suffered the effect of the international recession. The main proposal made to resolve this was to withdraw the social legislation extended to the island after the Second World War and to again permit a naked super-exploitation of labour.

Another variant of the 'export platform' model is Panama which, in recent years, has become a 'transnational service platform' — to use the expression of Panamanian economist Xabier Gorostiaga.[33] The Second World War years and the 1960s were a period of expansion based, at least partly, on the Panama Canal Zone, which in 1945 contributed one fifth of the Gross National Product. By the late 1960s, however, there was a shift away from the incipient import-substitution industrialisation towards a Hong Kong-type development based on a total foreign capital economy. The Colon Free Zone (which opened in the 1950s) became an active terminal for assembly and export for 600 firms. More importantly, liberal tax laws have led to a proliferation of 'paper' companies of which there are 55,000 there, engaged in tax evasion, illegal remittance of profits, etc. Most important of all, Panama has become an important international financial centre since 1970, along the lines of the Bahamas or Beirut — there were five banks in 1960, 20 in 1970 and 74 in 1976. Panama is thus becoming part of a global process to rearticulate commercial, banking and industrial capital to maximize accumulation. As Gorostiaga writes:

the financial centres are key axes in the whole process of unification and fusion of partial capitals, and in the process of concentration and centralization of capital in the periphery, the articulation of world finance capital.[34]

Puerto Rico and Panama are the advance posts of monopoly capital in the area, but the very nature of the dependent development model applied means that it cannot be generalised to all the countries of the area.

Personalist State

The 'normal' form of bourgeois rule entails a separation of executive and legislative powers, not to mention a distinction between particular governments and the underlying state form. In some countries of Central America these subtle distinctions hardly operated, nowhere more than in the Nicaragua of Anastasio Somoza. He came to power in 1936 through a coup engineered by the American-trained National Guard, which was ratified in a rigged election the following year. Thus began the Somoza dynasty in Nicaragua, with the father being replaced by Luis Somoza in 1957 and Anastasio Somoza II in 1967. The key to their relatively stable rule (until the mid 1970s) was the National Guard which, as Walker describes:

> rather than being a professional national police and military force, . . . was a sort of Mafia in uniform, which served simultaneously as the personal bodyguard of the Somoza family.[35]

Most forms of criminal activity were centralised by the Guard, much as the army in General Stroessner's Paraguay runs the smuggling business. This has the effect of giving the forces of repression a direct personal stake in the established order. It can, of course, get out of hand as in the way Somoza II handled the international aid provided after the Managua earthquake in 1972 to benefit his family and the Guard. At this point much of the bourgeoisie itself became discontented with the bourgeois order as it manifested itself in Nicaragua.

The main problem for the bourgeoisie was Somoza's blatant attempts to monopolise all profitable activities, something they termed *competencia desleal* or disloyal competition. The Somozas were engaged in cattle-raising, coffee-growing, gold mining, the agri-export sector, food processing, textiles, transport, etc. There was literally no branch of economic activity in which the Somoza group did not own major assets. In a sense, as Jung describes:

> the country's society and economy could not really be described as 'bourgeois' in the traditional sense of the term. Formally free and equal exchange, with all the social and political implications that follow from this, was overshadowed or suppressed, in broad sectors of the economy,

by measures of forcible appropriation sanctioned by political and military power.[36]

In short, Somoza personally summed up capital, the state and government; these latter were seen as his private property. In the long term this personalist rule created several problems. The normal mechanisms of capitalist competition were thwarted, there was little 'relative autonomy' between state and economy or state and government, and fundamentally, the armed forces could not act as the 'last resort' for the bourgeoisie in so far as they were involved in the day to day running of the country. Even the USA, which benefited from the Somoza rule for many years, was determined by the mid 1970s to obtain a peaceful switch to 'Somozaism without Somoza' before the inherent contradictions of this system became uncontrollable.

In the Dominican Republic, Rafael Trujillo ruled supreme between 1930 and his violent death in 1961. Marcel Niedergang writes, with only very slight exaggeration, that:

> by the end of his life, Trujillo was effectively and totally the owner of Santo Domingo. Either in his own name or those of members of his family he owned or controlled the whole of the country's economic activity, apart from those sectors in the hands of American firms.[37]

Nearly half the Dominican labour force was employed by the Trujillo family, he owned 13 of the 14 sugar-mills on the island, and so on. His power rested on a well equipped modern army of 25,000, and four separate bodies of secret police employing some 15,000 informers or *caliés*. Trujillo was more than willing to employ the repressive forces — in 1937 they murdered 20,000 Haitian seasonal agricultural workers in the border areas. Repression was not his sole policy however and during his mandate the 'Benefactor' built roads, a dam and houses, paid off the foreign debt and saw exports rise from $18 million to $140 million. That was because he considered the island as his own personal property and therefore a certain amount of paternalism existed. His North American partners who had helped him to power were, however, unhappy with their minority share of the economy. Particularly after the Cuban Revolution in 1959 they needed to secure a larger share of the island's sugar harvest and, alongside the excluded local bourgeoisie, they promoted his assassination in 1961.

Probably the most notorious personalist dictatorship of the area was that of 'Papa Doc' Duvalier in Haiti between 1957 and 1971 when he was succeeded by his son, 'Baby Doc'.[38] The tyrannical rule of the Duvaliers was supported by the notorious private militia of the *Tonton Macoutes* backed up by North American military aid and training. Niedergang wrote in the 1960s that 'Duvalier is under attack from the former governing class, whose privileges are slowly but surely being withdrawn . . . he draws his support basically from two sources: his militia and the United States.' The concentration of weath was unparalleled — by the mid 1970s barely one percent of the population received almost half the national income. The other side of the coin was poverty, illiteracy and a low life expectancy for the mass of the population. When François Duvalier died, in 1971, there was some hope in imperialist circles that his son Jean-Claude would modernise the structures of capitalism in Haiti. Cheap labour power attracted 230 new industrial plants from the US between 1970 and 1976. Between 1975 and 1978 US investment in the island actually trebled. The runaway plants set up by US capitalists in Puerto Rico were now relocating in Haiti. Only partial success was achieved, because Haiti's ruling oligarchy resolutely refused to develop a modern agri-business and, as Pearce reports, 'the extreme corruption of the Duvalier dynasty has continued, with an estimated 20–40% of the government's income going directly into the family coffers'.[39] In these conditions rational capitalist expansion and stable bourgeois rule is impossible.

In Central America as a whole the 1930s depression was to lead to a general imposition of dictatorial rule throughout the area. In El Salvador, Maximiliano Hernández Martínez ruled from 1931 to 1944, during the same period Jorge Ubico ruled in Guatemala, and from 1931 to 1948 Tiburcio Carias Andino reigned in Honduras. The 1929 slump led to a serious decline in Central American exports, and the peasantry were thrown back into the subsistence sector. This led to a period of stagnation which was to last until the Second World War. There were popular rebellions during this dictatorial phase of course: the 1932 peasants' revolt in El Salvador; the 1933 sugar workers' strike in Cuba; the 1934 plantation workers' strike in Costa Rica and so on.[40] These were all severely repressed, and a broad nationalist/populist movement led by the middle sectors did not appear on the scene. For one reason, the lack of social differentiation did not lead to a sizeable urban middle class. More importantly, these layers could choose between subordination to the oligarchic/dictatorial regimes or the mobilisation of the popular masses in what could be a risky venture. Given their own inherent weakness they were reluctant to attempt any co-optive mobilisation of the masses, and the economic and political structures passed through the years of the depression virtually unchanged.

In the post-Second World War period there was a gradual tendency towards industrialisation, as capitalist relations of production expanded outwards from the enclaves and into the urban centres. An urban bourgeoisie began to form in the cities and a small rural bourgeoisie emerged to challenge the previous total domination of the traditional oligarchy. Though the political rhythms varied from country to country, social differentiations led to an incipient class struggle, with unionisation in both the cities and the countryside imposing an element of popular rights. This process accelerated in the 1960s and, as Mario Posas writes for Honduras:

> different blocs of the bourgeoisie emerged with distinct political projects: one, composed of agrarian-bourgeois interests, linked to extensive exploitation of the land and urban industrialists and bankers and merchants associated with foreign capital, advocated a political

project of oligarchic content and limited social participation. Another, composed of a nucleus of industrial, financial and agro-industrial bourgeoisie, less linked to imperialist capital because it blocks its own ability to accumulate . . . advocates a reformist national project with broader social participation.[41]

My only reservation about this analysis is that it tends to follow Mao's understanding of 'comprador' bourgeoisie too closely – i.e., as a distinct fraction of the bourgeoisie, rather than as a range of functions that different sections of the bourgeoisie adopt at different times. The same capitalist can be engaged at the same time in 'national' and 'comprador' activities or functions.

The 1970s saw both an accentuation of the inter-bourgeois crisis and the challenge of the popular masses. The horizontal expansion of the market during the 1960s through the Common Market had created more tension in spite of its dynamising effect. International monopoly capital had basically defeated the nationalist-reformist project, but the social sectors promoting this orientation grew in strength. They were, in fact, precisely those sectors of the bourgeoisie opposed to Somoza in Nicaragua to such an extent that they would co-operate with an armed-struggle socialist organisation in his overthrow. The 1960s boom had for a while masked the concentrationist and socially exclusive effects of capitalist accumulation, but in the 1970s these become fully visible. Repression only intensified the popular protests that emerged – strikes put down by force led to workers accepting force as a legitimate means of struggle. The Central American bourgeoisie and their states turned increasingly to US imperialism to shore up their regimes – with aid and, of course, military hardware. The international recession of 1974–75, from which there has only been a partial and hesitant recovery since, served only to reduce the room for manoeuvre of the 'comprador' regimes. The class struggle had reached a pitch – again uneven over time and space – from which a climb-down and restoration of 'normal' bourgeois rule was difficult. The tendency is for those countries, such as Costa Rica, which have maintained a semblance of normality, to follow the course of El Salvador and Guatemala.

It is now clear that there is a fundamental difference between this type of state and that developed in the larger more 'advanced' republics of South America. This difference is well captured in the distinction which Gramsci drew between Russian and 'Western' type societies:

> in Russia the state was everything, civil society was primordial and gelatinous; in the West, there was a proper relation between state and civil society, and when the state trembled a sturdy structure of civil society was at once revealed. The state was only an outer ditch, behind which there stood a powerful system of fortresses and earthworks . . .[42]

In Somoza's Nicaragua, Trujillo's Dominican Republic or Duvalier's Haiti there was no such 'proper relation' between state and civil society, no 'powerful system of fortresses' behind the state. When the state trembled the whole society shook. As we shall see shortly, when Somoza's National Guard was defeated the bourgeois state simply collapsed. This is where the 'comprador' regimes differ most fundamentally from those of the larger countries of Latin America, particularly Mexico, Brazil and Argentina, where the bourgeoisie has developed a strong and articulate 'civil society' standing behind the 'outer ditch' of the state. Likewise, imperialist intervention becomes more necessary, unlike in countries such as Brazil in 1964 and Argentina in 1966 where counter-revolutionary movements were formed by *internal* class forces, even though aided by imperialism.

Under the 'comprador' regimes the national question clearly assumes a direct and extremely important role. There is often a total and transparent identification between the local ruling class and imperialism. When workers and peasants confront the bourgeoisie in struggle they are facing imperialism itself. The class struggle assumes a national character independently of the will of the participants. There is an unresolved colonial question in Puerto Rico, in many parts of the Caribbean and, until recently, in Belize.[43] There is an even greater semi-colonial question in most of the countries of the area where the local ruling class is merely an agent of imperialism. Revolutions in Cuba, more recently in Nicaragua and Grenada, as in Bolivia in 1952, show that the 'comprador' regime is particularly susceptible to revolutionary challenge. This is partly because it is unable to structure a durable social base, and the tendency towards personalist dictatorships even alienates part of the ruling class. These states also have an unresolved agrarian question which, as we have seen, is a potent and contemporary issue still. In conclusion, the comprador regime tends to lead to an inter-bourgeois crisis, manifests a lack of legitimacy as a bourgeois state, and is prone to overthrow by a broad anti-imperialist movement which perceives it as the direct enemy.

Imperialist Intervention

Central America (and the Caribbean) has become a byword for direct and naked imperialist intervention. This occurs when imperialist interests are threatened and the local ruling class is judged incapable of containing the subversion. In Figure 8.1 we see just some in the long series of imperialist interventions in Central America from 1898 to 1979. In the wake of the Civil War the North American bourgeoisie moved decisively to establish its overseas imperialist domain. Political domination was not always necessary, and an informal American empire began to take shape. As Stedman-Jones writes:

> the expansion of the frontier by trade into South America and the Pacific in the 1880s and early 1890s was increasingly associated with the idea of an ever expanding commercial frontier which would alleviate discontent at home.[44]

Figure 8.1
US Intervention in Central America (1898-1979)

1898-1902	U.S. troops occupy Cuba
1901	U.S. 'acquires' Puerto Rico
1905	U.S. Marines land in Honduras
1906-09	U.S. troops reoccupy Cuba
1908	U.S. troops sent to Panama
1912-33	U.S. Marines occupy Nicaragua
1914-34	U.S. Marines occupy Haiti
1916-24	U.S. Marines occupy Dominican Republic
1917-23	U.S. Marines occupy Cuba
1932	U.S. warships sent to El Salvador
1954	CIA backed invasion of Guatemala
1961	CIA backed invasion of Cuba (Bay of Pigs)
1965	U.S. Marines invade Dominican Republic
1979	U.S. 'military advisers' in El Salvador

Source: Pearce, J. (1981) *Under the Eagle*. London, Latin American Bureau, pp.6-7.

The war with Spain in 1898 put the seal on US domination over Central America and the Caribbean. Puerto Rico was seized as part of the 'spoils of war', Cuba was occupied by American troops from 1898 to 1902, then the Panama Canal Zone was acquired. An age of 'dollar diplomacy' and debt collection by gunboat had now begun. The expansion of US capitalism in Latin America would be underwritten by the military might of the rising imperialist power. One of the longest US military occupations was that of Nicaragua, where they occupied the national territory from 1912 to 1933 with only one year's break. For six years this occupation was resisted by the guerrilla army of Augusto César Sandino who gave his name to a new resistance movement in the 1960s.

The case of Panama is particularly revealing of the fusion of the economic, military and strategic objectives of US imperialism. The treaty signed on the country's nominal independence in 1903 charged the USA with 'maintenance of public order' in the territory. To this end the US Army supervised elections there in 1908, 1912 and 1918 and, after the completion of the Canal in 1914, established a permanent garrison in the Canal Zone. These were responsible for killing 24 people and injuring some 400 during nationalist demonstrations against the imperialist presence in 1964. Now the Canal is becoming obsolete and recent negotiations should lead to the withdrawal of the 14,000 American troops by 1999. The 1977 agreement, however, stipulates that the zone will continue to fulfil its counter-insurgency role for US imperialism and its Latin American allies. The notorious US Army School of the Americas sited in the Canal Zone has trained tens of thousands of Latin American military officers in the techniques of anti-guerrilla warfare. There is, in fact, an integrated counter-revolutionary military system based in Panama with its full panoply of intelligence, telecommunications, training and operational capabilities.[45] Through this medium (in which nearly $5,000 million dollars were invested by 1970) the USA has promoted the formation of the Central American Defence Council, which acts as the headquarters of the repressive apparatus of the region. Panama's Canal Zone, with the headquarters of the United States Southern Command, along with Puerto Rico and the Guantanamo base in Cuba, forms part of an imperialist ring of steel designed to ensure US hegemony in its 'backyard'.

In 1954 a CIA backed military coup overthrew the anti-imperialist government of Jacobo Arbenz in Guatemala.[46] In 1944 a student strike escalated into a general strike and led to the resignation of the dictator Ubico and, after a short transition government, an armed movement of workers, students and soldiers seized power. This led to the election of Juan José Arévalo as President in 1945, who proceeded to implement a broadly social-democratic nationalist programme. The urban labour movement made considerable advances but an agrarian reform was continually blocked. In the 1950 elections, Arévalo was replaced as President by the Minister of Defence, Jacobo Arbenz. His inaugural speech announced his aim of converting Guatemala:

> from a dependent nation with a semi-colonial economy to an economically independent country; second, to transform our nation from a backward nation with a predominantly feudal economy to a modern capitalist economy . . .[47]

This would be accomplished with the raising of the living standards of the masses. This industrialising, mildly redistributivist programme, was quite in accordance with prevailing United Nations recommendations for Latin America. The problem came when measures were taken to regulate certain operations of the United Fruit Company which, until then, had been a law unto itself.

In 1951 United Fruit resisted government attempts to mediate in a wage dispute and, when some of its land was seized to guarantee the payment of back wages, the company responded by closing down its shipping service and laying off 4,000 workers. The conflict became more serious in 1952 when Arbenz introduced an agrarian reform law which was basically aimed at idle lands. Early in 1953 some 100,000 peasants received land plots and 1,000 large plantations were affected. United Fruit Company, with more than half a million acres (of which less than one fifth were actually utilised) was due to have two thirds of its land expropriated to be compensated for at the value declared in the company's tax returns. A train of events was then set in motion which led to a bloody counter-revolution. The US State Department, which was tied through personal links to United Fruit, began to mobilise to meet the 'communist' threat of Arbenz. On the pretext of a small consignment of Czechoslovak arms sent to Guatemala, the CIA intensified its aid to

Castillo Armas and his mercenary army which was massing in neighbouring Honduras. In mid 1954 Castillo Armas began his invasion of Guatemala, backed up by CIA organised service operations. As Jonas concludes:

> the US could not tolerate the Guatemalan Revolution essentially
> because even a nationalistic independent capitalism directly threatened
> existing US interests there and called into question the feasibility of
> maintaining the area as a 'safe' preserve for future investments.[48]

Castillo Armas assumed power, reversed the land reform, launched a severe repression of the trade union and peasant movements, and opened the doors of the economy to foreign investment.

In 1965 the US Marines invaded Santo Domingo, the capital of the Dominican Republic.[49] After the death of the dictator Trujillo, in 1961, the mildly reformist Juan Bosch was elected to power in 1962 (after the token presidency of Balaguer). His Alliance for Progress type of programme drove the oligarchy into opposition, but his failure to dismantle the repressive apparatus of the state disillusioned his popular base. Having spent barely a year in power Bosch was overthrown by a reactionary military coup but a rebel movement began stirring within the armed forces who demanded a return to the Constitution. There was widespread middle-class and working-class support for the democratic anti-corruption programme of the rebels. The rising of April 1965 was set on a victorious course when the rebel soldiers handed out arms to the civilian population. The American Embassy called for US intervention 'to protect the lives and property of their nationals'. By mid-May there were 22,000 US marines and parachute troops on the island to save it from 'communism'. The rebels under Colonel Caamano resolutely faced up to imperialist intervention until they were defeated in September. After 3–4,000 Dominicans had been killed the country was once more made safe for the dollar.

Since Guatemala in 1954 and Santo Domingo in 1965 imperialist intervention has continued unabated in the area. There is now ample evidence that the USA did not cease in its efforts to destabilise the Cuban Revolution after the abortive Bay of Pigs invasion in 1961. With the victory of the Nicaraguan Revolution in 1979 US military intervention in the area intensified. Until his overthrow, the dictator Somoza was the largest recipient of US military aid in the area. When he was on the brink of collapse the US government attempted to persuade the Organisation of American States to send in a 'peacekeeping force'. All this failed, and then attention shifted to El Salvador. In 1981 an intensive large scale programme of counter-insurgency training was announced for El Salvador's soldiers and officers. In 1982, the US provided massive assistance for replacement of military aircraft destroyed by the guerrilla movement. Soon, US military 'advisers' were making their presence felt in the anti-guerrilla war. Guatemala, next in line according to the 'domino theory', also received its share of US aid. At a regional level there was a series of large scale naval 'exercises' designed to reassert US hegemony in the area. At the other extreme, covert operations were intensified in the region. To supplement the iron fist a large scale assistance programme for the Caribbean was put forward as a type of mini-Marshall Plan. This was more a part of the propaganda war and does not augur a return to the Alliance for Progress policy; today, strong dictators are seen as the best barrier to 'communism'.

Revolutionary Crisis

Today, Central America as a whole has become the 'weak link' of the imperialist chain in Latin America.[50] Cuba in 1959, and Nicaragua 20 years later in 1979, are the revolutionary highpoints of this imperialist crisis. It is clearly of vital importance to understand the underlying dynamic of current events in terms of the preceding analysis.

While imperialism could maintain its alliance with the local dominant pre-capitalist classes (basically the agrarian and commercial oligarchy) the typical 'comprador' state could be maintained in all its repressive simplicity. However, the capitalist mode of production inevitably generates contradictory elements, as industrialisation leads to the formation of a bourgeousie and, of course, a proletariat. The very success of 'modernisation' in the 1960s led to the revolutionary crisis of the 1970s; more specifically, it was the failure to achieve any measure of redistribution of wealth as capital accumulation accelerated. In Table 8.1 we can see graphically how unequal the distribution of wealth in Central America was in 1970. A small wealth owning class, representing 5% of the population, receives slightly less than one third of the total disposable income, whereas the poorest half of the population receives only 13% of total income. The annual per capita income of the various social sectors shows a particularly acute concentration of wealth, even by Latin American standards.

Poverty in itself does not necessarily lead to an explosive or revolutionary situation. Changes in the class structure of Central America since the 1960s do, however, point in this direction. In El Salvador, for example, the industrial proletariat in the 1970s comprised 42% of urban wage earners, which represents a big change since the 1930s. Between 1960 and 1975 the total number of wage earners not employed in agriculture grew by about one third, whereas the total of self-employed almost tripled over the same period. As Jung notes, this last element 'expresses on the one hand the sharp growth of an independent middle class, on the other a process of marginalization.'[51] Both these sectors, but for different reasons of course, will potentially represent an ally of the working class. The concentration of land, which accelerated throughout Central America in the 1960s, led to a massive proletarianisation of the peasantry, as well as chronic underemployment. It also led to a rapid shift of population to the cities where the poverty ridden *barrios* formed on the outskirts. The *barrios* were, in fact, a secure base for the revolutionary forces in Nicaragua, and now in El Salvador. In conclusion,

Table 8.1
Distribution of Income in Central America (1970)

Stratum	Percentage total population	Annual per capita income (pesos)	Strata of income (%)
High	5	17,600	31
Middle	15	5,680	30
Low	30	246	26
Very Low	50	74	13

Source: Torres-Rivas, E. (1980) The Central American Model of Growth. *Latin American Perspectives*, Vol. VII No. 2/3, p.36.

the anarchic development of capitalism in the 1960s created both bourgeois and popular forces opposed to the patrimonial 'comprador' regimes. This took the form of revolutionary nationalism which contained diverse class projects, such as the 'modernising' capitalist democracy of the embryonic 'national bourgeoisie', and the socially planned economy and popular democracy of the exploited classes.

The Cuban revolution is still the classic case of a 'comprador' state collapsing from its own internal contradictions, through a subversive threat that could have been contained in the more developed capitalisms of the Southern Cone. In the first place, there was the weakness of the local bourgeoisie and the fragility of its institutions. As Robin Blackburn wrote, with only slight exaggeration:

> No coherent ruling-class had ever established stable domination . . . there were no powerful institutions or ideology to oppose: only the isolated and opportunist Batista machine. . . . The enemy was a starkly corrupt and asocial machine. Its character determined the conditions of its overthrow.[52]

Cuba presented a relatively weak and unsophisticated bourgeoisie alongside a large and relatively politicised proletariat. The popular camp had accumulated valuable experience in the national and class struggles from the 30 years struggle for independence culminating in 1898; the 1933 rising to overthrow the Machado dictatorship to the 1953 attack on Moncada Barracks by the revolutionary nationalist forces of Fidel Castro. The ideology of the last and eventually victorious movement is well summed up in Fidel's 'History Will Absolve Me' speech from the dock. The basic thrust was to assert the need for national sovereignty, an agrarian reform and a redistirbution of wealth to aid the poorest in society. As Fidel was to say later:

> at the time of the Moncada, I was a pure revolutionary but not a Marxist revolutionary. In my defense . . . I outlined a very radical

revolution but I thought then that it could be done under the constitution of 1940 and within a democratic system.[53]

That an orientation only relatively more radical than that of Jacobo Arbenz in Guatemala led to socialism was due, at least in part, to the social forces which provided the base for the revolutionary war between 1956 and 1959. On one hand, the model 'comprador' regime of Fulgencio Batista, who had dominated Cuban politics since 1934, drove wide sectors of the bourgeoisie into opposition. Domination by the USA prevented the emergence of a sizeable national bourgeoisie with its own accumulation base. The prospects of the petty bourgeoisie, both urban and rural, were also threatened by imperialist-oligarchic domination. On the other hand, the sugar economy had produced a sizeable proletariat, both on the plantations and in the sugar-mills. The peasantry itself was closely linked to the proletariat through that 'semi-proletarian' force it provided to work on a seasonal basis on the plantations. There was, in fact, a relatively integrated popular camp with no significant urban/rural or skilled/unskilled division. When the rebels came to power, early in 1959, after a decisive general strike in the cities, the contradictions within the anti-imperialist coalition came out in the open. Gradually all the forces who had merely supported a return to constitutional rule and a stable national base for private capitalist accumulation deserted the rebels. The 'total transformation of Cuban life' promised by Castro in 1953 could not be achieved under independent capitalist rule, and in 1961 he was declaring the socialist character of the Cuban revolution (see Chapter 11).

After long years of failure, the victory of the Nicaraguan revolution in 1979 showed that the 'lessons of Cuba' were not yet outdated.[54] The success of the Sandinista liberation movement, in a fierce war which culminated in a popular insurrection, is due primarily to an intelligent assessment of inter-bourgeois contradictions and an uncompromising radicalism on all fronts. One interpretation articulated here by Norma Chinchilla maintains that:

> their ability to ally with sectors of the bourgeoisie, not only to over-throw Somoza but to contribute to a mixed economy . . . opens up a whole new chapter in the art of making revolution in Latin America.[55]

Now, several years after the revolution the prospects of a 'mixed economy' in the context of 'political pluralism' is less evident. Almost the whole of the Nicaraguan bourgeoisie threw its weight into the struggle against Somoza for the type of reason we examined in a previous section: to establish stable bourgeois rule to allow capitalist competition to flourish. They paid lip-service to a programme considerably more radical than that of Castro 20 years earlier, but they certainly had not been transformed into a 'progressive' social force. The intensified social conflict in Nicaragua since 1979 testifies to the Sandinistas own assessment that it would be 'easier' to seize power than to reconstruct the country in a socialist direction afterwards.

The phases of the Nicaraguan insurrection illustrate quite well the different social forces at work in the Central American revolutionary crisis. In 1978, the bourgeois opposition called what amounted to an employers' strike which paralysed large parts of the country. Later, a Broad Opposition Front was formed which, with US support, could have achieved a relatively peaceful *recambio* (changeover) of the regime. Towards the end of the year another national strike took on a much more radical content in the context of a military rising organised by the Sandinistas. Somoza, who had earlier engineered the assassination of the main opposition figure (Pedro Chamorro), now moved more decisively to block any compromise which could have saved capitalism, by dropping the regime. By 1979 the bourgeois opposition was overwhelmed by the radical mass mobilisations organised by the Sandinistas, and in the final victorious phase they were swept aside. Even at that late stage Panama — which along with Costa Rica, Venezuela, Mexico and European social democracy had supported the opposition to Somoza — tried to persuade the Sandinistas´to train the new Nicaraguan army in that country. It was too late for the bourgeoisie to save the basic organs of the bourgeois state, which had been so closely identified with Somoza as to make the collapse of the regime equivalent to the collapse of the state. If private capital remained in Nicaragua after 1979 it was on the conditions imposed by the radical Sandinista movement.

Today (1982) El Salvador is rapidly following in the footsteps of Nicaragua.[56] Fifty years earlier a communist led peasant insurrection had been put down with a massacre of tens of thousands. In the years since, a succession of brutal military dictatorships has ruled in El Salvador. From the start this country went through a process of development more organic and integrated than that of, say, Honduras or Nicaragua. The liberal reform of the 19th Century had been swift and thorough; there were no banana or mining enclaves then. Capitalist relations of production developed relatively rapidly with the formation of a concentrated proletariat and a rural semi-proletariat. Consequently, a relatively homogenous and strong oligarchy and later, bourgeoisie, have developed. This was consolidated by the overthrow of the dictator Martínez in 1944 in a movement led by an incipient industrial bourgeoisie. The 1960s were a prosperous phase for the bourgeoisie on account of the Common Market, as we saw earlier. The 1970s finally saw the beginning of a fierce war of liberation which has still not run its full course.

By the mid-1970s, three relatively clear political groupings could be distinguished: the regime and its supporters, the centrist or liberal opposition and the armed organisations of the revolutionary left. In the late 1970s, the armed struggle intensified as severe repression of the urban and rural social movements closed the door to all forms of legal protest. Even the Catholic Church, which had been a key supporter of the regime in the 1960s, was now severely persecuted and driven into radical opposition. In 1979 a military coup displaced the dictatorship of Romero, who had come to power in 1976 through fraudulent elections. Supported by the centrist opposition, and even for a time the Communist Party, the military junta launched a reformist programme, including an agrarian reform. This democratic counter-revolution, with US backing, was designed to cut the ground from under the feet of the guerrillas by winning over their social base of support. This type of strategy had been quite successful in Peru in 1968, when a reformist military regime had been able to break out of the 'comprador' mould and modernise the structures of domination. The 'reform plus repression' strategy failed, mainly because of the resistance of the socialist and popular movements to co-optation. The lessons of Nicaragua had been learned by the bourgeoisie of El Salvador. No matter how reasonable or rational the programme of the revolutionary movement, the dynamic of the class struggle, under conditions of extreme dependency as in Central America, would lead to a threat to the bourgeois order.

Guatemala is only slightly behind El Salvador in the intensity of its revolutionary crisis.[57] After the 1944–54 democratic interlude, Guatemala returned to the pattern of repressive regimes subordinated to imperialism. In the wake of the successful Cuban revolution, a number of guerrilla movements began to operate, reaching a peak in the mid-1960s. Towards the end of the decade they were all defeated, with the aid of the US counter-insurgency industry. Their basic failure was a lack of organic links with the masses, which was due to the *foquista* orientation, but also to the repression following the 1955 counter-revolution and the, as yet, tenuous class formation of the proletariat. Conditions changed with the 1960s wave of industrialisation and the shift in hegemony within the ruling bloc from the agro-export bourgeoisie to an industrial-financial fraction of the bourgeoisie. The 'new' working class which emerged in this period launched a series of militant strikes in the mid-1960s. With the election of the Lucas García government, in 1978, the class conflict sharpened, with mass mobilisations on the one side and intense repression on the other. As torture, kidnappings and massacres multiplied so did the social support of a new generation of guerrilla movements. The orientation of these was towards a combination of mass struggle and armed action with the perspective of a 'protracted people's war'. By 1982 the four main guerrilla organisations had united under a single command and had established their capacity to launch major operations. Indicative of their new orientation and its success was the number of indigenous people (who make up half the population) who joined the movement. Thus, the struggle in Guatemala, much more than in Nicaragua or El Salvador, contains a definite ethnic as well as class dimension. As the struggle intensifies the Guatemalan ruling class has closed ranks, and no swift victory, as in Nicaragua, seems likely. There is, of course, much more at stake in Guatemala for the USA as well, with the question of oil – not to mention the proximity to Mexico – making a direct military intervention at least possible. Increasingly, the prospect of 'socialism or barbarism' becomes a real and direct choice in Guatemala.

In conclusion, the 'comprador' regimes of Central America have become the 'weak links' of the imperialist chain in Latin America. This is fundamentally because the particular form of dependent capitalist development in these countries — from the 'enclave' economies to the Common Market — has accumulated a whole range of social contradictions. The contradictions engendered by monopoly capitalism are overlaid on those of competitive capitalism and even its pre-capitalist past. This leads to a 'condensation' of contradictions which are fused in an explosive mix which finds its expression through the, as yet, unresolved national question.

References

1. Mao Tse Tung (1967) *Selected Reading From the Works of Mao Tse Tung*. Peking, Foreign Language Press, p.11.
2. Torres-Rivas, E. (1970) *Problems of Development and Dependence of Central America*. Seminar on Modernisation and Development in Latin America, University of Essex, p.1. For an extended analysis see Torres Rivas, E. (1973) *Interpretación del Desarollo Social Centroamericano*. Costa Rica, EDUCA, and also Monteforte Toledo, M. (1972) *Centroamérica, subdesarollo y revolución*. Mexico, UNAM.
3. Cotler, J. (1979) State and Regime: Comparative Notes on the Southern Cone and the 'Enclave' Societies. *The New Authoritarianism in Latin America*, (ed) D. Collier. Princeton, NJ, Princeton University Press, p.263.
4. Cardoso, F.H. and Faletto, E. (1979) *Dependency and Development in Latin America*. Berkeley, University of California Press, p.102.
5. Galeano, E. (1973) *Open Veins of Latin America*. New York, Monthly Review Press, p.120.
6. See Burbach, R. and Flynn, P. (1980) *Agribusiness in the Americas*. New York, Monthly Review Press, Ch.11: A New 'Banana Republic': Del Monte in Guatemala.
7. Jonas, S. (1974) Guatemala. *Latin America: the struggle with dependency and beyond*, (ed) R. Chilcote and J. Edelstein. New York, Schenkman Publishing Co. p.100. See also Melville, T. and Melville, M. (1971) *Guatemala — Another Vietnam?*. London, Penguin Books.
8. Ibid., p.115.
9. Ibid., p.135.
10. Torres-Rivas, E. (1976) Síntesis Histórica del Proceso Político. *Centroamérica Hoy*, Torres-Rivas et al. Mexico, Siglo XXI, p.33. For a broad history of Costa Rica, see Denton, C. (1971) *Patterns of Costa Rican Politics*. Boston, Allyn and Bacon.
11. Ibid., p.60.
12. Ibid., p.22.
13. Manduley, J. (1980) Panama: Dependent Capitalism and Beyond. *Latin American Perspectives*, Vol.VII No.2/3:59. See also La Feber, W. (1978) *The Panama Canal: The Crisis in Historical Perspective*. New York, Oxford University Press.

14. See Fraginals, M.M. (1976) *The Sugarmill – The Socio-Economic Complex of Sugar in Cuba*. New York, Monthly Review Press.
15. Bray, D. and Harding, T. (1974) Cuba. *Latin America: the struggle with dependency and beyond*, p.594.
16. MacEwan, A. (1981) *Revolution and Economic Development in Cuba*. London, Macmillan, p.13.
17. See Rivas, D.C. (1980) *Acumulación de Capital y Empresas Trans- nacionales en Centroamérica*. Mexico, Siglo XXI; and Gorostiaga, X. et al., (1974) *La inversión extranjera en centroamérica*. Costa Rica, EDUCA.
18. Torres-Rivas, E. (1980) The Central American Model of Growth: Crisis for Whom? *Latin American Perspectives*, Vol.VII No.2/2:29.
19. Pearce, J. (1981) *Under the Eagle – US Intervention in Central America and the Caribbean*. London, Latin American Bureau, p.48.
20. Torres-Rivas, E. (1980) The Central American Model of Growth, p.33.
21. See Carias, M.V. and Slutsky, D. (eds) (1971) *La guerra inútil*. Costa Rica, EDUCA and Anderson, T. (1981) *The War of the Dispossessed: Honduras and El Salvador, 1969*. Lincoln Nebraska, University of Nebraska Press.
22. See Richter, E. (1980) Social Classes, Accumulation, and the Crisis of 'Over population' in El Salvador. *Latin American Perspectives* Vol.VII No.2/3:114-39.
23. Inter-American Development Bank, (1981) *Economic and Social Progress in Latin America*. Washington DC, Inter-American Development Bank, p.113.
24. Torres-Rivas, E. (1980) The Central American Model of Growth, p.42.
25. Winson, A. (1978) Class Structure and Agrarian Transition in Central America. *Latin American Perspectives*, Vol.V No.4:42.
26. Torres-Rivas, E. (1969) *Proceso y estructuras de una sociedad dependiente (Centroamérica)*. Santiago, Ed. Prensa Latinoamericana, p.151.
27. Jonas, S. (1974) Guatemala, p.174.
28. Ibid., p.179.
29. Torres-Rivas (1980) The Central American Model of Growth, p.42.
30. See Maldonado-Denis, M. (1972) *Puerto Rico: A Socio-Economic Interpretation*. New York, Random House; and *Latin American Perspectives*, Vol.III No.3 (1976) Puerto Rico: Class Struggle and National Liberation.
31. See Frobel, F., Heinrichs, J. and Kreye, O. (1980) *The New International Division of Labour*. Cambridge, Cambridge University Press. Part III: The world market oriented industrialisation of the developing countries: Free production zones and world market factories.
32. Villamil, J. (1979) Puerto Rico 1948-1976: The Limits of Dependent Growth. *Transnational Capitalism and National Development*, (ed) J. Villamil. Brighton, Harvester Press, p.253.
33. Gorostiaga, X. (1978) *Los centros financieros internacionales en los*

paises subdesarollados. Mexico, Instituto Latinoamericano de Estudos Transnacionales.

34. Ibid., p.110.
35. Walker, T. (1981) *Nicaragua: The Land of Sandino.* Boulder, Co., Westview Press, p.27. On the economy of Somozaism, see Wheelock, J.I. (1975) *Imperialismo y dictadura: crisis de una formación social.* Mexico, Siglo XXI.
36. Jung, H. (1979) *Behind the Nicaraguan Revolution.* New Left Review, No.117:71.
37. Niedergang, M. (1971) *The Twenty Latin Americas*, Vol.II, London, Penguin, p.262.
38. For a broad history see Nicholls, D. (1980) *From Dessalines to Duvalier: Race, Colour and National Independence in Haiti.* Cambridge, Cambridge University Press.
39. Pearce, J. (1981) *Under the Eagle*, p.91.
40. See respectively, Anderson, T. (1971) *Matanza. El Salvador's Communist Revolt of 1932.* Lincoln,Nebraska, University of Nebraska and Aguilar, L. (1972) *Cuba 1933: Prologue to Revolution.* New York, Norton.
41. Posas, M. (1980) Honduras at the Crossroads. *Latin American Perspectives*, Vol.VII No.2/3:49.
42. Hoare, Q. and Nowell Smith, G. (eds) (1971) *Selections from the Prison Notebooks of Antonio Gramsci.* London, Lawrence and Wishart, p.238.
43. On this last country, which we have not touched on here, see Grant, C. (1976) *The Making of Modern Belize.* Cambridge, Cambridge University Press; and Setzlkorn, W. (1981) *Formerly British Honduras: A Profile of the New Nation of Belize.* Ohio, Ohio University Press.
44. Stedman-Jones, G.I. (1972) The History of US Imperialism. *Ideology in Social Science*, (ed) R. Blackburn. London, Fontana, p.223. For a thorough history of US imperialism, see Kiernan, V. (1979) *America: The New Imperialism. From White Settlement to World Hegemony.* London, Zed Press.
45. See Etchison, D. (1975) *The United States and Militarism in Central America.* New York, Praeger Special Studies; and more generally on US military involvement in Latin America, Veneroni, H. (1971) *Estados Unidos y las Fuerzas Armadas de América Latina.* Buenos Aires, Ed. Periferia.
46. See Aybar de Santos, J. (1982) *Dependence and Intervention: the case of Guatemala in 1954.* Boulder, Co., Westview Press; and Schlesinger, S. and Kunzer, S. (1982) *Bitter Fruit — The Untold Story of the American Coup in Guatemala.* New York, Doubleday.
47. Cited in Jonas, S. (1974) Guatemala, p.156.
48. Ibid., p.165.
49. See Petras, J. (1970) The Dominican Republic: A Study in Imperialism. *Politics and Social Structure in Latin America.* J. Petras, New York, Monthly Review Press.

50. For an assessment of the area see, Ambursley, F., and Cohen, R., (eds) (1983) *Crisis in the Caribbean*. London, Heineman.
51. Jung, H. (1980) Class Struggles in El Salvador. *New Left Review* No.122: 8.
52. Blackburn, R. (1963) Prologue to the Cuban Revolution. *New Left Review* No.21: 81–2.
53. Cited in Bray, D. and Harding, T. (1974) *Cuba*, p.606. See also Lockwood, L. (1969) *Castro's Cuba, Cuba's Fidel*. New York, Vintage Press.
54. See, amongst others, Booth, J. (1982) *The End and the Beginning: The Nicaraguan Revolution*. Boulder Co., Westview Press; Weber, H. (1981) *Nicaragua: The Sandinist Revolution*. London, New Left Books; and Gilly, A. (1980) *La Nueva Nicaragua: anti imperialismo y lucha de clases*. Mexico, Editorial Nueva Imágen.
55. Chincilla, N. (1980) Class Struggle in Central America: background and overview. *Latin American Perspectives*, Vol VII, No 2/3:21.
56. Some of the more recent works are Montgomery, T.S. (1982) *Revolution in El Salvador – Origins and Evolution*. Boulder, Co., Westview Press; North, L. (1982) *Bitter Grounds: Roots of Revolution in El Salvador*. London, Zed Press; and Armstrong, R. and Schenk, J. (1982) *El Salvador: The Face of Revolution*. Boston, South End.
57. On the 1960s phase of the struggle, see Galeano, E. (1969) *Guatemala: Occupied Country*. New York, Monthly Review Press; Debray, R. (1978) *The Revolution on Trial*. London, Penguin, Ch.3. On more recent events consult Plant, R. (1978) *Guatemala: Unnatural Disaster*. London, Latin American Bureau, and the periodicals mentioned in the Bibliography.

9. Nationalist Regimes: Peronism in Argentina

> Caesarism — although it always expresses the particular
> solution in which a great personality is entrusted with the
> task of 'arbitration' over a historico-political situation
> characterised by an equilibrium of forces heading towards
> catastrophe — does not in all cases have the same historical
> significance. There can be both progressive and reactionary
> forms of Caesarism. . . .
>
> Antonio Gramsci[1]

The object of this chapter is to analyse the restoration of Peronism in Argentina
between 1973 and 1976 in terms of the movement's long term evolution.
Peronism, usually analysed in terms of 'populism' can also be seen as an
example of 'Caesarism' as described by Gramsci above. It is also, however, a
prime example — along with Varguismo in Brazil and Cardenismo in Mexico
— of nationalism in Latin America.[2] We therefore set our study of Peronism
in the context of the Marxist theory of nationalism. To that effect we discuss
some of the more recent contributions to this debate, bearing in mind that
traditionally, nationalism has been considered a 'blind spot' in Marxist theory.
On that basis we go on to see how Peronism has both a progressive and
reactionary side, which depend on the particular conjuncture of the class
struggle. In this way we avoid timeless 'definitions' or characterisations of
Peronism, in favour of a more historically based materialist analysis.

Nationalism

The unification of a national territory — and formation of a national market
— under the aegis of a nation-state was a prime task of the European bourgeois
revolutions.[3] In the particular conditions of domination in the Third World —
colonial, semi-colonial and dependent — this imperative gives rise to nationalist
movements and nationalist regimes. In theory, then, the 'national bourgeoisie'
or capital-owning class will be the main supporter of nationalist demands and
objectives. As we have seen in previous chapters, this social class tends in
practice to seek an accommodation with its metropolitan partners and, at

261

most, demands a renegotiation of the conditions of dependency. The unity of all 'patriotic' forces against foreign domination — economic, political or cultural — tends to be maintained as long as the nationalist movement has not seized state power. Once the movement becomes embodied in a nationalist regime the unresolved contradictions of class conflict once again come to the fore.

In any discussion of the 'national question' it is, therefore, vital to distinguish between the nation-state and nationalism; and, within the latter, one must distinguish the nationalism of the oppressed, which 'tends' towards a revolutionary or socialist direction. So goes the basic Marxist (or more specifically Leninist) thinking on the question of nationalism.[4] In recent years this has been the subject of serious criticism from outside and within Marxism.

According to Tom Nairn 'the theory of nationalism represents Marxism's great historical failure'.[5] Poulantzas goes even further and says that 'we have to recognize that there is no Marxist theory of the nation'.[6] Non-Marxist authors, not surprisingly, are equally dismissive of the Marxist heritage on the national question. Frank Parkin, in his self-titled 'bourgeois critique' of Marxism argues that:

> the Marxist preoccupation with the realm of production . . . obscures from view any recognition of the possibility that some line of cleavage other than that between capital and labour could constitute the *primary* source of political and social antagonism.[7]

One of the main areas neglected is, therefore, the question of inter-communal and ethnic conflict. Anthony Giddens equally dismisses existing Marxist work on nationalism, which he maintains 'is in substantial part a psychological phenomenon, involving felt needs and dispositions'.[8] From the Marxist camp comes a similar line of argument. Régis Debray writes that:

> this 'inadequate theory' [i.e., the Marxist theory of nationalism] is not accidental: the nation resists conceptualization because Marxism has no concept of nature. It has only concepts of what we produce. How could it have a concept of what we do not determine — that is, not of what we produce, but of that which produces us?[9]

We seem here to be returning to a conception of nationalism as something 'irrational' beyond theoretical comprehension and inimical to human progress. That is the position, for example, of Elie Kedourie for whom nationalism is 'an antiquarian irrelevance, a baneful invention of some misguided German philosophers'.[10]

There is certainly an 'irrational' element involved in nationalism. Marxist universalism — 'the proletariat has no nation' — proved to be a weak antidote to the patriotic fervour which took the European working class into the slaughter of the First World War. It is equally difficult to provide a 'rational' explanation for the recent war between the two ostensibly socialist states of China and Vietnam. Proletarian internationalism seems but a feeble antidote to the outbursts of apparently senseless primordial feelings. This is, of course, something to which Marxists are not immune, as testified by Regis Debray's recent bizzare confession:

> I even wonder if the whole 'anti-Boche' mythology and our [France's] secular antagonism to Germany may not be one day indispensable for saving the revolution, or even our national-democratic inheritance.[11]

This retreat from Marxism to naked chauvinism is hardly a contribution to a serious materialist theory of nationalism, and would seem to support Kedourie's negative prognosis.

There is also of course a 'positive' side to nationalism – that is the nationalism of the liberation movements and most successful socialist revolutions. Marxists in the advanced industrial societies were able to identify with the nationalist revolts in the Third World in the period following the Second World War. It was the very crisis of Stalinism in the late 1950s which fed the myth of Third Worldism which virtually transformed nationalism into socialism.[12] Every guerrilla movement in Latin America during the 1960s had, as its central slogan, a variation of *Patria o Muerte – Venceremos* (Fatherland or Death – to Victory). In Africa, Amílcar Cabral advanced the novel, and totally unrealistic, theory that the petty bourgeoisie which participated in the independence movement would either 'commit suicide as a class' or betray the revolution.[13] It invariably chose the latter course, and not surprisingly. The most basic distinction between bourgeois nationalism and proletarian nationalism would show that the class interests of the first were bound to emerge once the need for a multi-class independence movement was surpassed. The ideology of Third Worldism allowed the rhetoric of nationalism to obscure (and even deny the existence of) the underlying class struggle which must inevitably exist where different material class interests are at stake.

It is, of course, wrong to hold an 'either/or' conception of nationalism as though it was unequivocally regressive or progressive. Tom Nairn holds, quite correctly, that nationalism is a modern Janus standing over the doorway to 'modernity', looking back into the past to help it through the hard process of 'development'.[14] In mobilising the past to help move into the future it is inevitable that certain 'irrational' elements will emerge. In this sense nationalism 'worked', because it provided the masses with a culture more relevant to their concrete reality than the rationalism of the Enlightenment. Where Nairn seems to go too far is in arguing that this 'is something that class consciousness could never have furnished'.[15] This would deny the class, as well as national components of the Russian, Chinese, Vietnamese and Cuban revolutions. We must stress, however, the dual or contradictory nature of nationalism, which we can now conceive of as a complex historical process with its inherent tensions and multiple outcomes. As Horace Davis writes:

> a Marxist treatment of nationalism must be a dialectical treatment
> showing how nationalism arises in history, under what conditions,
> how it is related to other great movements such as democracy and
> socialism, and specifically, what is the relation of nationalism to the
> class struggle.[16]

This conception helps us move beyond the rather static definition of the
nation provided by Stalin, for whom it was simply 'a historically evolved,
stable community of language, territory, economic life and psychological
make-up manifested in a community of culture'.[17] Not only is this a restricted
definition, but its approach is basically scholastic and undialectical, listing
'factors' involved in nation-building as do the exponents of modernisation
theory. This can lead only to a pointless multiplication of different 'types'
of nationalism — heterogeneous, recession, irredentism, diaspora, pan- — into
which every country or movement can be neatly slotted.[18] This rather sterile
approach is rejected by Lenin, who always discussed nationalism in a *concrete*
setting — as with all general principles, it is relative to time and place.[19]
Fundamentally, it is nationalism's relation to democracy and socialism which
allows us to assess whether it is progressive or not — to distinguish Hitler
from Guevara or Mao from Perón.

In our study of Peronism we will certainly find that a nationalist movement
and regime cannot be reduced to a timeless, a-historical essence, nor can we
ignore the class content. In its classical phase (1946–55) Peronism was a
nationalist movement without the leadership of the national bourgeoisie, a
populist movement with strong Bonapartist features; during the Peronist
resistance (1955–73) it broke up into a revolutionary nationalist tendency
and a labour nationalist movement led by the unions; finally, when it regained
power (1973–76) the movement degenerated into a reactionary Bonapartism
marked by a severe repression of its progressive elements.[20] Peronism embodied
a historically necessary element for Argentina's development, but it also
contained inherent contradictions. Its socialist tendency (the Montoneros)
mistook the rhetoric of nationalism for its reality. Perón's movement was
based on the principle of *Justicialismo* (Justice) but this is as relevant as
Liberté, Egalité, Fraternité are to the French bourgeoisie. The illusion — so
violently destroyed in the mid 1970s — was that a populist-based nationalist
movement could create something called 'national socialism'.

The most sophisticated recent attempt to theorise nationalism and populism
is that made by Ernesto Laclau.[21] This author tries to counter what he sees as
a common Marxist trait to reduce ideologies to their class essence — 'class
reductionism'. In this sense, nationalism and democracy have been associated
with the rising bourgeoisie, and socialism as the ideology of the working class.
Against this view Laclau maintains that the class character of an ideological
discourse depends on its specific articulation with other ideological elements:

> Let us take an example: nationalism. Is it a feudal, bourgeois or
> proletarian ideology? Considered in itself it has no class connotation.

The latter only derives from its specific articulation with other
ideological elements.[22]

He goes on to show how, under feudalism, it could be linked to an authoritarian
system such as Bismarck's Germany; under capitalism it can combat feudal
particularism and maintain class unity at the expense of class struggle, as in
Germany; finally, a socialist movement might articulate nationalist themes
in the interests of the proletarian revolution. In their way Hitler, Mao and
Perón were all 'nationalists' and 'populists'. This notion of ideological
'relativism' is a useful one and helps us to understand certain paradoxes in
Argentina's political history. It can, however, lead to a dissolving of the
specificity of socialism *vis-à-vis* nationalism.

One of Laclau's critics points out that though there is no one-to-one
correspondence between classes and ideological themes, neither is there a
completely arbitrary relationship between the two.[23] The racist ruling class
of South Africa is unlikely to raise the banner of socialism; the military
rulers of Argentina would advance 'populist' themes only at the risk of losing
power; and a socialist movement which espouses racist or fascist notions
ceases to be socialist. Laclau maintains that 'popular-democratic' ideologies
are not class ideologies — they are themes which can be taken up by different
classes. To achieve socialism the working class must articulate these various
popular ideologies — above all nationalism — to draw 'the people' behind its
struggle. This, the revolutionary nationalist Peronist movement, the
Montoneros, did with considerable success. But, as we shall show, this did not
lead to socialism or even to strengthening the working class, rather it sowed
illusions in Perón and dampened the only element which could have advanced
socialism — the class struggle. Class reductionism can be replaced by a mythical
'classlessness' — in short democracy is *either* bourgeois democracy *or*
proletarian democracy — it does not float in the middle. The class 'sectarianism',
which Laclau rejects, can mean quite simply the self-organisation of the
working class in pursuit of its own objectives.

What Poulantzas, Debray, Nairn and Laclau all have in common is a
conception of nationalism as something separate from and somehow 'above'
classes. As Blaut notes 'for these scholars, nationalism is not a form of class
struggle, nor even a product of class struggle. It is an autonomous force, a
second motor of history.'[24] The classical Marxist position is, of course, that
the class struggle is the motor of history, and national struggle is a form of
class struggle. The struggle for independence is a struggle for state power,
which the proletariat as much as the bourgeoisie must engage in. This whole
conception is lost when the nation is reified to a metaphysical entity, as when
Debray says that 'we must locate the national phenomenon within general
laws regulating the survival of the human species . . . against death. Against
entropy. . . .'[25] Nairn endorses the conservative notion of nationalism as an
'idea', and Poulantzas similarly refers to the 'transhistorical irreducibility' of
the nation.[26] Our discussion of Peronism will try to show that there *is* a
material basis to nationalism and that the struggle between classes is the

motive force of historical development. We must relate the emergence of nationalism to the domination of imperialism, a perfectly material force ignored by the idealist theories. We must see the 'national question' as a stake in the class struggle, not something detached from it. Finally, we must demonstrate the complex relationship of bourgeoisie, petty bourgeoisie and proletariat to the nationalist movement/regime and how this is modified historically.

Peronism I

Marx once said that all great events and characters of world history occur twice: the first time as tragedy, the second as farce. History is made under the given and inherited circumstances which confront us and, in Marx's word 'the tradition of the dead generations weighs like a nightmare on the minds of the living'.[27] Certainly the Peronism of the 1970s can be understood only in relation to the 'classical' Peronism of 1946-55. Likewise, the vacillation and confusion within Peronism in the 1970s was, in great part, owing to the dead weight of the Peronist ideology inherited from an earlier period. Finally the degeneration of late Peronism can be seen to follow Marx's aphorism in a uncanny, but quite inevitable way, if Peronism is conceived of as part of the struggle between classes which, in 1973, many failed to do, turning instead to the 'leader' of days gone by. We shall now examine the social and political conditions of Peronism's return to power in 1973, and the growing contradictions of the movement between 1973 and 1976, a period closed by the military *coup d'etat* of March 1976, which ended the cycle of populism in Argentina.

The basic political and ideological co-ordinates of Peronism were set during its first phase in power (1946-55) to which we now turn our attention The first Peronist government was established in the context of a crisis in the economic system, as dependence on British imperialism and the dominan agrarian-export base of the economy were drawn into question by the crisis of 1929.[28] This led to the collapse of British imperialist domination over Argentina and to a growing process of industrialisation. Colonel Juan Domin Perón emerged on to the political scene at a crucial stage of transition when, for a certain period after 1945, neither Great Britain (weakened by the war and in decline) nor the United States (too busy restructuring Europe and Japan and the opening stages of the Cold War) could impose their policies or Argentina. This vacuum allowed the formation of an alternative power base – the rural and urban working class and a section of the petty bourgeoisie – on which Perón relied during his two administrations. With the expanding role of the state in the economy, this alliance was supported for most of its period of ascendancy by elements of the national bourgeoisie linked to the internal market rather than to imperialism. Peronism was, therefore, a politi movement based on a section of the army which attempted a project of independent capitalist development through a Bonapartist government whic

at the same time controlled and was based on the working class.[29] The working class, however, was not a simple puppet of Peronism; in a massive mobilisation, on the 17 October 1945, to support Perón against the right-wing attempt to prevent him coming to power, the working class entered the political arena in an explosive way. This was the basic contradiction of Peronism: its working-class base — massively unionised during this period and with an objectively anti-capitalist dynamic — and the bourgeois leadership of the movement.

Peronism had come to power in a unique historical conjuncture. The war in Europe led to a renewed demand for Argentine grain and meat, and the profit of this commerce built up the country's industrial base. It also provided the resources for Argentina's version of the welfare state and the prodigious growth of the trade unions. Additionally, what counts for a lot in political terms, the average industrial wage rose by 62% between 1943 and 1948. In foreign policy Perón's verbal anti-imperialism was, in fact, a fore-runner of today's 'non-aligned' position.[30] In practice, as the Cold War intensified, Perón was forced to rebuild the economic and military links with the USA. So, Peronism was not the 'Argentine road to socialism' as so many believed, nor was it the *Criollo* version of fascism as US academics, peeved by his anti-Yankee rhetoric, professed to believe. It was a form of populism in which the myth of the providential person comes to substitute for the ideological relationship on which social consensus is usually based.

Between 1953 and 1955 a change in the international and internal conditions was to lead to the fall of Perón. Deterioration of the terms of trade severely affected Argentine exports, which had provided the financial base for the industrial bourgeoisie. North American imperialism was on the rise, investing heavily in Latin America and undermining local competitiors with its superior technology. Faced with this situation, and with the growing militancy of the working class, part of the national bourgeoisie deserted the Peronist alliance and joined the US-backed coalition. By 1954, the system was in total crisis, and the options for Perón were simply a radicalisation of the regime through an agrarian reform (which was only talked about) and an extension of nationalisation or capitulation to imperialism and repression of the working class. Perón took the second option, but before the working class had been able to break from Peronist ideology and political organisations. The September 1955 coup (the *Fusiladora*, or 'executioner' for Peronists) was unleashed by the armed forces, and Perón — if not Peronism — was swept away.[31]

During the so-called Peronist Resistance, between 1955 and 1973, the movement was held together by the figure of Perón, but two distinct wings materialised. On the one hand, a powerful trade union bureaucracy consolidated its position within the workers movement and put forward a nationalist-reformist alternative. On the other, especially in the late 1960s, a radical brand of Peronism emerged to dominate the Peronist Youth and a class-struggle minority in the unions. Two slogans — *Patria Peronista* (Peronist Fatherland) and *Patria Socialista* (Socialist Fatherland) expressed the very different objectives, temporarily contained within the same Peronist movement.[32]

The period between 1955 and the return of Peronism to government in 1973, also saw fundamental modifications in the economic structure of the country. A steady inflow of foreign capital took over key dynamic sectors of industry, and consolidated the advance of monopoly capitalism. Between 1955 and 1972 the participation of international firms in industrial production grew from 8% to 40%, with US capital accounting for around 70% of total foreign investment.[33] The agrarian bourgeoisie, based on the fertile pampas, had for its part lost its dominant political role after 1930, but it remained a powerful economic agent into the 1960s. This led to a particular form of class balance within the dominant classes. As Juan Carlos Portantiero outlines:

> the political 'stalemate' between the different groups was articulated with a specific modality of capital accumulation in Argentina, based, in turn, on a situation of *shared economic power* which alternatively shifts between the Pampean agrarian bourgeoisie (provider of foreign reserves and therefore master of the situation in moments of external crisis) and the industrial bourgeoisie, totally turned towards the internal market.[34]

The military coup of 1966 attempted to resolve this particular stalemate in the class struggle. Its policies and ultimate failure are examined in Chapter 10 dealing with military dictatorships. It is important to note here that this coup was, in fact, tolerated, if not supported, by Perón. The trade union bureaucracy was even more enthusiastic, and they imagined they would get a fair slice of the cake in President Onganía's grandiose corporatist scheme.[35] But this was not to be and the process which was to lead to Perón's return began in 1969. The working class was to seal the fate of this version of militarist monopoly capitalism when it launched the massive semi-insurrection of 1969, known as the *Cordobazo*. This episode was the result of a process of working-class recovery from the downturn of the early 1960s, marked by such important episodes as the events of 1964, when three million workers took part in a massive strike movement, accompanied by nationwide factory occupations (see Chapter 5). The *Cordobazo* of 1969 opened up a pre-revolutionary period which placed Argentina at the centre of the class struggle in Latin America. Under the impact of the Cuban revolution, and more crucially because of the massive struggles after May 1969, a new social and political vanguard was formed, beginning to free itself from its traditional nationalist and reformist leadership. Workers and students entered into confrontation with the repressive bodies of the state in a wave of semi-insurrections — *Rosariazo, Tucumanazo*, etc. — which followed Córdoba.

The *Cordobazo* constitutes a decisive rupture in the rhythm of the class struggle in Argentina, being the most spectacular revolutionary upsurge for 30 years. It ushered in a new pre-revolutionary period characterised by:

1) an unstable governmental situation, in which the contradictions between the various fractions of the bourgeoisie were exacerbated by the rise of working-class struggle; 2) the growing opposition of the urban and rural petty bourgeoisie to the government faced by the growing advance of monopoly capital; and 3) a wave of strikes and other forms of activity which moulded a new working-class vanguard.[36] Its significance lies also in the blow it struck at the reconsolidation of the ruling bloc. Effectively, the Onganiato had been the most decisive attempt by Argentine capitalism to overcome the situation of organic crisis it had been in since 1955, and to consolidate the dominant class fraction at the socio-economic level (that linked to international monopoly capital) as the hegemonic fraction at the political level.

As Onganía's government fell under the impact of the *Cordobazo*, his successor, General Levingston, fell under the blows of a second *Cordobazo* in 1971, known as the *Viborazo*. The new government, led by General Lanusse, moved towards a controlled return to parliamentary structures, embodied in the *Gran Acuerdo Nacional* (Great National Agreement) which began to take shape in 1971. Mass protest actions against the military government did not stop in 1972, though the axis of protest had shifted from the industrial proletariat to impoverished sectors of the petty bourgeoisie, especially in the provinces. The movement in the provincial city of Mendoza (the *Mendozazo*) in 1972 was important in this regard, though it did not spread to other cities, as the dictatorship rapidly conceded the demands of the movement. The working class was contained fairly effectively by the trade union bureaucracy which was now collaborating closely with Lanusse to bring back the populist leader, Juan Domingo Perón.

Peronism II

What was the reason for *El Retorno* (i.e., Perón's return to Argentina) which his followers had preached and struggled for since 1955? It was precisely owing to the *Cordobazos* and *Rosariazos* under Onganía and Levingston, and the *Mendozazos* and *Rocazos* under Lanusse, which had demonstrated the strength and combativeness of the working class, and obliged the ruling bloc and the armed forces to reconsider their strategy. The aim of this new strategy, concretised through the GAN, was to prevent these partial struggles from becoming generalised and transformed into a conscious struggle for power. Perón was the only political figure who could possibly turn the working class towards a populist solution compatible with the continued dominance of capital in the Argentina of the 1970s. This is what made it an 'emergency government' as many contemporary observers called it. As a US State Department official noted 'I think this is the moment for Perón. He alone can bring cohesion to Argentina. There is no one else left. So he has come to represent opportunity. . . .'[37]

The leftist Peronist currents and their supporters, however, argued against the interpretation that Perón's return constituted the 'last card of the bourgeoisie'. Thus, Christopher Roper, for example, maintains this is incorrect because: 1) neither the bourgeoisie nor the trade union bureaucracy worked for the return of Perón in 1972, nor did Lanusse believe he would return; 2) Perón was expressly prevented from standing in the March 1973 elections. Why? If he was the last card of the bourgeoisie; and 3) the army attempted but failed to place conditions on the transfer of power in May 1973·defeated by the strength of popular mobilisations.[38] As to the first objection, clearly the bourgeoisie did not appeal to Perón without reservations and was quite conscious of the dangers involved in a turn towards populism. Nor is the historical significance of shifts in ruling-class strategy of this type faithfully and consistently mirrored in the consciousness of its participants. Likewise, the second objection relates to the complex political manoeuvres between Lanusse, Perón and the political parties, and in no way contradicts the *overall* orientation of the ruling bloc. Finally, the third objection raised by Roper only goes to show that the *aperturista* type strategy of the GAN had its dangers as it could unleash popular mobilisations before political control was established over the masses.

In 1973, however, illusions were widespread that Perón's return signalled the dawn of a new era, and many observers even saw Perón himself as some kind of nationalist-socialist leader, if not as Argentina's Lenin. For example Ernesto Laclau, comparing Peronism with other populist movements in Latin America, maintained that:

> only Peronism survived as a revolutionary force and, revitalising itself, continues to be so. The counter-revolution has, over seventeen years, *failed to co-opt Peronism as a political prop for the establishment.*[39]

The idealism contained in this type of analysis is related to the petty bourgeoisie, especially the intellectuals, turning to Peronism during the late 1960s. To compensate for the lateness of this turn they tried to outdo the working class in its faith and confidence in Perón, precisely when sections of the working class were beginning to question Peronism, both in organisational terms and also as a bourgeois ideology.

In many ways, a more lucid assessment of Perón's return is made by General Lanusse, himself a key participant in the event. For him the GAN was the *only* coherent political project possible in the circumstances of the period following the *Cordobazo*. He asks rhetorically what would have happened if all that anger had not been channelled into the escape valve of elections.[40] Basically, then, the GAN and Perón's return were a move to ensure the stability of bourgeois institutions under the watchful eye of the armed forces, but without their direct participation. In fact, each change in government since 1966 can be seen as a diversionary attempt by the ruling class block to offer legal, and hopefully harmless, outlets for popular discontent.

The elections were held and Perón's representative, Hector Cámpora, was elected President in March 1973, with nearly 50% of the vote, under the slogan 'Cámpora to government, Perón to power', coined by the Montoneros.[41] On assuming office in May, Cámpora outlined the new economic policy of Peronism, which included a series of measures to bring the economy under national control, and increase the power of the state to limit the scope of multinational corporations.[41] Perón's cherished hope for a massive flow of European and Japanese capital as a counterweight to US capital was, however, thwarted by the unfavourable world economic situation and a continued fear of the combativeness of Argentina's workers. Likewise, the effects of the world recession were felt more severely when the Common Market countries curbed the import of Argentine agrarian produce. The political effect of this was similar to that caused by the exhaustion of currency reserves in the 1950s. In this sense, the political capital of Peronism could not be easily replenished by economic concessions for very long.

The main axis of Peronist economic policy was the development of industrial exports and the capitalist rationalisation of the structures of production on the basis of this strategy. In Cámpora's words:

> the pacification of the country requires the forgetting of hatreds and the turning of energies until today consumed in fratricidal struggle, towards the pressing task of national reconstruction.[42]

The basis of Peronist governmental strategy was to contain popular mobilisation, even though Cámpora came to power on the wave of massive demonstrations of working-class strength. Thus, even as the masses were storming Villa Devoto prison to free the political prisoners, Cámpora signed a decree granting a general amnesty for political prisoners.

The lynchpin of the programme of 'National Reconstruction' was a 'Social Pact' between the CGT (General Workers Confederation) and the CGE (General Economic Confederation) which had been prepared before the Peronist return to power.[43] This was part of Perón's project in 1973 of establishing a form of 'integrated democracy' which could rebuild bourgeois hegemony over society as a whole. In return for a promise of price stability from the CGE, and of basic structural reforms by the government, the CGT gave a pledge of no strikes for a two year period. This, inevitably, led to a great deal of unease amongst the base of the CGT and was to result in a spate of strikes. When Cámpora came to power there was a wave of government office occupations by rival wings of the Peronist movement, but these were soon stopped with a strong reprimand from Perón. The workers' reaction to the 'Social Pact' was not, however, so easily quelled.

In a way similar to the early years of the first Peronist administration (1945–46) the workers' movement went on a real offensive during the second half of 1973, attempting to consolidate at the level of production what they had won on the electoral front.[44] This wave of strikes was not around wages and conditions only, but also contained a noticeable anti-bureaucratic element as the rank and file began to press for union democracy against the corrupt union leadership. Another series of demands raised in these strikes was aimed against repression, as by the end of the year trade union activists were being hard hit by the bureaucracy's *matones* (thugs) and the parliamentary forces of repression. Government strategy at first was simply to take over unions in struggle and forcibly break strikes, but by mid 1974 it had evolved a more subtle strategy aimed at maintaining a core of working-class support. It did this by granting wage increases to some privileged sections of the working class while focusing its repression against the militant labour leaders and left-wing forces actively organising the rank and file.

Cámpora was to last in office barely two months, then resigning to make way for Perón himself, as he had pledged when elected. Camporism had to go, partly to get rid of the irritating presence of left-wing Peronist intellectuals around the government, and also to make way for a new power formula which would include the trade union and political bureaucracies more centrally. His removal, however, became a matter of urgency for orthodox Peronism, including the trade union bureaucracy, because of his style of government which was to a certain extent 'open' and susceptible to pressure from mass mobilisations. Also, Perón had been seriously disturbed by such acts as the freeing of the political prisoners, and had practically broken with Cámpora. Not that his political programme was too advanced, the problem was rather the manner in which it was implemented. More precisely, Cámpora was seen as incapable of demobilising the masses, perhaps inevitably, given the weight of popular mobilisations during the period he came to power.

Without doubt, the main organisation involved in these mobilisations was that known as Montoneros, which had emerged as a mass force in the demonstrations following the Trelew massacre in 1972.[45] Its youth organisation, the J.P. or *Juventud Peronista* (Peronist Youth), was to achieve control of the national University when Cámpora came to power, and its 200,000 students were for a time its main power base. At the same time it began recruiting in the working class itself, creating the JTP or *Juventud Trabajadora Peronista* (Peronist Working Youth), which was to play an important role in the struggles of 1973–74. One current in these strikes was the 'old' combative sector of the trade union movement, such as the car workers of Córdoba and the unions following Raimundo Ongaro, which had been the driving force of the *Cordobazo*. A second layer, comprised of younger elements, was mobilised by the JTP which, for the first time, gave the struggles a *national* character. The mobilisation of the working class of the Greater Buenos Aires area posed for the first time the possibility of an *Argentinazo* as against the previous more localised mass struggles. That this did not materialise was in no small measure owing to the Montoneros' political subservience to Perón, mirrored in Roper's apologia when he says that 'while Perón lived, it was impossible to challenge his personal ascendancy' (adding, 'even though the Montoneros could and did question his judgement').[46]

At one level, the purely anti-imperialist and anti-oligarchic political programme of the Montoneros' 'national socialism' was not incompatible with Perón's economic project of 'national reconstruction', but their power of mass mobilisation was. This is what led to the Ezeiza massacre, when Perón returned definitively to Argentina in June 1973. After several months of intense mobilisation and conflicts between left- and right-wing Peronists some three million people gathered at Ezeiza airport to welcome Perón back. At first the rival wings simply chanted rival slogans such as *Patria Socialista* (Socialist Fatherland) against *Patria Peronista* (Peronist Fatherland) but then a Montonero column was fired on from the official platform by heavily armed union bureaucracy goon-squads. The 100 or so deaths, and the many others tortured or wounded that day, marked the beginning of an intense repression against the forces of leftist Peronism. Perón himself, speaking on television after the incident, clearly defined his own position and set the terms of his own government when he blamed the Montoneros for the bloodshed and condemned the 'infiltrators' within the Peronist movement.[47]

Perón assumed the Presidency in October 1973 (supported by 62% of the electorate) thus replacing the interim President, Raul Lastiri, who had already begun to turn towards repression of the mass movement and promoted the resurgence of the most reactionary elements in the Peronist coalition. The wave of mass mobilisations during the election campaign coincided with the bloody coup in neighbouring Chile which overthrew Salvador Allende's Popular Unity government. There were almost daily demonstrations up and down the country in solidarity with the Chilean people, and these in practice merged with the Peronist electoral campaign. The lessons of this were not lost on Perón himself who raised the bogey of the *Pinochetazo* (Pinochet's coup) to stay the hand of his movement's left wing — 'Do you want them to do to me what they have done to Allende?' The following May, the hypocrisy of this plea was made evident when he received President Pinochet himself in Buenos Aires; this resulted in mass protests ending in serious clashes with the police. The Montoneros, while criticising the reactionary elements within the Peronist movement, still called for support for Perón's strategy as 'the only possibility to achieve national liberation'.

The reactionary nature of the Peronist restoration was codified in a series of repressive laws which were in marked contrast to the popular legislation approved when Perón first came to power in 1946. Thus, the Law of Professional Associations gave the union bureaucracies the right to intervene in their regional bodies in order to overthrow combative leaders. Then the Law of Redundancy gave the University in particular the green light to fire 'excess personnel' i.e., undesirable political elements. The Law of Compulsory Arbitration practically outlawed the right to strike. The Reform of the Penal Code stepped up the penalties for 'political crimes'; and so on.[48]

The conflict between Perón himself and the Peronist Youth was to come to a head at the massive rally commemorating May Day in 1974. The Montoneros saw this as a chance to re-establish the mystical 'dialogue' between the leader and his followers, which had been the practice during the first Peronist period. Soon after Perón appeared at the rostrum, people began to chant — *'Qué pasa, qué pasa General, que está lleno de gorilas el gobierno popular'* (What's up, what's up, General, the popular government is full of 'gorillas' [i.e. reactionary elements]). At the sight of the hated trade union bureaucrats surrounding Perón on the platform another chant arose: *'Se vá a acabar, se vá a acabar la burocracia sindical'* (basically, 'the trade union bureaucracy will be finished'). Perón replied in a short and sharp speech which denounced the leftist 'infiltrators' as 'foreign mercenaries' and reaffirmed his support for the trade union leadership. Before Perón had finished some 60,000 demonstrators (over half of those at the rally) rolled up their banners and marched in orderly fashion out of the Plaza de Mayo.

The 1st of May 1974 marks an important turn in the history of the Peronist movement, when a decisive rupture occurred between its leader and the most representative mass base of the movement. The majority of the working class still remained sentimentally attached to Perón, but many began to see the flagrant contradictions between the movement's rhetoric and its practice. Left Peronism was baffled, as their old theory of a reactionary wall around Perón (*el cerco*) which prevented him from contacting the masses, simply crumbled. Now they could refer to only 'the metamorphosis of a leader'. The attempted *dialogo* with the leader had turned into a *desencuentro* (failure to meet).

One of the laws passed by the Peronist government was the Act of Obligation to National Security, which gave the federal government the right to intervene in the internal affairs of the provinces in the interest of 'national security'. A wave of federal 'interventions' in the provincial governments became an integral element in the orthodox Peronist campaign against leftist 'infiltrators' who were in any way responsive to the mass base of Peronism. Thus, in January 1974, Perón forced Oscar Bidegain (the governor of Buenos Aires) to resign because he was 'soft on terrorism', using as a pretext an ERP (People's Revolutionary Army) attack on Azul barracks. This was followed in February by a move against the leftist governor and vice-governor of Córdoba, Obregón Cano and Atilio López (a leader of the *Cordobazo*). Córdoba had been in the forefront of the mobilisations of 1973, and the government elected in March 1973 was far too close to the Peronist rank and file for Perón's comfort. He thus sanctioned a rebellion by Córdoba's police chief, Navarro, which displaced the elected government.[49] This reactionary mini-coup, known as the Navarrazo, was followed by further federal interventions in Mendoza, Santa Cruz, etc. If, until the Navarrazo, there was a certain minimal respect for democratic institutions on the part of the authorities, henceforth nothing was sacred in the war against 'subversion'.

The turn towards a clearcut reactionary orientation by the Peronist government had its effects in all spheres of national life. It was at this stage that the national university was attacked, and Rodolfo Puiggros and his project of a National and Popular University was shelved. Likewise, the Agrarian Leagues of the north-east had just seen an inter-provincial strike crushed by bloody repression reminiscent of General Lanusse's activity against them.

Perón Dies

In Perón's last speech to the masses, in June 1974, he made his usual attack on the left wing of his movement but also hit out against the oligarchy and the pressures of imperialism on his government. He ended with a phrase which helped repair some of the damage created by his May Day performance: *'Mi único heredero es el pueblo'* (My only heir is the people). These words were prophetic, for Perón died on the 1st of July, but his heir was Isabel Perón, who now stepped into his shoes from the Vice-Presidency. The circumstances of Perón's death could only please the architect of the GAN, General Lanusse, because:

> Perón died condemning the guerrilla and terrorism . . . if he had died in Madrid he would have died glorifying his 'special formations'. And I could not underestimate the influence this would have had on an immense section of the people. Perón would have been a revolutionary myth of special characteristics, capable of being used as a counter-image to the Armed Forces.[50]

In 1973, many had seen Perón as a sincere convert to an insurrectionary strategy, not understanding that his support for the armed Peronist organisation was purely a lever in negotiations with the dictatorship. The military had learned how a combative workers' movement and a deteriorating economic situation could wear out even a highly repressive government, and they were quite happy to see Perón lose his appeal amongst the radicalised youth. On the other hand, Perón's death deprived the bourgeoisie of the only credible Bonapartist figure it had, who could straddle the mass movement so skilfully.

Isabel Perón inherited the tarnished mantle of Peronism — and even the token loyalty of the Montoneros for a while — but also, a severe political crisis which was aggravated by the effects of the world recession on the Argentine economy. Isabel Perón did not represent any of the 'historical' currents of Peronism but was rather part of that declassé lumpen element which had always hung around the Peronist movement (of which her personal secretary, the notorious López Rega, was just a more visible specimen). López Rega, as Minister of Social Welfare, controlled vast sums of money expended on housing programmes, sports programmes, etc. as a means of patronage. In this process he took over many hospitals previously run by the trade unions, which deprived the union bureaucracy of an important function and source of income. In March 1975 he even tried to invade the metal workers' union central headquarters (a key bastion of the bureaucracy) but was repulsed by union bodyguards. López Rega clearly represented a semi-fascist tendency within the Peronist movement, and his strategy was to implement a 'preventive fascism' which would not, of course, have any mass base, but would hold the working class in terrorised passivity. To this end he set about organising the murderous AAA (Argentine Anti-Communist Alliance) together with certain police chiefs (especially Vilar and Margaride, notorious from the days of the military dictatorship and recently brought back by López Rega) and certain branches of the armed forces. The cold statistics of the number of political assassinations during 1973-75 give some idea of the terror. Whereas under the Cámpora government there were 18 victims of rightist terror and under General Perón 67, Isabel Perón's government (up to October 1975 alone) saw 535 victims of para-military action.[51] Those murdered included lawyers, doctors and other professionals, workers, students and political activists. These rightward moves intensified, particularly after a state of siege was imposed towards the end of 1974.

The economic and political crisis worsened under Isabel Perón, who clearly could not reconcile the contradictory tendencies within the Peronist movement of which she was nominally the leader. The impact of the international recession had become very serious by early 1975 and the room for manoeuvre by the bourgeoisie was seriously curtailed.[52] A declining rate of growth was followed by a rapidly accelerating rate of inflation, which was to lead to the emergence of a vast black market with its usual social consequences. At the political level this was reflected in a collapse of Peronist economic policy as articulated by José Gelbard. His resignation, in fact, entailed the collapse of the project of national capitalist development as put forward by Perón in 1973. As social and political contradictions were sharpened, his measures were increasingly seen as ineffective, especially as the masses were no longer blindly following Perón's demobilising directives. The Peronist movement was bursting at the seams and the congressional elections in Misiones province in April 1975 brought on to the scene a second Peronist party: the *Partido Peronista Auténtico*, which was led by old Peronist figures such as Andres Framini, but whose real base was provided by the Montoneros. This party, which aimed at creating a popular front with some of the opposition bourgeois parties, clearly set itself up against Isabel Perón, though it still revindicated the government of Juan Domingo Perón (forgetting that he had begun the offensive against the Peronist left).

The working class did not respond immediately to this wave of repression (resistance took the form of absenteeism, running at around 20% at the time) and for a long time it was the revolutionary organisations which suffered the brunt of the repression, in isolation from the mass movement. A number of important strikes in Córdoba, however, marked a gradual recovery of the workers' movement and there was a growing realisation that it was necessary to confront the Peronist government. The strike in Villa Constitución in early 1975 was to be the first large scale response to the government's offensive.[53] In December 1974, elections had been held in the local metal workers union which resulted in an overwhelming victory for the class-struggle slate which displaced the old Peronist bureaucracy. The new leadership demanded a 70% wage increase and, quite significantly, workers control over industrial health and the work pace. This led to an occupation of the big steel plants in the region and a month long struggle in which four successive strike committees were arrested. In spite of severe repression, the strike received widespread support throughout the country, and clearly demonstrated a militant determination to resist the economic policies and the repression of late Peronism.

The Villa Constitución strike did not achieve its objectives however, although it was not a defeat for the working class as a whole, since it marked an end of fragmented and defensive struggles and a turn towards a working-class offensive. As a contemporary observer noted:

> The government put its prestige on the line in this confrontation, and the test of strength, which was a prolonged one, did it damage. . . . Day after day the conflict was on the front page of the newspapers, and soon the automobile industry will be paralysed if the Villa factories do not start working again quickly. . . . Whatever negotiations the government may undertake, the masses of the country will see them as a triumph and will adopt the road and methods of Villa Constitución in order to push their own struggles forward.[54]

In the wake of the Villa Constitución strike the government yet again named a new Economy Minister, Celestino Rodrigo, who was clearly linked to the international financial centres and whose aim was to push through drastic austerity measures. This involved a new devaluation of the peso so as to stimulate exports, a big increase in the price of public services, and a severe limitation on wage increases, under the guise of holding down inflation – the government spoke of holding wage increases to 38–45% whereas the cost of living was going up by 150% per annum. The aim of the Rodrigo plan (or *Rodrigazo*) was clearly an attempt to reduce drastically mass consumption, even at the risk of provoking a deflationary turn so sharp that a serious economic recession would result.[55]

At this time, the periodic collective contracts of key sections of the working class – e.g., metal workers, construction workers, bank employees and public sector employees – were coming up for renewal. After wage increases of up to 100% had been negotiated the government stepped in and set a 50% limit, with an extra 15% in October and another 15% in January 1976. Isabel Perón also sharply attacked the workers for going back on the promise they made to her late husband the General to 'work harder and produce more'. She was at least conscious of the gravity of the situation:

> The Argentine nation is now facing what I would call the zero hour of our decision to obtain definitive freedom on all fronts. . . . Production is going down. Speculation seems to be spreading beyond all limits. . . .

Her solution was, predictably, to maintain 'a just and healthy austerity'.[56] Effectively, as real wages were dropping, the rate of unemployment was rising.

The working class did not accept this affront passively and launched a series of strikes which culminated in a 48 hour general strike in July, forced on the CGT by a massive wave of wildcat strikes which had spread throughout the country.[57] In Córdoba and Santa Fé provinces particularly, a new type of rank and file organisation was formed by co-ordinating bodies of factory activists and workers' commissions on a district level, known as *coordinadoras*. The emergence of the *coordinadoras* as a potential alternative leadership highlighted the crisis of Peronism, in which the tension between the rank and file and the leadership had never been as sharp as during this period. Workers had downed tools and marched to CGT headquarters to demand action without a word from their shop stewards — and without the transport which was usually laid on by the unions. Important sections of the working class broke socially with the bourgeois leadership of Peronism as embodied by the Isabel-López Rega clique. In fact, as well as ratifying the wage agreements, the government was forced to dismiss López Rega, thus satisfying one of the demands of the strike. However, this social break and the success of the first ever general strike against a Peronist government, was not consummated in a *political* break with Peronism, nor did an independent working-class political leadership emerge.

After the July 1975 general strike, which has been referred to as a *Cordobazo amortiguado* (*Cordobazo* with shock absorbers) there was a turn in bourgeois political strategy. The strike had effectively blocked the attempts to rationalise the economy on the basis of renewed integration with international monopoly capital.

As for the petty bourgeoisie, they went through an important shift during this period. Having supported the general strike to a large extent, they later became demoralised by what they saw as the political impotence of the workers movement in the face of the reactionary course of late Peronism. The growing decomposition of the Peronist regime drove the radicalised petty bourgeoisie towards apathy, and even towards supporting military intervention, in the absence of a clear-cut socialist alternative. The commercial petty bourgeoisie, hard hit by the economic crisis, decided to throw its weight behind the *paro patronal* (bosses' strike) staged in March 1976. The proletarianisation of the middle class, in fact, increased during the Peronist period: between January 1973 and June 1976 the real purchasing power of the middle-class salaried sectors went down by 70% (the industrial wage went down by nearly 50%, which also, of course, had its political impact). This complex evolution of the petty bourgeoisie lies at the base of the seemingly bizarre support given to the post-1976 military regime by the PCA (Argentine Communist Party) which, in a distorted way, reflects many of the sentiments of its largely middle-class social base. The very real chaos, terror and corruption of late Peronism was to provide a credible justification for military intervention, in the name of democracy and the restoration of 'order' and 'decency'.

Before the armed forces made their move, however, further divisions were to occur within the Peronist movement. After the López Rega current was liquidated, Peronism and the bourgeoisie still remained divided on how to deal with the renewed working-class struggles. This was not simply a conflict between the 'moderates' and the 'right' for control of the government. By the end of 1975 the split between the *verticalistas* — who showed unquestion-ing loyalty to Isabel — and the emerging *anti-verticalistas* — who questioned her leadership of the Peronist movement — had become particularly sharp, spreading to the trade union bureaucracy where one current was calling for Isabel's resignation. Victor Calabró, a metal workers' union leader and governor of Buenos Aires, was even expelled from the Peronist movement for 'insubordination'. Briefly, it could be said that the *verticalistas* were striving to set the government on a renewed semi-Bonapartist course, whereas the *anti-verticalistas* (also known as *acuerdistas* or agreement seekers) were looking towards a new GAN, which would be mediated through the parliamentary process. The military knew that when the 'vertical column' of the Peronist movement, the trade unions, were split they could begin to think of a coup, but not before Isabel Perón's government had thoroughly discredited itself in the eyes of the masses. The divisions amongst the Peronist trade union bureaucracy had already made its impact on mass mobilisations. On 17 October 1975 — the 30th anniversary of the 1945 events — in spite of a massive propaganda campaign and free transport, only 30,000 people turned up to the CGT rally, and most of these were trade union employees, and 'lumpen' elements, with a marked absence of shop-steward committee banners. Meanwhile, some half a million workers were on strike up and down the country.

A Coup is Prepared

As the crisis of late Peronism became more acute towards the end of 1975, the most reactionary wing of the air force responded to the growing call for a coup to deal with inflation, government corruption, and 'labour unrest'. Brigadier General Capellini, who had a fascist background, led a five day revolt which included taking over an air base. He received the support of ex-President General Onganía and some bourgeois political figures of the extreme right. However, although the bulk of the armed forces were sympathetic towards the putsch attempt it was considered premature and General Videla decided to take a hard line against it. The CGT called a strike only towards the end of the coup dress-rehearsal, and its failure was a good indicator for the military in regard to popular response to a real coup.

The army was, of course, already playing an important role in the field of repression, mainly against the rural guerrilla campaign launched by the ERP in Tucumán during 1974.[58] Towards the end of 1975 a massive ERP attack on an army barracks in Monte Chingolo (in Buenos Aires province) moved more sections of the armed forces towards intervention, as did the Montoneros' attack on a regiment in the northern province of Formosa. These activities of the guerrilla organisations no doubt accelerated military intervention, but the major determinants of this lay in the class struggle of the organised working class.

Tension mounted in the first months of 1976, with constant rumours of a new military *coup d'etat*. Two main orientations had crystallised amongst the military hierarchy. The first, represented by General Bessone (based in Rosario) and General Menendez (based in Córdoba) was known as the 'hard line' which favoured a generalised and long term repression of the mass movement, the second, majority current, led by General Videla and Army Chief of Staff Viola, incorrectly labelled as 'moderates', favoured a more selective and temporary repression of trade union and political activists. The aims of the two currents were the same: to inflict a decisive defeat on the organised working class so as to restore the profitability of Argentine capitalism. They differed only in terms of the tactics they proposed to use, something not perceived by those who supported Videla as against a mythical Argentine Pinochet. Towards the end of February 1976, General Videla was setting the timetable for military intervention. It was agreed that the armed forces should seize power at the earliest opportunity, in order to counter the anticipated wave of strikes against the new austerity plan then being prepared. It was hoped to inflict minimum damage on the Peronist movement and to avoid alienating the population as a whole. A *Pinochetazo* was rejected in favour of 'national reconciliation', with the purpose of restricting the coup to putting an end 'to misgovernment, corruption and subversion'.

Meanwhile, though the defeat of the government in the *Rodrigazo* triggered off a political crisis, the economic measures Rodrigo had tried to implement were still necessary and, therefore, Economy Minister Mondelli launched the sixth attempt at 'economic pruning' since Peronism's return to power. This time, not only were rigorous wage limits set, but there was a proposal to sack around half a million public sector employees (there had been a 24% increase in state employment between 1972 and 1975) to counter the increasing fixed deficit. The CGT was shaken out of its original acceptance of the plan by a powerful and spontaneous working-class response. A wave of strikes lasting two weeks rocked the industrial belt around the capital and spread to the provinces. Then a section of the trade union bureaucracy, led by Victor Calabró, decided (for its own reasons) to call for a series of 24 and 48 hour strikes. This was followed by another week of isolated actions as Calabró vacillated, even though the broad masses were in sympathy with the strikes against the Mondelli hunger-plans and were waiting for concerted action. However, Calabró (conscious of the impending coup) began to negotiate with a wing of the military conspirators and retreated, while the inter-factory co-ordinating committees were unable to offer an alternative leadership at a national level. It must be noted that most of the left-wing parties did not throw their full weight behind the fight against the allegedly inevitable coup, thus weakening the only process which would defeat the coup: a development of the mobilisation, which had begun against the economic plan.

As one contemporary observer noted:

> The road was finally open to the putschists. There was no leadership
> or force sufficient to detonate a generalised mobilization of the entire
> working class. Thus Peronism, while preparing its own defeat, rendered

the capitalist system one last great service: the division, disillusionment, and lack of confidence it provoked among the masses in turn deprived the masses of the only leadership they had known.[59]

The final military intervention came on 23 March, when Isabel Perón's government was overthrown by a military junta led by General Videla. The timing of the military intervention related to an accentuation of the economic crisis — the International Monetary Fund refused credits to the last Peronist cabinet, the Central Bank was in the red, and inflation was totally out of control — the rate of inflation in 1975 was 335% and for the first six months of 1976 it was 197%. On top of this, the regular wage negotiations for the various branches of industry (the *paritarias*), were coming up in April with the prospect of more strikes, etc. On the political front the meeting of all the bourgeois political parties (known as the *multipartidaria*) had not provided a coherent strategy for the ruling class and could only agree on its opposition to a coup. Finally, there was very little confidence in the ability of the Peronist government to guarantee the forthcoming elections.

If there was one, prime underlying cause of the coup it was the failure of the Peronist project to contain the combativeness of the working class within a framework of 'national unity' and class collaboration, under a charismatic Bonaparte supported by a powerful trade union bureaucracy able to maintain hegemony over the working class. The key element, with Perón himself dead, was the trade union bureaucracy, and it had begun to lose control over sections of the rural proletariat in the north, such as the sugar workers, the core sections of the Córdoba proletariat, and sections of the steel workers and other dynamic industries in the Greater Buenos Aires region.

The military regime (see Chapter 10) filled the political vacuum that resulted from the crisis and disintegration of late Peronism, which was also of course a crisis of bourgeois political domination. Peronism had evolved in three years from a mass nationalist movement to a form of reactionary Bonapartism with very little mass support. As the economic crisis worsened the material basis for the Peronist movement became exhausted, but the failure of the workers' movement to produce an alternative leadership meant that the turn to a military 'solution' was inevitable. In spite of important struggles around the time of the coup, including a general strike in Córdoba the day before, the working class did not respond to defend a government it no longer saw as its own. By 1976 the pre-revolutionary situation had been exhausted, and the working class was on the defensive, not through direct confrontation with the ruling class, but rather from the effects of a 'popular' government.[60] The working class was isolated and demoralised, hard hit by the crisis of populism and unable to see an alternative in the substitutionism of the armed organisations.

Figure 9.1
Chronology of Late Peronism (1973–1976)

Period	Economy	Government	Working Class
1973	Social Pact signed. Prices frozen, curbs on foreign investment. *Plan Trienal* announced.	*Gran Acuerdo Nacional* implemented. Cámpora elected then sacked by Perón. Lastiri interlude. Perón elected.	Ezeiza massacre. Wave of factory occupations. Amnesty for political prisoners. Anti-bureaucracy strikes.
1974	Perón/Gelbard economic strategy implemented. Wage increase threatens Social Pact. Gelbard resigns. Collapse of Social Pact. Economic crisis worsens.	Bidegain resigns. Navarrazo and other federal interventions. Perón dies – Isabel to power. AAA activity stepped up. State of siege declared.	Azul barracks attack. May Day clash with Perón. SMATA strike in Córdoba. Montoneros go underground. Combative unions intervened.
1975	Gómez Morales plan fails. Rodrigo measures announced. Cafiero plan fails. Agrarian sector rebels. Fiscal deficit, inflation rising rapidly.	*Partido Peronista Autentico* formed. Misiones elections. López Rega falls. Luder interlude. Capellini Air Force revolt.	Tucamán *foco* defeated. Villa Constitución and general strike. Formosa barrack and Monte Chingolo attacks.
1976	Mondelli measures announced. MARTÍNEZ DE HOZ PLAN	*Verticalista – antiverticalista* dispute sharpens. Bosses' strike. MILITARY COUP	*Coordinadoras* developed. Anti-Mondelli strikes. CGT INTERVENED

References

1. Hoare, Q. and Nowell Smith, G. (1971) *Selections from the Prison Notebooks of Antonio Gramsci*. London, Lawrence and Wishart, p.219.
2. On these movements, see respectively Andrade, R.C. (1977) *Perspectives in the Study of Brazilian Populism*. Toronto, Latin American Research Unit, Working Paper No.23; and Ciria, A. (1977) *Cardenismo and Peronismo: A Needed Comparison*. Houston, Joint Meeting of LASA and

ASA.

3. On the European experience, see Tilly, C. (1975) *The Formation of National States in Europe*. Princeton, NJ, Princeton University Press.

4. For a full exposition see Davis, H.B. (1973) *Nationalism and Socialism. Marxist and Labor Theories of Nationalism to 1917*. New York, Monthly Review Press; also the article by Lowy, M. (1977) Marxism and the National Question. *Revolution and Class Struggle* (ed) R. Blackburn. London, Fontana.

5. Nairn, T. (1975) The Modern Janus. *New Left Review* No.94:3. For a commentary on Nairn's and other approaches see Zubaida, S. (1978) Theories of Nationalism. *Power and the State* (ed) G. Littlejohn et al. London, Croom Helm.

6. Poulantzas, N. (1980) *State, Power and Socialism*. London, New Left Books, p.93.

7. Parkin, F. (1979) *Marxism and Class Theory – A Bourgeois Critique*. London, Tavistock, p.5.

8. Giddens, A. (1981) *A Contemporary Critique of Historical Materialism*. London, Macmillan, p.193.

9. Debray, R. (1977) Marxism and the National Question. *New Left Review* No.105:30.

10. Cited by Giddens, A. (1981) *A Contemporary Critique*, p.182.

11. Debray, R. (1977) Marxism and the National Question, p.41.

12. For a critique of 'Third Worldism' by an author who previously expounded this view see Chaliand, G. (1977) *Revolution in the Third World – Myths and Prospects.* Brighton, Harvester Press.

13. On Cabral, see Andrade, M. de (1980) *Amilcar Cabral – Essai de biographie politique*. Paris, Maspero.

14. Nairn, T. (1975) The Modern Janus, p.18.

15. Ibid., p.22.

16. Davis, H.B. (1978) *Toward a Marxist Theory of Nationalism*. New York, Monthly Review Press, p.86.

17. Stalin, J. (1945) *Marxism and the National Question*. Moscow, Foreign Language Publishing House, p.11.

18. See Smith, A.D. (1971) *Theories of Nationalism*, London, Duckworth, p.228.

19. Lenin, V.I. (1967) *Lenin on the National and Colonial Questions*. Peking, Foreign Language Press.

20. Hodges, D.C. (1976) *Argentina, 1943-1976. The National Revolution and Resistance*. Albuquerque, University of New Mexico Press, p.139.

21. Laclau, E. (1977) *Politics and Ideology in Marxist Theory*. London, New Left Books.

22. Ibid., p.160.

23. Mouzelis, N. (1978) Ideology and Class Politics: A Critique of Ernesto Laclau. *New Left Review* No.112:53.

24. Blaut, J.M. (1982) Nationalism as an Autonomous Force. *Science and Society* Vol.XLVI No.1:1.

25. Debray, R. (1977) Marxism and the National Question, p.27.
26. Poulantzas, N. (1978) *State, Power, Socialism*, p.94.
27. Marx, K. and Engels, F. (1973) *Surveys from Exile*. London, Penguin, p.146.
28. For a background to the Peronist period see Falcoff, M. and Dolkart, R. (ed) (1975) *Prologue to Perón. (Argentina in Crisis and War, 1930-1943).* Berkeley, University of California Press; and Ciria, A. (1974) *Parties and Power in Modern Argentina*. Albany, NY, State University of New York Press; and Smith, P. (1974) *Argentina and the Failure of Democracy (Conflict Among Political Elites (1904-1955))*. Madison, University of Wisconsin Press.
29. For a more thorough discussion of Peronism's class base see Ciria, A. (1974) Peronism Yesterday and Today. *Latin American Perspectives*, Vol.I No.3:21-41; Hodges, D.C. (1976) *Argentina, 1943-1976* and Waldmann, P. (1981) *El Peronismo 1943-1955*. Buenos Aires, Editorial Sudamericana.
30. On Perón's foreign policy see Conil Paz, A. and Ferrari, G. (1964) *Política externa argentina 1930-1962*. Buenos Aires.
31. The most thorough analysis of the 1955 coup and its causes, in Godio, J. (1975) *La Caida de Perón*. Buenos Aires, Granica Editor.
32. For an overview of this period see Rock, D. (1975) The Survival of Peronism. *Argentina in the Twentieth Century*, (ed) D. Rock, London, Duckworth.
33. North American Congress on Latin America (NACLA) (1975) *Argentina in the Hour of the Furnaces*. New York, NACLA, p.24.
34. Portanteiro, J.C. (1977) Economía y política en la crisis argentina: 1958-1973. *Revista Mexicana de Sociologia*. Vol.   No.2:533.
35. For an account of the *Onganiato* see O'Donnell, G. (1982) *1966-1973 El Estado Burocrático Autoritario*. Buenos Aires, Editorial de Belgrano.
36. This interpretation is developed by González, E. (1974) *Que fué y que és el Peronismo*. Buenos Aires, Ed Pluma, and also, Gèze, F. and Labrousse, A. (1975) *Argentine: Révolution et Contre-Revolutions*. Paris, Ed du Seuil.
37. Cited in NACLA (1975) *Argentina In The Hour Of The Furnaces*. p.27.
38. Roper, C. (1977) Montoneros and the liberation of Latin America. *Revolutionary Socialism* No.1:21.
39. Laclau, E. (1973) Peronism and Revolution. *Latin American Review of Books*, No.1:128.
40. Lanusse, A. (1977) *Mi Testimonio*. Buenos Aires, Laserre Editores, p.264.
41. For a detailed analysis of these elections see Moray Araujo, M. and Llorente, I. (eds) (1980) *El Voto Peronista*. Buenos Aires, Editorial Sudamericana.
42. Cámpora, H. (1973) Discurso al asumir la Presidencia Argentina. *Panorama Económico*, No.278:23.
43. On the Social Pact see Ayres, R. (1976), The Social Pact as anti-

inflationary policy: The Argentine experience since 1973. *World Politics*, Vol.XXVIII No.4.

44. For an overall assessment of strikes in this period see Jelin, E. (1979) Labour Conflicts under the second Peronist regime, Argentina 1973-76. *Development and Change*, Vol.10 No.2:233-58; also Torre, J.C. (1974) The meaning of current workers' struggles. *Latin American Perspectives*, Vol.1 No.3.

45. For a full length analysis of the Montoneros see Gillespie, R. (1982) *Soldiers of Perón: Argentina's Montoneros*. Oxford, Oxford University Press; see also James, D. (1976) The Peronist Left, 1955-1975. *Journal of Latin American Studies*, Vol.8 No.16.

46. Roper, C. (1977) Montoneros and the liberation of Latin America, p.22.

47. For this and other events in the 1973-76 period see the following chronology and narratives: Sobel, L.A. (ed) (1976) *Argentina and Perón 1970-75*. New York, Facts on File Inc., Terragno, R. (1974) *Los cien días de Perón*. Buenos Aires, Editorial Cuestionario; and Kandel, P. and Monteverde, M. (1976) *Entorno y Caida*. Buenos Aires, Editorial Planeta.

48. On this wave of repressive legislation, see Nadra, F. (1974) *Un Año de Gobierno Peronista*. Buenos Aires, Ediciones Silaba, also Corradi, J. et al (1976) Argentina 1973-1976: The Background to Violence. *Latin American Studies Association Newsletter*, Vol.VII No.3.

49. On this mini-coup see Balvé, B. (1978) Crisis institucional, experiencia y conciencia del poder. *Estudios Sociales Centroamericanos*, No.20.

50. Lanusse, A. (1977) *Mi Testimonio*, p.231.

51. According to Argentine Commission to Support the Russell Tribunal. The repression of this period is analysed most thoroughly in Marin, J.C. (1980) *Argentina 1973-1976: Armed events and Democracy*. Toronto, Latin American Research Unit Working Paper No.28.

52. On the economic problems of the 1973-76 period see Di Tella, G. (1982) *Argentina under Perón: 1973-76. The Nation's Experience under a Labour-Based Government*. London, Macmillan; also Canitrot, A. (1977) La viabilidad económica de la democracia: un analisis de la experiencia peronista 1973-1976. *Estudios Sociales CEDES*, No.11; and Ferrer, A. (1977) *Crisis y alternativas de la politica económica argentina*. Buenos Aires, Fondo de Cultura Económica.

53. For a detailed account of this strike see Galitelli, B. (1980) La huelga de Villa Constitución. *Apuntes*, No.2.

54. Rasin, E. (1977) Villa Constitución. *Inprecor*, No.29: 15.

55. For a day by day account of the *Rodrigazo* and reaction against it Della Costa, D. (1977) Hace Dos Años: el Rodrigazo. *Todo Es Historia*, No.121:38-51.

56. Speech cited in Kandel, P. and Monteverde, M. (1976) *Entorno y Caída*, p.182.

57. On this strike see Thompson, A. (1982) *Labour Struggles and Political Conflict, Argentina: The General strike of 1975 and the crisis of Peronism*

through an historical perspective. MA dissertation, Institute of Social Studies, The Hague.

58. For a critique of the ERP see Flores, L. (1980 & 1981). La cuestión de 'Las vías' en Argentina. *Rearme*, Vol.II No.6 and No.7; more generally on the armed struggle during this period, see Dias, M. (1977) *A guerra da Argentina.* Lisbon, A Regra do Jogo.
59. Rodriguez, F. (1977) Argentina: one year after the coup. *Inprecor,* No.68:6.
60. An interpretation developed brilliantly in Landi, O. (1979) Argentina 1973-1976: La génesis de una nueva crisis política. *Revista Mexicana de Sociologia.* Vol.XLI No.1.

10. Military Regimes: Argentina Since the Coup

> If the ruling class has lost its consensus; i.e. is no longer 'leading' but only 'dominant', exercising coercive force alone, this means precisely that the great masses have become detached from their traditional ideologies, and no longer believe what they used to believe previously, etc. The crisis consists precisely in the fact that the old is dying and the new cannot be born. . . .
>
> Antonio Gramsci[1]

There was undoubtedly a 'crisis of authority' or 'hegemonic crisis' in Argentina after the death of Perón in 1974. Yet the new had not been born either — the break with Peronism was incomplete and a socialist alternative failed to materialise. In that context the military coup of 1976 aimed to re-establish the conditions for capital accumulation and a recomposition of bourgeois ideology. Some analysed the new regime as a form of 'fascism', others opted for the theory of the 'bureaucratic-authoritarian' state. We consider these two alternatives and our own perspective of a 'modern' military dictatorship, and then move on to an analysis of the various military regimes in Argentina since the fall of Perón in 1955, concentrating on developments since the 1976 coup which drove his widow, Isabel Perón, from power.

The military coup of 1976 in Argentina closed a counter-revolutionary cycle in the Southern Cone of Latin America which had begun with the military intervention in Brazil in 1964, continued with the fall of the Popular Assembly in Bolivia in 1971, and the military coups in Uruguay and Chile in 1973.[2] Clearly, the 1964 coup in Brazil was 'different' from previous military interventions in that country and in relation to the classical *cuartelazo* (barracks coup). It was not simply a question of one military faction or *caudillo* seizing the reins of government to displace another military ruler, or a civilian president, without fundamentally altering the nature of the state. The armed forces of Brazil came to power with a long term economic and political project (a bourgeois revolution even) which was to fundamentally alter the physiognomy of Brazilian capitalism (see Chapter 7).

Dependent Fascism

It was the ferocity of repression in Chile after the 1973 coup which gave rise to the wide currency of 'fascism' as a characterisation of the 'new' dictatorships. The solidarity movement in Europe particularly was based on Communist and Social Democratic movements in which the struggle against fascism had deep historical roots. But I would say that the description of these dictatorships as 'fascist' was politically 'overdetermined' by the current strategy of the Communist parties of Latin America, as codified in the 1975 International Congress of the area's parties in Havana.[3] Once the parallels with fascism were established, it followed inexorably that the struggle to overthrow the military regime would be of an 'anti-fascist' and 'democratic' nature. The Chilean CP thus prioritised an alliance of the ex-Popular Unity parties with the Christian Democrats led by Eduardo Frei, who had been an ardent supporter of the coup but who would now come to his democratic senses and oppose 'fascism'. It is now clear that how one characterises the 'new' military dictatorships is thus inextricably linked up with the question of what political strategies are appropriate for the workers' movement.

According to an important Latin American communist statement on the issue:

> actual social development has confirmed the definition of fascism as an overt terroristic dictatorship of the most reactionary section of the monopoly bourgeoisie, closely allied with the reactionary militarists, the counter-revolutionary bureaucracy and the big landowners. As in Europe forty or fifty years ago, it is finance capital, some local but most of it foreign, that has the leading role to play in this bloc in present-day Latin America.[4]

This definition of fascism, based on Dimitrov's famous report to the 1935 Seventh Congress of the Communist International, has the effect of narrowing down the supporters of the 'new' military regimes.[5] This is also made explicit in the document when it says that:

> it must be stressed, however, that by no means all the bourgeoisie supports the fascist 'project' and that some branches of the international corporations do not reject the idea of working out and possibly applying other 'stand-by' projects.[6]

The logic becomes clearly one of seeking out allies for the working class amongst 'dissident' capitalists, and exploiting the 'contradictions' amongst the armed forces. What this ignores is that Brazil 1964, Chile 1973 and Argentina 1976 were the result of a *unified* bourgeois response to working-class insurgency.

There are several analytical reasons why 'fascism' is a totally inappropriate category to describe the military regimes of Latin America. Writers such as

Atilio Borón and Emir Sader have shown conclusively it is a totally forced historical analogy with the quite distinct conditions which gave rise to European fascism.[7] The historical function of fascism is abruptly to transform the conditions of production and realisation of surplus value to the advantages of the key sectors of monopoly capitalism.[8] The violent centralisation of political power which this entails is accompanied by a mass movement of the petty bourgeoisie, combining extreme nationalism with intense hatred of the organised workers' movement. To fulfil its historical role, the workers' movement must be ground down before the seizure of power, achieving the complete destruction of all workers' organisations and the atomisation of the working class. The imperialist expansionism of classical fascism by the dependent states of Latin America is clearly ruled out, in spite of a certain credence given to the idea of a Brazilian 'sub-imperialism' and Argentina's role in recent military coups in Bolivia.[9] Furthermore, in a recessive phase of the world capitalist economy, there is little basis for an accelerated accumulation of capital in, say, Chile or Argentina, which could compare with that of Nazi Germany. The main differences, however, lie in the vastly different situation of the petty bourgeoisie and of the working class in these countries. Basically, the repressive regimes of Brazil, Chile and Argentina, have been able only to structure middle-class support very briefly, and only prior to their accession to power. The fervent anti-communist and 'law and order' ideology of a section of the Brazilian middle class in 1964, or the Chilean middle class in 1973 was not translated into a mass fascist party in the years which followed. The acquiesence of the middle class in Argentina in 1976, faced with the corruption and inefficiency (for capitalism or socialism) of late Peronism, only gave the military rulers a brief breathing space, but not a solid and durable social base. The proletarianisation of the middle sectors, and the failure of the military economic policies to create a new bureaucratic petty bourgeoisie, means that an essential component of fascism is missing. Most crucially, there is a failure to correctly compare the position of the working class in both regimes. Unlike the situation under fascism, the Latin American regimes have not even tried to establish new organisational and ideological co-ordinates for the working class which could change the axis of their social initiatives.[10] There are no fascist trade unions or appeals to supra-class ideological elements (e.g., race) in the Latin American case. Above all, the working class has maintained the ability (albeit partially and unevenly) to resist the economic and political reorganisation of dependent capitalism at their expense. In conclusion, the Latin American military state differs from classical fascism, most critically in its inability to maintain the active mobilisation of significant layers of the petty bourgeoisie and to destroy totally the organisations of the workers' movement and disintegrate the working class as a class.

Dos Santos is aware that the CP interpretation is a forced analogy, so he has coined the term 'dependent fascism' the better to describe the situation.[11] Dos Santos has pointed to the main elements which would distinguish these regimes from 'classical' fascism; (1) repression is carried out by an armed élite rather than through mass reactionary mobilisations; (2) a weak fascist movement is relatively independent from the fascist state, which is dominated instead by a business, military and technocratic élite; (3) the internal contradictions of these regimes produce a limited political space for the activity of a popular movement; and (4) these regimes survive on the basis of mass political apathy, rather than through the active political support of the petty bourgeoisie.[12] The rather obvious conclusion of this analysis is that 'dependent fascism' is politically weaker than its metropolitan counterpart. Having indicated all the fairly major ways in which the Latin American regimes differ from European fascism it seems futile to carry on using the term even with the 'dependent' qualification.

The Chilean *Movimiento de la Izquierda Revolucionaria*, (Movement of the Revolutionary Left) opposed the Communist Party characterisation of the Pinochet regime in Chile as fascist, though later they agreed to characterise the resistance as 'anti-fascist' and even agreed to co-operation with the Christian Democrats.[13] Their Argentine counterparts of the Castroist *Partido Revolucionario de los Trabajadores – Ejército Revolucionario del Pueblo* (Revolutionary Workers' Party – People's Revolutionary Army) have from the beginning characterised 'their' regime as fascist. According to the PRT-ERP:

> the term fascist is not simply an agitational term, but a scientific category which has its base in the class character of the regime. We can say that the transition of dependent capitalism towards monopoly dependent capitalism is a natural tendency of the development of capitalism in Latin America, a tendency which is not always accompanied by Fascism (Venezuela and Mexico). But when this transition is endangered by the threat of revolution, fascism appears. Because of the dependent character of our economy, we must speak of dependent fascism.[14]

Theoretically this analysis is fundamentally economistic in so far as political regimes are seen to follow inexorably from economic transformations. Politically, this brings the radical Castroist organisations into line with CP orthodoxy, as ratified by the 1975 Congress of Latin American and Caribbean parties. In Argentina, the Communist Party has *not* characterised the military regime as fascist. This is not because of any theoretical disagreement with the theory pioneered by their Chilean counterparts, rather, they maintained that President Videla was, in fact, a democrat trying to stave off Argentina's Pinochet, who was supposedly lurking in the wings. The military regime was thus supported on the basis that it stood in the way of a fascist takeover. This position owes more to the prioritised trade links between the Soviet Union and Argentina (now the main Soviet trading partner in America after Cuba) than to serious political analysis.

Bureaucratic-Authoritarianism

A second theory, of 'bureaucratic-authoritarianism', has been developed in a more academic milieu in order to account for the specificity of the 'new' dictatorships in Latin America. This analysis is particularly associated with Fernando Henrique Cardoso and Guillermo O'Donnell, for whom:

> the bureaucratic authoritarian state is a system of exclusion of the popular sector, based on the reaction of the dominant sectors and classes to the political and economic crises to which populism and its developmentalist successors led.[15]

The main difference with the traditional military regime is located in the strong link forged with international capital in this current stage. The aim of this new type of regime is 'social order' and economic stability as preconditions to attract domestic and international capital investment. O'Donnell lists five main general characteristics of the bureaucratic-authoritarian state: 1) it is dominated by the bureaucracies of the state, business and armed forces; 2) it carries out the political exclusion of the popular sectors through repression and corporatist controls; 3) it results in the economic exclusion of the popular sectors; 4) it poses the 'technical' resolution of social and political problems through a process of depoliticisation; and 5) it corresponds to a 'deepening' of the productive structures of dependent capitalism.[16] In a general sense, the bureaucratic authoritarian state is seen as a reaction to the crisis of hegemony in Latin America since 1930 and, more precisely, results from a sharpening of the class struggle on the one hand and the internationalisation of capital on the other. Without doubt this constitutes an original and sensitive attempt to come to grips with a new situation, but there are several criticisms to be made.

First there are 'internal' problems, or those of consistency. Much of the discussion in North America has been directed towards a rather formal typology of states, and discussion of O'Donnell's work as a closed theoretical system in much the same way as 'dependency theory' was received. Karen Remmer and Gilbert Merkx have recently tried to demonstrate that:

> O'Donnell's hypothesis linking prior threat levels to variations in patterns of repression, political deactivation, economic policy and performance, political alignments, and elite cohesion are not supported by comparative data.[17]

O'Donnell's reply shows a much greater dialectical imagination, noting for example how:

> the higher the level of crisis and previous threat, the greater the degree of economic orthodoxy which tends to be applied. The greater the degree of orthodoxy, the deeper the damage to economic and

institutional interests of a good part of the supporters of the coup that installed the BAs — the middle sectors and not a few segments of the bourgeoisie.[18]

This would seem to be a fruitful research guide for the case of Argentina. It is essential to guard against unwarranted generalisations, such as in respect of the case of Mexico, but in his more recent works O'Donnell himself has warned against this.

If we take each of the terms in the 'bureaucratic-authoritarian state' definition we discover certain weaknesses. First these regimes are more technocratic than bureaucratic, and one would hardly call Argentina's rather fluid and unpredictable military policies 'bureaucratic' in the strict Weberian sense of rational norms. The term 'authoritarian' is far too vague (Pinochet, Thatcher, Stalin, Hitler and the Ayatollah Khomeini are all authoritarian) and acts essentially as a euphemism for repression. Collier defines the 'new authoritarianism', rather coyly, as:

> a type of political regime that is distinct from both democracy and totalitarianism and that in certain respects, particularly with regard to the degree of limitation of political pluralism, is an intermediate type.[19]

The degree and extent of repression *essential* to these regimes is thus seriously underestimated. Finally, the analysis of O'Donnell is at a level of abstraction more appropriately placed at the more concrete level of 'regime' than that of state.[20] Definitional critiques are, however, less important than substantive ones.

The 'bureaucratic-authoritarian' line of analysis tries constantly to avoid the various forms of reductionism, an economism which reduces the political forms to mere epiphenomena of the capital-labour relation, and a politicism which accords an undue weight to political voluntarism in accounting for historical developments. The danger is, of course, that one may fall into an empiricism which recognises the changing situation, but fails to identify the dynamic of the whole process i.e., the class struggle. Certainly the class struggle is not 'absent' since, for O'Donnell, this type of state is 'a reaction to extended political activation by the popular sector'.[21] But he then goes on to question the importance of the low level of militancy and organisation of the working class in accounting for the relative stability of the military regime in Brazil after 1964 compared to the instability of the regime which came to power in Argentina in 1966. In itself this could be quite legitimate, if one advanced a coherent alternative explanation, but it is indicative that this comment is relegated to a footnote.[22] As to the sources of instability in these regimes, O'Donnell argues that 'the Achilles heel of the Bureaucratic Authoritarian State' is 'the problem of presidential succession'.[23] Again, this is a real problem, but it is not central — the real 'Achilles heel' of every capitalist state is the class destined to be its grave-digger: the proletariat. Even a liberal writer, such as Skidmore, recognises the centrality of the working class in the prospects of the new military dictatorships, noting how:

> variations in the character of the labor movement (which may in turn be attributable to the level of economic development) is the most important single variable in explaining the success or failure of economic stabilisation programs.[24]

Norberto Lechner, who has also developed this current of analysis, maintains correctly that 'one cannot explain the authoritarian State as a simple "preventive counter-revolution" to a sharpening of the class struggle'.[25] Certainly, one cannot ignore the level of capital accumulation and the form of integration into the international circuit of capital accumulation, nor does one ignore the specific historical mediations between the class struggle and the type of regime which ensues. But, in their constant bid to avoid 'class reductionism' this current ends up displacing the class struggle from the core of their analysis, with an inevitable effect on the political practice advised. The bureaucratic-authoritarian theorists seldom make explicit the political conclusions of their analysis but when they do, we find them coming close to the Communist Party prescription. Thus, Cardoso refers vaguely to a 'reactivation of civil society' as a way of combating these 'essentially demobilising regimes', with an emphasis on what the ruling class should do to avoid 'shameful forms of fascism' by moving away from 'anachronistic authoritarianism'.[26] Lechner, rather more specifically, says that:

> If the problematic of *revolution* was the focus of Latin American societies during the sixties (say from the victory of the Cuban Revolution in 1959 until the overthrow of Allende in 1973), the *leitmotif* of the present period is *democracy*.[27]

This, after the 1979 revolution in Nicaragua, is at least questionable. For his part, O'Donnell, in his concrete study of Argentina, continually emphasises the role of bourgeois opposition, such as that of the internal industrial bourgeoisie, to the 'bureaucratic authoritarian' state, thus displacing attention from the independent self-organisation of the masses which alone can ensure the overthrow of the military dictatorships.[28]

The 'Modern' Dictatorship

Having identified the analytical/political shortcomings in the dominant political paradigm (dependent fascism) and the dominant academic paradigm (bureaucratic-authoritarian state) it is incumbent on us to provide an alternative. Military dictatorships are a form of 'exceptional state' — to use the terminology developed by Poulantzas — along with fascism and Bonapartism.[29] It shares with these certain general characteristics:

1) it corresponds to political crises and comes into being to remedy a crisis of hegemony *within* the power bloc and in its relations with the masses;
2) it involves a radical change in the relationship between the repressive and the ideological state apparatus marked by a resurgence of organised physical repression;
3) the relative autonomy of the exceptional state form in relation to the dominant classes is particularly necessary given the need to reorganise hegemony and the power bloc;
4) there is a marked increase of state intervention in the economic field to readjust its conditions of reproduction.[30]

The modern military dictatorship can be said to unite and, in practice, fuse the state, the government and the armed forces. The armed forces, in acting as the 'political party' of the bourgeoisie, no longer operates as the last resort for the bourgeoisie. The 'wear and tear' of exercising political power directly will have a direct effect on the armed forces. In this situation, a threat to the government becomes automatically a threat to the stability of the capitalist state. We would not want to follow Dimitrov, who deliberately stressed the weakness of fascism and saw it practically as a direct prelude to socialism. The resort to military dictatorships by the Latin American bourgeoisie is, however, a sign of the fundamental instability of capitalist rule in those countries and their inability to structure a stable system of bourgeois hegemony.

It may well be objected that military dictatorship covers equally the Paraguay of Stroessner, the Nicaragua of Somoza, and Argentina and Brazil under the generals. As we have already noted, in the latter cases there is an institutional intervention of the armed forces marked by a 'deepening' of the productive structure through integration with the world economy. I would provisionally refer to these as 'modern' dictatorships, in so far as they lead to the development of the forces of production and 'rationalise' capitalist rule in these countries.[31] Philip O'Brien has rightly pointed out in relation to studies by Schneider and Stepan on Brazil's 'modernising' military rulers that:

> much of this analysis would be more useful stripped of its belief in 'modernisation' (which begs the essential question of what kind of modernisation, with what chances of success and for whose benefit and whose loss).[32]

This is correct, but I do not think we need accept the whole 'sociology of modernisation' perspective when we refer to the intensified capitalist penetration and acceleration of the social division of labour as 'progressive' in the Marxist sense. Politically, there are no obvious conclusions from this perspective. All I would say is that it stresses that these are *capitalist* states with all that implies for working-class objectives; both perspectives analysed above stress democratic as against socialist aims. Having said that, the democratic tasks are obviously primary under a state of exception. What is important is not *what* is fought for but *how* it is fought for — whether there will be a subordination of the working class to bourgeois forces and methods, or whether the working class organises autonomously and fights with its own weapons (from the strike to the insurrection).

Argentine Coups

The armed forces of Argentina have played a major role in the political history of that country.[33] Our concern will be limited to the post-Second World War period which really shaped the military of today. As we saw in the previous chapter, a section of the army played an important role in the rise to power of Peronism between 1943 and 1945. The particular nationalist-statist ideology of Peronism proved attractive to a middle-ranking element of the armed forces, much influenced by Mussolini's Italy. The prospect of Argentina as an important regional power, with the heavy industry necessary to produce modern armaments, was quite persuasive.

Armed forces, however, do not exist in a vacuum. They operate in a class society and their behaviour is inevitably influenced (some would say determined) by the dominant social classes. A broad middle-class alliance had consolidated in the struggle against Perón by 1954, and it exercised a strong influence on the military, as did the withdrawal of Church support from Perón. Perhaps more decisive was the threat by radical elements within Peronism to form workers' militias to defend the regime. Even pro-Peronist officers were aghast at this threat to the traditional armed forces' monopoly over the use of arms. And so the military prepared the *coup d'etat* of 1955.

On 16 June 1955 a formation of Gloster Meteors flew over the government house, dropping bombs on the crowded streets below, killing over 1,000 people. But this was just a 'trial run', and most of the armed forces remained loyal to Perón — at least until 16 September, when a military revolt led by General Aramburu forced Perón to resign. Sporadic resistance occurred in the working-class districts, but huge middle-class (and student) demonstrations greeted the *Revolución Libertadora* (Liberating Revolution). Soon the heterogeneous anti-Peronist coalition began to quarrel, and a new 'coup within the coup' took place in November 1955, displacing the caretaker president Leonardi and bringing the fiercely anti-Peronist Aramburu himself to the Presidency. But repression of Peronism was not in itself a coherent political programme, and the bourgeoisie as a whole opted for a civilian government in 1958. Having broken the power of the unions — at least temporarily — the military could withdraw to their traditional role. For some years, civilian governments, with sporadic intervention by the armed forces, would rule Argentina, with Peronism safely banned by law.

This led to the Frondizi period (1958–62) which, much like Kubitschek in Brazil (1955–60), promoted the expansion of monopoly capitalism and the economic consolidation of an 'internationalised' fraction of the bourgeoisie (that is, integrated into the international circuit of capital accumulation). This was not, however, translated into a clear-cut hegemony by this sector. Frondizi's government was, in fact, a hostage of the armed forces who were concerned with his 'soft' line on Peronism. When a Peronist candidate won the Buenos Aires provincial elections, in 1962, the time had come for a new military intervention. The Vice-President of the Senate, José María Guido, took over under the watchful eye of the military. One of his economic ministers was to be Martinez de Hoz who had his first chance at the monetarist policies to be applied after the 1976 coup. Meanwhile, severe conflicts wracked the armed forces. The *azules* (blues) wanted to call elections to steal Perón's thunder, while the *colorados* (reds) were set for a long stay in power. A brief military confrontation in 1963 led to a new round of elections, duly won by the Radical Party of Arture Illia with only two and a half million votes (Peronism was still banned).

The civilian government of Illia could not deal effectively with the severe social and economic conflicts which dominated Argentina. The military were soon preparing a new coup, but this time, unlike in 1955, with the support of a sophisticated technocratic element. The military dictatorship of General Onganía, which came to power in 1966, represented the most coherent attempt of this sector to break the particular 'stalemate' which had characterised Argentina since 1955. In Gramscian terms, it was an attempt to resolve in its favour the situation of organic crisis and transform its (economic) *predominance* into (political) *hegemony*.[34] A project was launched to completely restructure and modernise the economy to the benefit of monopoly capitalism. Primarily this involved the economic repression of the working class, but also the ruin of certain sectors of the petty bourgeoisie and the 'rationalisation' of peripheral areas of the economy such as Tucumán, where more than a third of the sugar-mills were forcibly closed down. Many of the short term objectives of the military-monopolist plan were accomplished in terms of promoting the concentration of capital, reduction of wages, stabilisation of inflation etc.

The strategic aims of the dictatorship were not, however, achieved, and a chain of events was set off which led to the return to power of Perón in 1973. One element of the strategy launched in 1966 — modelled on the Brazilian 'economic model' — was to maintain military rule long enough for the new stage of capital accumulation to create a bureaucratic petty bourgeoisie, which could provide it with a social base.[35] But the project backfired, as the independent (or traditional) petty bourgeoisie was squeezed by the expansion of monopoly capitalism resulting in widespread proletarianisation of these social layers. The 'rationalisation' of the economy led vast sectors of the petty bourgeoisie to abandon their traditional anti-Peronism and link their fate to that of the organised workers' movement. Opposition to the Onganía regime was building up and led to a defensive class alliance between the petty bourgeoisie, the workers' movement, and even sections of the industrial bourgeoisie linked to the internal market, which was affected by the decline of mass purchasing power. As O'Donnell points out, this sporadic, defensive class alliance was able to check the hegemonic project of the internationalised fraction of the bourgeoisie, but it was not able to impose a coherent capitalist alternative, as became abundantly clear between 1973 and 1976 when, as a governing alliance, it came up against its own internal contradictions.[36]

This heterogeneous class alliance was, however, sufficiently strong to inflict a serious defeat on the military plans. The workers' movement and the radicalised petty bourgeoisie entered a series of mass struggles provoked by the anti-dictatorship mobilisation of the students' movement. The *Cordobazo* of 1969, which was followed by a wave of semi-insurrections in other provincial cities (the *Rosariazo, Tucumanazo* etc), sealed the fate of Onganía. He was replaced by General Levingston, who implemented an economic policy more attuned to the needs of the 'internal' industrial sectors. This government in turn was swept away by the second *Cordobazo* in 1971, after which General Lanusse came to power with a clear policy of 'institutionalisation', which was effectively a retreat by the military to pave the way for a return of Perón. Our analysis in the previous chapter of the 1973–76 period need not be repeated here. Suffice it to say that Peronism Mark II was unable to reconcile the exigencies of a dependent capitalist economy with the demands of a highly organised and combative working class.

Many commentaries on the 1966 military coup refused to see any relationship between it and the course of the class struggle. The pre-emptive role of the dictatorship, faced by a recomposition of the working class, has since been recognised in spite of the appearance at the time that it was emerging 'in the cold', as it were. In 1976, the military coup which brought General Videla to power was analysed in a similar manner. It was seen as a simple response to the 'power vacuum' left by the crisis of late Bonapartism. This ignores the fundamental factor in prompting the military intervention, which was not so much the constant hammering of the guerrilla organisations but the big strikes of 1975, which outflanked the trade union bureaucracy and posed the critical danger of a workers' movement beginning to break organisationally from Peronism.

Compared to 1966, the class struggle in 1976 was reaching a peak in spite of the great confusion and demoralisation amongst the working class as they perceived the degeneration of 'their' movement and the betrayal by 'their' government. This points to a key element perceptively analysed by O'Donnell, namely that:

> the greater the threat level, the greater the polarization and visibility of the class content of the conflicts that precede implantation of the bureaucratic-authoritarian state. This, in turn, tends to produce a stronger cohesion among the dominant classes, to prompt a more complete subordination of most middle sectors to them, and to provoke a more obvious and drastic defeat of the popular sector and its allies.[37]

The alliance forged between the working class and the petty bourgeoisie in the *Cordobazo* of 1969 and consolidated in the years after was severely shaken by the reactionary turn of late Peronism. This milieu, converted to Peronism as part of its turn to the workers' movement, was full of expectation and hopes in 1973. When these were rudely shattered by the reality of Peronism in government they were easy prey for the official explanation of the 1976 coup, namely the restoration of 'order and decency'. As to the cohesion of the dominant classes, this was decisively reinforced by the greater prior level of threat in 1976. Four years after Videla came to power no significant section of the bourgeoisie had broken with the military junta and no coherent bourgeois alternative had materialised (no doubt partly owing to the decomposition of the Peronist movement).

The military dictatorship, which came to power in 1976, immediately took a number of measures which indicated its class nature. It stamped out the few remaining democratic rights which had already been seriously eroded under the Peronist government, parliament and all other national and provincial authorities were closed down, political parties were outlawed or 'suspended', and so on. The dictatorship intensified repression, particularly of the 'industrial guerrilla', i.e., factory militants. This resulted in the long list of deaths and 'disappearances' which symbolised the Argentine dictatorship abroad.[38]

Economic Rearticulation

The economic policy of the military regime was articulated by minister Martínez de Hoz, who symbolised through his personal interests the unity of agrarian, industrial and financial concerns. The first impression was that the economic measures would be more 'gradual' than those applied by the 'Chicago boys' in Chile after the 1973 coup.[39] This was probably due more to political expediency and the fear of precipitating a premature political confrontation than any qualms about the efficacy of monetarist prescriptions. The main measures taken were:

1) the reduction of real wages by nearly 50% in relation to the previous five years, increase in the price of public services, and an end to the subsidy of social services such as health and housing;
2) a programme of progressive reduction of import tariffs, no subsidies to non-traditional exports, encouragement of agricultural exports;
3) a liberalisation of the exchange and financial markets;
4) the reduction of government expenditure and employment, the reprivatisation of state owned firms.[40]

We shall now examine how these four major principles were applied in practice in the course of the six years after March 1976 (i.e., until the Falklands/Malvinas crisis which opens up a whole new period).

The first phase of the economic process was one of reordering affairs, renegotiating the foreign debt and the signing of a stand-by agreement with the International Monetary Fund.[41] Inflation was significantly reduced and, because unemployment did not increase, a certain social stability prevailed. In mid-1977 the financial reform was put into effect which freed interest rates and prompted a spectacular growth of finance companies. Practically overnight huge financial empires — the *financieras* — were built, such as Sasetru, which soon overshadowed the traditional firm of Bunge and Born in the commercialisation of agricultural products. 'Hot' money poured into Argentina seeking a rapid speculative profit. Between 1976 and 1980 the financial sector grew by 45%. Finance capital — a fusion of banking and industrial capital — became the hegemonic fraction within the ruling class bloc. These financial interests established an intimate relationship with the military rulers of Argentina, to such an extent that some commentators began to refer to a new 'financial/military' ruling class. The financial reform was no doubt the institutional transformation of most far reaching effects carried out by the military regime and most vital to its long term monetarist project.

Central to the conception of a free enterprise market economy is the free operation of the capital market. This entailed, of course, an increased penetration of foreign capital into Argentina. This reversed a tendency under the 1973–76 Peronist government which had renationalised seven major commercial banks bought by foreign financial interests during the late 1960s. These were returned to their former owners, and a number of state owned subsidiaries, manufacturing, mining and petroleum, were offered up to tender. For example, BANADE, the state development bank, decided early on to sell off its interests in nearly 200 manufacturing and service companies. A further limit to this tendency was the sizeable interests of the armed forces themselves in industry, particularly armaments. It is then, with only slight exaggeration that Julian Martel can write that:

> one of foreign capital's major objectives in Argentina has been to gain control of its public sector, and more specifically its state-owned enterprises. The present military regime is offering the international bankers and industrialists the opportunity to accomplish it.[42]

The important point to retain is that since 1976 international finance capital has increased its role in Argentina. High interest rates, and the subsequent increase level of local firms' debt, have attracted the financiers who have reaped a considerably increased portion of the economic surplus produced in the country. Ironically, the 1976 coup leaders had pledged a turn away from a 'speculative' to a 'production' economy.

It was perhaps, predictable, that without a solid recovery of the productive sector this financial euphoria would be limited in time. Effectively, in the first months of 1980 one after another of the big financial concerns began to collapse — Sasetru, Oddone, Grecco, etc. This followed the liquidation of the

Banco de Intercambio Regional (Regional Exchange Bank), which led to a
total crisis of confidence in the local financial sector. Further banks were
taken over by the Central Bank and the conglomerates which had sprung
up after the 1977 'reform' now just as rapidly began to collapse. A process
of concentration ensued which resulted in a serious reduction of the number
of banks and financial companies from around 400 to 300. Those who had
preached 'efficiency', or the survival of the fittest, for the industrial sector
were now facing the same kind of relentless concentration and centralisation
of capital. By the end of 1980 and the beginning of 1981, it was widely
recognised that the monetarist policies had brought the financial and
productive structures of the country to the brink of collapse. In this artificial
situation it was estimated that 25% of the total holdings of the financial
sector — that is over $10,000 million — was impossible to collect. Meanwhile,
the growing debt of the private sector was generating costs which could not
be paid.

Intimately linked to the financial reform was the opening of the economy
towards the world market. The aim here was to eliminate the 'inefficient'
units of industrial capital and, hopefully, weaken the traditionally strong
union organisation as well. The reduction of protective tariffs was the main
instrument of this policy; in 1980, all tariffs were lifted on goods not
produced in the country, and a maximum of 55% (to be reduced to 20%
by 1984) was set on goods produced in the country. The entry of foreign
capital and the transference of technology was also liberalised considerably.
This orientation towards the international market was not aimed at increasing
the level of non-traditional exports (manufactured exports were one-third of
the total in 1974) as in Brazil. On the contrary this policy was simply putting
into practice a longstanding belief that Argentine industry had been built up
artificially behind protective tariff barriers since Perón took power in 1946.
A return to the pre-1930 golden era, based on Argentina's 'comparative
advantages' in the agricultural sector, was no doubt a dream for certain
ideologues. More realistically, the policies aimed at a drastic restructuring
of the productive structure — agricultural and industrial — to bring it more
into line with the requirements of international monopoly capital. This does
not mean an adoption of a crude conspiracy theory, but simply an objective
convergence between these requirements and the strategy of the most
'dynamic' fractions of capital in Argentina. This line of interpretation is
only a starting point, but it is preferable to that of Aldo Ferrer for whom
'one of the greatest paradoxes of the Argentine experience is the difficulty
in identifying its benificiaries'.[43]

One of the first aims of the military government was to eliminate the
traditional tax on agricultural exports and to raise prices in this sector.
Industry, defined as the main 'problem sector', was, on the contrary, to lose
any fiscal, credit or tariff advantages. The reduction of wages after 1976 did
not lead to the hoped for reduction in prices, and in 1977 a 120 day long
price freeze was imposed on the major firms. Then the financial reform and
reduction of protectionism began to have their effects by 1978. Some firms

benefited by a renewal of their machinery when the price of imported capital goods fell. But those sectors involved in the production of consumer goods for the home market were hard hit — the textiles industry was virtually destroyed by the influx of cheap imports. The motor industry has been rationalised considerably and, for the winners, perhaps represents a vindication of the government's aim to bring manufacturing costs into line with international costs at the expense of some inevitable bankruptcies. On the other hand, the tractor industry has virtually collapsed. Employment in the industrial sector as a whole declined by 26% between 1975 and 1980, which gives an idea of the magnitude of the 'shake out'. By 1981 some observers estimated that industry was operating at only 50% of installed capacity. It is hardly an exaggeration to speak of deindustrialisation in Argentina, although this has not resulted in a significant direct increase in denationalisation, in so far as foreign productive capital has been remarkably reluctant to invest in Argentina (only 5% of US investment in Latin America goes there). This pruned down industrial sector, whatever its sectoral difficulties, did benefit from the military government's labour policy. This is manifest in the evolution of wages, labour productivity and, particularly, of labour costs in relation to final prices in the industrial sector enterprises. Industrial labour costs plunged from 103 in 1975 (1970:100) to 73.2 in 1980. Product per 'man/hour' increased dramatically in some sectors of industry between 1975 and 1980 — 43% in textiles, 31% in machine-making, 27% in the wood industry and 25% in the chemical industry. The overall figures for industry are just as eloquent — the early, brutal reduction of wages being the indispensable starting point for capital's concerted drive to reduce labour costs in the long term. The slight recovery of wages in 1979 and 1980 resulted directly from the increased labour resistance in these years, which will be examined in more detail in a subsequent section. (In 1981, however, wages dropped again.) It is hard to see how Ferrer felt unable to find any beneficiaries of the military/monetarist policies since 1976. Clearly, some fractions of capital have to be sacrificed in the common interest of the class, and every grouping will have its own particular complaints, but this should not hide the overall trend of events.

As with all monetarists, even 'reformed' monetarist Martínez de Hoz and his military backers made a reduction of the role of the state a prime objective. The public sector's role in the economy had increased substantially during the 1973–76 Peronist administration. Martínez de Hoz set two main objectives: the reduction and rationalisation of public spending, and the denationalisation of (some?) state companies. The offensive against state employees was considerably successful — the number of personnel in the State Railway Company fell from 158,003 in 1976 to 96,000 in 1980 (a 40% reduction), the Economy Ministry shed 100,000 of its 500,000 employees (a 20% reduction) and so on.[44]

Thus, although the 1975 peak reached during the Peronist period has been reduced, the figures are still above the 1970 figures. The programme of denationalisation of state firms achieved its 'successes' — the current list of companies put out to tender included Siam SA, Argentine State River Company,

Austral Argentina, four television stations and nine radio stations, 40 small hotels, etc. When we take the global figures, however, we find that the relation between public expenditure and Gross National Product fell from 39% in 1975, to 34% in 1977, only to recover and reach the 1975 level by 1979. Furthermore, in spite of early rhetoric, the major productive and services concerns ran by the state have not been affected, often for the very good reason that they are not profitable and would not attract private buyers.

Taking a long term view of Argentina's economic development, clearly an element of state capitalism is inevitable in a situation of late dependent industrialisation. Five or six years of anti-statist measures (or intentions) have not altered that fact. There were even clashes between economy minister Martínez de Hoz and the armed forces over the crucial *Fabricaciones Militares* complex, with the military obviously getting the upper hand. As to the fiscal crisis of the state – so obvious in 1976 – the monetarist measures did have some effect – although by 1980 expenditure was rising again. If one takes an overall look at state functions in Argentina what is most noticeable is a dramatic decline of its 'legitimation' operations, particularly its withdrawal from a commitment towards building a welfare state, which began under its first Peronist administration. This bid to dismantle the welfare elements of the state – be it housing, health or education, follows from an ideological offensive against the previous 'demagogic and populist' state form. This particular element of privatisation is bound to have far- · reaching social effects which will continue under future civilian administration.

The agrarian oligarchy had ruled supreme in Argentina until 1930. The depression of the 1930s led to a limited industrialisation which accelerated under Perón in the post-war period. In spite of the liberal restoration in 1955, this sector never regained full political power and it became even more economically marginalised in the expansive industrialisation of the 1960s. Nevertheless, many observers detected the hand of the agrarian oligarchy in the measures taken after 1976, as though they were trying to put the clock back 50 years.[45] Clearly, the emphasis of the military government was on the export potential of Argentina's agriculture and livestock industries. Measures were taken to particularly favour the integration of transnational companies into this area, to promote a real agri-business sector. The differential exchange rates, which had previously constituted an effective tax on agrarian exports, were eliminated. Favourable government policies did, in fact, lead to an agrarian boom in the first years of military rule, helping amongst other things to build up a favourable balance of payments. Cereal exports in 1977 were nearly 75% higher than the level achieved during the 1973–76 Peronist period. By 1978, the Pampa producers' organisation CARBAP (*Confederación de Asociaciones Rurales de Buenos Aires*) was threatening to not pay increased tax demands. Furthermore, as with other sectors, they were vehemently opposed to paying positive interest rates on their loans, having for many years become accustomed to negative interest rates, given the high level of inflation.

The aim of modernising agriculture was not too successful either. In 1978, a CARBAP statement gave the simple reason: in 1973 it took 120 cows to buy a tractor, in 1974 it was 340 and by 1978 500 cows were required. Clearly the political instability of the country would not favour heavy investment in modernisation either. If one were to seek an explanation for the export agrarian boom of the first few years after the coup, this would lie with the level of modernisation achieved in the previous 20 years and the drastic reduction of internal consumption.[46] By 1980, agrarian production levels were beginning to fall and the prioritised trade links with the Soviet Union were the main frail (and risky) lifeline. The verbal protests of the big producers in the Pampas against the government's economic policies were joined by a series of strikes by smaller farmers, particularly in the fruit producing areas. The acute crisis of the provincial economies became an important component of the generalised crisis situation opened up in 1980–81. Once the aims of the military coup had been achieved — defeat of the guerrillas and disarticulation of the labour movement — its backers began to count the costs more carefully.

In March 1981, after an unprecedented (for Argentina) five years in control of the economy Martínez de Hoz was replaced by Lorenzo Sigaut. Since March 1976, monetarist policies backed up by military power had tackled forcefully the alleged lack of 'labour discipline' and the various 'distortions' and sources of 'inefficiency' in the economy. What seemed the main gain of this period — the high level of foreign reserves — was also steadily disappearing. Sigaut announced a 23% devaluation of the peso and a new injection of credit via the Central Bank, both aimed at salvaging a debt-ridden industrial sector. These stop-gap measures could do very little to contain the overall tendency towards a recession. Some ministers seemed committed to a reactivation of industry above the fight against inflation but those such as Industry Minister Oxenford, were soon forced to resign. The only optimists were the foreign bankers, who continued moving in to markets vacated by the collapse of their competitors. As after the *Cordobazo* of 1969, a rapid succession of military rulers began; in March 1981 General Videla was replaced by Viola, and by December he was replaced by General Galtieri, in what appears to have been a 'coup within a coup'. In 1982 Roberto Alemann had taken over as economy minister and, against some expectations of a change of course, announced exactly the same objectives as had Martínez de Hoz in 1976. This direct representative of finance capital embarked on his programme regardless of its political consequences. President Galtieri, on the other hand, began negotiations on a political timetable with the political parties, setting 1984 as the target for elections. Were it not for the Falklands/Malvinas crisis beginning in April 1982, a gradual 'decompression' of military rule such as that carried out by General Lanusse in 1973 or that embarked on in recent years by the Brazilian generals could have been predicted. By mid 1982 political criteria became dominant as the economy slipped further into recession, aggravated of course by military adventurism on the South Atlantic.

The failure of monetarism-militarism yet again in Argentina must be seen in the context of these policies in the Southern Cone of Latin America generally.[47] The 'economic genocide' practised in Chile, and to a certain extent in Uruguay, was not possible in Argentina given the still substantial weight of the national industrial bourgeoisie and the cohesion and combativeness of the labour movement. The monetarist faith in the operation of the market neglects the overriding role of the international context in the semi-industrialised dependent economies. Likewise, the belief that private capital can do everything (except perhaps in the area of defence) better than the state leads the monetarists to a politically and economically counter-productive assault on this bastion of stable capitalist rule. Political realities have, however, kept the opening of the economy and its privatisation within certain limits in Argentina. This points to the limitation of a purely 'internal' critique of monetarism and its logical inconsistencies. The growing band of bankrupt capitalists are quite aware of the effects of Milton Friedman's doctrines, but they also know that to oppose them is a risky political choice. The pendulum is swinging again towards a broad coalition of bourgeois and popular forces against the dictatorship but, significantly, even the Peronists accept the basic framework set by the military monetarists. The Keynesianism practised by earlier populist governments was unable to overcome the long-term stagnation of dependent capitalism in Argentina. In 1982 we see this long-term tendency joined by an acute conjunctural crisis. For the six years from 1976 to 1981, industrial production showed positive growth rates only in 1977 and 1979. In 1978 there was a 10.9% *decline* of industrial production and in 1981 a 12.7% decline. Inflation, which for some was the *raison d'être* of military intervention, has declined from the dizzy heights of 1976 (444%) but in 1981 it was still running at 138%, hardly a normal situation (see Table 10.1).

Political Recomposition

If, as we have seen, the capital market was rationalised by the military dictatorship the labour market would be affected no less. The recomposition of capital leads inevitably to the restructuring of labour. During the first two years of military rule there was an explicit commitment to prevent the logic of monetarism resulting in widespread permanent unemployment. Low rates of unemployment, of 3–4%, were proudly held up as proof of the military commitment to 'social peace'. By 1980, however, there were one million unemployed out of a working population of seven and a half million. Even these figures are masked by a withdrawal of immigrants (returned to neigh-bouring countries) and women (returned to the home) from the labour market, the wave of skilled labour which has emigrated, and the massive rise in the number of 'self-employed' workers in the 'informal' sector. Deindustrialisation has meant that whereas in 1976 there were 1,030,000 industrial workers, by 1980 there were only 790,000. In 1976 there were 1,700,000 state workers, in 1980 there were 1,200,000. Of the 120,000 textile workers in 1976, in 1980 there were 40,000. The workplaces which remain are increasingly subject to technological change (containerisation of the Buenos Aires port for example) resulting in redundancies and deskilling. Wage differentials have increased dramatically, driving a wedge into a working class previously united both economically and politically (through Peronism). As the labour market is reshaped, hundreds of thousands of workers and employees are shifted around geographically, adding to the disorganisation of the class achieved by naked repression.

Economists tend to forget that labour is not just a 'factor of production' but is also a conscious agent with an obstinate will of its own. If we were to seek one overriding reason for the failure of the monetarist policies of the military regime that would be the continued resistance of the labour movement since 1976. The early pattern of resistance was centred around 'go-slows' and the famous *trabajo a tristeza* (literally 'sad working'). In spite of unprecedented levels of repression, directed particularly against a militant layer of shop stewards, more generalised expressions of labour discontent emerged, culminating in the general strike of April 1979. We can see the overall trend of strikes in Table 10.2. There were strikes at the ports, the railways, the big car plants and nearly every branch of industry. Though the bare figures themselves testify to the continuous nature of labour resistance, it is important to note the qualitative change between 1976 — when absenteeism was a more common form of protest — and 1979 onwards when factory occupations and street demonstrations became once again common features. The divided trade union bureaucracy — committed to the opposition grouping, the *Multipartidaria* — has played a role in containing this new upsurge of labour activity. Nevertheless, as in the period 1969-73, the working class has been the backbone of resistance to the military government.[48]

The first years of the 1980s were dominated by the struggle against legislation passed in November 1979, designed to 'democratise and depoliticise' the unions. Amongst other measures, national union federations and the CGT

Table 10.1
Argentina: Economic Indicators (1976-81)

Year	Annual Growth Rate of Industry	Industrial Labour Costs (1970:100)	Total Foreign Debt ($billion)	Consumer Price Index
1976	−2.0	64.2	8,280	444
1977	5.9	58.2	9,678	176
1978	−10.9	58.5	12,496	176
1979	9.1	62.5	19,035	160
1980	−3.5	73.2	27,162	101
1981	−12.7	−	32,000	138

Source: Adapted from A. Canitrot (1981) Teoría y práctica del liberalismo. *Desarollo Económico*, Vol.21 No.82.

Table 10.2
Strikes in Argentina (1976–1981)

Year	No. of Strikes	No. of Strikers
1976	89	191,660
1977	100	514,710
1978	40	212,140
1979	188	1,818,020
1980	261	362,447
1981	360	–

Source: Adapted from *Vencer* No.8, 1981, pp.6–7.

(*Central General de Trabajadores*) were banned, the social services previously administered by the unions were taken over by the state, and the unions are barred from political activity. The balance of forces is difficult to assess, but in March 1979, for the first time since the coup, the Ministry of Labour allowed the election of *delegados sindicales* (union delegates) by sections in all plants. The renewal of the *comisiones internas* (internal commissions) proceeded apace in the course of the 1979 strikes, and there was a dramatic increase in internal union life. There has even been a restructuring of the inter-factory *coordinadoras*, not, as in 1975, restricted to anti-bureaucratic elements, but drawing in the middle cadre of the union bureaucracy as well. All in all, it can be said that the working class is passing through a phase of recomposition and that a solid leadership seems to be re-emerging. It is important to note that the 'plan of action' mounted by the leadership against this legislation in 1980 received widespread support amongst the bourgeois political forces (obviously for their own reasons). This again shows that the 'labour question' is absolutely central to the prospects of consolidation of a military dictatorship, and that the bourgeois opposition shapes its strategy according to its development. The recomposition of the labour movement was probably achieved definitively in the May 1982 demonstrations against the dictatorship just before the Malvinas war. This was consolidated in the wake of the war in an upsurge of strikes, demonstrations and factory occupations.

The military dictatorship had set out with a plan known as the 'Process of National Institutional Reorganisation' which aimed at achieving a durable recomposition of the ruling bloc by the mid 1980s. Though the first objective of crushing the armed guerrilla movements was achieved virtually within their first year in power, the military were frustrated in their long term plan to inflict an irreversible defeat of the mass movement. To achieve 'normalisation', a cowed working class would have to be incorporated into a stable social democratic organisation acting as its *interlocutor válido* (acceptable representative). This has not happened, though the more openly collaborationist fractions of Peronism would gladly occupy that role. Some of these projects are simply unrealistic, as with Admiral Massera (ex-Junta member) who suddenly discovered his populist vocation and offered the Peronists a new 'charismatic' leader. The working class today remains 'Peronist' but not because of nostalgia for days gone by, rather expressing the political unity of the working class. That is why the revolutionary nationalist Montonero movement has remained committed to the unity of Peronism, even when its leadership is hardly progressive.[49] This position also, of course, reinforces popular illusions of the viability of a renewed Peronist-type project.

In the course of political events since 1976 the bourgeois opposition, and even some military leaders, have expressed misgivings about the *Proceso*. A favourite area for political comment after the coup was the diagnosis of various 'wings' within the armed forces. The most persistent version saw General Videla as a 'moderate', even 'democratic' element, faced with 'hard' or 'fascist' elements in the army and the navy as a whole. Rather crudely perhaps, we would maintain against this that all political currents and disputes within the dictatorship ultimately reflect the role of the masses, or rather they are debates on *how* to carry on the class struggle most effectively so as to safeguard the capitalist system. As Poulantzas says, these internal differences:

> can only be appreciated at their true significance if behind this or that measure or policy in favour of this or that fraction of capital, we see clearly the spectre of the struggle of the popular masses.[50]

The tendency to spot 'internal contradictions' within the military dictatorship is matched by an incorrect estimation of bourgeois opposition to the Junta. Ricardo Balbin, leader of the Radical Party in Argentina, began after a while to voice criticisms of the military dictatorships, as Eduardo Frei of Chile's Christian Democrats was doing with Pinochet's regime. Both these political representatives of capital (now dead) supported the implantation of the military dictatorships. Today, to a greater or lesser extent their successors are critical, but not because they support 'democracy'. The reason for their muted, never organised opposition is that they fear the *consequences* of the economic and politically repressive measures of 'their' dictatorships. In 1981, Nestor Vicente, a leader of the Christian Democrats in Argentina, declared that:

> It is impossible to observe passively how the social explosions are beginning in the country, we must interpret them and translate into politics the anger (*la bronca*) of the Argentines.[51]

This, of course, was the worry of the bourgeois opposition — that the effects of the military dictatorship would exacerbate social conflict to a degree with which even they could not cope when constitutional rule was re-established. At the same time, the politicians were quite prepared to allow the military a longer period in office if necessary. Thus, Conrado Storani of the Radical Party was saying in 1981, that 'for the rest of this century and for several

decades of the next one there will not be *populist adventures* in Argentina in
the style of Radicalism and Peronism.'[52] Naturally, when the military did
begin to stumble in the following year, all the bourgeois parties began jockey-
ing for positions in the new *abertura* politics.

The stage had now arrived at that described by General Lanusse when he
began the 1971–73 retreat to barracks, 'the real discussion was not whether
or not to institutionalise the Republic. The real discussion was *how* and
when institutionalisation should be carried out.'[53] The military began their
rule saying *'la Junta no tiene plazos, sino objetivos'* (the Junta has no fixed
term only objectives). Though they have only partially met their objectives
their term has now run out. This process of 'normalisation' has, of course,
severe limits. In the first place, the dictatorship is conceiving of the above
process as co-existing with a permanent role for the armed forces in
government. More fundamentally, the very nature of this process and its
rhythm is dictated by the development of the class struggle. This process
cannot be a smooth one and will be marked by sharp outbursts of the class
struggle. This is because, as Poulantzas has pointed out:

> just as an exceptional form of state (fascism, dictatorship, bonapartism)
> cannot develop out of a parliamentary democratic state by a
> continuous and linear route, imperceptibly as it were, by successive
> steps, so a parliamentary democratic state cannot develop in this way
> out of an exceptional state.[54]

In the wake of the Malvinas war, President Galtieri was replaced by General
Bignone who had been forced to govern – initially, at least – without the
support of a Junta comprising the navy and air force as well.[55] There are
signs that a 'Peruvianist' wing of the armed forces may yet draw drastic
conclusions from the fiasco in the South Atlantic. A retreat from monetarism
now seems certain, as Dagnino Pastore (a technocrat who served under Onganía)
takes over the economic ministry with a brief to salvage the industrial sector
and allow wages to rise. An event possibly prompted directly by labour
agitation (the Malvinas repossession) has now led to a distinctly more
favourable prospect for a democratic renewal process. This outside event
has unleashed an internal dynamic of incalculable effects. Some observers
even feel that a period similar to 1943–45 has emerged in which the military
(or a section thereof) will launch a nationalist renewal. More likely is a
renewal of the cycle of weak and unstable civilian regimes followed by
military rule. The basic 'pendulum' of Argentine politics does not seem to
have been broken in so far as Peronism remains the dominant ideology
within the popular camp.

The Peronism of the 1980s lacks the dominant central figure of Perón
and is divided into multiple tendencies.[56] His widow, Isabel Perón, clings
to a leadership position amongst the 'historic' current of the movement,
but this is due more to the principle of 'verticalism' than any independent
political capacity. This current, which brings together the main figures of the

1973-76 government, could be said to be centrist in terms of its willingness to negotiate with the military. A more openly collaborationist wing preaches a broad unity of the armed forces, the church and the political parties. On the other hand an 'intransigent' or 'hard' wing maintains, at least in principle, that popular mobilisation will be the only means to displace the military regime. Outside of this mainstream are the Montoneros who have gone through several splits since 1976 and, after the severe repression of the years since, is effectively an exiled force. At the moment the more militant wing of Peronism is to the fore, reflecting the immense pressure from the rank and file. Today, Peronism is no longer a movement tied to one political figure but represents rather the political identity of the working class. Having said that, there is still an insuperable contradiction between the militant rank and file of the movement and the ranks of the movement's political and trade union bureaucracy engaged in intrigue. Without doubt Peronism remains the major political force in Argentina, although the middle-class Radicals may yet gain something from Peronism's disastrous performance in 1973-76.

A similar division was seen in the trade union camp. Two main currents crystallised within the trade union bureaucracy after the coup — both trying to become the representatives of labour before the military dictatorship. One was the Group of 25, which mainly organised a series of unions not 'intervened' by the military dictatorship. This current, which maintains the labour bureaucracy support for Peronism, was at first critical of the government, but then turned to 'accommodating' themselves with the state. A second federation was then organised — the *Comisión Nacional de Trabajo* (CNT: National Commission of Labour), which put forward a 'professional' image, ostensibly concerned solely with trade union matters. The CNT organised many of the large 'intervened' unions, such as the textile workers, metal workers, construction workers, and power workers, many of the 'big battalions' of the CGT union central. The first current was supported by the *desarollista* political tendency and the reactionary nationalist elements within the army. The second, which fits in best with the 'social-democratic' alternative, was supported by the international trade union bureaucracy and the most lucid currents of the dictatorship. In September 1979 the two tendencies joined to form the CUTA (*Conducción Unica de Trabajadores Argentinos*) which could effectively take the place of the CGT, the previous union central. After various reshuffles, by 1982 there were two CGT's — CGT Azopardo based on a 'professional' orientation, and CGT Brasil (both named after the streets in which the main office is sited) with a traditional Peronist orientation. The first is now negotiating with the transitional government and will probably back a governmental formula along the same pragmatic lines as North American or European unions. The second remains effectively the trade union branch of the Peronist movement.

In 1976 the bourgeoisie of Argentina launched a global offensive to restructure the class relations and relaunch the capital accumulation process. This was the most thoroughgoing hegemonic project since the 1880s and aimed to end the cycle of working-class resistance begun in 1945. In the first place this 'modernising' project involved an offensive against the medium and national sectors of capital through the economic policy outlined above. The second main plank of this project — probably the fundamental one — was aimed at breaking the social and political cohesion of the working class through deindustrialisation and terror. Having changed the mechanisms of capital reproduction, it was hoped then to remove the material basis for the reproduction of the old nationalist-populist alliance. The economic, political and social physiognomy of the country has no doubt changed dramatically since 1976. There was, however, a fundamental constraint on the monetarist-militarist project, namely the steady and gradually more organic and massive resistance of the working class. Peronism has remained the main source of working-class indentity, but only with difficulty (arid for a limited period) will it be able to provide an alternative strategy to either modernise capitalism or build socialism in Argentina. In that sense Argentina is a country which is 'blocked' — 'the old is dying and the new cannot be born', as Gramsci said. It remains to be seen whether Britain's 'Task Force' was the unwitting element which led to an 'unblocking' of this society.

References

1. Hoare, Q. and Nowell Smith, G. (1971) *Selections from the Prison Notebooks of Antonio Gramsci*. London, Lawrence and Wishart, pp.275-€
2. On these other military interventions see respectively: Stepan, A. (ed) (1973) *Authoritarian Brazil – Origins, Policies and Future*. New Haven, Yale University Press; Zavaleta, R. (1972) Bolivia. Military nationalism and the Popular Assembly. *New Left Review* No.73; Kaufman, E. (1978) *Uruguay in Transition*. New Brunswick, Transaction Books; and Valenzuela, A. (1976) *The Breakdown of Democratic Regimes: Chile*. Baltimore, Johns Hopkins University Press. For a broad overview see Rouquié, A. (1982) *L'État Militaire en Amérique Latine*. Paris, Ed Seuil.
3. This congress is covered in Ratcliff, W. (1976) *Castroism and Communism in Latin America, 1959-1976*. Washington, American Enterprise Institute.
4. Barrios, J. et al. (1978) Fascism in Latin America: Origins and Futures. *World Marxist Review* Vol.21 No.4:91.
5. Discussed in Claudin, F. (1975) *The Communist Movement – From Comintern to Cominform*. London, Penguin.
6. Barrios, J. et al. (1978) op.cit., p.97.
7. See Borón, A. (1977) El Fascismo como categoría histórica: en torno al problema de la dictaturas militares en América Latina. *Revista Mexicana de Sociología*. Vol.XXXIX No.2; and Sader, E. (1975) Fascismo e ditadura militar na América Latina. *Brasil Socialista*. Vol.1 No.3.

8. On European fascism see amongst others Kitchen, M. (1976) *Fascism*. London, Macmillan; and Machiochi, M. (ed) (1976) *Éléments pour une analyse du fascisme* 2 vols. Paris, 10/18.

9. The sub-imperialism thesis is advanced by Marini, R.M. (1972) Brazilian Sub-imperialism. *Monthly Review* Vol.23 No.9.

10. This is argued in more detail by Sidicaro, R. (1982) Elementos para un análisis sociológico de las relaciones entre regimenes autoritarios y clase obrera en Argentina y Chile. *Sindicalismo y Regimenes Militares en Argentina y Chile* (eds) B. Galitelli and A. Thompson. Amsterdam, CEDLA.

11. Santos, T. dos (1977) Socialismo y fascismo en América Latina hoy. *Revista Mexicana de Sociología*. Vol.XXXIX No.2.

12. Ibid., p.187.

13. On the MIR's policies see MIR (1976) *Dos Años de la resistencia popular del pueblo chileno 1973-1975*. Bilbao, Edita Zero.

14. Partido Revolucionario de los Trabajadores. *Argentina*. London, n.d. p.12.

15. O'Donnell, G. (1978) Reflections on the Pattern of Change in the Bureaucratic Authoritarian State. *Latin American Research Review*. Vol.XIII No.1:13.

16. Ibid., p.6.

17. Remmer, K. and Merkx, G. (1982) Bureaucratic-Authoritarianism Revisited. *Latin American Research Review*. Vol.XVII No.2:33.

18. O'Donnell, G. (1982) Reply to Remmer and Merkx. *Latin American Research Review*. Vol.XVII No.2:47.

19. Collier, D. (ed) (1979) *The New Authoritarianism in Latin America*. Princeton New Jersey, Princeton University Press, p.399.

20. A point developed by Riz, L. de (1977) Formas de Estado y desarollo del capitalismo en América Latina. *Revista Mexicana de Sociología*. Vol.XXXIX No.2.

21. O'Donnell, G. (1978) Reflections of the Patterns of Change, p.6.

22. Ibid., p.33.

23. Ibid., p.26.

24. Skidmore, T. (1977) The politics of economic stabilization in postwar Latin America. *Authoritarianism and Corporatism in Latin America* (ed) J. Malloy. Pittsburgh, University of Pittsburgh Press, p.179.

25. Lechner, N. (1971) *La Crisis del Estado en América Latina*. Caracas, El Cid Editor, p.20.

26. Cardoso, F.H. (1975) *Autoritarismo e democratizacão*. São Paulo, Paz e Terra, p.236.

27. Lechner, N. (1981) *State and Politics in Latin America*. Toronto, Latin American Research Unit Working Paper No.31, p.1.

28. See O'Donnell, G. (1978) State alliances in Argentina 1956-1976. *The Journal of Development Studies*. Vol.15 No.1.

29. See Poulantzas, N. (1974) *Fascism and Dictatorship*. London, New Left Books.

30. Ibid., pp.313-8.
31. Rouquié, A. (1978) *Pouvoir militaire et société politique en République Argentine*. Paris, CNRS, refers to the 'traditionalisme modernisateur' of the military.
32, O'Brien, P. (1977) The Emperor has no clothes: class and state in Latin America. *The State and Economic Development in Latin America*. (ed) E.V.K. Fitzgerald et al. University of Cambridge, Centre of Latin American Studies, p.57. The studies referred to are: Schneider, R. (1971) *The Political System of Brazil: Emergence of a 'Modernizing' Authoritarian Regime*. New York, Columbia University Press; and Stepan, A. (1971) *The Military in Politics – changing patterns in Brazil*. Princeton, Princeton University Press.
33. On the role of the military in Argentina see Potash, R. (1969) *The Army and Politics in Argentina, 1928–1945: Yrigogen to Perón*. Stanford, Stanford University Press; and Potash, R. (1980) *The Army and Politics In Argentina, 1945–62. Perón to Frondizi*. London, Athlone Press. For a general history of Argentina during this period see Luna, F. (1974) *De Peron a Lanusse 1943/1973*. Buenos Aires, Editorial Planeta; and Fayt, C. (1971) *El Politíco Armado. Dinámica del Proceso Politíco Argentino 1960/1971*. Buenos Aires, Ediciones Pannedille.
34. An argument elaborated in Portantiero, J.C. (1974) Dominant Classes and Political Crisis. *Latin American Perspectives*. Vol.1 No.3:94–120.
35. See Laclau, E. (1970) Argentina: Imperialist Strategy and the May Crisis. *New Left Review* No.62:3–21.
36. See O'Donnell, G. (1978) State alliances in Argentina.
37. O'Donnell, G. (1977) Reflections on the Patterns of Change, p.7.
38. For an overview of repression during this period see Araujo, C.V. (1976) *Argentina: De Perón al golpe militar*. Madrid, Ediciones Felmar; and, for a personal report, Timerman, J. (1982) *Prisoner Without a Name, Cell Without a Number*. London, Penguin.
39. On the post-1973 Chilean economy see Frank, A.G. (1976) *Economic Genocide in Chile*. Nottingham, Spokesman Books.
40. Expanded in Canitrot, A. (1980) Discipline as the central objective of economic policy: an essay on the economic programme of the Argentine Government since 1976. *World Development* Vol.8:913-28.
41. For an overview of the economy since 1976 see Ferrer, A. (1981) *Nacionalismo y orden constitucional*. Buenos Aires, Fondo de Cultura Económica, of which one chapter is translated: Ferrer, A. (1980) The Argentine Economy 1976–79. *The Journal of Interamerican Studies and World Affairs*. May.
42. Martel, J. (1978) Domination by Debt-Finance in Argentina. *NACLA Report on the Americas* Vol.XII No.4:21.
43. Ferrer, A. (1981) *Nacionalismo y orden constitucional*. p.162.
44. On the state sector see Green, R. (1981) Les enterprises publiques en Argentine face á la nouvelle stratégie économique (1976-1980). *Problémes d'Amérique Latine*. Vol.61.

45. For example, Comercio Exterior (1976) Argentina: la politica económica despues del golpe. *Comercio Exterior*, Vol.26 No.9.

46. On agriculture, see Sidicaro, R. (1978) Les grands propriétaires et les problèmes agraires en Argentine (1973–1978) *Problèmes d'Amérique Latine*. Vol.L, Decembre.

47. For an overview see Thorp, R. and Whitehead, L. (ed) (1979) *Inflation and Stabilisation in Latin America*. London, Macmillan; and on the more recent period, Monetarism and the Third World. *Institute of Development Studies Bulletin* (1981) Vol.13 No.1.

48. On labour resistance see Munck, R. (1982) Restructuración del capital y recomposición de la clase obrera en Argentina desde 1976. *Sindicalismo y Regimenes Militares en Argentina y Chile* (eds) B. Galitelli and A. Thompson. Amsterdam, CEDLA.

49. For the Montonero position see interview in *NACLA Latin America and Empire Report*. Vol.XI No.1.

50. Poulantzas, N. (1976) *Crisis of the Dictatorships*. London, New Left Books, p.82.

51. Alende, O. et al. (1981) *El Ocaso del "Proceso"*. Buenos Aires, El Cid Editor, pp.175-6.

52. Ibid., p.401.

53. Lanusse, O. (1977) *Mi Testimonio*, p.264.

54. Poulantzas, N. (1976) *Crisis of the Dictatorships*, p.90.

55. On current developments see *Latin America Weekly Report*.

56. This draws on the Argentine press, particularly the newspaper *El Clarin*.

11. Socialist Regimes: The Cuban Revolution

> Socialist democracy is not something which begins only in
> the promised land after the foundations of socialist economy
> are created; it does not come as some sort of Christmas
> present for the worthy people who, in the interim, have
> loyally supported a handful of socialist dictators. Socialist
> democracy begins simultaneously with the beginnings of
> the destruction of class rule and of the construction of
> socialism . . . It is the same thing as the dictatorship of the
> proletariat.
>
> Rosa Luxemburg[1]

Following Luxemburg we intend to apply a critical analysis to Cuba's
revolution, focusing particularly on the question of socialist democracy.
It should, however, be quite clear that this critical perspective should be
matched by an understanding of the material obstacles to the construction
of socialism in one island. Even further, any comparison of 'actually existing
socialism' in Cuba should be made not against an abstract notion of
socialism 'as it should be', but rather related to the abysmal conditions of
life in similar geographical locations, such as neighbouring Haiti. The analysis
thus proceeds from a discussion of some of the general issues involved in the
transition to socialism in the Third World to the concrete study of economic
and political transformations in Cuba since 1959.

The Transition

Any serious discussion of the politics of underdevelopment must tackle the
attempts made throughout the Third World to establish a socialist development process. The majority of socialist revolutions have occurred in countries
without a strong industrial working class, apparently contradicting Marx's
predictions. So, can there be a 'transition to socialism' in the Third World?[2]
   A socialist revolution entails the seizure of state power by the working
class and the building of a new society in which the means of production
become socialised. The communist mode of production, where social classes

disappear (because there is no longer a class struggle) and where the state 'withers away' (because only things and no longer people need to be administered) is preceded by the 'dictatorship of the proletariat'. This is seen as the centralised organisation of working-class power over the old dominant classes. In this transitional phase the principle means of production — factories, mines and large estates — pass into the hands of the state. This allows for a national planning of the economy in accordance with the needs of the people as a whole, rather than the interests of private profit. This phase is governed by the principle 'to each according to his labour', which only later, when labour ceases to be a commodity, becomes 'to each according to his needs'. In this transitional phase a major aim is to overcome the division between mental and manual labour, and between city and countryside, characteristic of capitalism.[3]

Most of the so-called socialist regimes in the Third World do not seem to display these characteristics. Two essential components are missing: 1) a powerful economic base which will allow the 'socialisation of plenty' rather than the 'socialisation of misery' and, 2) a large, highly educated industrial working class which can become the conscious actor in this process, and itself administer the economic and political system. Furthermore, the socialist tasks and aims of these Third World movements are inextricably bound up with those of the bourgeois nationalist revolution. What we see emerging instead is more akin to what Marx described as the 'asiatic mode of production' — communal relations of production coexisting with a state élite become a new exploiting class.[4] The analogy with the asiatic mode of production is of limited value, given the quite distinct historical phenomena with which we are dealing. It does, however, point us towards the existence of a state bureaucracy ('bureaucratic collectivism') which emerges in the post-revolutionary period and tends towards the crystallisation of a state bourgeoisie. It also indicates the massive difference between 'the transition' in the countries of the Third World and those where capitalism is fully developed. As Marx says:

> What we have to deal with here is a communist society . . . which is thus in every respect, economically, morally and intellectually, still stamped with the birth marks of the old society from whose womb it emerges.[5]

The conditions of underdevelopment impose the need for a process of 'primitive socialist accumulation' in the Third World transition. This was a term coined by the Soviet economist Preobrazhensky in the 1920s.[6] Whereas capitalism was born out of a process of primitive accumulation in a non-capitalist milieu, its socialist counterpart accumulates in the hands of the state material resources lying outside the complex of state economy. As Preobrazhensky notes, 'this accumulation must play an extremely important part in a backward peasant country. . . .'[7] Primitive or preliminary socialist accumulation lays the basis for a superior mode of production, but for a whole historical period it coexists with the (capitalist) law of value in determining the distribution of means of production and of labour power in the economy. The rapid development of industry was seen by Preobrazhensky as the only way to break out of backwardness, and this would entail the forcible alienation of the peasant's product. Aware of the problems of accumulation in backward Russia, Preobrazhensky was also forced to reject the possibility of 'socialism in one country'. What is more questionable in Preobrazhensky's discourse, is the emphasis on primitive socialist accumulation as an economic *law* when, in fact, the dynamic of the transition period is determined by political factors. In short, socialist accumulation is a stage in the building of socialism and not a law.

Given the difficulties of achieving even the preconditions for a transition to socialism in the Third World, some authors have diagnosed a particular 'non-capitalist' path to development. This theory is one widely supported by Soviet line Communist parties and, since 1975, the Cuban leadership. The 'non-capitalist' path is based on an alliance of the oppressed layers with the urban and rural petty bourgeoisie, and even sections of the national bourgeoisie, for a whole historical epoch. As one Soviet author, Ulianovsky writes:

> at this particular stage the national democrats upholding the non-capitalist path of development are coming to grips with the tasks of an anti-feudal, anti-imperialist nature, ie general democratic tasks the implementation of which is also in the interests of a certain section of the national bourgeoisie.[8]

A critique of this conception is based on the understanding of Third World social formations developed in earlier chapters, particularly regarding the subordinate position of the so-called 'national bourgeoisie'. Furthermore, the class struggle cannot be 'frozen' and the 'non capitalist' path must sooner or later become fully capitalist or break with this rationality and become socialist. In fact, as Clive Thomas notes, 'the non-capitalist way may be more consistent with state interests than it is with those of the working class. . . .'[9] Apparently representing a break with the utopianism of those who would 'build communism' in the Third World, this theory represents a profoundly conservative outlook and is also, in its way, utopian, because it has no long term prospects of success.

The conditions of underdevelopment do not, however, preclude the necessity for political democracy in the transition to socialism. Democracy is reduced to a 'bourgeois illusion' and an unnecessary luxury in the hard conditions of Third World transitions to socialism. Yet Lenin was always clear that the dictatorship of the proletariat would lead to more not less democracy than under capitalism. Clive Thomas points to the dangers involved in forgetting this, noting how 'rationalizations of the need to curb freedoms in order to further so-called progress have no place in the building of a socialist society. . . .'[10] The self-emancipation of the masses is essential to socialism, since it cannot be built by decree. Likewise, socialism is not solely (or even mainly) the development of the forces of production, but entails the transformation of the relations of production. To quote Philip Corrigan and his co-authors:

> The struggle for socialism, then — conceived *as* a struggle for production — does *not* lie between 'backwardness' and 'modernisation'. It lies between what Marx in 1867 described as the *political* economies of capital and labour.[11]

And that means a different rationality — from a system based on production for private profit to one geared towards social need. It is not economic laws, but concrete struggles between classes which determine the success or otherwise of this process.

In conclusion I will present five general hypotheses to be borne in mind when we turn to the study of the Cuban revolution.

1) The vast majority of socialist revolutions have, until the present occurred in relatively 'backward' countries: Russia, China, Vietnam, Korea, Algeria, Cuba, Nicaragua, etc. This means that Marx's vision of a fairly rapid transition to a new socialised mode of production was impeded. Instead, a long transition period, more correctly described as 'state socialism', has become established. This does not radically question the primacy of the capitalist relations of production or the capitalist labour process. The heavy legacy of imperialist domination — a distorted economic structure, corruption, bureaucracy, illiteracy, etc. — has proved to be the main barrier to a socialist transformation of Third World society. Furthermore, the enforced factory discipline of capitalism cannot be replaced overnight by 'socialist emulation', with the result being seen in high rates of absenteeism, low productivity, etc.

2) The whole notion of building 'socialism in one country', coined by Stalin for the Soviet Union of the 1920s, has been proven illusory. Most socialist countries, and even more a small island such as Cuba, are highly integrated into the predominantly capitalist world economic system. Short of a totally inward looking system, such as that attempted by the Khmer Rouge in Kampuchea with disastrous results, or a world revolution, this will place tremendous objective constraints on any socialist process.[12] However, the constraints of external reproduction operate only on the basis of their determination by the *internal* capitalist forms of reproduction.

3) It is important not to confuse socialist with nationalist regimes. The language of Marxism has become popular in many so-called developing nations because of its stress on industrial development and conscious activity. This does not mean that socialism is being constructed there. The experience of Algeria, Tanzania, and the general evolution of 'Third World socialism' is amply illustrative in this respect. The social movement against foreign domination may be part and parcel of a socialist process in

the Third World, but socialism can never be reduced to radical nationalism. In the same way, socialisation of the means of production cannot be reduced to the *statisation* (state control) which usually occurs.

4) Each socialist revolution is shaped by the particular historical circumstances in which it is born. The particular social structure, political traditions, and international situation give rise to distinct 'paths' to socialism. What seems certain, however, is that a 'peaceful road' to socialism in the Third World does not exist. The example of Chile, which has been analysed so thoroughly, seems to be ample proof of this.[13] There is confirmation of this, in the opposite sense, in the Nicaraguan insurrection of 1979, which only overthrew the Somoza dictatorship after a bloody civil war. Quite simply, no privileged group gives up its position without a struggle.

5) And finally, what does socialism offer the people of the Third World? Certainly no magic answers, as we shall see for Cuba, which in many ways is the showcase for socialism in the Third World. Undoubted gains in the fields of health and education and the eradication of gross inequalities have not been matched by comparable economic growth or political democracy. The question of whether Cuba has exchanged one form of dependency (on the USA) for another (the USSR) naturally arises. In a strict sense I think this does not apply, in so far as the Soviet Union supports Cuba financially, rather than exploits it. Politically, however, we will see how the 'Soviet model' has gradually achieved its sway over Cuban society. But this, certainly, is not inevitable and one should bear in mind that there are other 'models' based on self-organisation, workers' councils and genuine socialist democracy.[14]

The First Decade

In December 1956, proceeding from Mexico, Fidel Castro and a handful of comrades landed in the Oriente province of Cuba. After initial setbacks this small band of guerrillas began to organise amongst the impoverished peasants of that region. Three years of campaigning, against tremendous military odds (3,000 guerrillas to 80,000 Batista troops) but with growing support from vast sectors of the population, led to victory.[15] A general strike early in January 1959 (which capped a long resistance campaign in the cities) ensured the total success of the revolutionary forces. After the dictator Batista fled the rebels began systematically to dismantle the old state apparatus. The avowed aims of the revolutionaries were democratic and nationalist. But the dynamic of the revolutionary process was such that, in Che Guevara's words, there was 'an uninterrupted development of the revolution' whereby 'a logical progression led from the first to the last'.[16]

One can distinguish three relatively distinct phases of the Cuban Revolution up until 1961. The first was limited in its aims and methods to a programme of 'moralising' the old regime. The bourgeois-democratic aims of the Fidelista movement were matched by a programme of agrarian reform, becoming more and more radical. The popular revolutionary forces signed a pact with the middle-class democratic political representatives during this phase. A second phase opened up in 1959, which saw the accession of the traditional politician Urrutia to the Presidency, with the Fidelistas remaining in the background. This phase was, however, also marked by the first revolutionary conquests in the economic and social fields and, above all, by the implementation of the agrarian reform. In 1960, a third phase opened up which saw the definitive break of the Fidelistas with the conservative-liberal political system. It was then that a wave of nationalisations took place; in October 1960 the principal industrial and commercial concerns of the Cuban and international bourgeoisie, together with the banks, were taken over. Faced with a growing opposition from the ruling classes as a whole (supported by the US) the Fidelistas could either capitulate or move forward decisively. They took the second course, and by 1961 Castro was declaring the socialist nature of the Cuban Revolution.

It is now generally admitted that the intensely hostile attitude of the US government actually accelerated the course of the revolution. In June 1960 US firms in Cuba refused to refine oil that had arrived recently from the Soviet Union; in July all sugar imports from Cuba were cut; in October the US ambassador was withdrawn from Havana. In 1961 there was a US backed invasion of Cuba, repulsed by the militias at the Bay of Pigs, and by 1962 there was a total US embargo on trade with Cuba. So, the turn to the USSR was, in the circumstances, probably inevitable. This was the period in which the Committees for the Defence of the Revolution were formed and strengthened. These were neighbourhood committees which were organised in most urban areas taking over many administrative and also defence tasks. The Bay of Pigs invasion in 1961, and the so-called Missile Crisis of 1962, led to a great radicalisation of the Cuban people as a whole.

The Cuban Revolution clearly did not give birth to a 'healthy' fully developed socialist state by any standard or definition. Castro himself has highlighted some of these deformations quite dramatically:

> What happened was that when the Revolution took power the bourgeois state didn't exist any more. . . . Once our revolutionary government was established, the laws were enacted by decree. And, in this situation, some vestiges of the bourgeois state – such as the administrative appar-atus – still remained. Remained? Some vestiges of the bourgeois state remain even now in Cuba. I only wish we could say there weren't any. It is quite possible that some of the organisations we created were even more bourgeois than the old bourgeois state.[17]

The first few years of the 1960s were dominated by the attempt to institute a centralised system of planning, backed up by technical aid from the Soviet Union.[18] The Missile Crisis of 1962 led to a certain questioning of the Soviet 'model' and, between 1963 and 1966, there was a lively 'economic debate' over the appropriate form of planning; this also brought out into the open the

319

question of 'moral' versus 'material' incentives at work, and generally, the meaning of the socialist 'New Man' which was the aim of the process.[19] The radical alternative to Soviet orthodoxy won out, culminating in the 'Revolutionary Offensive' of 1968. This was a period of mass mobilisations, a belief that communism itself could be built in Cuba in the relatively short term. It was a period which saw serious attempts to spread the revolution abroad — as with the early Bolsheviks, the 'Fidelista' leaders believed that the survival of Cuba depended absolutely on breaking out of the economic and political isolation in which they found themselves.

Politically speaking, Castro's admission of 1971 quoted above is significant. The Committees of Defence of the Revolution (CDR) were the neighbour-hood vigilance bodies, which could have been extended into Soviet type formations — i.e., organs of self-representation of the working people with power vested in a sovereign congress of workers' and peasants' councils. However, their duties were gradually reduced to a type of voluntary social work — donating blood, collecting empty bottles etc. Systematic violations of democracy were rare, but so too was the operation of proletarian democracy. Ultimately this phase was characterised by voluntarism, laced with a paternalistic and moralising approach, which could not substitute for revolutionary Marxism. We see this in the Fidelistas' 1962 purge against sectarianism, and even more in the 1968 purge of the Escalante 'micro-faction' elements from the old communist party, the PSP (Popular Socialist Party), within the now unified revolutionary party. These events were part of a struggle against administrative methods and the growing weight of the bureaucratic apparatus — Aníbal Escalante aimed to bring Cuban socialism more into line with the Soviet model. So, Castro, though acting in pursuit of anti-bureaucratic objectives, was employing bureaucratic (perhaps even 'Stalinist') methods to deal with the problem. Escalante was gaoled, not because of any crimes against the revolution, or even for his politics, but simply because he was 'guilty' of forming a political faction. The temporary banning of factions in the Bolshevik Party in the extremely difficult conditions of 1921 has thus passed down to us a 'natural' state of affairs in post-revolutionary societies.

Certainly the overall trend in this period after 1966 was one of denunciation and bureaucratic methods (particularly in the trade unions) and genuine attempts were made to involve the masses more directly in the organisation of society. Nevertheless, it also reflects the essentially commandist methods of the Castro leadership itself. The Fidelistas created structures of a bureaucratic sort (using them for revolutionary ends for the most part) because their background and the nature of the process which brought them to power gave them no experience of or contact with the democratic traditions of the workers movement. Even the fight against bureaucracy focused more on 'red-tape' and administrative maladministration, showing little awareness of the social process involved in the bureaucratisation of the Russian Revolution for example. This is not necessarily contradictory with the assessment by Livio Maitan that:

> Fidel Castro's self criticism . . . revealed a clear potential for fighting
> bureaucratism and showed, in any case, that the group around Fidel
> was conscious of what was at stake. . . .[20]

Being conscious of what is at stake did not mean that the Fidelistas were
able to confront the challenge successfully, and the only conclusion we can
draw is that their project failed largely owing to its own inherent weaknesses,
rather than to Soviet pressure or Stalinist influence, which in any case was
very restricted at this period.

The achievements of the revolution during the first decade were, however,
considerable. As we saw in Chapter 8, before 1959 Cuba was dominated by
what was known as 'the slavery of sugar'. Effectively, sugar represented 81%
of all exports and three quarters of total production came from 22 companies,
13 of which were US owned. As employment was seasonal, sugar workers
were unemployed for seven or eight months of each year. The social
condition of the vast majority of Cuba's population was characterised by
unemployment (17%), inadequate housing (85% of rural houses had no
electricity), malnutrition (90% of rural families did not have milk, 95% did
not have meat, and 98% did not eat eggs), illiteracy (45% in the countryside)
and bad health (15% of the rural population had tuberculosis).

In the industrial field the gains of the revolution were less obvious. As with
most dependent capitalist countries, Cuba's industrial base was very weak in
1959. Having substantial iron ore deposits it was logical after the revolution
to create a steel industry which could spawn a process of diversification,
and thus reduce the dependence on sugar. But there were huge problems,
including the reliance on the US for spares, the lack of technicians, and
basically, the lack of financial resources. By 1963 a decision had been taken
to concentrate on the country's comparative advantages and produce . . .
sugar. The mechanisation of agriculture, seen as the axis of development, is
now a major priority. In other fields big advances were also made – in 1958
Cuba's merchant navy consisted of 14 ships (57,000 tons capacity), by 1971
it had grown to 50 ships (500,000 tons capacity). Overall, by the late 1960s,
Cuba had acquired a sizeable industrial base (particularly for consumer goods)
but the setback of 1963 remained a heavy burden.

One of the worst legacies of 'underdevelopment' was no doubt the low
educational and cultural level to which the population was restricted.[22] In
1959 alone 10,000 rural schools were built across the country and a real
'army of educators' volunteered to take the skills of reading and writing to
the countryside. In one year the illiteracy rate was reduced from 24% to 3%
and Cuba had become a model case for UNESCO. This was followed up by a
campaign to take everyone up to secondary level education standards. A
general characteristic of Cuban education today is its 'polytechnic' nature-
students receive an integrated scientific, technical, cultural and physical
education. Most importantly too, the educational system is closely linked to

the world of work. The rural schools often have a farm attached, which is cultivated by the students and teachers; in the towns students work up to 20 hours weekly in an appropriate field of productive labour. The counterpart to this breakdown of manual and intellectual labour is the organisation of further education courses at the workplaces — in 1973 one in every five students was a worker. Educational establishments are run by councils composed of trade union and peasant representatives, the parent representatives, student organisers and representatives of the mass organisations (e.g. Party, Cuban Women's Organisation, etc.).

The health standards of Third World populations are generally extremely precarious, and pre-revolutionary Cuba was no exception. There were only 6,300 doctors in 1958 and they mainly attended the well-off in the capital, Havana. Preventive medicine was virtually non-existent. Today, there is one doctor per 650 inhabitants, compared to one per 6,000 in neighbouring Haiti. Compared to the 53 hospitals of 1958 there were 250 in 1973, as well as 350 clinics, 100 rural medical centres, etc. The effects of this priority accorded to preventive medicine have been remarkable. Polio, malaria, tetanus, have all been eliminated. Infant mortality is down from over 60 per 100 live births in the pre-revolutionary period to 20 in 1976. In pre-revolutionary Cuba, to get a hospital bed, one had to be 'recommended' by a politician in return for one's own, and the family, vote. In the rural areas, 'witch doctors' compensated for the lack of trained personnel. By 1968 the World Health Organisation had recognised Cuba as the most advanced country of Latin America in health-care.

To the average person a 'revolution' does not mean all that much, unless it results in a change in his socio-economic condition. Within days of entering Havana the rebels had reduced rent, gas and electricity charges by half, and wages were increased by an average of 35%. Unemployment was rapidly absorbed by a vast programme of public works; an urban reform eliminated property speculation and limited rents to 10% of a workers' income. A comprehensive social security programme was extended to the whole population. Housing has advanced, but in 1974 25% of Havana's houses were still considered 'average', and 27% 'mediocre' to scarcely inhabitable. In relation to the capital city (which holds 20% of the population) there has been an attempt to stem the rural/urban migration. This has been done by promoting economic activities in the rural areas and generally improving the standard of living there. Havana also has its 'green belt' where the inhabitants grow fruit and vegetables. Overall, there is a conscious effort to break down the dichotomy between city and countryside.

Institutionalisation

It was the failure of the projected ten million ton sugar harvest in 1970 which provided a chance for a general reassessment of the whole period preceding it, and after which the move towards 'institutionalisation' of the revolution began in earnest.[23] The giant *zafra* had been a major objective of the Cuban leadership (to which the Soviet Union kept it) and one which the whole economy was geared towards, together with massive human resources. Fidel Castro's speeches after the failure to achieve this target drew up an extremely self critical balance sheet which denounced administrative methods and the lack of popular participation in the processes of economic management. Castro spoke of 'replacing the administrative work habits of the first years of the Revolution' and of substituting 'democratic methods for the administrative methods that run the risk of becoming bureaucratic methods.'[24] The failure to meet the 1970 sugar target was not only critical because of the consequent dislocation of the economy, but more importantly, because it became the political watershed in the Cuban revolutionary process. Fidel's balance sheet expressed an aspiration that might have been translated into real forms of proletarian democracy, on condition that Fidel and his supporters were prepared to launch the kind of offensive that they had in 1966. However, this point in history, in the wake of humiliating and economically costly reverses at home, and in the context of several seeming successes for 'democratic and anti-imperialist' experiments in Peru, Chile, etc., was perhaps the last in which such an occurrence could be expected. Moreover, granted the heights of 'dirigisme' and militarisation attained in the sugar harvests of the previous two years, there was plenty of room for increases in mass participation which would involve meaningful changes but at the same time remain within the Soviet mould.

One of the key areas where the new orientation of the Cuban leadership was expressed was the question of work incentives. It is generally accepted that after the failure to meet the 1970 sugar target there was a turn away from moral incentives and towards material incentives, such as production bonuses and overtime pay. To assume that moral incentives had failed, or that the goals of a new society (the 'New Person') had been renounced, would be simplistic, ignoring the complex economic and social realities involved in this question.[25] Prior to 1970, socialist emulation and voluntary labour had been successfully encouraged in a bid to increase political consciousness, with the 1970 *Zafra* itself representing perhaps the largest mass mobilisation in Cuban history. In the aftermath of its failure, demoralisation set in and absenteeism seems to have run as high as 20%. The emphasis has been shifted since to a systematic reorganisation and rationalisation of the economy, in which material incentives have inevitably become dominant. Socialist emulation as it now stands is a means of increasing production and productivity through individual workers and enterprises 'competing' against each other, and an increase in wage differentials.

Fundamentally related to the question of work incentives is the reorganisation of the trade unions, and in particular the CTC (Confederation of Cuban Workers). Prior to 1970 the emphasis on moral incentives had led to the trade unions becoming largely replaced by the so called 'Advanced Workers Movement'. In effect, they had been turned into instruments of the plant administration and the Party, and then almost ceased to exist, as both of these did their jobs better than the trade unions could. After 1970 there was a decisive turn towards rebuilding the trade unions, with island-wide elections being held to create the local unions first.[26] This process was consolidated at the 13th Congress of the CTC in 1973, which defined the unions as mass organisations to which all workers would belong regardless of political opinion, and they are seen neither as part of the state apparatus nor as part of the party. The 'political guidance' of the Communist Party is, however, clearly recognised, and the situation that has developed is that the unions have become defined explicitly as 'transmission belts' for the party, working best at feeding party policies downward, and only sporadically (and in an unstructured way) serving to transmit workers' views upwards. This is clearly not in accordance with Lenin's views, on the need for trade union independence during the transition periods, as expressed in the 1920s Trade Union debate.[27]

The decisive element in the post 1970 'institutionalisation' of the Cuban revolution was the process of democratic elections, which began with an experiment in Matanzas province during 1974.[28] The regional elections were evaluated by the First Party Congress in 1975 and then extended to the national level. Finally, in December 1976, the National Assembly of People's Power held its first meeting, marking the culmination of the process of institutionalisation. The Organs of People's Power which have been formed are defined in the new constitution as the central institutions of the Cuban state, to become its supreme constituent and legislative authority. The democracy involved in the People's Power structures, however, is to a certain extent formal. Elections are not held on the basis of political platform but on the strength of individual biographies. The electoral unit is not the workplace, as with the original Soviets, but rather the neighbourhood. The Party dominates all proceedings – in 1976, 72.2% of the locally elected delegates were members of the CP or the Youth organisation, a proportion rising to 96.7% at the level of the National Assembly.

The Organs of People's Power have served fundamentally as a means of administrative decentralisation and as a curb to bureaucratic tendencies at the local level. Popular participation and involvement at a local level has increased, but overall decision making remains a highly centralised affair with little room for control by the masses. In spite of the intention to depersonalise power, Fidel Castro still concentrates an immense amount of power in one person – he is now President of the Council of State, President of the Council of Ministers, Commander-in-Chief of the Armed Forces and of course First Secretary of the Communist Party. At the national level, therefore, these structures can act only as a safety valve for popular grievances, not as sovereign assemblies of producers. The comment of two French Communist writers on the question of the mass organisations generally can, I think, be applied to the People's Power experience as a whole:

> It is true that at the start, when neither the party nor the state were fully constituted, the mass organisations – especially the CDRs –

played a particularly important role. But they never held 'People's Power'. It is also true that the consolidation of the party and then of the state have reduced the role of the mass organisations. In a nutshell, the mass organisations are not and have never been organs of self-managing democracy.[29]

We must clearly reassess whether there were really two possible 'solutions' to the situation in 1970 — the one technocratic and authoritarian, the other based on mass mobilisations and a more real participation in administration than in the past. One perceptive observer, Mesa-Lago, has since noted clearly the difference between what Castro promised in his post-1970 speeches and the reality which emerged:

> The image projected in the second half of 1970 by Castro's promised reform was of a decentralized, democratic, independent and mass-participation movement, in the mobilization style that was typical in Cuba during the 1960s. In real life there has been an institutionalisation trend characterized by central controls, dogmatism, administrative-bureaucratic features and limited mass participation resembling the Soviet system.[30]

The reason for this evolution does not lie in Castro's 'machiavellianism' but rather in the fact that the Organs of Popular Power which emerged in fact corresponded to the conception of socialist democracy held by the Cuban leadership. As Trotsky noted in the context of the Chinese Revolution:

> To create an elected soviet is not an easy matter. It is necessary that the masses know from experience what a soviet is, that they understand its form, that they have learned something in the past to accustom them to an elected soviet organisation.[31]

These traditions clearly did not exist in the Cuban case either. Certainly the various analyses of the Cuban 'institutionalisation' process have suffered from confusion on this point. Thus, we have one of the better studies of this process asserting in the first place that, 'The principal aim of the OPP as was the fundamental aim of the soviets in Lenin's words is — ". . . to draw the whole of the poor into the practical work of administration . . ." ' only to end up concluding that:

> the Cuban OPP are not the product of the spontaneous organizing activity of the people (as the first soviets were), although they do indeed respond to the people's demand for participation. They have been organised from above. . . .[32]

Participation though, is simply not equivalent to socialist democracy.
The first Congress of the Cuban Communist Party in 1975 served to

consolidate the process of institutionalisation begun in 1970; this was then embodied in the first socialist Constitution of the Republic of Cuba in 1976.[33] In the economic field, there was a process of 'rectification' which entailed rejecting the previous emphasis on eliminating the operation of the law of value. Attention now would be focused on the 'objective economic laws' and full use would be made of 'monetary-market relations'. This was a far cry from the hopes in the early days that money itself would soon be unnecessary in Cuba. In the factories the manager would henceforth be vested with sole authority, although provision was made for an advisory council with trade union representation. Perhaps symbolically, Cuba's formal integration into the Soviet international economic system in 1972 served to ratify full Cuban membership in the Soviet camp. Clearly the economic problems of the late 1960s required a change in orientation, but this was not necessarily the only possibility. It would be wrong to see the shift as one purely dictated by 'Moscow' and imposed on the basis of the massive Soviet subsidy to the island's economy (approaching one million dollars per day). Rather, it represents an internal evolution perhaps 'overdetermined' by the international reality of two opposed 'camps'.

The 1975 Congress also reasserted the primacy of the Communist Party in the period of transition to socialism. This, in any case, is ensured by the clear predominance of Party members in the leadership of society, a predominance which becomes virtually exclusive as one moves up the hierarchy. In the National Assembly the 80% of the population who are not members of the Party (or its Youth organisation) are represented by only 3% of the deputies. Of the Central Committee members in 1975, 28.6% were involved in political areas of activity, 17.9% in the bureaucracy, 32.1% were from the military, and only 6.3% were from the mass organisations. The growing involvement of ex-PSP (Popular Socialist Party) members is also significant – the congress elected three of these to the Political Bureau for the first time. One of these was Carlos Rafael Rodriguez who represented the prerevolutionary communist party in Batista's cabinet in the early 1940s, who now emerged as the second most important figure in the regime along-side Raúl Castro.

The relationship between the Party and the organs of popular power and the other mass organisations has clearly become one of subordination. Fidel Castro had said before the Congress that:

> the party, in accordance with the principles of Marxism-Leninism, regulates and guides society and the state. The party does not administer the state. The state must be administered by the masses through their organs of people's power.[34]

Yet shortly afterwards, Raúl Castro could state that the Party 'directs not only other party organisations and their members, but also directs the organs of people's power.'[35] There is no qualitative structural difference between the Cuban political system and the orthodox Soviet model, in spite of a more democratic or 'populist' style and more mass involvement. There is room for criticism from below but not for decision making from below. There are, however, still no definitive signs that the Cuban leadership has become a hardened bureaucratic caste with economic privileges of such a magnitude as to create distinct non-proletarian class interests.

Twenty years after the victory of the Cuban Revolution the balance sheet must be a sober one, in keeping with that of the Cubans' own Second Party Congress in 1980 which represents a serious attempt to confront the present difficulties.[36] We have concentrated on a process of what might be called 'structural assimilation' by which Cuba, in many aspects, became a 'normal' Soviet type state far removed from the dreams of 1961. The economic balance sheet must be a contradictory one – on the one hand the mass of the population have improved their living standards, but on the other hand economic problems remain.[37] Cuba has obviously been adversely effected by the international capitalist recessions of the late 1970s and the only partial breaking of the island's reliance on a single commodity (sugar) for trade, but the effect of the economic policies adopted cannot be neglected.

The background to the Second Congress was one of increasing economic difficulties – Raul Castro, in January of 1980, is quoted as saying that 'Cuba is haunted by the spectre of economic disaster and bankruptcy with its sequel of famine and hundreds of thousands of unemployed.'[38] However that may be, the 1981–85 plan for social and economic development confirms the trend towards allowing the market forces a greater role. Thus, incentive pay schemes (bonuses to form up to 25% of take-home pay) are to be extended; the *mercado libre campesino* (small farmers' free market) is to be consolidated, etc. The economic growth rate for 1976–80 was only 4% (against a target of 6%) and the main cause isolated was 'inefficiency', the absence of production norms, labour indiscipline and a 'bureaucracy characterised by absenteeism and mismanagement'. Ties with the Soviet Union have increased greatly – whereas in 1975 48% of the island's total trade was with the USSR (58% with Comecon as a whole) in 1979 this had risen to 67% (78% with Comecon). A further rise in trade with Comecon is expected for the coming five-year plan, and loans from the Comecon are expected to double.[39] In 1982, Soviet aid was put at $3,000 million and Cuba's debt to private Western banks (mainly Canadian and Japanese) ran at a similar figure.

Foreign Policy

What importance does foreign policy have in assessing the overall nature of a particular social formation? According to Gramsci the answer to the question 'Do international relations precede or follow (logically) fundamental social relations?' is that:

> There can be no doubt that they follow. Any organic innovation in the social structure, through its technical-military expressions, modifies

327

organically absolute and relative relations in the international field too.[40]

This is clearly in accordance with our own analysis in previous chapters which accords a primacy to internal factors. It does not, however, disallow the ability of external factors to react back upon the internal situation, as Gramsci also points out. This can also mean, as Gramsci notes, that:

> the more the immediate economic life of a nation is subordinated to international relations the more a particular party will come to represent this situation and to exploit it, with the aim of preventing rival parties gaining the upper hand.[41]

This 'foreigners' party' usually refers to those representatives of a comprador bourgeoisie who maintain the subordination of their country to imperialism. It is also true, however, that the position of the Cuban Communist Party — its hegemony — is underwritten by the second most powerful nation on earth — the USSR.

The early 1960s was a period of enthusiastic, one might even say adventurist, attempts to spread the revolution. This peaked with Guevara's slogan to create 'two, three, many Vietnams', and his death in action in Bolivia in 1967.[42] A gradual rapprochement with the Soviet Union — and acceptance of its foreign policy principles — began, perhaps symbolically, with Fidel Castro's support (albeit guarded) of the Soviet invasion of Czechoslovakia in 1968. That same year the nationalist military regime in Peru was highly praised and later the presidents of Mexico and Panama were welcomed to Cuba, in spite of their repressive policies at home.[43] What was happening was that Cuba had recognised the failure of its earlier 'voluntaristic' policy abroad and was now seeking to alleviate its isolation on the continent. At this stage diplomatic recognition of a regime did not preclude concrete support to revolutionaries in that country; in fact, the second half of the 1960s saw an offensive towards Latin America. A cynical interpretation of this is that the economy had run out of steam, and workers had to be motivated to work harder for less pay. Binns and Gonzalez claim that:

> to convince the workers to do this, they had to be shown that it was part of a crusade: one aimed at the whole of Latin America and with fairly immediate prospects of success.[44]

This may or may not be the reason for the interventionist policy of these years, but it does not mean that the line was 'mainly rhetorical', as these authors claim. The interesting point is that one must bear in mind the inter-relation between internal evolution and foreign policy and not just take the latter at face value.

The Cuban reaction to the Popular Unity government in Chile (1970-73) was highly contradictory and exemplifies the different tendencies in Cuba's foreign policy. On the one hand Allende was supported uncritically and built up into a mythical figure, but on the other, Castro, during his visit to Chile, did offer some effective advice on the problems involved in the reformist project of Popular Unity. More to the point, perhaps the Castroists in Chile (the MIR – Movement of the Revolutionary Left) were unable to offer an alternative to Popular Unity. This is probably the most important effect of Cuban foreign policy – its education of a whole generation of Latin American revolutionaries in a direction shaped by the Cubans' own particular experience. Hence the great effect of Régis Debray's simplified formulas – the general stress on 'marginal' layers of the population and guerrilla heroism, as against the organised activity of the working class.[45] The second half of the 1970s saw a different type of influence as the Cubans strove – with considerable success – to bring the Castroist organisations in Latin America into line with Soviet orthodoxy.

The evolution of the Castroist organisations in a pro-Soviet direction is perhaps clearest with the Chilean MIR (Movement of the Revolutionary Left) and the Argentine ERP (People's Revolutionary Army). When the MIR was formed, in 1965, it maintained that 'peaceful coexistence represents a provisional agreement between the socialist bureaucrats and imperialism designed to prevent or delay revolutions.'[46] In 1978, the MIR leadership in exile was declaring that the socialist countries 'promoted the world revolution' and 'represented models of economic and social organisation genuinely alternative to capitalism.'[47] The Cuban revolution had led to the emergence of a continent-wide vanguard inspired by Che Guevara's slogan of 'socialist revolution or caricature of revolution?' The internal 'sovietisation' of Cuba, and the crushing defeats of the 1970s in the Southern Cone, led to a real-politik in the redefinition of political alliances. In Argentina, the ERP, which, until 1972 had been a member (albeit a maverick one) of the Trotskyist Fourth International was, by the late 1970s, a firm supporter of the Soviet 'two camps' theory. In 1978, the 'International Communist Movement' (while it supported Argentina's military dictatorship) was seen as 'the principal promoters of proletarian internationalism and of the struggles for peace, democracy, freedom and socialism in the world.'[48] The Cuban leadership declared in 1975 that it would no longer tolerate an 'anti-Soviet' left in Latin America and the days of OLAS (Organization of Latin American Solidarity) and the Second Declaration of Havana, were put firmly behind.

From the mid 1970s on, Cuba turned to Africa in a serious way, as well as taking a central role in the movement of non-aligned countries.[49] The revolutionary internationalism of Cuba's support for the Angolan liberation struggle, particularly when attacked by South Africa, is not in doubt. Cuba is clearly not a simple 'surrogate' in Africa for 'Soviet imperialism' but having said that, Cuban policy is clearly advancing the aims of Soviet foreign policy there. There are serious doubts about the actual political role of Cuba's presence in Angola, and whether they are actually aiding a transition to democratic socialism there. Cuban intervention in Ethiopia since 1977 is perhaps even more open to question.[50] No one doubts the right of any anti-imperialist government to call on the aid of another, but is the Ethiopian regime a socialist one? Furthermore, one must question the rather one-sided approach to Somalia, and even more to the continued Ethiopian aggression against the people of Eritrea. The liberation movement of Eritrea had received Cuban aid in the 1960s and now, in all probability, they are facing Cuban 'advisers' on the battlefield. The point is that there is a thin dividing line between internationalism and involvement in the internal affairs of other liberation movements or struggles. In fact, if we examine the list of 'progressive' African states that Cuba regularly supports — Guinea Bissau, Guinea Conakry, Benin, Angola, Congo, Mozambique, Ethiopia, Tanzania, Seychelles, Madagascar — we see that Cuban support is not always conditioned by the fact of an ongoing revolution or foreign aggression.

Our rather sketchy summary of Cuban foreign policy culminates symbolically in 1979 with the victory of the Nicaraguan revolution. The unstinting Cuban aid to the new and free Nicaragua is of great importance and seems to signal a return to a new 'hard line' in Latin America. Through all the fluctuations in Cuban foreign policy we can detect a revolutionary intention, even when there has been an acceptance of the Soviet framework of 'peaceful coexistence'. What Nicaragua (and El Salvador) show is that Cuba is not a frozen entity, it is still evolving, and premature judgements are ill-advised. Clearly, El Salvador, and later Guatemala, will be severe tests for Cuba's foreign policy, but one can detect a clearly revolutionary line. But there does seem to be a contradiction between this and the Cuban endorsement of the military coup against Solidarity in Poland in 1981. Accepting the 'two camps' version of international politics leads to a simplist 'if you are my enemy's friend you are my enemy.' That the vast majority of the Polish people do not accept 'actually existing socialism' and that the Solidarity trade union movement was pursuing democratic socialism and not the restoration of capitalism is ignored when big power politics calls for an alignment of its allies.[51] This 'pragmatic' approach to international alignments cannot but have its effect on internal politics and reduce the prospects for a genuine socialist democracy in Cuba.

A New Dependency?

Two authors, Gouré and Weinkle argue that:

> Moscow has attempted to exercise political control by exploiting Cuba's economic dependence on the Soviet Union. This strategy has proved increasingly effective as Cuba has faced growing economic difficulties at home and Castro's revolutionary ambitions abroad have gone unfulfilled.[52]

The proponents of Cuba's 'new dependency' on the USSR find no lack of facts to show the growing economic integration and political assimilation, as we have seen above. For the critics of Marxism and dependency theory generally this supposedly 'proves' Cuba's continued dependence and, by implication, the hypocrisy of their revolutionary message for other Third World countries. Not all the proponents of this thesis are Cold War warriors however. One of these authors is Kosmas Tsokhas, who argues persuasively that 'the history of Cuban-Soviet relations is one of transition from independence to integration with a Soviet dominated sphere of influence.'[53] This is not put down to Soviet manipulation or 'imperialism' but more realistically to:

> a convergence between the views of a section of the ruling party in Havana, the economic problems created by its attempts to revolutionize Cuba, and the objectives of the USSR.[54]

The right-wing and left-wing critics of Cuba seem to agree that economic dependence has led to political subservience abroad and the imposition of Soviet style socialism at home.

The early 'tourists of the revolution' in Cuba brought back glowing reports on the island, as had earlier generations for the Soviet Union in the 1930s, and then for China in the 1960s.[55] Critical socialist visitors report differently. Samuel Farber says bluntly that 'Cuba is a totalitarian country'.[56] Carlos Franqui, a leader of the revolution who went into exile after Castro's support for the Soviet invasion of Czechoslovakia, reaches similar conclusions. He reports that:

> At first, there was a genuine festival of freedom. . . . What problems does Cuba face today? Soviet domination. Statism. *Caudillism*. Militarism. Sugar monoculture. Complete lack of freedom.[57]

Fidel Castro becomes a classic Latin American *caudillo*, with a deep mistrust for the people, who allowed the revival of a small discredited Communist Party to provide the country with a bureaucracy and links with a major super power. All forms of opposition, resistance and dissidence are eliminated, and power is concentrated in the hands of a small élite — in short, 'totalitarianism'. Tsokhas even sees Cuba as fitting O'Donnell's bureaucratic-authoritarian state model:

> Growing dependence on the USSR led Cuba to adopt a bureaucratic and authoritarian political and economic structure. Divisions between mental and manual labor, between party and masses were widened. 'Commandism' triumphed over the 'mass-line'.[58]

Other authors go on to draw the logical conclusion that the Cuban working class will have to overthrow the 'bureaucratic ruling class' before socialism can be built in Cuba.[59]

The response to the 'new dependency' thesis has been at various levels. It

331

has been shown that the economic relations of dependence (in terms of trade, foreign debt, etc) were inevitable given the realities of international politics. It can also be argued, as Joel Edestein does, that 'the Cuban leadership has implicitly accepted a period of dependency as necessary on Cuba's path to independent socialist development.'[60] It is also necessary to take into account that Cuba's 'socialist dependency' of today is dictated by the structures engendered by hundreds of years of capitalist dependency. Then, even when Cuba is following a Soviet line in foreign policy a certain element of 'relative autonomy' must be allowed for. So far, we can say that the dependency argument has been relativised, placed in its historical context, or accepted as a temporary stage. The evidence, as such, is not radically contested, only its interpretation. Robin Blackburn, in criticising the account of Binns and Gonzalez cited above, agrees that 'Sugar looms large in Cuban exports but its sale to the Soviet Union is governed by long term contracts and guaranteed prices. . . .'[61] He goes on to say that:

> Cuba's policies in the field of culture and education, the operation of its judicial and penal system, all differ markedly from Soviet models. However in terms of fundamental categories of political analysis there is certainly a family resemblance between Cuba and the Soviet Union. . . .[6]

The difference in this analysis is that the resemblance is not such that a 'political revolution' and overthrow of the ruling bureaucracy is as yet necessary in Cuba.

A more full blooded critique of the 'Sovietization' thesis is that of Frank Fitzgerald, who argues that:

> not only does it exaggerate the depth and irreversibility of Cuban dependence on the Soviet bloc, but it also misinterprets the post-1970 changes in Cuban socialism as well.[63]

The shift away from moral incentives is seen as no problem at all, because 'the inequality-generating tendencies of material incentives have been limited. . . .'[64] More broadly, 'Soviet and Cuban interests seem to be converging, with considerable advantage accruing to the Cubans.'[65] In short, we still have the best of all possible worlds and the aim of the New Person remains the lodestar of all Cuba's policies. There is here a serious failure to engage critically with the evidence presented by a whole range of sympathetic observers.[66] The one positive element is, I believe, a rejection of the simple 'Soviet imperialism' thesis which sees external factors as dominant. As MacEwan concludes in his carefully documented book:

> there is ample evidence to explain the evolution of Cuba's major internal policies without reference to Soviet influence (aside from the obvious fact that Soviet aid and trade created certain possibilities that otherwise would not have existed).[67]

For example, Cuba's continued reliance on sugar is not due simply to Soviet imposition of this role on the country in accordance with the 'socialist division of labour' as the critics mention.

It is difficult to 'choose' between the two lines of interpretation advanced above. Certainly our own empirical evidence points towards a growing convergence between Cuban and Soviet conceptions of socialism since 1970. Some critics of the 'Sovietization' thesis do not so much deny the evidence, but say simply that the Soviet model of socialism *is* socialism. More critical writers see present dependency as a phase before 'independent' socialism can be achieved. This would appear to be highly utopian, given the integration of the world economy and Cuba's necessary links with it at all levels (witness the 1982 negotiations with the capitalist countries over the foreign debt). None of these points, however, validates the nightmare vision of a semi-police state presented by disillusioned socialist critics. In terms of foreign policy, not even the CIA presented real evidence that in Angola 'Castro was acting as Brezhnev's agent' as some of these critics maintain.[68] The weakest point on both sides of the debate is the one-sided nature of evidence put forward — it is never presented in its full context and all its contradictions examined. In fact there is a large element of idealism in the discussions — one side taking the rhetoric of a revolution for its reality and the other advancing an abstract ideal model of socialism against which the rather more complex material reality is judged as wanting.

It is, in fact, worth considering the underlying assumption in these discussions that Cuba is a socialist society or at least in transition to one. Against the official discourse in Cuba, Charles Bettelheim speaks of:

> an ideology and a political line which concentrate all power in the hands of a ruling group, and which therefore do not create the necessary conditions — ideological, organizational, and political — for the democratic exercise of proletarian power.[69]

Whatever our assessment of Bettelheim's verdict on Cuba specifically, we must agree with his break from a teleological conception of the transition to socialism. The revolution (which only with difficulty can be classed as a workers' one) created the preconditions for the break with capitalism, but not its necessity. As Bettelheim writes elsewhere:

> the dissolution of the capitalist mode of production does not create *all* the conditions for its succession by the socialist mode of production unless the political and ideological conditions for this succession are present as well.[70]

There is, in short, no unilinear development towards socialism, and (though its forms are debatable) a restoration of capitalism is clearly one possibility. The simple teleological schema of the expanding forces of production entering into contradiction with the relations of production as the inexorable motor of social change is no longer tenable. It is clearly the class struggle — certainly under different forms after the overthrow of the capitalist state — which provides the dynamic element of the transition period.

It may be useful to introduce the concept of a 'transition to the transition' in discussing the post-revolutionary process. This, according to Tim Wohlforth, would 'mediate the disjuncture between the immediate impossibility of pure Soviet democracy and its longer-term necessity. . . .'[71] Its short term impossibility is owing to the immense economic pressures faced by the new state and the consequent need for centralisation. With a similar effect the conditions of underdevelopment produce the material causes of a growing bureaucracy. The 'free association of producers' cannot emerge overnight, but the building of a 'monolithic, statist, and oppressive system' in the transition makes it simply impossible.[72] The transition to socialism involves not only nationalisation of the means of production but a genuine socialisation which sees a change in the content as well as the form of social relations. The need for central planning by a strong state will (until the 'withering away' of the state with the disappearance of social classes) be in contradiction with the requirements of maximum political decentralisation. The point is to recognise this but incorporate mechanisms to minimise it. Wohlforth is therefore correct to insist that:

> A transitional society must not only contain elements of the society from which it is emerging — in this case the most advanced democracy produced by the old regime — but also elements of the society towards which it seeks to evolve: the free association of producers expressed embryonically in factory councils.[73]

What is strangely absent from most of the discussions on the nature of Cuban society is a detailed consideration of social classes. This is partly owing to the fact that the Cuban leadership does not emphasise the continuing class struggle under socialism, as was once the case in China. If classes continue to exist, it would seem that a form of class struggle will persist, unless one can show that these classes exist in 'non-antagonistic' contradictions with one other. Direct producers in Cuba do not exercise social control over the means of production in so far as the state dominates the social process of appropriation and controls the objects and instruments of labour. As David Slater notes:

> there has also emerged an increasingly significant social group or class of enterprise managers, administrators and technicians whose location and role in the social organization of labour is qualitatively different from that of the direct producers.[74]

This bureaucratic layer (or arguably, class) exercises managerial and leadership functions at all levels of Cuban society, from the economy through to scientific research. Their material privileges are certainly less than under capitalist society, but real nonetheless, and, therefore, a source of potential class struggle. Carlos Franqui writes bitterly that:

> This bureaucratic bourgeoisie enjoys the privileges taken from the capitalist regime: houses, beaches, villas, motor-cars, restaurants, trips, a higher standard of living. And in addition, it has the privilege of giving orders and being obeyed.[75]

We have returned full circle to our opening quotation from Rosa Luxemburg on the inescapable requirement for a successful transition to socialism: proletarian democracy. The key question is whether authors like Fitzgerald are correct when they state that the 'Organs of Popular Power ... are representative bodies that promise to involve the masses heavily in the day-to-day administration of the state.'[76] Other writers have argued that these bodies were created to help consolidate the regime and overcome certain inefficiencies in terms of distribution at the local level.[77] I think we must recognise *both* the pragmatic reasoning behind their introduction and the possibilities they open up for increased popular participation. However, as Machover and Fantham argue in relation to China:

> mass participation at a local level does not equal mass democracy. Such participation that exists takes place in structures which are controlled by, and on terms that are set by, the ruling bureaucracy. Mass democracy would involve the control of the masses over these structures and terms.[78]

A mode of production based on the voluntary co-operation of labour simply cannot be brought into being through anything other than socialist democracy, which can never be substituted for by a benevolent or paternalist *caudillo*.

Figure 11.1
Phases of the Cuban Revolution (1959–79)

Period	International	Economic	Political
1959-60	Relations with the USSR established. Ill-prepared guerrilla expeditions abroad.	Industrialisation, diversification away from sugar.	Mass mobilisation. Workers' militia.
1961-63	Confrontation over Missile Crisis (1962). Conflict with Latin American Communist Parties as Cuba supports guerrilla movements.	Centralized planning. Decline of material-individual incentives.	Purge of Escalante. Labour mobilisation begins.

Period	International	Economic	Political
1963-66	Accommodation with USSR — long-term economic agreements. Compromise with Latin American Communist Parties.	Return to priority of sugar. Decentralization, emphasis on managerial skills.	Cuban Communist Party established (1965). Professionalization of army.
1966-70	OLAS set up. *'Foco'* theory promoted. Castro supports Czechoslovakia invasion.	Emphasis on 1970 sugar harvest. Emphasis on moral incentives.	Forging of 'New Man'. Party and administration fused.
1970-73	Cuba enters COMECON. Move away from 'guerrilla road' to power.	Move away from central planning. Labour mobilization decreased.	Egalitarianism criticized. Militia phased out. New army ranks established.
1973-79	Move towards relations with US. Intervention in Angola and Ethiopia. Aid to Nicaraguan revolution.	Market mechanisms emphasised. Soviet methods and techniques predominate. ('Economic management system').	Move towards 'institutionalization' — Organs of Popular Power consolidated.

Source: Draws on Mesa Lago, C. (1974) *Cuba in the 1970s*. Albuquerque, University of New Mexico Press, pp.2–4.

References

1. Waters, M.A. (ed) (1970) *Rosa Luxemburg Speaks*. New York, Pathfinder Press, pp.393–4.
2. See Munslow, B. (1983) Is Socialism Possible in the Periphery? *Monthly Review*. Vol 35 No.1 and the case studies in White, G., Murray, R. and White, C. (eds) (1983) *Revolutionary Socialist Development in the Third World*. Brighton, Wheatsheaf Books.
3. See Ollman, B. (1977) Marx's Vision of Communism. A Reconstruction. *Critique*. No.8:4–42.
4. An interpretation developed by Melotti, U. (1977) *Marx and the Third World*. London, Macmillan.
5. Marx, K. (1970) *Selected Works* Vol.2. London, Lawrence and Wishart, p.23.
6. In Preobrazhensky, E. (1965) *The New Economics*. Oxford, Clarendon Press. On the broader debate see Lewin, M. (1975) *Political Undercurrents in Soviet Economic Debates*. London, Pluto Press; and more

directly, Boukharin, N., Preobrazhensky, E. and Trotsky, L. (1972) *Le Débat Soviétique Sur la Loi de la Valeur*. Paris, Maspero. On Stalin's conception and practice of 'socialism in one country' see Carr, E.H. (1970) *Socialism in One Country 1924–1926* Vol.2. London, Penguin.

7. Preobrazhensky, E. (1972) Socialist Primitive Accumulation. *Socialist Economics* (eds) A. Nove and M. Nuti. London, Penguin, p.132.
8. Cited in Thomas, C. (1978) 'The Non-Capitalist Path' as theory and practice of decolonization and socialist transformation. *Latin American Perspectives*. Vol.V No.2:16.
9. Ibid., p.26.
10. Ibid., p.23.
11. Corrigan, P., Ramsay, H. and Sayer, D. (1978) *Socialist Construction and Marxist Theory*. London, Macmillan, p.153.
12. For a thorough analysis see Kiernan, B. and Boua, C. (1982) *Peasants and Politics in Kampuchea, 1942–1981*. London, Zed Press.
13. On Chile see, amongst others, Smirnow, G. (1979) *The Revolution Disarmed: Chile 1970–1973*. New York, Monthly Review Press; Sweezy, P. and Magdoff, H. (ed) (1977) *Revolution and Counter-revolution in Chile*. New York, Monthly Review Press; and Marini, R.M. (1976) *El reformismo y la contrarevolución – Estudios Sobre Chile*. Mexico, Ediciones Era.
14. See the differing perspectives of Mattick, P. (1978) *Anti-Bolshevik Communism*. London, Merlin Press; and Mandel, E. (1979) *Revolutionary Marxism Today*. London, New Left Books.
15. On the background to the revolution see Bonachea, R. and San Martín, M. (1974) *The Cuban Insurrection 1952–1959*. New Brunswick, Transaction Books; and Bambirra, V. (1976) *La Revolución Cubana – una reinterpretación*. Mexico, Editorial Nuestro Tiempo.
16. Guevara, E. (1968) *Textes Militaires*. Paris, Maspero.
17. Castro, F. (1972) *Fidel in Chile*. New York, International Publishers, p.83.
18. On developments in the 1960s see, amongst others, Mesa Lago, C. (ed) (1971) *Revolutionary Change in Cuba*. Pittsburgh, University of Pittsburgh Press; Bonachea, R. and Valdes, N. (eds) (1972) *Cuba in Revolution*. New York, Anchor Books; and Horowitz, I.L. (ed) (1977) *Cuban Communism*. New Brunswick, Transaction Books.
19. On this debate see Silverman, B. (1971) *Man and Socialism in Cuba: The Great Debate*. New York, Atheneum.
20. Maitan, L. (1976) Problems of the Cuban workers state. *Intercontinental Press*. 15 March, p.410.
21. On the agrarian reform and other achievements of the early years see Huberman, L. and Sweezy, P. (1970) *Socialism in Cuba*. New York, Monthly Review Press.
22. For a sector by sector analysis, including education and culture, see Barkin, D. and Manitzas, (eds) (1973) *Cuba: The Logic of Revolution*. Andover, Mass., Warner Modular; and for the 1970s, Griffiths, J. and

Griffiths, P. (eds) (1979) *Cuba: The Second Decade*. London, Writers and Readers Publishing Cooperative.

23. On the 1970s generally see Mesa-Lago, C. (1978) *Cuba in the 1970's – Pragmatism and Institutionalization*. Albuqueque, University of New Mexico Press; Dominguez, J. (1978) *Cuba: Order and Revolution*. Cambridge, Mass., Harvard University Press; and Valdes, N. (1979) The Cuban Revolution: Economic Organization and Bureaucracy. *Latin American Perspectives*. Vol.VI No.1:13–37.

24. *Granma* (30 August 1970), p.4.

25. See Karl, T. (1975) Work Incentives in Cuba. *Latin American Perspectives*. Vol.11 No.4:21–41.

26. See Perez-Stable, M. (1975) Whither the Cuban Working Class? *Latin American Perspectives*. Vol.II No.4: 21–41.

27. On which, see Harding, N. (1981) *Lenin's Political Thought Vol 2* London, Macmillan, Ch.12: The Trade Union Debate.

28. On popular power, see particularly Harnecker, M. (1980) Cuba: *Dictatorship and Democracy*. Westport, Conn., Lawrence Hill, which is a remarkable study based on oral history.

29. Demichel, A. and Demichel, F. (1979) *Cuba*. Paris, Libraire Generale de Droit et de Juisprudence. Vol.XXXI, p.102.

30. Mesa-Lago, C. (1978) *Cuba in the 1970s*, p.115.

31. Trotsky, L. (1976) *On China*. New York, Pathfinder Press, p.318.

32. Casal, L. (1975) On Popular Power: the Organization of the Cuban State During the Period of Transition. *Latin American Perspectives*. Vol.II No.4:79 and 85.

33. See the Congress report in Comité Central del Partido Comunista de Cuba (1976) *La Unión Nos Dio La Victoria*. La Habana, Instituto Cubano del Libro.

34. *Granma* (4 August 1974).

35. *Granma* (8 September 1974).

36. See the Congress report in Castro, F. (1980) *Il Congreso del Partido Comunista de Cuba – Informe Central* – La Habana, Editora Política.

37. For a global economic assessment see Mesa-Lago, C. (1981) *The Economy of Socialist Cuba: A Two Decade Appraisal.*. New York, New York University Press.

38. Vergara, F. (1980) Cuba: vingt années de transformations économiques, trois stratégies pour un échec. *Les Temps Modernes*. No.413:1006.

39. Latin American Weekly Report (20 February 1981).

40. Hoare, Q. and Nowell Smith, G. (1971) *Selections from the Prison Notebooks of Antonio Gramsci*. London, Lawrence and Wishart, p.176.

41. Ibid.

42. This period is examined in Debray, R. (1977) *A Critique of Arms*, Vol.1. London, Penguin.

43. This turn is covered in Blaiser, C. and Mesa-Lago, C. (eds) (1979) *Cuba in the world*. Pittsburgh, University of Pittsburgh Press; see also Weinstein, M. (ed) (1979) *Revolutionary Cuba in the World Arena*.

Philadelphia, Institute for the Study of Human Issues.

44. Binns, P. and Gonzalez, M. (1980) Cuba, Castro and Socialism. *International Socialism*. No.8:18.

45. See Debray, R. (1967) *Revolution in the Revolution?* New York, Monthly Review Press.

46. *Principios del MIR* (1965) Santiago de Chile, p.4.

47. Tesis Fundamentales (1978) *Correo de la Resistencia* No.5, p.18.

48. PRT Argentina (1978) *Solidaridad Internacional*. London, p.16.

49. See articles in Blaiser, C. and Mesa-Lago, C. (eds) (1979) *Cuba in the World*. Also Thomas, G. (1981) Cuba and Africa: the international politics of the liberation struggle. *Latin American Perspectives*. Vol. VIII No.1.

50. See the Cuban analysis of the situation in Vivó, R.V. (1977) *Ethiopia: the unknown revolution*. La Habana, Editorial de Ciencias Sociales; compare with the account in Halliday, F. and Molyneux, M. (1981) *The Ethiopian Revolution*. London, New Left Books.

51. See amongst others the report in Acherson, N. (1982) *The Polish August*. London, Penguin. The term 'actually existing socialism' is derived from Bahro, R. (1978) *The Alternative in Eastern Europe*. London, New Left Books.

52. Gouré, L. and Weinkle, J. (1972) Cuba's New Dependency. *Problems of Communism*. March/April:69. See also Gonzalez, E. (1976) Castro and Cuba's New Orthodoxy. *Problems of Communism* January/February: 1-19.

53. Tsokhas, K. (1980) The Political Economy of Cuban Dependence on the Soviet Union. *Theory and Society*. No.9:357.

54. Ibid., p.321.

55. See for example Sartre, J.P. (1961) *Sartre on Cuba*. New York, Ballentine Books, and even Huberman, L. and Sweezy, P. (1960) *Anatomy of a Revolution*. New York, Monthly Review Press.

56. Farber, S. (1981) Going Home to Cuba. *Critique* No.13, p.139.

57. Franqui, C. (1979) The Soviet Model and 'Caudillism' in Cuba. *Power and Opposition in Post-revolutionary Society*. London, Ink Links, p.211.

58. Tsokhas, K. (1980) The Political Economy of Cuban Dependence on the Soviet Union, p.359.

59. For example, Binns, P. and Gonzalez, M. (1980) Cuba, Castro and Socialism, p.34.

60. Edelstein, J. (1981) The Evolution of Cuban Development Strategy, 1959-1979. *From Dependency to Development* (ed) H. Muñoz. Boulder Co, Westview Press, p.226.

61. Blackburn, R. (1980) Class forces in the Cuban Revolution: a reply to Peter Binns and M. Gonzalez. *International Socialism* No.9:89.

62. Ibid.

63. Fitzgerald, F. (1978) A Critique of the 'Sovietisation of Cuba' Thesis. *Science and Society*. Vol.XLII No.1:31.

64. Ibid.

65. Ibid., p.19.
66. For example, the work cited above of Mesa-Lago, Dominguez and Valdes.
67. MacEwan, A. (1981) *Revolution and Economic Development in Cuba.* London, Macmillan, pp.222–3.
68. Binns, P. and Gonzalez, M. (1980) Cuba, Castro and Socialism, p.32.
69. Sweezy, P. and Bettleheim, C. (1971) *On the Transition to Socialism.* New York, Monthly Review Press, p.22.
70. Bettelheim, C. (1975) *The Transition to Socialist Economy.* Brighton, Harvester Press, pp.20–21.
71. Wohlforth, T. (1981) Transition to the Transition. *New Left Review.* No.130:68. Cf. Buick, A. (1975) The Myth of the Transitional Society. *Critique* No.5:59–70.
72. Ibid., p.68.
73. Ibid., p.80.
74. Slater, D. (1982) State and territory in post-revolutionary Cuba. *International Journal of Urban and Regional Research.* Vol.6, No.1:7.
75. Franqui, C. (1979) The Soviet Model and 'Caudillism' in Cuba, p.211. For a more rigorous discussion of the bureaucracy in post-revolutionary society see Mandel, E. (1974) Ten Theses on the Social and Economic Laws Governing the Society Transitional Between Capitalism and Socialism. *Critique* No.3:5–25.
76. Fitzgerald, F. (1978) A Critique of the 'Sovietization of Cuba' Thesis, p.31.
77. For example, Horowitz, I. (1979) Institutionalisation as integration: the Cuban Revolution at age twenty. *Cuban Studies.* Vol.9 No.2:84–90.
78. Machover, M. and Fantham, J. (1979) *The Century of the Unexpected – a New Analysis of Soviet Type Societies.* Liverpool, Big Flame Publications p.14.

PART IV
Conclusion

12. Dependent Politics

> When we consider a given country politico-economically,
> we begin with its population. . . . It seems to be correct to
> begin with the real and the concrete, with the real precon-
> dition, thus to begin, in economics, with e.g. the population,
> which is the foundation and the subject of the entire social
> act of production. However, on closer examination this
> proves false. The population is an abstraction if I leave out,
> for example the classes of which it is composed. These
> classes in turn are an empty phrase if I am not familiar
> with the elements on which they rest. E.g. wage labour,
> capital, etc. . . . The concrete is concrete because it is the
> concentration of many determinations, hence unity of the
> diverse.
>
> Karl Marx[1]

Marx here breaks down a complex and concrete concept like that of population
into simpler concepts or determinations. Populations consist of social classes
which in turn are based on wage-labour, capital, etc. So, if we are to study
population (or Latin America) we find that this actual starting point is 'a
chaotic conception of the whole' until we move analytically to the simpler
concepts or determinations. Then Marx says:

> the journey would have to be retraced until I had finally arrived at the
> population again, but this time not as the chaotic conception of a whole,
> but as a rich totality of many determinations and relations.[2]

In that way the concrete reality of population (or Latin America) appears to
us as 'the concentration of many determinations'. The aim is to achieve 'the
reproduction of the concrete by way of thought.'[3] This concrete reality we
are investigating is both the 'real starting point' and the final result of our
theoretical enterprise.

Marx's method is, to quote Lenin, 'a double analysis, deductive and
inductive — logical and historical'.[4] Lenin goes on to say that at every stage
of the analysis we must ensure control either by facts or by practice.[5] In our

343

enquiry we must try 'to track down the inner connection' of the material gathered.[6] This is not only to discover the 'essence' of any particular relation but also to move towards an understanding of its superficial appearances. Through a process of mediation we can, as Marx says, 'approach step by step the form in which they appear on the surface of society . . . and in the everyday consciousness of the agents of production themselves.'[7] Our theory is not a simple 'model' abstracted from empirical reality but must guide us towards an integration of essence and appearance. If the Marxist method is materialist (against the idealism of Hegel) it is also historical — social facts are inseparable from the historical process of their formation. The objective structures and relations of society are the product of a definite historical epoch — capitalism — not timeless abstractions. The 'unity of diverse elements' which make up the concrete totality of society can only be understood historically. As Mandel stresses 'the intellectual reproduction of reality, or in Althusser's language, "theoretical practice", must remain in constant contact with the actual movement of history.'[8]

If one were to classify the numerous textbooks on Latin American politics in terms of method we would see two broadly defined camps: the empiricist and the rationalist. Those defined by the first criteron would be primarily the country by country introductions to Latin American politics.[9] These tell us all we need to know — from A to Z — about each country from Argentina to Venezuela. There are obviously good and bad texts within this category, but the basic problem is that the category 'Latin America' is taken as a self-evident given rather than theoretically constructed. Another variant is to focus on 'Latin America' and discuss at a broad level of generality the various social categories: i.e., businessmen, workers, students, the clergy, etc.[10] The problem here is that each category is taken as a self-contained element rather than in its interrelations with other groups in society. It assumes that society is some kind of jigsaw, in which, if we study the individual components then we need simply fit the pieces together to see how the whole functions. The most simple empiricist text is the chronology, the narrative history which collapses the complex and differential 'time' of social reality into a succession of discrete events. We can no longer accept the model of traditional historians of a continuous and homogeneous time.[11] The different temporalities of the economic, political and social dimensions make it impossible to theoretically account for any event in this simplistic manner.

The empiricism which runs through these diverse categories of text starts from the assumption that knowledge springs from the facts.[12] Scientific research consists simply of verifying these facts, bringing them together and synthesising them for efficient communication. Facts are seen as 'given', pre-existing the activity of the researcher whose job is to simply observe 'objectively' without 'preconceptions'. However, theory *cannot* be conceived as a simple inductive operation carried out after the facts have been collected; on the contrary, it is the very means of production of scientific facts. No observation or collection of facts is possible without a previous process of categorization — in short, facts are not given but theoretically constructed.

The polar opposite of empiricism is formalism, which instead of ignoring the element of theoretical construction isolates and elevates it to an undue extent. Theoretical reflection is seen as self-sufficient by virtue of its internal coherence and logical rigour. Concepts multiply through a process of internal generation which need not confront material reality. Scientific work as a process of production is replaced by abstract speculation as the point of departure and of arrival in the production of knowledge. Formalism systematically inverts the propositions of empiricism, but it pertains equally to the idealist theory of knowledge. The Marxist method, on the contrary, is historical and materialist.

Texts in the formalist mould adopt a particular social theory into which selected fragments of reality are added. Traditionally, these have followed the concepts of 'economic development' and 'political development' advanced by modernisation theory, which we have already criticised in our opening chapter. The underlying concepts of a 'traditional' and a 'modern' society, which still underpin a number of studies, are theoretically impoverished no matter how many refinements are added.[13] One variant is to look at 'system capabilities' and 'system demands' and conclude, as one text does, that in spite of the 'growing gap between rising demands and declining effectiveness of the system' producing tension, Latin America's characteristic 'politics of immobility' blocks change.[14] The relation to real history here is very tenuous indeed. It becomes even more remote in a recent text *The Politics of Latin American Development* by Gary Wynia which is the epitome of formalism.[15] Wynia views politics as a 'game' with rules, players, contests for power, winners and losers, played out in an imaginary Latin American 'country' of his own construction. Thus we are introduced to the 'military authoritarian game' and the 'revolutionary game' with their various 'players' and the 'rules of the game'. History is here reified into a meaningless formalised contest equivalent to a game of Monopoly. The sophistication of games theory leaves little room for the crude social reality of Latin America and its class struggle.

Class Conflict: Internal/External Determinations

The class struggle as the motor of history is the touchstone of Marxism, but can this still be true if the ruling class is 'external' to the nation-state, as many writers on the Third World suggest? We have seen in the course of this book that this is at least a partial if not an incorrect notion. Even in the so-called 'comprador regimes', where the local ruling classes are almost totally subordinated to a foreign power they have a certain level of 'relative autonomy'. We should, therefore, retain the centrality of the class struggle in any analysis of the 'laws of motion' of Third World social formations. Having said that, we should clearly assess the relative weight of the internal and external determinations which shape the class struggle in the Third World. We start by examining the correct unit of analysis — world economy or nation-state, mode of production or social formation.

Trotsky stated unambiguously that:

> Marxism takes its point of departure from world economy, not as a
> sum of national parts but as a mighty and independent reality which
> has been created by the international division of labour and the world
> market, and which in our epoch imperiously dominates the national
> markets.[16]

I do not think we can quarrel with the conception of world economy as a
'point of departure' in analysis of a Third World social formation. Immanuel
Wallerstein and his followers go much further, however, and argue that
processes in any sub-system of the world economy are due to the contradictions in the system as a whole. So, for example, liberation movements in the
Third World are seen 'to arise out of the structural contradictions of the
capitalist world-economy'.[17] This shifts attention away from class struggle at
the level of the nation-state, which remains (by simple observation) the locus
of proletarian resistance and nationalist rebellion. The conception of class
formation at a world level is equally dubious. There is no real evidence for
world-wide classes or for that matter of world-wide states. There are, of course,
relations between nation-states and international bodies but it is very difficult
to locate an 'international system' which is somehow greater and more far-
sighted than its individual components. One possible resolution to the debate
over internal/external primacy is suggested by João Quartim, who advances
the proposition that dependency is a specific form of domination determined
in the first instance, by the internal class struggle and the development of
capitalism and, in the last instance, by the periodisation of capital accumulation on a world scale.[18] The most interesting question for Quartim is the
genesis of dependency, to which we might add the laws of motion of
dependent reproduction. In this situation internal factors are seen as the
major determinants though the external system — the international capitalist
economy — remains determinant in the last instance. Clearly, in certain
situations — comprador regimes for example — this determination is brought
to bear constantly, otherwise it is 'in reserve'.

One reaction to the global statements of dependency theory was to focus
on the Marxist concept of 'modes of production'. A rigorous set of concepts
— forces and relations of production, etc., — would replace the global
simplifications of Gunder Frank and others (see Chapter 1). For different
reasons than the world system theorists attention was focused away from the
nation-state (or social formation), this time towards a narrower area. Thus,
studies multiplied on various pre-capitalist modes of production, of which
the social formation became just a concrete 'realisation'. The failure here
was to mediate between essence and appearance as outlined above. Another
tendency was to extend unduly the concept of mode of production to
embrace the whole social formation — as in the 'colonial mode of production'
discussion. In some cases there were problems of empiricism — note some
particularity (e.g. colonialism) and establish a new 'mode of production'.

A far greater problem was one of formalism with the internal generation of concepts around the mode of production idea. The need to confront reality at every step of the research enterprise went by the board. History became idealised, as with Hegel, whose concepts have a life of their own (the 'self-delivering concept') which become the active subjects of reality rather than men and women. As with the world system analysis, this leads us away from sustained attention to the concrete formation of social classes and the antagonism between them.

To say that an analysis should be 'dialectical' is often seen as a cliché — a way out of a dilemma, which sounds right but does not say much. Lenin, in his fragmentary Philosophical Notebooks, constantly stressed one element in Hegel's dialectics — its 'all-sidedness'.[19] Flexibility of concepts if applied subjectively led to eclecticism, but, said Lenin, 'flexibility, applied *objectively*, i.e., reflecting the all-sidedness of the material process and its unity, is dialectics, is the correct reflection of the eternal development of the world.'[20] We should study the totality of all sides of the phenomenon and their reciprocal relations (or contradictions). On this basis it is easy to reject any false counterposition of analysis in terms of 'modes of production' or 'social formations' (or, as Laclau says, 'economic systems'). Laclau points out, quite correctly:

> that Marxist thought in Latin America has found considerable difficulty in moving *simultaneously* at the level of *modes of production* and at that of *economic systems*, and that its most frequent mistakes derive from a unilateral use of one or other of the two levels.[21]

We have seen a certain 'theoretical inflation' of the mode of production concept which tends to subsume the more concrete 'social formation' category. On the other hand, we are faced with a concept of world capitalist economy in writers such as Wallerstein and Frank, which 'is not the *result* of a theoretical construction but the *starting point* of analysis'.[22] In other words, Marx's move, from the abstract concept (population) to its complex of theoretical determinations (classes, etc) and back again to uncover the 'unity in diversity' which makes up the first, is ignored.

Dependent Reproduction and State Forms

As Harry Goulbourne writes, 'there is still no systematic theoretical discussion of the specificity of the political (politics and the state) in [Third World] formations.'[23] This is largely owing to the fact that the major thrust of the critique of modernisation theory occurred at the economic level. A certain economism in much of the dependency writers (Cardoso and Faletto being a signal exception) is now undeniable. Our aim here will be to extend our earlier concept of 'dependent reproduction' (see Chapter 1) to embrace the different 'state forms' present in Third World social formations.

In Chapter 7 on Brazil we proposed a procedure of 'state derivation', whereby specific state forms were related to particular patterns of capital accumulation. By focusing on the 'logic of capital' the danger is, of course, that of reductionism — as though the political could be simply 'read-off' the economic. Furthermore, as Bob Jessop points out:

> one should not artificially separate the logic of capital from its historical conditioning through class struggle nor oppose a determinate, eternal logic of capital to an indeterminate, contingent historical process.[24]

Abstracting from the historical process and the class struggle may lead us into a theoretical cul-de-sac, as with some of the modes of production writings. State derivation can lead to a form of idealism which ignores that the state is a synthesis of *many* determinations. Its strength is that it breaks with an earlier conception of the state as the mere instrument of social classes and shows the necessary relation between capitalist reproduction and the state.

A totally opposed approach to this takes up the proposition made once by Poulantzas, that the 'political' is the 'dominant' instance in modern capitalism. State intervention displaces market forces as the dominant element in the reproduction of the capital relation. The tendency here is, of course, towards an 'over politicisation' of our analysis, which reduces the Marxist concept of economic determination in the last instance to a verbal token. Some variants of dependency theory, such as the work of Cardoso, tends towards making the political level the 'prime mover' of society in Latin America. Colin Henfrey has recently presented this view more systematically and argued for the dominance of the political in the history of the dependent social formations: 1) in the export economies, where the economic centre is external:

> the ruling class rules disproportionately through the political mechanisms of its relations with other classes, rather than through economic ones, which it controls either incompletely or scarcely at all,

and 2) where the social relations of production are not fully capitalist and are therefore, 'reproduced largely by ideological and political rather than economic forms of coercion'.[25]

We are dealing here with a situation typical of the comprador regimes and the enclave economies. More broadly, we can refer to a process in Latin America in which the class structure is constituted more in terms of political domination than the relations of production, because only in the political sphere can generalised class interests be established.[26]

One way out of the dilemma between determination of the political by the economic, and dominance of the political is to refer to the 'relative autonomy' of the political and the state. Clearly the capitalist state retains a degree of independence from the dominant classes, the better to organise the conditions of dependency. Alavi argues that:

this problem is of particular importance in peripheral capitalist societies where we may have more than one dominant class, eg. not only the indigenous bourgeoisie, but also the metropolitan bourgeoisie and landowning classes.[27]

One element in this 'relative autonomy' is the massive economic resources controlled by the peripheral state. It is also perpetuated by denying all classes (including the dominant ones) organic and effective means of political representation. We must point firstly to the fact that 'relative autonomy' indicates a theoretical problem, but hardly resolves it. More substantially, we must question whether the 'relative autonomy' of, for example, state capital in the Third World is more apparent than real. Nora Hamilton argues correctly against this type of approach that:

> an examination of the more advanced contemporary Latin American states suggests that there is no necessary relation between increased state access to and even control over economic resources and greater autonomy with respect to structural constraints.[28]

The enduring strength of this perspective is that it clearly belies the instrumentalist conception of the state, which sees it as an object manipulated by an undistinguished 'ruling class'.

So far our analysis points to a general lack of integration in theories of capital and the state, a false counterposition of levels. We will now sketch in an alternative perspective. Except for a few spirited defences, the 'primitive' Marxist thesis of the primacy of the forces of production is now rejected.[29] This does not mean that the construction of socialism can, for example, take place *independently* of the level of development of the productive forces. It entails, however, a rejection of technological determinism, and a focus on the relations of production, to explain 'the entire social structure' and 'the specific form of state' as Marx notes but does not develop.[30] The social relations of production in any society determine the distribution of the means of production and the mode of appropriation of surplus labour. Furthermore, following Simon Clarke:

> The economic, political and ideological are forms which are taken by the relations of production. Political and ideological relations are as much relations of production as are strictly economic forms of the social relations within which production takes place.[31]

From this perspective then, we can escape the dilemma between 'economic determination' and 'relative autonomy'. The state is now neither an 'instrument' nor part of some 'superstructure', rather, in a sense it is itself a relation of production.[32] The outdated topographic metaphor of economic 'base' and political 'superstructure' can now be finally dispensed with.

It is the Italian 'workerist' Marxists such as Mario Tronti and Antonio Negri who have developed a set of concepts which take us beyond this rejection of Second International Marxism. Modern capitalist society has become a 'social factory', as all elements within are subsumed under the role of capital. This is the era of 'social capital' which, in Tronti's words:

> is not merely the total capital of society; it is not the simple sum of individual capitals. It is the whole process of socialization of capitalist production; it is capital . . . as social power.[33]

When we think in terms of the 'social factory' and 'social capital' we can see how capitalist reproduction involves all the institutions of bourgeois society and, above all, the state. The class struggle is absolutely central to the dynamic of this system, a class struggle which 'takes the form of cycles of offensive/ defensive strategies employed by capital in response to the resistance of the working class', as Bell puts it.[34] These cycles of class struggle were clearly evident in our Latin American case studies, and they emerge only when we integrate our economic, political and social analyses. Labour power is an integral element of the capital relation and, in the long waves of capital accumulation, the working class is constantly made and remade. The capitalist cycle profoundly modifies the whole structure of the social relations of production in each phase.

The capitalist cycle and the crisis can now be reinterpreted in a way which avoids economism. Crisis is a rupture in the expanded reproduction of the capital relation in which the working class is an active element and not a mere spectator. That is why, as Negri explains:

> we now see the formation of the State-as-Crisis, the Crisis-State, on the following lines: to divide up the overall thrust of the working class; to control it from within the mechanisms of its own accumulation; and to forestall it, by attacking it in its class composition.[35]

This understanding of the restructuring and recomposition of bourgeois society leads us to reject any separation of the economic and political 'levels' of society. One cannot analyse capitalist development first and political struggle later. We must start with the struggle of the working class 'to which the political mechanisms of capital's own reproduction must be tuned', as Tronti says.[36] The development of capitalism is inseparable from the struggle of the working class. This should not, however, be taken in an apocalyptic sense, as seemed to occur in the later development of the Italian 'autonomists'. Nor can one credit capitalism with the sort of far-sightedness which 'provokes' crisis, cleverly 'uses' reforms to subordinate workers, etc. In short, this perspective is an effective critique of orthodoxy but does not yet offer a fully rounded alternative. Furthermore, it ignores the complexity of imperialism's forms of domination in the Third World and the contradictory nature of nationalism.

Political Power and Social Class

It would be misconceived, I believe, to try somehow to 'apply' or 'translate'
Poulantzas' *Political Power and Social Classes* to the Third World.[37] This
could result only in a rather mechanical succession of theoretical proposition
and empirical reality, without any real integration (or mediation). It does
seem a useful starting point, in so far as it represents the most sophisticated
attempt to theorize the political 'level' in the capitalist mode of production.
For Poulantzas, the *political* is constituted by the 'juridico-political superstructure of the state' and *politics* refers to 'political class practices', in other
words, the class struggle.[38] Some authors have suggested that in the Third
World the political embraces politics and subsumes it, leading to the appearance of a muted class struggle. The overriding influence of nationalism, and
the preponderant role of the state in development, leads to a lesser role for
'normal' politics. According to Harry Goulbourne 'these developments tend
to accentuate the "centrality" of the state in these formations vis-à-vis the
social and economic structures.'[39] This is correct in the development of
capitalism where the state 'forces' the emergence of new relations of
production, and in the latest phase of monetarism-militarism where the state
has become a new Leviathan. It leads, amongst other things, to a more
directly 'political' class struggle because it is the state more than the capitalist
class which is identified as the key element in the social formation.

Poulantzas distinguishes between the 'normal' and the 'exceptional' form
of state and, as we have seen, the latter predominates in the Third World.[40]
One objection is that the distinction is Eurocentric, but more important is
the point made by Bob Jessop that:

> not only is the crucial concept of 'hegemony' underdeveloped relative
> to the explanatory burden placed upon it, but the arguments for the
> benefits of 'normal' forms are largely asserted and depend for proof on
> the contra-indications of 'exceptional' regimes.[41]

Effectively, it is assumed that bourgeois democracy is the 'best possible
political shell' for capitalism. Also, the distinguishing feature between the two
forms — the ability of the ruling class to establish 'hegemony' over society —
is still largely underdeveloped. If Poulantzas had as his two main formative
influences the structural Marxism of Althusser and the political writings of
Gramsci the task now is to develop the latter. In fact, we note a growing
influence of his thought in the critical social science of Latin America.[42]
Finally, we must question the general analysis, based on Poulantzas, in terms
of 'fractions of capital'. This type of analysis tends to focus on the struggle
between fractions of capital, and this neglects the struggle between capital
and labour. Its main problem, as Simon Clarke explains is that:

> instead of showing how political conflicts arise as *developed forms* of
> class struggles constituted at the level of the relations of production by

351

> showing how various political and semi-political institutions develop
> on the basis of struggles centred on specific barriers to the valorisation
> of capital . . . the procedure is reversed and simplified and the key to
> the class struggle is sought *immediately* in the relation between political
> organisations.[43]

If there is one concept that is central to our understanding of the political
development of the Third World it is that of 'bourgeois revolution'. In general,
we can say that the economic and political tasks of the bourgeois revolution
have been only partially fulfilled in the Third World. The condition of
dependency has prevented the indigenous bourgeoisie from acting as the
social force that would carry out this revolution. This should not, however,
lead us to a static conception of bourgeois revolutions as events, because
clearly they have occurred as a historical *process* in the Third World. It is
this historical process of class formation and achievement of hegemony by
the bourgeoisie which should be a major theme in any analysis of political
power and social class in the Third World. The crisis of the oligarchic state
led to a transition phase, in which there was a recomposition of the power
structures and a gradual configuration of bourgeois power and bourgeois
domination. Today, as Florestan Fernandes writes:

> the central problem of historical-sociological investigation of the
> bourgeois transition . . . consists in the *crisis of bourgeois power*,
> which is located in the present era and emerges as a consequence of
> the transition from competitive capitalism to monopoly capitalism.[44]

In this analysis we must dispense with any unilinear model — whether liberal
or Marxist — which expects historical replication in today's Third World of
what happened in Western Europe in the last century.

It would be suggestive in this respect to relate Barrington Moore's classic
Social Origins of Dictatorship and Democracy to Latin America.[45] His first
development route — the bourgeois revolution from below — has occurred
only to a certain extent in Mexico (1910) and Bolivia (1952). They were also
partially comparable to Moore's third variant of 'peasant revolution', in
which a revolutionary peasantry rather than a revolutionary bourgeoisie clears
the way for modernisation. In fact, we can detect in these cases a fourth
variant following the path of agrarian populism to corporatism, as argued by
Harvey Kaye.[46] The 'revolution from above', similar to Gramsci's concept of
the 'passive revolution', has been more common. This term should not be
restricted to fascist-led modernisation, as with Moore. Roxborough points
out correctly that the term:

> may be used more generally to refer to any attempt by an elite other
> than the bourgeoisie to use its control of the state to oversee an attempt
> at rapid economic development.[47]

Examples would be Brazil's Estado Nôvo and Peru's military government after 1968. The failure of the bourgeoisie to complete its own 'historic' tasks and the, as yet underdeveloped nature of the working class (which should take over according to the theory of 'permanent revolution') leads to the emergence of a petty bourgeois or bureaucratic stratum (possibly military) which 'leads' the bourgeois revolution.

The bourgeois revolution in Latin America was neither classically democratic, nor fascist, nor communist revolutionary. The victory of the land-owning and mercantile classes in the wars of independence foreclosed the North American 'farmer' road to capitalism. Instead, a dependent modernisation route began, which was partly a 'revolution from above' but one led not by an industrialising force, but rather agrarian based and 'open' to the international economy. This route generated only an incomplete modernisation and led to a general cyclical instability of the social formation; neither did this dependent capitalist development generate stable democratic structures. This late and partial modernisation did not create the preconditions for the emergence and development of democracy. The state became the dominant power over civil society; legitimacy was achieved through order and development, not respect of individual liberties; and the industrial bourgeoisie emerged in subordination to the dependent oligarchic state.[48] One can also mention the acute social contradictions of this society – from peasant insurgency to proletarian revolt – which has created the conditions for authoritarian bourgeois rule. We can conclude with García Delgado that:

> Late modernization was marked by (apparently) insoluble contradictions between accelerated development and democracy, between liberalism and nationalism, and finally between the cultural ideal and social reality.[49]

Our periodisation of capitalist development in Latin America focuses on three main state forms: the oligarchic, populist and military. The main determinants of each will be summarised in a broad theoretical synthesis which perforce neglects national particularities. The dependency approach provides our broad focus – the mediation between the economic/political articulation of society and its external/internal determinants. The modes of production theory leads us to reject the conception of this society as simply capitalist, and distinguish between the various non-capitalist relations of production.

The essential element in the emergence of the oligarchic state form in Latin America is that it was not constituted on the foundation of a feudal absolutist state but rather in the vacuum created by the dissolution of social and political structures based on an external monarchy.[50] The rhythms and form taken by this transition out of colonialism were to a certain extent dictated by the pressure of the masses, but this was essentially a political rather than a social revolution. By 1825, the so-called 'colonial pact' had been broken nearly everywhere, and by 1850, the elements of the new liberal-oligarchic state had been formed. This state emerged basically as a military machine to conduct the independence struggle and overcome the period of 'anarchy' and regionalism which preceded it.

The main elements of the liberal-oligarchic state were effectively consolidated between 1870 and the end of the century, as the process of primitive accumulation was completed and the nation-state secured. The atomisation and dispersion of political power of the earlier period was replaced by this new state form, corresponding to the implantation of capitalism as the dominant mode of production. This oligarchic state was, as Agustín Cueva points out, 'the fundamental lever of the first phase of capitalist accumulation, its very authoritarianism constituting an economic power.'[51] In spite of their differences, the following regimes follow this essential pattern: the 'Porfiriato' in Mexico (1876-1910); the 'First Republic' in Brazil (1889-1930); Chile's parliamentary republic (1891-1920); Argentina's presidential regimes after Roca (1880-1930); the Cabrera tyranny in Guatemala (1899-1920), and the Vicente Gómez dictatorship in Venezuela (1908-35). These regimes varied in terms of the level of contradictions within the dominant bloc — as Atilio Borón notes, 'this variety expressed the specific national conditions of the oligarchic pact between bourgeois fractions, landowning gentry and imperialist capital.'[52] The resistance of the labouring masses was also a key difference, which set apart, for example, Argentina, where the tenets of liberalism (such as free trade, etc) were reflected even in the working-class parties, and Mexico where a more naked form of bourgeois domination prevailed.

The economic basis of this state form was the so-called agro-export system. This was the mode of economic organisation to which the oligarchic mode of domination corresponded. It coincided with the emergence of British imperialism as hegemonic power and the integration of the Latin American economies into the international system took place under its aegis. In spite of the severe impact of international economic crises, and the growing indebtedness of the Latin American economies, the system functioned relatively smoothly. The railways were a key element in the agrarian export economy, and these in turn led to the first steps towards an industrial economy. The metropolis required growing supplies of foodstuffs and minerals, and the Latin American economies were integrated on this basis. The generalisation of commodity production in this period leads equally to the formation of a financial sector, tied by multiple links to the City of London, the lynchpin of imperialism in this era. This period is characterised by Cardoso and Faletto as one of 'consolidation of external linkage and the bourgeois-oligarchic domination'.[53] This bourgeois domination was not the product of a bourgeois revolution however — its rationality was determined externally, and the nation is a purely territorial entity with little social and political integration or development of a national collective identity.

The oligarchic state was characterised by the essentially pre-capitalist matrix of its relations of production. The abolition of African and Indian slavery had led to an acute problem of labour supply. Immigration was one solution, particularly in Argentina, Uruguay and Brazil. Elsewhere — Peru and Mexico particularly — Chinese coolies were introduced. Between these two extremes of free and 'unfree' labour was a whole range of capitalist relations of production — *huasipungaje* in Ecuador, *pongaje* in Peru, *cambão* in Brazil, and so on, characterised by the extra-economic coercion typical of servitude. The debate over the 'feudal' or 'capitalist' nature of Latin America during this period has been largely surpassed. The overall domination of capitalism is exercised by 'external' factors. This did not preclude the existence, and in fact expanded reproduction, of non-capitalist relations of production. Even the wage relation could be used to impose servitude, as in the case of debt peonage. Merchant or usury capital could take over agrarian exploitation to the benefit of capitalism without changing the production regime on which it was based. Towards the end of the century the feudal, slave and petty commodity production forms of labour were definitively transformed. This did not, however, take a revolutionary course — the generalisation of free labour — but a conservative Junker type road in which the old was transformed the better to serve the new.

The liberal-oligarchic state entered a period of crisis in the first decades of the 20th Century — the Mexican revolution began in 1910, the Radical Party took power in Argentina in 1916, and the Batlle regime in Uruguay, particularly after 1911, made its first moves towards social democracy. If the political crisis of the oligarchic state pre-dated the great slump it was this international event which 'overdetermined' the conjuncture of the 1930s and converted it into a watershed throughout Latin America. On the one hand there was a series of confused rebellions, partly fuelled by pre-capitalist motives, as with the 1848 revolutions in Europe. On the other hand, there was a succession of military interventions in Chile, Argentina, Brazil and many countries of Central America. Lechner proposes that 'these social-political eruptions are a consequence of an economic restructuring and must be analysed as a moment in the reordering of the world economy.'[54] The international crisis acted as a detonator for more long term structural transformations within these societies. The breaking of international commercial relations, as with the First World War earlier, led to a restructuring of the agro-export economy and an incipient industrialisation. In Argentina, whereas the agrarian oligarchy reimposed its political rule after the democratic interlude of the Radicals (a similar process occurred in Uruguay) it was forced to carry out a number of industrialising measures during the 1930s. In other countries, such as Colombia, the oligarchic-export system continued after 1930 and social differentiation proceeded very slowly.

The nationalist-populist state was essentially an interlude between the crisis of the oligarchic state and the re-establishment of stable bourgeois hegemony. It did not emerge automatically from the results of the 1929 crisis. In fact, in Chile the non-capitalist relation of *inquilinaje* was actually reinforced in the countryside. In other countries the crisis led simply to economic stagnation, most noticeably in Cuba where this state of affairs lasted virtually until 1959. If industrialisation on a continental scale had to wait until after the Second World War, in three major countries — Argentina, Brazil and Mexico — it began in the 1930s and 1940s under nationalist-populist regimes. In Argentina, Peronism (1946–55) accelerated pre-existing trends, in Brazil, Varguismo (1930–55) used the state to 'force' industriali-sation, and in Mexico, the Cárdenas regime (1934–40) consolidated the only truly popular democratic revolution in Latin America. The Popular Front in Chile (1938–47) can also be considered a variant of this type of state, as too can the nationalist regimes after the Bolivian revolution (1952–64), and the various regimes of Velazco Ibarra in Ecuador between 1934 and 1972. In these last two cases, however, as in Peru, the economics of the oligarchic system were largely untouched and the bourgeois revolution as historical process was not completed until the 1970s. A certain prior level of the social division of labour and development of capitalist relations of production is necessary to achieve a full transition to the bourgeois-capitalist mode of production.[55]

This state form is characterised by a strong element of Bonapartism — a modern form of state according to Engels, which arises:

> when the nobility no longer needed protection against the onrush of the bourgeoisie and it became necessary to protect all the propertied classes against the onrush of the working class. . . .[56]

This does not mean that the old ruling class — the Junkers and the comprador bourgeoisie — lose their economic predominance. As Engels says, 'the substance remains, being merely translated from the feudal into the bourgeois dialect.'[57] It was necessary to incorporate a new industrial bourgeoisie into the power bloc, so as more effectively to carry out the transition required by the 1930s collapse. The oligarchic state had been one which was effectively 'captured' by the ruling class, for which it acted as a simple political extension. Now the state had at least to appear above particular classes, expressing the global interests of the dominant classes. This 'benefactor' state was no longer a class object and became universalised as a class relation. As Octavio Ianni writes:

> the populist pact appears as a Bonapartist type *intermezzo* in the transition from oligarchic hegemony to properly bourgeois domination, understood as a bourgeoisie with an urban or industrial base.[58]

One of its main tasks was to generate the material conditions and class alliances which could carry out a process of industrialisation.

The national-populist state is marked by the consolidation of social classes with the definitive separation of workers from the means of production. This working class came on to the scene even before a solid industrial bourgeoisie had consolidated its position. It was a case, as Engels wrote about Britain, in which 'the industrial and commercial middle class had . . . not yet succeeded in driving the landed aristocracy from political power when another competitor, the working class, appeared on the stage.'[59] The task of incorporating or co-opting the working class took place by different means. In Chapter 5 we discussed the cases of Argentina and Brazil; we might also mention the case of Mexico where the legitimacy of the revolution allowed for a stable political-trade union incorporation of the working class which lasted until recently. This does not mean that the bourgeoisie becomes a truly national class with a hegemonic project in Gramscian terms. On the one hand, its rationality is external and its class autonomy is very limited. On the other, as Lechner writes, it is unable to unify the different social groups in national form:

> it fails to relate the urban and rural worlds, it fails to root bourgeois values as the common sense of the whole population [and] it fails to develop political institutions with a broad political participation.[60]

As with the liberalism of the oligarchy, the democracy of the new bourgeoisie is more formal than real.

The crisis of this state form was much more clearly internal in its dynamic than was the earlier crisis of the oligarchic state. The emergence of democratic regimes in the post-Second World War period is not unconnected with an international conjuncture.[61] Their closure, however, beginning with the 1964 coups in Bolivia and Brazil, has no identifiable external causation. The basic contradiction of the nationalist-populist regimes was the working class it created. The first phase of industrialisation, up until the 1940s, did not fundamentally change the organic composition of capital and hence resulted in a rapid incorporation of workers into wage labour. Later, more capital intensive industrialisation prevailed and the question of 'marginality' became apparent. Inside the factories the earlier, formal subordination of labour to capital, which did not alter the labour process, gave way to the real subordination of labour and the generation of a clearly identified proletariat. Against the aims of the 'populist pact' this class was rapidly politicised, and even when this was on a purely nationalist basis it entered into conflict with a system increasingly subordinated to foreign capital. Conversely, an industrial-financial bourgeoisie was growing in economic power and eager to impress its political mark on society. These contradictions were most clearly manifested in the 1964 'bourgeois revolution' in Brazil, which became the trend-setter for the Latin American bourgeoisie in the 1970s.

The crisis of hegemony in Latin America began, in retrospect, with the victory of the Cuban revolution in 1959, and particularly in 1961 when its socialist character became clear. The impact of this revolution was quite as important as was the effect of the Russian revolution in Europe from 1917 into the 1920s. The collapse of the populist regimes was also the acknowledgement of the failure of reformism in Latin America. The economic and social conditions of bourgeois rule could allow for only brief interludes of democracy with a growing trend towards the militarisation of society. When democratic rule was reinstated — as in Argentina between 1973 and 1976 —

its inherent contradictions under conditions of dependent capitalism proved insuperable. The case of Venezuela, where stable democratic rule has been possible, is clearly related to the income generated by oil and its redistributive potential; this, however, should not lead us to fall into economism. More generally, the dynamic leading to the 'modern military' regimes or the 'bureaucratic-authoritarian' state cannot be reduced to economic transformations imposing their logic on the political system. Having said that we note that in spite of the differences imposed by the class struggle in each situation there are sufficient cases of repressive military regimes — Brazil and Bolivia 1964, Argentina 1966 and 1976, Chile and Uruguay 1973 — along with the incorporative (i.e. reformist) military regimes, most noticeably Peru since 1968 but also Ecuador and Panama, to constitute a general trend. The tendency towards recession in the international economy, from the mid 1970s onwards, was a factor in perpetuating this internal dynamic towards a strong state.

What is the way out for the 'bureaucratic-authoritarian' state? Obviously this will depend on particular historical circumstances and the concrete unfolding of the class struggle. We can, though, distinguish generally between 'internal' and 'external' causes of democratisation.[62] An example of the first would be the 'decompression' engineered by the Geisel regime in Brazil between 1975 and 1979, on the basis of decisions internal to the 'bureaucratic-authoritarian' alliance. A prime example of the second course was the liberalisation led by the Lanusse regime in Argentina between 1971 and 1973, which was imposed from outside the alliance. A key element in this process is whether the working class is either too weak (as, initially, in Brazil) or organised in reformist political parties (as in Spain and Chile) which will allow a peaceful transition back to democratic rule. In this respect, the remarkably stable post-Francoist period in Spain — at least in relation to expectations — serves as a model for the rulers of countries contemplating a *recambio* (changeover) of regimes. There is a growing tendency in this direction marked by elections, even in the Dominican Republic in 1978, after 50 years of dictatorship. This is, of course, an unstable process as witnessed by the recurrent elections and coups in Bolivia since 1978. The other side of the coin is a growing tendency towards a 'bureaucratic authoritarian state' in such countries as Colombia (and perhaps Venezuela in the longer term) which had apparently remained as an exception to the rule with relatively stable democratic forms. Finally, Nicaragua in 1979 showed, as Cuba had done 20 years earlier, that there was a viable *revolutionary* alternative to dependent capitalist development.

Noting the direction of recent research on Latin America, Alain Touraine wrote that 'the principal actors in recent Latin American history appear to be not the bourgeoisie and the proletariat . . . but rather foreign capital and the state.'[63] No one would wish to exclude the last two from our analysis, but it does seem that attention to the fundamental classes of capitalism is now overdue. There is, in fact, a growing body of research on the Latin American bourgeoisie which has moved beyond the demystification of the

the 'national bourgeoisie' concept.[64] The 1960s conception of this class as a demiurge of a process of national autonomous development was replaced in the 1970s by an equally simplified view of it as a captive of the state, or swallowed up by foreign capital. Now we have studies based on 'classical' concepts, such as finance capital, but built on detailed empirical investigation.[65] The other side of capital is labour, and here again we have broken from the simplifications of workers as *either* submissive to paternalist/populist rule *or* fully fledged leaders of the socialist revolution.[66] The traditional patterns of labour politics under the nationalist regimes have, however, been studied in greater detail than the more recent position and role of labour under the military dictatorships. In conclusion, since the capital-wage labour relation has become the axis of bourgeois society in Latin America, our attention must be focused on its two main elements and the relations between them.

The question of hegemony must now be explored further because it is crucial to a global understanding of the political process in Latin America. Referring to an element of 'moral leadership' over and above simple domination, the term hegemony can apply either to a working-class strategy (extension of the worker-peasant alliance) or to a mechanism of bourgeois rule. Our concern is with the latter, and starts from Gramsci's algebraic definition of the bourgeois state as 'dictatorship + hegemony'.[67] He goes on to analyse the balance between coercion and consent in the modern bourgeois state, showing how the latter element is essential if the bourgeoisie is to 'lead' society and not simply dominate it. Gramsci refers to the 'dual perspective' in politics: 'the levels of force and of consent, authority and hegemony, violence and civilisation. . . .'[68] Though this formulation changes in the course of his writing, Gramsci refers to the state as the site of coercion/domination and hegemony/direction as pertaining to 'civil society' — the 'private' associations of church, school, family, etc.[69] In Latin America taken as a whole, and with a broad historical sweep, we can speak of a relative absence of hegemony in this sense. Civil society is weakly developed and, even worse, its elements often come into contradiction with actually existing bourgeois rule, as with the recent radical role of the Catholic church in Central America. The state is everything, but its very strength and omnipotence shows the unstable basis of bourgeois rule. Consent is replaced by naked terror as the cement of bourgeois society. The 'armed bodies of men' on which the state is based are no longer the ultimate recourse for the bourgeoisie but a pre-condition for their day to day survival in many countries. The 'moral leadership' of the bourgeoisie does not even extend to its own 'organic intellectuals' who practice a cynical short term 'politics'. In short, 'coercion' has become the overriding element in the new monopolist-monetarist mode of accumulation, to an extent that makes the establishment of stable hegemonic rule highly unlikely if not impossible.

If we were to characterise Latin America today it would not be in terms of 'underdevelopment' — witness the quadrupling of Gross National Product in the region over the last 25 years — but rather in terms of an 'organic crisis'. According to Gramsci, this

> crisis of the ruling class's hegemony . . . occurs either because the ruling class has failed in some major political undertaking for which it has requested, or forcibly extracted, the consent of the broad masses (war for example), or because huge masses . . . have passed suddenly from a state of political passivity to a certain activity, and put forward demands which taken together, albeit not organically formulated, add up to a revolution.[70]

This 'general crisis of the state' is reflected in Argentina and Brazil for precisely these reasons. Elsewhere, as in Nicaragua yesterday and Chile tomorrow, the simplest democratic demands add up to a fundamental threat to bourgeois rule given the general 'crisis of authority' in these countries. As Bismarck used to say, you can do many things with bayonets except sit on them — at least for any length of time.

Finally, what constitutes the unity of Latin America in analytical terms? One answer, favoured by North American authors, focuses on the so-called 'Iberian tradition' and Catholic social thought, which has led to the predominance of 'corporatism'.[71] The stress is on cultural continuity since the days of the Conquest and the society's 'patrimonialist' structures — and hence traditional forms of domination. The approach is totally unhistorical however — today's generals are not yesterday's *caudillos* — and shades imperceptibly into racism in attributing immutable cultural characteristics to a whole society. Our own conclusion is that Latin America as an object of analysis is constituted by the 'condition of dependency' — external domination over the capital accumulation process and structural heterogeneity of the relations of production. It is the contradictions engendered by this process, and not the 'Iberian tradition', which lead to the condition of 'political instability' that so fascinates observers. We have seen throughout the text that there are common trends — both economic and political — running across the continent in spite of the 'differential historical time' of each country. Unity goes deeper than this however, and springs from the aim of the 19th Century independence struggle leaders, such as Simon Bolívar, to combat the 'balkanization' of the continent. As with the unification of the Arab or African nations, this national task can take place only through socialist revolution. The legacy of Bolívar and Che Guevara is embodied in the slogan of a United Socialist States of Latin America which is essential to permanently overcome the present conditions of servitude.

References

1. Marx, K. (1973) *Grundrisse*. London, Penguin, pp.100–101. For a critical comment on this text see Carver, T. (ed) (1975) *Karl Marx: Texts on Method*. Oxford, Basil Blackwell.
2. Ibid., p.100.

3. Ibid., p.101.
4. Lenin, V.I. (1963) *Collected Works* Vol.38. *Philosophical Notebooks*. Moscow, Foreign Languages Publishing House, p.320.
5. Ibid.
6. Marx, K. (1976) *Capital* Vol.1. London, Penguin, p.102.
7. Marx, K. (1981) *Capital* Vol.3, London, Penguin, p.117.
8. Mandel, E. (1975) *Late Capitalism*. London, New Left Books, p.18. For a further discussion of Marx's method see Sayer, D. (1979) *Marx's Method*. Brighton, Harvester Press.
9. For example Kantor, H. (1969) *Patterns of Politics and Political Systems in Latin America*. Chicago, Rand McNally; and Fitzgibbon, R. (1971) *Latin America: A Panorama of Contemporary Politics*. New York, Meredith Corporation.
10. For example, Adie, R. and Poitras, G. (1974) *Latin America: The Politics of Immobility*. Englewood Cliffs, NJ, Prentice Hall Inc., and Williams, E. and Wright, F. (1975) *Latin American Politics: A Developmentalist Approach*. California, Masfield Publishing Co.
11. On the Marxist conception of history, see McLennon, G. (1981) *Marxism and the Methodologies of History*. London, New Left Books.
12. This discussion draws on Castels, M. and Ipola, E. de (1973) Pratique épistémologique et sciences sociales. *Theorie el Politique*. No.1 (December):30–61.
13. For a critique of the 'political development' literature, see Kesselman, M. (1973) Order or Movement. The literature of political development as ideology. *World Politics*. Vol.26 No.1.
14. Adie, R. and Poitras, G. (1974) *Latin America. The Politics of Immobility*. p.270.
15. Wynia, G. (1978) *The Politics of Latin American Development*. Cambridge, Cambridge University Press.
16. Trotsky, L. (1971) *The Permanent Revolution*. London, New Park Publications, p.22.
17. Wallerstein, I. (1980) *The Capitalist World Economy*. Cambridge, Cambridge University Press, p.64.
18. Quartim, J. (1972) Le statut théorique de la notion de dépendence. *Dépendence et structure de classes en Amérique Latine* (eds) E. Anda et al. Paris, Centre Europe-Tiers Monde.
19. See Lenin, V.I. (1963) *Collected Works* Vol.38. *Philosophical Notebooks*, p.110, 146, 159 and 196.
20. Ibid., p.110;
21. Laclau, E. (1979) *Politics and Ideology in Marxist Theory*. London, New Left Books, p.42.
22. Ibid., p.44.
23. Goulbourne, H. (1979) Some problems of analysis of the political in backward capitalist social formations. *Politics and State in the Third World* (ed) H. Goulbourne, London, Macmillan, p.11.
24. Jessop, B. (1982) *The Capitalist State*. Oxford, Martin Robertson, p.134.

25. Henfrey, C. (1981) Dependency, Modes of Production, and the Class Analysis of Latin America. *Dependency and Marxism* (ed) R. Chilcote, Boulder, Colorado, Westview Press, p.29–30.

26. Lechner, N. (1977) *La Crisis del Estado en América Latina*. Caracas El Cid Editor, p.160. See also Lechner, N. (ed) (1981) *Estado y Politica en América Latina*. Mexico, Siglo XXI.

27. Alavi, H. (1982) State and Class Under Peripheral Capitalism. *Introduction to the Sociology of 'Developing' Societies*, (eds) H. Alavi and T. Shanin. London, Macmillan, p.293.

28. Hamilton, N. (1981) State autonomy and dependent capitalism in Latin America. *British Journal of Sociology*. Vol.32 No.3:325.

29. For example, Cohen, G. (1978) *Karl Marx's Theory of History: A Defence*. Oxford, Oxford University Press, for a critique of which see Levine, A. and Wright, E.O. (1980) Rationality and Class Struggle. *New Left Review* No.123:47–68.

30. Marx, K. (1981) *Capital* Vol.3, p.927; for a development of this theme see Callinicos, A. (1982) *Is There a Future for Marxism?* London, Macmillan, Ch.8: Relations of Production.

31. Clarke, S. (1977) Marxism, Sociology and Poulantzas' theory of the state. *Capital and Class* No.2:10.

32. See Corrigan, P., Ramsay, H., and Sayer, D. (1980) The State as a Relation of Production. *Capitalism, State Formation and Marxist Theory* (ed) P. Corrigan. London, Quartet Books.

33. Tronti, M. (1973) Social Capital. *Telos* No.17 (Fall):105.

34. Bell, P. (1978) 'Cycles' of Class Struggle in Thailand. *Journal of Contemporary Asia*. Vol.8 No.1:54.

35. Negri, T. (1979) Capitalist domination and working class sabotage. *Working Class Autonomy and the Crisis*. London, CSE Books/Red Note p.103.

36. Tronti, M. (1979) Lenin in England. *Working Class Autonomy and the Crisis*. p.1.

37. Poulantzas, N. (1973) *Political Power and Social Classes*. London, New Left Books.

38. Ibid., pp.41–2.

39. Goulbourne, H. (1979) Some problems of the analysis of the political in backward capitalist social formations, p.26.

40. See Poulantzas, N. (1974) *Fascism and Dictatorship*. London, New Left Books.

41. Jessop, B. (1982) *The Capitalist State*. p.189.

42. For example, Portantiero, J.C. (1974) Dominant Classes and Political Crisis. *Latin American Perspectives* Vol.1 No.3: 94–120.

43. Clarke, S. (1978) Capital, Fractions of Capital and the State: 'neo-Marxist' Analyses of the South African State. *Capital and Class* No.5:36

44. Fernandes, F. (1973) Revolução burguesa e capitalismo dependente. *Debate e Critica* No.1, p.60.

45. Moore, B. (1966) *Social Origins of Dictatorship and Democracy*.

London, Penguin.

46. Kaye, H. (1978) Barrington Moore's Paths to Modernisation: Are they Applicable to Latin America. *Bulletin of the Society for Latin American Studies*. No.28:24–41.

47. Roxborough, I. (1979) *Theories of Underdevelopment*. London, Macmillan, p.143.

48. On the crisis of bourgeois domination in Latin America see Benítez Zenteno, R. (ed) (1981) *Clases Sociales y Crisis Política en América Latina*. Mexico, Siglo XXI, and the theoretically informed histories in González Casanova, P. (ed) (1982) *América Latina: Historia de Medio Siglo*. 2 vols. Mexico, Siglo XXI.

49. García Delgado, D. (1981) Modernización dependiente y democracia. Un comentario a la obra de Barrington Moore. *Crítica y Utopía* No.4: 191.

50. Cavarozzi, M. (1978) Elementos para una caracterización del capitalismo oligárquico. *Documento CEDES* No.12, p.9.

51. Cueva, A. (1977) *El Desarollo del Capitalismo en América Latina*. Mexico, Siglo XXI, p.141.

52. Borón, A. (1981) Latin America: Between Hobbes and Friedman. *New Left Review*. No.130:58.

53. Cardoso, F. and Faletto, E. (1979) *Dependency and Development in Latin America*. Berkeley, University of California Press, p.54.

54. Lechner, N. (1977) *La Crisis del Estado en América Latina*. p.55.

55. See the theoretical development of this point in Oliveira, F. (1975) A Emergência do Modo de Produção de Mercadorias: Uma Interpretação Teórica da Economia da República Velha no Brasil. *O Brasil Republicano 1º Volume. Estructura de Poder e Economia (1889–1930)* (ed) B. Fausto, São Paulo, DIFEC.

56. Engels, F. (1969) *The Peasant War in Germany*. London, Lawrence and Wishart, p.18.

57. Ibid., p.19.

58. Ianni, O. (1975) *A Formação do Estado Populista na América Latina*. Rio de Janeiro, Editora Civilização Brasileira, p.45.

59. Marx, K. and Engels, F. (1970) *Selected Works in one volume*. London, Lawrence and Wishart, p.391.

60. Lechner, N. (1977) *La Crisis del Estado en América Latina*, p.64.

61. See Therborn, G. (1979) The Travail of Latin American Democracy. *New Left Review* No.113/114:86.

62. See O'Donnell, G. (1979) Notas para el estudio de procesos de democratización política a partir del estado burocrático-autoritario. *Estudios CEDES*. Vol.2 No.5.

63. Touraine, A. (1976) *Les Sociétés Dépendantes – Essais sur l'Amérique Latine*. Paris, Duculot, p.92.

64. See the dossier on the Latin American bourgeoisie in *Amerique Latine* No.5 (1981), Paris, CETRAL.

65. See the excellent collection, Estevez, J. and Lichtensztejn (eds) (1981)

Nueva fase del capital financiero. Elementos teóricos y experiencias en América Latina. Mexico, Editorial Nueva Imágen.

66. See the dossier on Latin American trade unionism in *Amérique Latine* No.7 (1981), Paris, CETRAL.

67. Hoare, Q. and Nowell Smith, G. (eds) (1971) *Selections from the Prison Notebooks of Antonio Gramsci.* London, Lawrence and Wishart, p.239.

68. Ibid., p.170.

69. These differences are developed in Anderson, P. (1977) The Antinomies of Antonio Gramsci. *New Left Review.* No.100:5–80; see also Portelli, H. (1973) *Gramsci y el Bloque Histórico.* Buenos Aires, Siglo XXI.

70. Hoare, Q. and Nowell Smith, G. (eds) (1971) *Selections from the Prison Notebooks*, p.210.

71. See, for example, Wiarda, H. (1973) Towards a Framework for the Study of Political Change in the Iberic-Latin Tradition: The Corporative Model. *World Politics.* Vol.25 No.2:206–35.

Bibliography

This is composed of three sections corresponding to those of the book: dependent development, class and politics. Clearly some overlap will result but the titles chosen try to fit in with the themes of the chapters contained within each section. It is restricted to titles in English which is less of a constraint than it once was, especially if the periodicals listed separately are followed closely, in so far as they often carry translations. A few books in each section, which are considered essential for further reading on the main topics raised by each chapter, are highlighted.

Dependent Development

Chilcote, R. (ed) (1982) *Dependency and Marxism – Towards a Resolution of the Debate*. Boulder, Co., Westview Press. A useful collection of survey type and polemical articles on dependency, modes of production and world systems theories.

Evans, P. (1979) *Dependent Development: The Alliance of Multinational, State and Local Capital in Brazil*. Princeton, NJ, Princeton University Press. One of the best concrete studies emerging from the 'new dependency' school, providing a systematic account of the current patterns of dependent development.

Weaver, F.S. (1981) *Class, State and Industrial Structure – The Historical Process of South American Industrial Growth*. Connecticut, Greenwood Press. A sophisticated theoretical framework for an understanding of the historical patterns of industrialisation.

Arruda, M. et al (1975) *Multinationals and Brazil*. Toronto, Latin American Research Unit.

Baer, W. (1979) *The Brazilian Economy: Its Growth and Development*. Columbus, Grid Publishing Co.

Barraclough, S. and Collarte, J.C. (1973) *Agrarian Structure in Latin America*. Lexington, Mass., Heath-Lexington Books.

Brown, J. (1979) *A Socio-Economic History of Argentina, 1776–1860*. Cambridge, Cambridge University Press.

Burbach, R. and Flynn, P. (1980) *Agribusiness in the Americas*. New York, Monthly Review Press and NACLA.

Carl, G. (1977) *Venezuelan Economic Development: A Political and Economic Analysis*. Greenwich, JAI Press.

Carrière, J. (ed) (1979) *Industrialization and the State in Latin America*.

Amsterdam, CEDLA.

Chilcote, R. and Edelstein, J. (ed) (1974) *Latin America: the Struggle With Dependency and Beyond*. New York, John Wiley and Sons.

Cockcroft, J. et al. (1972) *Dependence and Underdevelopment: Latin America's Political Economy*. New York, Anchor.

—————— (1982) *Mexico: Class Formation, Capital Accumulation and the State*. New York, Monthly Review Press.

Dean, W. (1969) *The Industrialization of São Paulo: 1880–1945*. Austin, University of Texas Press.

De Vylder, S. (1976) *Allende's Chile: The Political Economy of the Rise and Fall of the Unidad Popular*. Cambridge, Cambridge University Press.

Diaz Alejandro, C. (1970) *Essays on the Economic History of the Argentine Republic*. New Haven, Yale University Press.

Feder, E. (1977) *Strawberry Imperialism: An Enquiry into the Mechanisms of Dependency in Mexican Agriculture*. Mexico, Ed. Campesina.

Finch, H. (1981) *A Political Economy of Uruguay since 1870*. London, Macmillan.

Fitzgerald, E.V.K. (1976) *The State and Economic Development: Peru since 1968*. Cambridge, Cambridge University Press.

—————— (1979) *The Political Economy of Peru 1956–78: Economic Development and the Restructuring of Capital*. Cambridge, Cambridge University Press.

Fraginals, M.M. (1976) *The Sugar Mill: The Socio-Economic Complex of Sugar in Cuba.* New York, Monthly Review Press.

Frank, A.G. (1969) *Capitalism and Underdevelopment in Latin America – Historical Studies of Chile and Brazil*. London, Penguin.

—————— (1969) *Latin America: Underdevelopment or Revolution*. New York, Monthly Review Press.

—————— (1972) *Lumpen bourgeoisie: Lumpen development. Dependence, Class and Politics in Latin America*. New York, Monthly Review Press.

Furtado, C. (1968) *The Economic Growth of Brazil*. Berkeley, University of California Press.

—————— (1970) *Economic Development in Latin America: A Survey from Colonial Times to the Cuban Revolution*. Cambridge, Cambridge University Press.

Galeano, E. (1973) *Open Veins of Latin America. Five Centuries of the Pillage of a Continent*. New York, Monthly Review Press.

Graham, R. (1968) *Britain and the Onset of Modernization in Brazil, 1850–1914*. Cambridge, Cambridge University Press.

Grayson, G. (1980) *The Politics of Mexican Oil*. Pittsburgh, University of Pittsburgh Press.

Griffin, K. (ed) (1971) *Financing Development in Latin America*. London, Macmillan.

Grunwald, J. (ed) (1978) *Latin America and World Economy: A Changing International Order*. Beverly Hills, Sage Publications.

Halperin Doughi, T. (1973) *The Aftermath of Revolution in Latin America*. New York, Harper.

—————— (1975) *Politics, Economics and Society in Argentina in the Revolutionary Period*. Cambridge, Cambridge University Press.

Inter-American Development Bank (1981) *Economic and Social Progress in*

Latin America. 1980-81. Washington D.C., Inter-American Development Bank.

Jenkins, R.O. (1977) *Dependent Industrialization in Latin America.* London, Martin Robertson.

MacEwan, A. (1981) *Revolution and Economic Development in Cuba.* London, Macmillan.

Mallon, R.D. and Sourrouille, J. (1975) *Economic Policymaking in a Conflict Society: The Argentine Case.* Cambridge, Cambridge University Press.

Mesa-Lago, C. (1982) *The Economy of Socialist Cuba: A Two Decade Appraisal.* Albuquerque, University of New Mexico Press.

Mitchell, S. (ed) (1981) *The Logic of Poverty: The Case of the Brazilian Northeast.* London Routledge and Kegan Paul.

Moran, E. (ed) (1982) *The Dilemma of Amazonian Development.* Bloomington, Indiana University Press.

Moran, T. (1974) *Multinational Corporations and the Politics of Dependence: Copper in Chile.* Princeton, NJ, Princeton University Press.

Morris, A. (1981) *Latin America: Economic Development and Regional Differentiation.* London, Hutchinson.

N.A.C.L.A. (1971) *Yanqui Dollar: The Contribution of U.S. Private Investment to Underdevelopment in Latin America.* New York, North American Congress on Latin America.

O'Connor, J. (1970) *The Origins of Socialism in Cuba.* Ithaca, Cornell University Press.

Odell, P. and Preston, D. (1981) *Economies and Societies in Latin America.* Chichester, John Wiley and Sons.

Palacios, M. (1980) *Coffee in Colombia 1850-1870: an Economic, Social and Political History.* Cambridge, Cambridge University Press.

Palmer, R.W. (1979) *Caribbean Dependence on the United States Economy.* New York, Praeger.

Randall, M. (1978) *An Economic History of Argentina in the 20th Century.* New York, Columbia University Press.

Reynolds, C.W. (1970) *The Mexican Economy. Twenthieth Century Structure and Growth.* New Haven, Yale University Press.

Roett, R. (ed) (1972) *Brazil in the Sixties.* Nashville, Vanderbilt University Press.

————— (1976) *Brazil in the Seventies.* Washington, American Enterprise Institute.

Sigmund, P. (1980) *Multinationals in Latin America. The Politics of Nationalization.* Madison, University of Wisconsin Press.

Sideri, S. (ed) (1979) *Chile 1970-73 – Economic Development and its International Setting.* The Hague, Nijhoff.

Stallings, B. (1978) *Class Conflict and Economic Development in Chile, 1957-1973.* Stanford, Stanford University Press.

Stein, S. and Stein, B. (1970) *The Colonial Heritage of Latin America: Essays on Economic Dependence in Perspective.* New York, Oxford University Press.

Street, J. and James, D. (ed) (1979) *Technological Progress in Latin America: The Prospects for Overcoming Dependency.* Boulder Co. Westview.

Taylor, K.S. *Sugar and the Underdevelopment of Northeast Brazil, 1500-1970.* Gainsville, University Presses of Florida.

Thorp, R. and Bertram, G. (1978) *Peru 1890-1977: Growth and Policy in an*

Open Economy. London, Macmillan.

Thorp, R. and Whitehead, L. (eds) (1979) *Inflation and Stabilisation in Latin America*. London, Macmillan.

Wynia, G. (1978) *Argentina in the Postwar Era: Politics and Economic Policy Making in a Divided Society*. Albuquerque, University of New Mexico Press.

Class

Janvry, A. de (1981) *The Agrarian Question and Reformism in Latin America*. Baltimore, The Johns Hopkins University Press. A sophisticated and comprehensive analysis of the agrarian question as it affects Latin America.

Latin American and Caribbean Women's Collective (1980) *Slaves of Slaves — The Challenge of Latin American Women*. London, Zed Press. A readable introduction to the still understudied problematic of women in Latin America.

Spalding, H. (1977) *Organized Labor in Latin America — Historical Case Studies of Workers in Dependent Societies*. New York, Harper and Row. A broad comparative focus on the Latin American labour movement from its origins until the nationalist phase.

Alexander, R. (1957) *Communism in Latin America*. New Brunswick, Rutgers University Press.

Baily, S. (1967) *Labor, Nationalism and Politics in Argentina*. New Brunswick, Rutgers University Press.

Balan, J. et al. (1973) *Men in a Developing Society: Geographic and Social Mobility in Monterrey, Mexico*. Austin, University of Texas Press.

Barrios, D. (1978) *Let Me Speak! Testimony of Domitila, a woman of the Bolivian mines*. London, Stage 1.

Blanco, H. (1972) *Land or Death — The Peasant Struggle in Peru*. New York, Pathfinder Press.

Chaney, E. (1979) *Supermadre: Women in Latin American Politics*. Austin, University of Texas Press.

Chaplin, D. (1967) *The Peruvian Industrial Labor Force*. Princeton, NJ, Princeton University Press.

Corradi, J. et al. (ed) (1977) *Ideology and Social Change in Latin America*. New York, Gordon and Breach.

Duncan, K. and Rutledge, I. (ed) (1977) *Land and Labour in Latin America. Essays on the development of agrarian capitalism in the nineteenth and twentieth centuries*. Cambridge, Cambridge University Press.

Eckstein, S. (1977) *The Poverty of Revolution — The State and Urban Poor in Mexico*. Princeton, NJ, Princeton University Press.

Erickson, K.P. (1977) *The Brazilian Corporative State and the Working Class*. Berkeley, California University Press.

Espinoza, J. and Zymbalist, A. (1978) *Economic Democracy: Workers Participation in Chilean Industry 1970-1973*. New York, Academic Press.

Forman, S. (1975) *The Brazilian Peasantry*. New York, Colombia University Press.

Germani, G. (1981) *Marginality*. New Brunswick, Transaction Books.

Goodman, D. and Redclift, M. (1981) *From Peasant to Proletarian: Capitalist*

Development and Agrarian Transitions. Oxford, Blackwell.

Gott, R. (1971) *Guerilla Movements in Latin America*. London, Penguin.

Gudeman, S. (1978) *The Demise of a Rural Economy: From Subsistence to Capitalism in a Latin American Village.*. London, Routledge and Kegan Paul.

Hahner, J. (1976) *Women in Latin American History*. Los Angeles, UCLA Latin American Center.

Hemming, J. (1978) *Red Gold: the Conquest of the Brazilian Indians*. London, Macmillan.

Horowitz, I. (ed) (1970) *Masses in Latin America*. New York, Oxford University Press.

Huizer, G. (1972) *The Revolutionary Potential of the Peasants in Latin America*. Lexington, Mass., Heath.

Humphrey, J. (1982) *Capitalist Control and Worker Resistance in the Brazilian Auto Industry*. Princeton, NJ, Princeton University Press.

Kruijt, D. and Vellinga, M. (1979) *Labour Relations and Multinational Corporations: The Cerro de Pasco Corporation in Peru (1902-1974)* Essen, Van Gorcum.

Laite, J. (1981) *Industrial Development and Migrant Labour*. Manchester, Manchester University Press.

Latin American Bureau (1980) *Unity is Strength: Trade Unions in Latin America*. London, Latin American Bureau.

Lavrin, A. (1978) *Latin American Women: Historical Perspectives*. Westport, Conn. Greenwood Press.

Lora, G. (1977) *A History of the Bolivian Labour Movement (1848-1971)*. Cambridge, Cambridge University Press.

Loveman, B. (1976) *Struggle in the Countryside – Politics and Rural Labor In Chile, 1919-1973*. Bloomington, Indiana University Press.

Lundhall, M. (1979) *Peasants and Poverty: A Study of Haiti*. New York, St. Martins Press.

Mellafe, R. (1975) *Negro Slavery in Latin America*. Berkeley, University of California Press.

Morner, M. (ed) (1970) *Race and Class in Latin America*. New York, Columbia University Press.

Nash, J. (1979) *We Eat the Mines and the Mines Eat Us – Dependency and Exploitation in Bolivian Tin Mines.*New York, Columbia University Press.

Nash, J. and Safa, H.I. (ed) (1980) *Sex and Class in Latin America*. London, Zed Press.

Payne, J. (1965) *Labor and Politics in Peru: The System of Political Bargaining*. New Haven, Conn., Yale University Press.

Pearse, A. (1975) *The Latin American Peasant*. London, Frank Cass.

Perlman, J.E. (1976) *The Myth of Marginality. The Urban Squatter in Brazil*. Berkeley, University of California Press.

Pescatello, A. (ed) (1975) *The African in Latin America*. New York, Knopf.

————— (ed) (1979) *Female and Male in Latin America*. Pittsburgh, University of Pittsburgh Press.

Petras, J. and Zemelman, H. (1972) *Peasants in Revolt*. Austin, University of Texas Press.

Post, K. (1978) *Arise Ye Starvelings: The Jamaican Labour Rebellion of 1938 and its Aftermath*. The Hague, Nijhoff.

Quartim, J. (1971) *Dictatorship and Armed Struggle in Brazil*. London, New

Left Books.

Randall, M. (1981) *Women in Cuba: Twenty Years Later*. Brookly, Smyrna.

———————— (1982) *Sandino's Daughters: Testimonies of Nicaraguan Women in Struggle*. London, Zed Press.

Redclift, M. (1978) *Agrarian Reform and Peasant Organization on the Ecuadorean Coast*. London, Athlone Press.

Rodney, W. (1981) *A History of the Guyanese Working People 1881–1905*. Baltimore, The Johns Hopkins University Press.

Route, L.B. (1976) *The African Experience in Spanish America. 1502 to the Present Day*. New York, Cambridge University Press.

Ruiz, R.E. (1976) *Labour and the Ambivalent Revolutionaries: Mexico, 1911–1923*. Baltimore, The Johns Hopkins University Press.

Safa, H.I. (1974) *The Urban Poor of Puerto Rico: A Study of Development and Inequality*. New York, The Johns Hopkins University Press.

Saffiotti, H.B. (1978) *Women in Class Society*. New York, Monthly Review Press.

Seligson, N. and Booth, J. (eds) (1979) *Political Participation in Latin America* Vol II: *Politics and the Poor*. New York, Holmes and Meier.

Silveira de Queiroz, D. (1981) *Women of Brazil*. New York, Vantage Press.

Steenland, K. (1977) *Agrarian Reform under Allende: Peasant Revolt in the South*. Albuquerque, University of New Mexico Press.

Toplin, R.B. (1981) *Freedom and Prejudice: The Legacy of Slavery in the United States and Brazil*. Westport, Greenwood Press.

Urrutia, M. (1969) *The Development of the Colombian Labor Movement*. New Haven, Yale University Press.

Vellinga, M. (1979) *Economic Development and the Dynamics of Class. Industrialization, Power and Control in Monterrey, Mexico*. Assen, Van Gorcum.

Wauchope, R. (ed) (1970) *The Indian Background of Latin American History*. New York, Knopf.

Zeitlin, M. (1970) *Revolutionary Politics over the Cuban Working Class*. New York, Harper and Row.

Politics

Cardoso, F.H. and Faletto, E. (1979) *Dependency and Development in Latin America*. Berkeley, University of California Press. The basic theoretical statement on dependency integrating economic and political analysis.

Collier, D. (ed) (1979) *The New Authoritarianism in Latin America*. Princeton, NJ, Princeton University Press. A wide ranging theoretical and historical survey of what is probably the most important topic of current research.

Wiarda, H. and Kline, H. (ed) (1979) *Latin American Politics and Development*. Boston, Houghton Mifflin Company. An elementary country by country introduction with useful bibliographies.

Bernhard, J.P. et al. (1973) *Guide to the Political Parties of Latin America*. London, Penguin.

Black, G. (1981) *Triumph of the People – The Sandinista Revolution in Nicaragua*. London, Zed Press.

Bouricaud, F. (1970) *Power and Society in Contemporary Peru*. New York,

Praeger.

Casanova, P.G. (1970) *Democracy in Mexico*. New York, Oxford University Press.

Ciria, A. (1974) *Parties and Power in Modern Argentina, 1930–1946*. Albany, State University of New York Press.

Conniff, M. (ed) (1982) *Latin American Populism in Comparative Perspective*. Albuquerque, University of New Mexico Press.

Cotler, J. and Fagen, R. (eds) (1974) *Latin America and the United States*. Stanford, Stanford University Press.

Cueva, A. (1981) *The Process of Political Domination in Ecuador*. New Brunswick, Transaction Books.

Dix, R. (1967) *Colombia: The Political Dimensions of Change*. New Haven, Yale University Press.

Dominguez, J. (1978) *Cuba: Order and Revolution*. Cambridge, Mass., Harvard University Press.

Einaudi, L. (ed) (1974) *Beyond Cuba: Latin America Takes Charge of its Future*. New York, Crane, Russak and Co.

Fagen, R. (ed) (1979) *Capitalism and the State in U.S.-Latin American Relations*. Stanford University Press.

Feinberg, R. (ed) (1982) *Central America: International Dimensions of the Crisis*. New York, Holmes and Meier.

Flynn, R. (1978) *Brazil: A Political Analysis*. London, Benn.

Germani, G. (1977) *Authoritarianism, National Populism and Fascism*. New Brunswick, Transaction Books.

Gilly, A. (1982) *The Mexican Revolution*. London, New Left Books.

Goldwert, M. (1972) *Democracy, Militarism and Nationalism in Argentina, 1930–66*. Austin, University of Texas Press.

Gorman, S. (ed) (1982) *Post-Revolutionary Peru – The Politics of Transformation*. Boulder, Co., Westview.

Handelman, H. and Sanders, T. (eds) (1981) *Military Government and the Movement Towards Democracy in South America*. Bloomington, Indiana University Press.

Harnecker, M. (1980) *Cuba: Dictatorship or Democracy?* Westport, Lawrence Hill.

Hodges, D. (1976) *Argentina 1943–76. The National Revolution and Resistance*. Albuquerque, University of New Mexico Press.

Hurtado, O. (1981) *Political Power in Ecuador*. Albuquerque, University of New Mexico Press.

Ianni, O. (1970) *Crisis in Brazil*. New York, Columbia University Press.

Jaguaribe, H. (1973) *Political Development: A General Theory and a Latin American Case Study*. New York, Harper and Row.

Johnson, D. (ed) (1973) *The Chilean Road to Socialism*. New York, Anchor Books.

Jonas, S. and Tobis, D. (eds) (1974) *Guatemala*. Berkeley, NACLA.

Kaufman, E. (1978) *Uruguay in Transition*. New Brunswick, Transaction Books.

Kline, H. (1982) *Colombia*. Boulder, Co., Westview.

Latin American Bureau (1982) *Falklands/Malvinas – Whose Crisis?* London, Latin American Bureau.

Levine, D. (1973) *Conflict and Political Change in Venezuela*. Princeton, NJ, Princeton University Press.

Lewis, P. (1980) *Paraguay and Stroessner*. Chapel Hill, University of North Carolina Press.

Linz, J. and Stepan, A. (eds) (1978) *The Breakdown of Democratic Regimes: Latin America*. The Johns Hopkins University Press.

Lowenthal, A. (ed) (1975) *The Peruvian Experiment – Continuity and Change under Military Rule*. Princeton, NJ, Princeton University Press.

Lynch, J. (1973) *The Spanish-American Revolutions, 1808–1826*. New York, Norton.

Maldonado-Denis, M. (1972) *Puerto Rico: A Socio-Historic Interpretation*. New York, Random House.

Malloy, J. (1970) *Bolivia: The Uncomplete Revolution*. Pittsburgh, Pittsburgh University Press

——————— (ed) (1977) *Authoritarianism and Corporatism in Latin America*. Pittsburgh, University of Pittsburgh Press.

Martz, J. and Myers, D. (eds) (1977) *Venezuela: The Democratic Experience*. New York, Praeger.

Mesa Lago, C. (ed) (1970) *Revolutionary Change in Cuba*. Pittsburgh, University of Pittsburgh Press.

——————— (1978) *Cuba in the 1970s*. Albuquerque, University of New Mexico Press.

Mitchell, C. (1977) *The Legacy of Populism in Bolivia: From the MNR to Military Rule*. New York, Praeger.

Morris, J.A. (1982) *Honduras*. Boulder, Co., Westview.

North American Congress on Latin America (1973) *New Chile*. New York, NACLA.

——————— (1975) *Argentina in the Hour of the Furnaces*. New York, NACLA.

Needler, M. (1977) *An Introduction to Latin American Politics*. Englewood Cliffs, New Jersey, Prentice-Hall Inc.

North, L. (1982) *Bitter Grounds: Roots of Revolution in El Salvador*. London, Zed Press.

O'Brien, P. (ed) (1976) *Allende's Chile*. New York, Praeger.

O'Donnell, G. (1973) *Modernization and Bureaucratic-Authoritarianism. Studies in South American Politics*. Berkeley, University of California Press.

Pearce, J. (1981) *Under the Eagle – U.S. Intervention in Central America*. London, Latin American Bureau.

Petras, J. et al. (1981) *Class, State, and Power in the Third World – With Case Studies on Class Conflict in Latin America*. London, Zed Press.

Plant, R. (1978) *Guatemala: Unnatural Disaster*. London, Latin American Bureau.

Potash, R. (1980) *The Army and Politics in Argentina 1945–62: Peron to Frondizi*. London, Athlone Press.

Quijano, A. (1971) *Nationalism and Capitalism in Peru: A Study in Neo-Imperialism*. New York, Monthly Review Press.

Reyna, J.L. and Weinert, R. (eds) (1977) *Authoritarianism in Mexico*. Philadelphia, Institute for the Study of Human Issues.

Rock, D. (ed) (1975) *Argentina in the Twentieth Century*. Pittsburgh, University of Pittsburgh Press.

——————— (1976) *Politics in Argentina 1890–1930 – the Rise and Fall of Radicalism*. Cambridge, Cambridge University Press.

Roett, R. (1978) *Brazil: Politics in a Patrimonial Society*. New York, Praeger.

Roxborough, I. et al. (1977) *Chile: The State and Revolution*. London, Macmillan.

Skidmore, T. (1967) *Politics in Brazil, 1930–1964*. New York, Oxford University Press.

Smith, P. (1969) *Politics and Beef in Argentina*. New York, Columbia University Press.

Stein, S. (1980) *Populism in Peru: the Emergence of the Masses and the Politics of Social Control*. Madison, University of Wisconsin Press.

Stepan, A. (1971) *The Military in Politics*. Princeton, NJ, Princeton University Press.

——————— (1978) *The State and Society – Peru in Comparative Perspective*. Princeton, NJ, Princeton University Press.

Tugwell, F. (1975) *The Politics of Oil in Venezuela*. Stanford, Stanford University Press.

Tulchin, J. (ed) (1973) *Problems in Latin American History – The Modern Period*. New York, Harper and Row.

——————— (ed) (1975) *Latin America in the Year 2000*. California, Addison Wesley.

Valenzuela, A. and Valenzuela, J. (eds) (1976) *Chile: Politics and Society*. New Brunswick, Transaction Books.

Van Niekerk, A. (1974) *Populism and Political Development in Latin America*. Rotterdam, Rotterdam University Press.

Veliz, C. (ed) (1965) *Obstacles to Change in Latin America*. New York, Oxford University Press.

——————— (ed) (1967) *The Politics of Conformity in Latin America*. New York, Oxford University Press.

Walker, T. (ed) (1982) *Nicaragua in Revolution*. New York, Praeger.

Weinstein, M. (1975) *Uruguay: The Politics of Failure*. Westport, Greenwood Press.

White, R. (1978) *Paraguay's Autonomous Revolution*. Albuquerque, University of New Mexico Press.

Wiarda, H. and Kryzanek, M. (1981) *The Dominican Republic: A Caribbean Crucible*. Boulder, Co., Westview.

Wilkie, J. et al. (eds) (1976) *Contemporary Mexico*. Berkeley, University of California Press.

Williams, E. (1970) *From Columbus to Castro – The History of the Caribbean, 1492–1969*. New York, Harper and Row.

Woodward, R. (1976) *Central America: A Nation Divided*. New York, Oxford University Press.

Wynia, G. (1978) *The Politics of Latin American Development*. Cambridge, Cambridge University Press.

Periodicals

Latin American Perspectives (California). A lively radical quarterly offering focus issues on different countries and themes.

NACLA's Report on the Americas (New York). A more directly political approach than the above, providing up-to-date bi-monthly introductions to topical subjects.

Bibliography

Latin American Research Review (North Carolina). Appears three times a year — noted for extensive bibliographical essays and scholarly debates on historical and theoretical questions.

Bulletin of Latin American Research (Oxford). A new bi-annual journal similar in outlook to the above, presenting original research in all the disciplines.

Journal of Latin American Studies (Cambridge). A bi-annual focus on traditional historiography with occasional articles on more political subjects.

Latin American Weekly Report. A well-informed London-based weekly useful for current developments.

There are numerous journals dedicated to development studies generally with occasional articles on Latin America, including: *Development and Change, The Journal of Developing Areas, World Development, The Journal of Development Studies, Institute of Development Studies Bulletin, Studies in Comparative International Development*, etc.

Other journals which deal with specific social groups also focus on Latin America in some issues, including: *Critique of Anthropology, Journal of Peasant Studies, Race and Class, Feminist Review, Signs* (Journal of Women in Culture and Society), *Labour, Capital and Society, Newsletter of International Labour Studies*, etc.

Journals dealing with other areas of the Third World often carry material relevant to research on Latin America: *Review of African Political Economy, African Marxist, Journal of Contemporary Asia, MERIP Report*, etc.

Finally, the general radical journals often carry material relevant to the theoretical aspects of Latin American research: *New Left Review, Monthly Review, Economy and Society, Review, Capital and Class, Review of Radical Political Economy, Contemporary Marxism, Kapitalistate, Insurgent Sociologist, Socialist Register, Science and Society*, etc.